W9-BPL-741

BELIEVE

LIVING THE STORY OF THE BIBLE
TO BECOME LIKE JESUS

SELECTIONS FROM THE NEW KING JAMES VERSION

BELIEVE

LIVING THE STORY OF THE BIBLE
TO BECOME LIKE JESUS

GENERAL EDITOR
RANDY FRAZEE

ZONDERVAN®

ZONDERVAN
Believe, NKJV
Copyright © 2015 by Zondervan

The Holy Bible, New King James Version
Copyright © 1982 by Thomas Nelson Inc. All rights reserved.

Requests for information should be addressed to:
Zondervan, 3900 *Sparks Drive SE, Grand Rapids, Michigan, 49546*

Assistant Editor: Randy Larson

The text of the New King James Version (NKJV) may be quoted or reprinted without prior written permission with the following qualifications:

(1) up to and including 1,000 verses may be quoted in printed form as long as the verses quoted amount to less than 50% of a complete book of the Bible and make up less than 50% of the total work in which they are quoted;
(2) all NKJV quotations must conform accurately to the NKJV text.

Any use of the NKJV text must include a proper acknowledgment as follows:

Scripture taken from the New King James Version. Copyright © 1979, 1980, 1982 by Thomas Nelson, Inc. Used by permission. All rights reserved.

However, when quotations from the NKJV text are used in church bulletins, orders of service, Sunday School lessons, church newsletters and similar works in the course of religious instruction or services at a place of worship or other religious assembly, the following notice may be used at the end of each quotation: "NKJV."

For quotation requests not covered by the above guidelines, write to Thomas Nelson Publishers, Bible Rights and Permissions, P.O. Box 141000, Nashville, TN 37214-1000.

All rights reserved.

Cover design: Extra Credit Projects

Printed in the United States of America

---

15 16 17 18 19 20 21 22 23 24 25 26 /DCI/ 15 14 13 12 11 10 9 8 7 6 5 4 3 2 1

Table of Contents

Preface | *7*
Introduction | *9*

THINK

What Do I Believe?

Chapter 1. God | *15*
Chapter 2. Personal God | *29*
Chapter 3. Salvation | *46*
Chapter 4. The Bible | *64*
Chapter 5. Identity in Christ | *80*
Chapter 6. Church | *95*
Chapter 7. Humanity | *114*
Chapter 8. Compassion | *131*
Chapter 9. Stewardship | *149*
Chapter 10. Eternity | *166*

ACT

What Should I Do?

Chapter 11. Worship | *183*
Chapter 12. Prayer | *200*
Chapter 13. Bible Study | *218*
Chapter 14. Single-Mindedness | *234*
Chapter 15. Total Surrender | *249*
Chapter 16. Biblical Community | *266*
Chapter 17. Spiritual Gifts | *284*
Chapter 18. Offering My Time | *299*
Chapter 19. Giving My Resources | *314*
Chapter 20. Sharing My Faith | *330*

BE

Who Am I Becoming?

Chapter 21. Love | *349*
Chapter 22. Joy | *363*
Chapter 23. Peace | *379*
Chapter 24. Self-Control | *395*
Chapter 25. Hope | *411*
Chapter 26. Patience | *428*
Chapter 27. Kindness/Goodness | *445*
Chapter 28. Faithfulness | *462*
Chapter 29. Gentleness | *478*
Chapter 30. Humility | *493*

Epilogue | *511*
Chart of References | *513*

Preface

A distinguished sociologist embarked on a quest to answer this question, "How did the marginal Jesus movement become the dominant religious force in the Western world within just a few centuries?" By his estimates the number of Christians grew to 33,882,008 believers by AD 350.[1] A movement that started with Jesus and a handful of His followers grew at an amazing rate! This professor was not a personal follower of Jesus but was mesmerized by the influence of Jesus' life on the entire world.

What he discovered in his adventures through history was a group of very common, ordinary folks who ended up doing uncommon, extraordinary things. These people valued others who were looked down upon. When two devastating epidemics of measles and smallpox wiped out one-fourth to one-third of the population of the Roman Empire, these Christ-followers not only nursed their own but also took in those whose families cast them out into the streets to die. People flocked to this new community, a community founded on a rare expression of love. Anyone who said "yes" to Jesus' invitation to life was welcomed.

At the end of the unbelieving social scientist's extensive search he wrote these words: "Therefore, as I conclude this study, I find it necessary to confront what appears to me to be *the ultimate factor* in the rise of Christianity ... I believe that it was the religion's particular doctrines that permitted Christianity to be among the most sweeping and successful revitalization movements in history. And it was the way these doctrines took on actual flesh, the way they directed organizational actions and individual behavior that led to the rise of Christianity."[2]

In a nutshell, the early Christians BELIEVED. They simply, by faith, believed with their whole hearts the powerful truths taught in the Scriptures. It changed them from the inside out. Their loving and courageous actions toward their family, neighbors and

1. Rodney Stark, *The Rise of Christianity: A Sociologist Reconsiders History* (New Jersey: Princeton University Press, 1996), 10.

2. Ibid., 211.

even strangers were merely outpourings of the love that was flowing from inside them. What are the core truths these followers believed that so radically changed their lives for the good? These truths make up the content of the book you now hold in your hands—*Believe.*

As you read the first core belief about God, remember *Believe* is an action word. God is personally watching over you as you embark on this journey. He doesn't want you to just believe in your head these truths; He wants you to believe with your whole heart His Word as the operating system for your life. He wants to transform your life and family for good and forever. He wants you to join the movement. He wants to put the "extra" in your "ordinary" so you can live an "extraordinary" life in Christ. What He did so radically in the beginning, He is doing again today, if you will only BELIEVE.

Here is my prayer for you:

"Father, you fully know the reader who holds this book in their hands. You know them by name. You love them deeply—always have, always will. As they embark on this amazing journey, give them the faith to believe your truths with their whole heart. Work within them. Let that good work push out to their mouth, ears, hands and feet to positively affect the people you have placed around them. As they finish reading the last page, may they whisper to you and then shout to the world—I BELIEVE!"

—Randy Frazee
General Editor

Introduction

All Scripture is *given by inspiration of God, and* is *profitable for doctrine, for reproof, for correction, for instruction in righteousness.* *2 Timothy 3:16*

Book Sections

As you journey through *Believe*, you will read three ten-chapter sections:

THINK. The first ten chapters of *Believe* detail the core BELIEFS of the Christian life. Together they answer the question, "What do I believe?"

ACT. The second ten chapters discuss the core PRACTICES of the Christian life. Together they answer the question, "What should I do?"

BE. The final ten chapters contain the core VIRTUES of the Christian life. Together they answer the question, "Who am I becoming?"

Scripture

Believe includes the actual, God-breathed words of the Bible. This is not one person's or one church's words on these important, life-altering topics. The Bible text alone is our source of teaching on each of these truths. *Believe* contains portions of Scripture that were thoughtfully and carefully excerpted from the Bible because they speak directly to the core belief, practice or virtue. You will read an Old Testament story, a New Testament story and several supporting texts from throughout the Bible. The Scripture text used in *Believe* is taken from the New King James Version (NKJV).

Chapter Structure

Each chapter contains several elements to guide you through your *Believe* journey.

THINK

CHAPTER

2

Personal God

KEY QUESTION

Does God care about me?

KEY IDEA

I believe God is involved in and cares about my daily life.

KEY VERSE

I will lift up my eyes to the hills—
From whence comes my help?
My help *comes* from the LORD,
Who made heaven and earth.
Psalm 121:1–2

29

The Keys

Key Question

The key question poses the problem or issue the chapter will grapple with.

Key Idea

The key idea gives you words to use to express your beliefs. Try memorizing the key ideas so you "know that you know" what you believe.

Key Verse

The key verse for each belief is the most important Scripture about that subject. The 30 key verses are also important to commit to memory, so you have the power of God's Word at the ready when you need it.

30 | BELIEVE

OUR MAP

The God of the Bible is the only true God—Father, Son and Holy Spirit. He is the one all-powerful, all-knowing eternal God. But is He good? Is He involved in His creation? Does He love us? Does He have a plan for us? Is He interceding and intervening to move the events of our life and world toward His intended purpose?

We can consider these questions as we read the Scripture passages in this chapter that explore three ways God shows us He is a personal God:

- *God Is Good*
- *God Has a Plan*
- *God Cares for Us*

GOD IS GOOD

Abraham and Sarah—the great patriarch and matriarch of the Israelite people—were first named Abram and Sarai. God had promised Abraham that he would be the father of a great nation, but how can you father a nation when you have no children?

As you read the passage below from Genesis 16, look for some ways in which God showed His goodness to Abraham, Sarah and Hagar. What impact did this have on them?

Now Sarai, Abram's wife, had borne him no children. And she had an Egyptian maidservant whose name was Hagar. So Sarai said to Abram, "See now, the LORD has restrained me from bearing children. Please, go in to my maid; perhaps I shall obtain children by her." And Abram heeded the voice of Sarai. Then Sarai, Abram's wife, took Hagar her maid, the Egyptian, and gave her to her husband Abram to be his wife, after Abram had dwelt ten years in the land of Canaan. So he went in to Hagar, and she conceived. And when she saw that she had conceived, her mistress became despised in her eyes.

Then Sarai said to Abram, "My wrong *be* upon you! I gave

Our Map

The Our Map section orients you to the belief, practice or virtue you are about to explore. You will get the big picture of what the chapter is about and see a preview of the topics that will be covered.

30 | BELIEVE

OUR MAP

The God of the Bible is the only true God—Father, Son and Holy Spirit. He is the one all-powerful, all-knowing eternal God. But is He good? Is He involved in His creation? Does He love us? Does He have a plan for us? Is He interceding and intervening to move the events of our life and world toward His intended purpose?

We can consider these questions as we read the Scripture passages in this chapter that explore three ways God shows us He is a personal God:

- *God Is Good*
- *God Has a Plan*
- *God Cares for Us*

GOD IS GOOD

Abraham and Sarah—the great patriarch and matriarch of the Israelite people—were first named Abram and Sarai. God had promised Abraham that he would be the father of a great nation, but how can you father a nation when you have no children?

As you read the passage below from Genesis 16, look for some ways in which God showed His goodness to Abraham, Sarah and Hagar. What impact did this have on them?

Now Sarai, Abram's wife, had borne him no children. And she had an Egyptian maidservant whose name was Hagar. So Sarai said to Abram, "See now, the LORD has restrained me from bearing children. Please, go in to my maid; perhaps I shall obtain children by her." And Abram heeded the voice of Sarai. Then Sarai, Abram's wife, took Hagar her maid, the Egyptian, and gave her to her husband Abram to be his wife, after Abram had dwelt ten years in the land of Canaan. So he went in to Hagar, and she conceived. And when she saw that she had conceived, her mistress became despised in her eyes.

Then Sarai said to Abram, "My wrong *be* upon you! I gave

Transitions

The transition paragraphs between the Scripture text appear *in italic*. They were written to guide you through the chapter and connect the dots between each story. The transitions have been carefully crafted to avoid telling you what to believe; it is important that the Scripture itself be the driver of what you decide to believe. These segments aid you in digging into the meaning and significance of the Scripture.

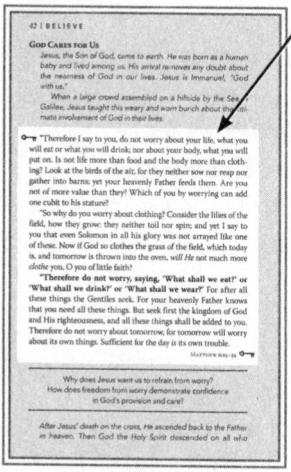

42 | BELIEVE

God Cares for Us

Jesus, the Son of God, came to earth. He was born as a human baby and lived among us. His arrival removes any doubt about the nearness of God in our lives. Jesus is Immanuel, "God with us."

When a large crowd assembled on a hillside by the Sea of Galilee, Jesus taught this weary and worn bunch about the intimate involvement of God in their lives.

"Therefore I say to you, do not worry about your life, what you will eat or what you will drink; nor about your body, what you will put on. Is not life more than food and the body more than clothing? Look at the birds of the air, for they neither sow nor reap nor gather into barns; yet your heavenly Father feeds them. Are you not of more value than they? Which of you by worrying can add one cubit to his stature?

"So why do you worry about clothing? Consider the lilies of the field, how they grow: they neither toil nor spin; and yet I say to you that even Solomon in all his glory was not arrayed like one of these. Now if God so clothes the grass of the field, which today is, and tomorrow is thrown into the oven, will *He* not much more *clothe* you, O you of little faith?

"Therefore do not worry, saying, 'What shall we eat?' or 'What shall we drink?' or 'What shall we wear?' For after all these things the Gentiles seek. For your heavenly Father knows that you need all these things. But seek first the kingdom of God and His righteousness, and all these things shall be added to you. Therefore do not worry about tomorrow, for tomorrow will worry about its own things. Sufficient for the day is its own trouble.

Matthew 6:25–34

Why does Jesus want us to refrain from worry?
How does freedom from worry demonstrate confidence in God's provision and care?

After Jesus' death on the cross, He ascended back to the Father in heaven. Then God the Holy Spirit descended on all who

Key Stories

Look for Key Story symbols at the beginning and end of one Old Testament and one New Testament story in each chapter. The Bible characters in these stories best exemplify that belief, practice or virtue.

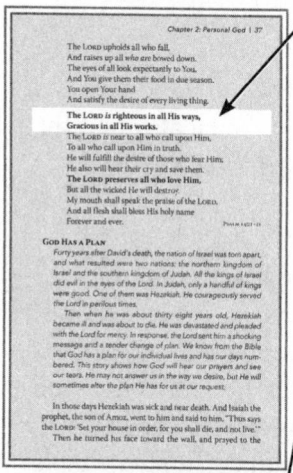

Chapter 2: Personal God | 37

The Lord upholds all who fall,
And raises up all who are bowed down.
The eyes of all look expectantly to You,
And You give them their food in due season.
You open Your hand
And satisfy the desire of every living thing.

The Lord *is* righteous in all His ways,
Gracious in all His works.
The Lord *is* near to all who call upon Him,
To all who call upon Him in truth.
He will fulfill the desire of those who fear Him;
He also will hear their cry and save them.
The Lord preserves all who love Him,
But all the wicked He will destroy.
My mouth shall speak the praise of the Lord,
And all flesh shall bless His holy name
Forever and ever.

Psalm 145:1–21

God Has a Plan

Forty years after David's death, the nation of Israel was torn apart, and what resulted were two nations: the northern kingdom of Israel and the southern kingdom of Judah. All the kings of Israel did evil in the eyes of the Lord. In Judah, only a handful of kings were good. One of them was Hezekiah. He courageously served the Lord in perilous times.

Then when he was about thirty-eight years old, Hezekiah became ill and was about to die. He was devastated and pleaded with the Lord for mercy. In response, the Lord sent him a shocking message and a tender change of plan. We know from the Bible that God has a plan for our individual lives and has our days numbered. This story shows how God will hear our prayers and see our tears. He may not answer us in the way we desire, but He will sometimes alter the plan He has for us at our request.

In those days Hezekiah was sick and near death. And Isaiah the prophet, the son of Amoz, went to him and said to him, "Thus says the Lord: 'Set your house in order; for you shall die, and not live.'"

Then he turned his face toward the wall, and prayed to the

Core Truths

As you read the Scripture text, you will see core truths or main ideas bolded. The core truth is the essence of the message of that Scripture and helps you understand why that particular passage was selected to convey that truth.

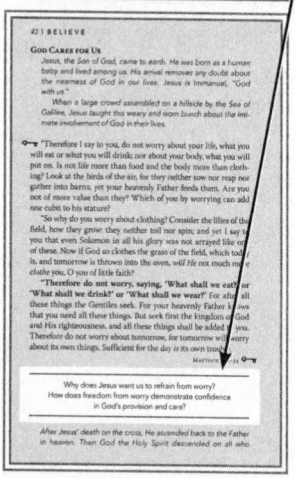

42 | BELIEVE

God Cares for Us

Jesus, the Son of God, came to earth. He was born as a human baby and lived among us. His arrival removes any doubt about the nearness of God in our lives. Jesus is Immanuel, "God with us."

When a large crowd assembled on a hillside by the Sea of Galilee, Jesus taught this weary and worn bunch about the intimate involvement of God in their lives.

"Therefore I say to you, do not worry about your life, what you will eat or what you will drink; nor about your body, what you will put on. Is not life more than food and the body more than clothing? Look at the birds of the air, for they neither sow nor reap nor gather into barns; yet your heavenly Father feeds them. Are you not of more value than they? Which of you by worrying can add one cubit to his stature?

"So why do you worry about clothing? Consider the lilies of the field, how they grow: they neither toil nor spin; and yet I say to you that even Solomon in all his glory was not arrayed like one of these. Now if God so clothes the grass of the field, which today is, and tomorrow is thrown into the oven, *will He* not much more *clothe* you, O you of little faith?

"Therefore do not worry, saying, 'What shall we eat?' or 'What shall we drink?' or 'What shall we wear?' For after all these things the Gentiles seek. For your heavenly Father knows that you need all these things. But seek first the kingdom of God and His righteousness, and all these things shall be added to you. Therefore do not worry about tomorrow, for tomorrow will worry about its own things. Sufficient for the day is its own trouble.

Matthew 6:25–34

Why does Jesus want us to refrain from worry?
How does freedom from worry demonstrate confidence in God's provision and care?

After Jesus' death on the cross, He ascended back to the Father in heaven. Then God the Holy Spirit descended on all who

Reflection Questions

There are five reflection questions embedded in each chapter. These questions and suggestions are there to help you get the most out of your reading. When you come to a question, pause and reflect. You will grow to understand the Bible better if you take the time to explore the issues raised by these questions. You can record your answers and observations in a journal, the companion study guide or right in your book. Then talk about your discoveries with someone. Sharing your thoughts with others is a great way to dig deeper into what you've learned.

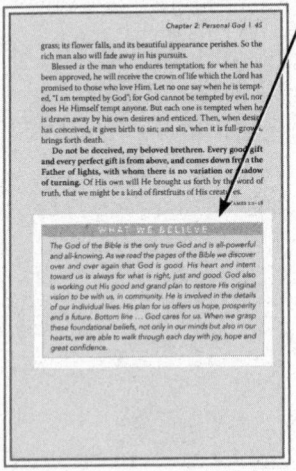
Chapter 2: Personal God | 45

grass; its flower falls, and its beautiful appearance perishes. So the rich man also will fade away in his pursuits.

Blessed is the man who endures temptation; for when he has been approved, he will receive the crown of life which the Lord has promised to those who love Him. Let no one say when he is tempted, "I am tempted by God"; for God cannot be tempted by evil, nor does He Himself tempt anyone. But each one is tempted when he is drawn away by his own desires and enticed. Then, when desire has conceived, it gives birth to sin; and sin, when it is full-grown, brings forth death.

Do not be deceived, my beloved brethren. Every good gift and every perfect gift is from above, and comes down from the Father of lights, with whom there is no variation or shadow of turning. Of His own will He brought us forth by the word of truth, that we might be a kind of firstfruits of His creatures.

JAMES 1:1–18

WHAT WE BELIEVE

The God of the Bible is the only true God and is all-powerful and all-knowing. As we read the pages of the Bible we discover over and over again that God is good. His heart and intent toward us is always for what is right, just and good. God also is working out His good and grand plan to restore His original vision to be with us, in community. He is involved in the details of our individual lives. His plan for us offers us hope, prosperity and a future. Bottom line . . . God cares for us. When we grasp these foundational beliefs, not only in our minds but also in our hearts, we are able to walk through each day with joy, hope and great confidence.

What We Believe

At the conclusion of each chapter, the What We Believe section wraps it all up. The big ideas of the belief, practice or virtue are recapped in a helpful summary so you can recall everything you learned in the chapter and put it all together in a cohesive way.

Back of the Book

At the back of the book, the epilogue gives you an idea of the global impact this story has had on the world. You'll also find the Chart of References, which lists every Scripture reference in the book.

Take It to the Next Level

Believe is a full Bible-engagement campaign with resources for an entire church, school or small group to experience together. If you have experienced *The Story* and are wondering what's next and how to go deeper, then *Believe* is the next step for you. If you haven't experienced *The Story* and are looking for a tool to help you and your church, organization or small group understand the Bible as one overarching narrative, then *The Story* will also be a useful resource for you to explore your faith. For more on *Believe* and *The Story*, check out www.thestory.com and www.believethestory.com.

THINK

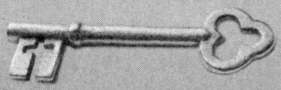

What Do I Believe?

A good man out of the good treasure of his heart
brings forth good; and an evil man out of the evil treasure
of his heart brings forth evil. For out
of the abundance of the heart his mouth speaks.
Luke 6:45

What we believe in our hearts will define who we become. God wants you to become like Jesus. This is who God created you to be. It is the most truthful and powerful way to live. The journey to *becoming* like Jesus begins by *thinking* like Jesus.

The following ten chapters will introduce and expose you to the key beliefs of the Christian life. These beliefs were not only taught by Jesus but also modeled by Jesus when He walked this earth. Because we live from the heart, embracing these core truths in both our minds and our hearts is the first step to truly becoming like Jesus.

Each of the following chapters contains Scripture passages from Genesis to Revelation focused on a particular belief. You are about to discover what God wants you to know and believe about these important topics. Embark on each page with a passion to learn and understand. Then prayerfully ask, "What do *I* believe?"

Fully adopting these fantastic truths in your heart may not come at the end of reading the chapter. If you are honest, it may take a while, and that is okay. The Christian life is a journey. There are no shortcuts. As each of the key concepts takes up residence in your heart they, with the amazing help of God's presence in your life, will change your life for the good.

When you start *thinking* like Jesus, you are well on your way to *becoming* like Jesus.

CHAPTER

1

God

KEY QUESTION

Who is God?

KEY IDEA

I believe the God of the Bible is the only true God—
Father, Son and Holy Spirit.

KEY VERSE

The grace of the Lord Jesus Christ,
and the love of God, and the communion
of the Holy Spirit *be* with you all. Amen.
2 Corinthians 13:14

OUR MAP

Belief in God is the very foundation of the Christian faith. Christianity is the only spiritual belief system that emanates from a Creator-God who had no beginning, who interacts with His creation as a plural entity and who exhibits preeminence over all other gods and beings.

We will be reading Scripture passages in this chapter that describe how we know about God, aspects of His essence and what they mean to us:

- *God Reveals Himself*
- *The One True God*
- *God in Three Persons: Father, Son and Holy Spirit*
- *The Trinity in Our Lives*

God Reveals Himself

Everything begins with God. The Bible never seeks to defend the existence of God. It is assumed. God has revealed Himself so powerfully through His creation—both at the macro and micro level—that at the end of the day, no one will have an excuse for not putting their trust in Him.

In the beginning God created the heavens and the earth.

Genesis 1:1

The heavens declare the glory of God;
And the firmament shows His handiwork.
Day unto day utters speech,
And night unto night reveals knowledge.
There is no speech nor language
Where their voice is not heard.
Their line has gone out through all the earth,
And their words to the end of the world.

In them He has set a tabernacle for the sun. Psalm 19:1–4

For since the creation of the world His invisible *attributes* are clearly seen, being understood by the things that are made, *even* His eternal power and Godhead, so that they are without excuse.

Romans 1:20

In what ways do you see
the invisible qualities
of God revealed in nature?

The One True God

From beginning to end, the Bible reveals that there is only one true God. But who is He? The book of Deuteronomy looks back at how Moses had led the Israelites out of slavery in Egypt. During that time God, through the ten plagues, had revealed Himself as the one true, all-powerful God over Pharaoh. Now a new generation had grown up in the wilderness and was poised to inherit the land God had promised Abraham. Moses offered the second generation a series of farewell speeches to remind them to choose, worship and follow the one true God—the God of Abraham, Isaac and Jacob. If they did, all would go well for them.

"Now this *is* the commandment, *and these are* the statutes and judgments which the Lord your God has commanded to teach you, that you may observe *them* in the land which you are crossing over to possess, that you may fear the Lord your God, to keep all His statutes and His commandments which I command you, you and your son and your grandson, all the days of your life, and that your days may be prolonged. Therefore hear, O Israel, and be careful to observe *it,* that it may be well with you, and that you may multiply greatly as the Lord God of your fathers has promised you—'a land flowing with milk and honey.'

"Hear, O Israel: The Lord our God, the Lord *is* one! You shall love the Lord your God with all your heart, with all your soul, and with all your strength.

"And these words which I command you today shall be in your heart. You shall teach them diligently to your children, and shall talk of them when you sit in your house, when you walk by the way, when you lie down, and when you rise up. You shall bind them as a sign on your hand, and they shall be as frontlets between your eyes. You shall write them on the doorposts of your house and on your gates."

Deuteronomy 6:1–9

What are some of the main points of God's requirements for His people? Why do you think He emphasized these things?

After Moses died, Joshua became the next great leader of the Israelites. He was charged with leading the people into the promised land. God was with them and fought for them as they began conquering the land. Under Joshua's leadership the Israelites remained steady in their devotion to God. Before Joshua died, he gathered the people together and issued them a stiff challenge to choose to serve the Lord, the one true God.

Then Joshua gathered all the tribes of Israel to Shechem and called for the elders of Israel, for their heads, for their judges, and for their officers; and they presented themselves before God. And Joshua said to all the people, "Thus says the LORD God of Israel: 'Your fathers, *including* Terah, the father of Abraham and the father of Nahor, dwelt on the other side of the River in old times; and they served other gods. Then I took your father Abraham from the other side of the River, led him throughout all the land of Canaan, and multiplied his descendants and gave him Isaac. To Isaac I gave Jacob and Esau. To Esau I gave the mountains of Seir to possess, but Jacob and his children went down to Egypt. Also I sent Moses and Aaron, and I plagued Egypt, according to what I did among them. Afterward I brought you out.

'Then I brought your fathers out of Egypt, and you came to the sea; and the Egyptians pursued your fathers with chariots and horsemen to the Red Sea. So they cried out to the LORD; and He put darkness between you and the Egyptians, brought the sea upon them, and covered them. And your eyes saw what I did in Egypt. Then you dwelt in the wilderness a long time. And I brought you into the land of the Amorites, who dwelt on the other side of the Jordan, and they fought with you. But I gave them into your hand, that you might possess their land, and I destroyed them from before you. Then Balak the son of Zippor, king of Moab, arose to make war against Israel, and sent and called Balaam the son of Beor to curse you. But I would not listen to Balaam; therefore he continued to bless you. So I delivered you out of his hand. Then you went over the Jordan and came to Jericho. And the men of Jericho fought against you—*also* the Amorites, the Perizzites, the Canaanites, the Hittites, the Girgashites, the Hivites, and the Jebusites. But I delivered them into your hand. I sent the hornet before you which drove them out from before you, *also* the two kings of the Amorites, *but* not with your sword or with your bow. I have given you a land for which you did not labor, and cities which you did not build, and you dwell in them; you eat of the vineyards and olive groves which you did not plant.'

"Now therefore, fear the LORD, serve Him in sincerity and in truth, and put away the gods which your fathers served on the other side of the River and in Egypt. Serve the LORD! And if it seems evil to you to serve the LORD, choose for yourselves this day whom you will serve, whether the gods which your fathers served that *were* on the other side of the River, or the gods of the Amorites, in whose land you dwell. But as for me and my house, we will serve the LORD."

So the people answered and said: "Far be it from us that we should forsake the LORD to serve other gods; for the LORD our God *is* He who brought us and our fathers up out of the land of Egypt, from the house of bondage, who did those great signs in our sight, and preserved us in all the way that we went and among all the people through whom we passed. And the LORD drove out from before us all the people, including the Amorites who dwelt in the land. We also will serve the LORD, for He *is* our God."

But Joshua said to the people, "You cannot serve the LORD, for He *is* a holy God. He *is* a jealous God; He will not forgive your transgressions nor your sins. If you forsake the LORD and serve foreign gods, then He will turn and do you harm and consume you, after He has done you good."

And the people said to Joshua, "No, but we will serve the LORD!"

So Joshua said to the people, "You *are* witnesses against yourselves that you have chosen the LORD for yourselves, to serve Him."

And they said, "*We are* witnesses!"

"Now therefore," *he said,* "put away the foreign gods which *are* among you, and incline your heart to the LORD God of Israel."

And the people said to Joshua, "The LORD our God we will serve, and His voice we will obey!"

So Joshua made a covenant with the people that day, and made for them a statute and an ordinance in Shechem.

Then Joshua wrote these words in the Book of the Law of God. And he took a large stone, and set it up there under the oak that *was* by the sanctuary of the LORD. And Joshua said to all the people, "Behold, this stone shall be a witness to us, for it has heard all the words of the LORD which He spoke to us. It shall therefore be a witness to you, lest you deny your God." So Joshua let the people depart, each to his own inheritance.

Now it came to pass after these things that Joshua the son of Nun, the servant of the LORD, died, *being* one hundred and ten years old. And they buried him within the border of his inheritance at Timnath Serah, which *is* in the mountains of Ephraim, on the north side of Mount Gaash.

Israel served the LORD all the days of Joshua, and all the days of the elders who outlived Joshua, who had known all the works of the LORD which He had done for Israel. JOSHUA 24:1–31

Unfortunately the Israelites failed to keep their promise to follow only God. Through the people's repeated disobedience, God weakened Israel's influence—445 years after Joshua died—by dividing them into two kingdoms: the northern kingdom of Israel and the southern kingdom of Judah. Israel did not have one good king during its more than 200 years of existence. King Ahab was particularly wicked, as he introduced the worship of the pagan god Baal to Israel. But God demonstrated through the prophet Elijah that He, the Lord, not Baal or any other "god," is the one true God.

Ahab went to meet Elijah.

Then it happened, when Ahab saw Elijah, that Ahab said to him, "*Is that* you, O troubler of Israel?"

And he answered, "I have not troubled Israel, but you and your father's house *have,* in that you have forsaken the commandments of the LORD and have followed the Baals. Now therefore, send *and* gather all Israel to me on Mount Carmel, the four hundred and fifty prophets of Baal, and the four hundred prophets of Asherah, who eat at Jezebel's table."

So Ahab sent for all the children of Israel, and gathered the prophets together on Mount Carmel. **And Elijah came to all the people, and said, "How long will you falter between two opinions? If the LORD *is* God, follow Him; but if Baal, follow him."** But the people answered him not a word. Then Elijah said to the people, "I alone am left a prophet of the LORD; but Baal's prophets *are* four hundred and fifty men. Therefore let them give us two bulls; and let them choose one bull for themselves, cut it in pieces, and lay *it* on the wood, but put no fire *under it;* and I will prepare the other bull, and lay *it* on the wood, but put no fire *under it.* Then you call on the name of your gods, and I will call on the name of the LORD; and the God who answers by fire, He is God."

So all the people answered and said, "It is well spoken."

Now Elijah said to the prophets of Baal, "Choose one bull for yourselves and prepare *it* first, for you *are* many; and call on the name of your god, but put no fire *under it.*"

So they took the bull which was given them, and they prepared *it,* and called on the name of Baal from morning even till noon, saying, "O Baal, hear us!" But *there was* no voice; no one answered. Then they leaped about the altar which they had made.

And so it was, at noon, that Elijah mocked them and said, "Cry aloud, for he *is* a god; either he is meditating, or he is busy, or he is on a journey, *or* perhaps he is sleeping and must be awakened." So they cried aloud, and cut themselves, as was their custom, with knives and lances, until the blood gushed out on them. And when midday was past, they prophesied until the *time* of the offering of the *evening* sacrifice. But *there was* no voice; no one answered, no one paid attention.

Then Elijah said to all the people, "Come near to me." So all the people came near to him. And he repaired the altar of the LORD *that was* broken down. And Elijah took twelve stones, according to the number of the tribes of the sons of Jacob, to whom the word of the LORD had come, saying, "Israel shall be your name." Then with the stones he built an altar in the name of the LORD; and he made a trench around the altar large enough to hold two seahs of seed. And he put the wood in order, cut the bull in pieces, and laid *it* on the wood, and said, "Fill four waterpots with water, and pour *it* on the burnt sacrifice and on the wood." Then he said, "Do *it* a second time," and they did *it* a second time; and he said, "Do *it* a third time," and they did *it* a third time. So the water ran all around the altar; and he also filled the trench with water.

And it came to pass, at *the time of* the offering of the *evening* sacrifice, that Elijah the prophet came near and said, "LORD God of Abraham, Isaac, and Israel, let it be known this day that You *are* God in Israel and I *am* Your servant, and *that* I have done all these things at Your word. Hear me, O LORD, hear me, that this people may know that You *are* the LORD God, and *that* You have turned their hearts back *to You* again."

Then the fire of the LORD fell and consumed the burnt sacrifice, and the wood and the stones and the dust, and it licked up the water that *was* in the trench. **Now when all the people saw *it*, they fell on their faces; and they said, "The LORD, He *is* God! The LORD, He *is* God!"**

And Elijah said to them, "Seize the prophets of Baal! Do not let one of them escape!" So they seized them; and Elijah brought them down to the Brook Kishon and executed them there. 1 KINGS 18:16–40

Why did God have to prove over and over that He is the one true God?

GOD IN THREE PERSONS: FATHER, SON AND HOLY SPIRIT

Throughout the Old Testament, people were invited to worship the one true God, but what do we know about this God of miracles and creative wonder? Christians believe God is actually three persons, a "Trinity." Though the word "Trinity" isn't found in the Bible, in the very beginning of God's story, the creation story, we see hints that God is plural. Genesis 1:26 says, "Then God said, 'Let Us make man in Our image, according to Our likeness.'" God is Himself a mini-community.

The creation story tells us we were created in God's image. When He made the first human (Adam), God wanted him to experience the community and relationship that has eternally existed within the Trinity. That's why He made Eve. Notice that Adam and

Eve were not two separate beings. Eve came out of Adam, and they became two distinct persons who shared one being, like God. God is three distinct persons who share a single being.

This *is* the history of the heavens and the earth when they were created, in the day that the LORD God made the earth and the heavens, before any plant of the field was in the earth and before any herb of the field had grown. For the LORD God had not caused it to rain on the earth, and *there was* no man to till the ground; but a mist went up from the earth and watered the whole face of the ground.

And the LORD God formed man *of* the dust of the ground, and breathed into his nostrils the breath of life; and man became a living being.

The LORD God planted a garden eastward in Eden, and there He put the man whom He had formed. And out of the ground the LORD God made every tree grow that is pleasant to the sight and good for food. The tree of life *was* also in the midst of the garden, and the tree of the knowledge of good and evil. GENESIS 2:4–9

Then the LORD God took the man and put him in the garden of Eden to tend and keep it. And the LORD God commanded the man, saying, "Of every tree of the garden you may freely eat; but of the tree of the knowledge of good and evil you shall not eat, for in the day that you eat of it you shall surely die."

And the LORD God said, "*It is* not good that man should be alone; I will make him a helper comparable to him." Out of the ground the LORD God formed every beast of the field and every bird of the air, and brought *them* to Adam to see what he would call them. And whatever Adam called each living creature, that *was* its name. So Adam gave names to all cattle, to the birds of the air, and to every beast of the field. But for Adam there was not found a helper comparable to him.

And the LORD God caused a deep sleep to fall on Adam, and he slept; and He took one of his ribs, and closed up the flesh in its place. **Then the rib which the LORD God had taken from man He made into a woman, and He brought her to the man.**

And Adam said:

"This *is* now bone of my bones
And flesh of my flesh;
She shall be called Woman,
Because she was taken out of Man."

Therefore a man shall leave his father and mother and be joined to his wife, and they shall become one flesh.

GENESIS 2:15–24

Recalling Genesis 1:26, "Then God said, 'Let Us make man in Our image, according to Our likeness,'" God as a plural being is clearly evident from the very beginning of the Bible. But what are the identities of the individual persons of God, and how are they just one being? How do they interact? The opening words of John's Gospel makes the answer more clear.

In the beginning was the Word, and the Word was with God, and the Word was God. He was in the beginning with God. All things were made through Him, and without Him nothing was made that was made. In Him was life, and the life was the light of men. And the light shines in the darkness, and the darkness did not comprehend it.

JOHN 1:1–5

The "Word" here refers to Jesus. John refers to him as "God," as divine. John also says Jesus was there in the beginning. Jesus, the divine Word, partnered with God to create all that we see and all that we have yet to see.

So who were the other members of the Trinity? The second sentence of the Bible tells us that the Holy Spirit was also present at creation: "The earth was without form, and void; and darkness was on the face of the deep. And the Spirit of God was hovering over the face of the waters" (Genesis 1:2). Jesus and the Spirit were at the creation of the world; these two persons are God. Is that it? Who else makes up the person of God? Fast-forward to the baptism of Jesus at the age of 30 to discover the answer. As you read this account, look for the appearance of all three persons of the Trinity.

Now in the fifteenth year of the reign of Tiberius Caesar, Pontius Pilate being governor of Judea, Herod being tetrarch of Galilee, his brother Philip tetrarch of Iturea and the region of Trachonitis, and Lysanias tetrarch of Abilene, while Annas and Caiaphas were high priests, the word of God came to John the son of Zacharias in the wilderness. And he went into all the region around the Jordan, preaching a baptism of repentance for the remission of sins, as it is written in the book of the words of Isaiah the prophet, saying:

> *"The voice of one crying in the wilderness:*
> *'Prepare the way of the LORD;*
> *Make His paths straight.*
> *Every valley shall be filled*
> *And every mountain and hill brought low;*
> *The crooked places shall be made straight*
> *And the rough ways smooth;*
> *And all flesh shall see the salvation of God.'"* LUKE 3:1–6

Now as the people were in expectation, and all reasoned in their hearts about John, whether he was the Christ *or* not, John answered, saying to all, "I indeed baptize you with water; but One mightier than I is coming, whose sandal strap I am not worthy to loose. He will baptize you with the Holy Spirit and fire. His winnowing fan *is* in His hand, and He will thoroughly clean out His threshing floor, and gather the wheat into His barn; but the chaff He will burn with unquenchable fire."

And with many other exhortations he preached to the people.

LUKE 3:15–18

When all the people were baptized, it came to pass that Jesus also was baptized; and while He prayed, the heaven was opened. And the Holy Spirit descended in bodily form like a dove upon Him, and a voice came from heaven which said, "You are My beloved Son; in You I am well pleased."

Now Jesus Himself began *His ministry at* about thirty years of age, being (as was supposed) *the* son of Joseph. LUKE 3:21–23

Three distinct persons are fully revealed in Scripture to make up the identity of the one true God: the Father, the Son Jesus and the Spirit. And all three were involved at the baptism of Jesus—the Father spoke, the Son was baptized and the Holy Spirit descended on the Son. Throughout the centuries, followers of Jesus have come to call the one true God the Trinity, three persons who share one being. As difficult as this concept is to understand, it is important to our lives.

In what ways have you experienced God as Father?
As Jesus the Son? As the Holy Spirit?

The Trinity in Our Lives

In the spirit of Joshua of the Old Testament, in the early church Paul called people to declare the identity of the one true God. During his travels Paul went to the great Areopagus in Athens, Greece. The intellectual people who lived there created an altar to many gods. Notice how they even created an altar dedicated "to the unknown God" in case they missed one and therefore offended them. Paul declares the identity of this God as the one who created everything in the beginning (see Genesis 1–2) and is now revealed in the second person of the Trinity, Jesus Christ. His words to the people of Athens are applicable to all those who believe—God is everywhere and there is nothing in this world that His hand has not touched. The Trinity is woven into every aspect of our lives.

Now while Paul waited for [Silas and Timothy] at Athens, his spirit was provoked within him when he saw that the city was given over to idols. Therefore he reasoned in the synagogue with the Jews and with the *Gentile* worshipers, and in the marketplace daily with those who happened to be there. Then certain Epicurean and Stoic philosophers encountered him. And some said, "What does this babbler want to say?"

Others said, "He seems to be a proclaimer of foreign gods," because he preached to them Jesus and the resurrection.

And they took him and brought him to the Areopagus, saying, "May we know what this new doctrine *is* of which you speak? For you are bringing some strange things to our ears. Therefore we want to know what these things mean." For all the Athenians and the foreigners who were there spent their time in nothing else but either to tell or to hear some new thing.

Then Paul stood in the midst of the Areopagus and said, "Men of Athens, I perceive that in all things you are very religious; for as I was passing through and considering the objects of your worship, I even found an altar with this inscription:

TO THE UNKNOWN GOD.

Therefore, the One whom you worship without knowing, Him I proclaim to you: **God, who made the world and everything in it, since He is Lord of heaven and earth, does not dwell in temples made with hands. Nor is He worshiped with men's hands, as though He needed anything, since He gives to all life, breath, and all things.** And He has made from one blood every nation of men to dwell on all the face of the earth, and has determined their preappointed times and the boundaries of their dwellings, so that they should seek the Lord, in the hope that they might grope for Him and find Him, though He is not far from each one of us; for in Him we live and move and have our being, as also some of your own poets have said, 'For we are also His offspring.' **Therefore, since we are the offspring of God, we ought not to think that the Divine Nature is like gold or silver or stone, something shaped by art and man's devising. Truly, these times of ignorance God overlooked, but now commands all men everywhere to repent, because He has appointed a day on which He will judge the world in righteousness by the Man whom He has ordained. He has given assurance of this to all by raising Him from the dead."**

And when they heard of the resurrection of the dead, some mocked, while others said, "We will hear you again on this *matter.*" So Paul departed from among them. However, some men joined him and believed, among them Dionysius the Areopagite, a woman named Damaris, and others with them. ACTS 17:16–34

What is meant by the phrase Paul quoted: "For in Him we live and move and have our being?" Why do you think this needed to be said to this group of Athenians?

The power and identity of the one true God is highlighted throughout Paul's writing, including the last words of 2 Corinthians, which he penned with the benediction below.

The grace of the Lord Jesus Christ, and the love of God, and the communion of the Holy Spirit *be* with you all. 2 CORINTHIANS 13:14

Notice how all three members of the Trinity are involved in our lives. God, the Father, loves us and sought a way for us to come back into a relationship with Him. Jesus, the second person of the Trinity, provided the way back to God by offering Himself as a sacrifice in our place. Now that we believe, the Holy Spirit, the third person of the Trinity, fellowships with us as we journey through life, guiding and comforting us every step of the way.

WHAT WE BELIEVE

The Bible never tries to prove the existence of God—His existence is simply an assumed fact. God has clearly revealed Himself through creation, in events such as Jesus' baptism and in our own consciences, leaving everyone without excuse in the end. The key question we asked at the beginning of this chapter comes down to the declaration of who the one true God is. The God who protected Israel and demonstrated power over false gods declares, "I AM!"

The journey of faith begins with our belief in God. Like the Israelites of the Old Testament and the early Christians of the New Testament, we too are called to make a personal declaration. Do we believe in the one true God? Do we accept the Bible's revelation that God exists in three persons?

THINK

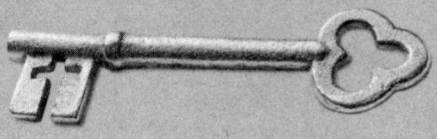

CHAPTER

2

Personal God

KEY QUESTION

Does God care about me?

KEY IDEA

I believe God is involved in and cares
about my daily life.

KEY VERSE

I will lift up my eyes to the hills—
From whence comes my help?
My help *comes* from the LORD,
Who made heaven and earth.
Psalm 121:1–2

OUR MAP

The God of the Bible is the only true God—Father, Son and Holy Spirit. He is the one all-powerful, all-knowing eternal God. But is He good? Is He involved in His creation? Does He love us? Does He have a plan for us? Is He interceding and intervening to move the events of our life and world toward His intended purpose?

We can consider these questions as we read the Scripture passages in this chapter that explore three ways God shows us He is a personal God:

- *God Is Good*
- *God Has a Plan*
- *God Cares for Us*

God Is Good

Abraham and Sarah—the great patriarch and matriarch of the Israelite people—were first named Abram and Sarai. God had promised Abraham that he would be the father of a great nation, but how can you father a nation when you have no children?

As you read the passage below from Genesis 16,
look for some ways in which God showed
His goodness to Abraham, Sarah and Hagar.
What impact did this have on them?

Now Sarai, Abram's wife, had borne him no *children.* And she had an Egyptian maidservant whose name was Hagar. So Sarai said to Abram, "See now, the Lord has restrained me from bearing *children.* Please, go in to my maid; perhaps I shall obtain children by her." And Abram heeded the voice of Sarai. Then Sarai, Abram's wife, took Hagar her maid, the Egyptian, and gave her to her husband Abram to be his wife, after Abram had dwelt ten years in the land of Canaan. So he went in to Hagar, and she conceived. And when she saw that she had conceived, her mistress became despised in her eyes.

Then Sarai said to Abram, "My wrong *be* upon you! I gave

my maid into your embrace; and when she saw that she had conceived, I became despised in her eyes. The LORD judge between you and me."

So Abram said to Sarai, "Indeed your maid *is* in your hand; do to her as you please." And when Sarai dealt harshly with her, she fled from her presence.

Now the Angel of the LORD found her by a spring of water in the wilderness, by the spring on the way to Shur. And He said, "Hagar, Sarai's maid, where have you come from, and where are you going?"

She said, "I am fleeing from the presence of my mistress Sarai."

The Angel of the LORD said to her, "Return to your mistress, and submit yourself under her hand." Then the Angel of the LORD said to her, "I will multiply your descendants exceedingly, so that they shall not be counted for multitude." And the Angel of the LORD said to her:

> "Behold, you *are* with child,
> And you shall bear a son.
> You shall call his name Ishmael,
> Because the LORD has heard your affliction.
> He shall be a wild man;
> His hand *shall be* against every man,
> And every man's hand against him.
> And he shall dwell in the presence of all his brethren."

Then she called the name of the LORD who spoke to her, You-Are-the-God-Who-Sees; for she said, "Have I also here seen Him who sees me?" Therefore the well was called Beer Lahai Roi; observe, *it is* between Kadesh and Bered.

So Hagar bore Abram a son; and Abram named his son, whom Hagar bore, Ishmael. Abram *was* eighty-six years old when Hagar bore Ishmael to Abram.

GENESIS 16:1–16

Abraham and Sarah tried to "help God out" by having Abraham father a child with Hagar. What resulted was a debacle for everyone involved. But in this story, we see the beginning of a pattern—God takes our messes and turns them into something good. Hagar involuntarily became party to Abraham's and

Sarah's lack of faith. Yet God heard her cries and helped her. The story continues . . .

And the LORD visited Sarah as He had said, and the LORD did for Sarah as He had spoken. For Sarah conceived and bore Abraham a son in his old age, at the set time of which God had spoken to him. And Abraham called the name of his son who was born to him—whom Sarah bore to him—Isaac. Then Abraham circumcised his son Isaac when he was eight days old, as God had commanded him. Now Abraham was one hundred years old when his son Isaac was born to him. **And Sarah said, "God has made me laugh, *and* all who hear will laugh with me."** She also said, "Who would have said to Abraham that Sarah would nurse children? For I have borne *him* a son in his old age."

So the child grew and was weaned. And Abraham made a great feast on the same day that Isaac was weaned.

And Sarah saw the son of Hagar the Egyptian, whom she had borne to Abraham, scoffing. Therefore she said to Abraham, "Cast out this bondwoman and her son; for the son of this bondwoman shall not be heir with my son, *namely* with Isaac." And the matter was very displeasing in Abraham's sight because of his son.

But God said to Abraham, "Do not let it be displeasing in your sight because of the lad or because of your bondwoman. Whatever Sarah has said to you, listen to her voice; for in Isaac your seed shall be called. Yet I will also make a nation of the son of the bondwoman, because he *is* your seed."

So Abraham rose early in the morning, and took bread and a skin of water; and putting *it* on her shoulder, he gave *it* and the boy to Hagar, and sent her away. Then she departed and wandered in the Wilderness of Beersheba. And the water in the skin was used up, and she placed the boy under one of the shrubs. Then she went and sat down across from *him* at a distance of about a bowshot; for she said to herself, "Let me not see the death of the boy." So she sat opposite *him,* and lifted her voice and wept.

And God heard the voice of the lad. Then the angel of God called to Hagar out of heaven, and said to her, "What ails you, Hagar? Fear not, for God has heard the voice of the lad where

he *is*. Arise, lift up the lad and hold him with your hand, for I will make him a great nation."

Then God opened her eyes, and she saw a well of water. And she went and filled the skin with water, and gave the lad a drink. So God was with the lad; and he grew and dwelt in the wilderness, and became an archer. He dwelt in the Wilderness of Paran; and his mother took a wife for him from the land of Egypt.

GENESIS 21:1–21

Even though Hagar and Ishmael weren't the main characters in the Biblical story line, God still provided for them and promised to bless their descendants. He did this because He is a compassionate and personal God.

Another Biblical character in whose life we see how much God is involved and cares about His people is David, the poet, singer, shepherd, warrior and king, who wrote and sang from a deep well of faith as he journeyed through life and encountered the one true God. David composed many of the psalms found in our Bible: he wrote as a shepherd boy while gazing at the billions of stars God created; he wrote while being chased down by King Saul; he wrote while he was king of Israel; and he wrote as he was coming to the end of his life on earth. The songs that David and the other psalmists wrote express their personal and intimate relationship with God.

O LORD, our Lord,
How excellent *is* Your name in all the earth,
Who have set Your glory above the heavens!

Out of the mouth of babes and nursing infants
You have ordained strength,
Because of Your enemies,
That You may silence the enemy and the avenger.

When I consider Your heavens, the work of Your fingers,
The moon and the stars, which You have ordained,
What is man that You are mindful of him,
And the son of man that You visit him?

For You have made him a little lower than the angels,
And You have crowned him with glory and honor.

You have made him to have dominion over the works
of Your hands;
You have put all *things* under his feet,
All sheep and oxen—
Even the beasts of the field,
The birds of the air,
And the fish of the sea
That pass through the paths of the seas.

O LORD, our Lord,
How excellent *is* Your name in all the earth! PSALM 8:1–9

The LORD *is* my shepherd;
I shall not want.
He makes me to lie down in green pastures;
He leads me beside the still waters.
He restores my soul;
He leads me in the paths of righteousness
For His name's sake.

Yea, though I walk through the valley of the shadow
of death,
I will fear no evil;
For You *are* with me;
Your rod and Your staff, they comfort me.

You prepare a table before me in the presence of my
enemies;
You anoint my head with oil;
My cup runs over.
Surely goodness and mercy shall follow me
All the days of my life;
And I will dwell in the house of the LORD
Forever. PSALM 23:1–6

O LORD, You have searched me and known *me*.
You know my sitting down and my rising up;

You understand my thought afar off.
You comprehend my path and my lying down,
And are acquainted with all my ways.
For *there is* not a word on my tongue,
But behold, O LORD, You know it altogether.
You have hedged me behind and before,
And laid Your hand upon me.
Such knowledge *is* too wonderful for me;
It is high, I cannot *attain* it.

Where can I go from Your Spirit?
Or where can I flee from Your presence?
If I ascend into heaven, You *are* there;
If I make my bed in hell, behold, You *are there.*
If I take the wings of the morning,
And dwell in the uttermost parts of the sea,
Even there Your hand shall lead me,
And Your right hand shall hold me.
If I say, "Surely the darkness shall fall on me,"
Even the night shall be light about me;
Indeed, the darkness shall not hide from You,
But the night shines as the day;
The darkness and the light *are* both alike *to You.*

For You formed my inward parts;
You covered me in my mother's womb.
I will praise You, for I am fearfully *and* wonderfully made;
Marvelous are Your works,
And *that* my soul knows very well.
My frame was not hidden from You,
When I was made in secret,
And skillfully wrought in the lowest parts of the earth.
Your eyes saw my substance, being yet unformed.
And in Your book they all were written,
The days fashioned for me,
When *as yet there were* none of them.

How precious also are Your thoughts to me, O God!
How great is the sum of them!

If I should count them, they would be more in number
than the sand;
When I awake, I am still with You. PSALM 139:1–18

How have you experienced God's personal knowledge of you? When have you known He was searching your heart? What was the result?

I will extol You, my God, O King;
And I will bless Your name forever and ever.
Every day I will bless You,
And I will praise Your name forever and ever.
Great *is* the LORD, and greatly to be praised;
And His greatness *is* unsearchable.

One generation shall praise Your works to another,
And shall declare Your mighty acts.
I will meditate on the glorious splendor of Your majesty,
And on Your wondrous works.
Men shall speak of the might of Your awesome acts,
And I will declare Your greatness.
They shall utter the memory of Your great goodness,
And shall sing of Your righteousness.

The LORD *is* gracious and full of compassion,
Slow to anger and great in mercy.
The LORD *is* good to all,
And His tender mercies *are* over all His works.

All Your works shall praise You, O LORD,
And Your saints shall bless You.
They shall speak of the glory of Your kingdom,
And talk of Your power,
To make known to the sons of men His mighty acts,
And the glorious majesty of His kingdom.
Your kingdom *is* an everlasting kingdom,
And Your dominion *endures* throughout all generations.

The LORD upholds all who fall,
And raises up all *who are* bowed down.
The eyes of all look expectantly to You,
And You give them their food in due season.
You open Your hand
And satisfy the desire of every living thing.

The LORD *is* righteous in all His ways,
Gracious in all His works.
The LORD *is* near to all who call upon Him,
To all who call upon Him in truth.
He will fulfill the desire of those who fear Him;
He also will hear their cry and save them.
The LORD preserves all who love Him,
But all the wicked He will destroy.
My mouth shall speak the praise of the LORD,
And all flesh shall bless His holy name
Forever and ever.

PSALM 145:1–21

GOD HAS A PLAN

Forty years after David's death, the nation of Israel was torn apart, and what resulted were two nations: the northern kingdom of Israel and the southern kingdom of Judah. All the kings of Israel did evil in the eyes of the Lord. In Judah, only a handful of kings were good. One of them was Hezekiah. He courageously served the Lord in perilous times.

Then when he was about thirty-eight years old, Hezekiah became ill and was about to die. He was devastated and pleaded with the Lord for mercy. In response, the Lord sent him a shocking message and a tender change of plan. We know from the Bible that God has a plan for our individual lives and has our days numbered. This story shows how God will hear our prayers and see our tears. He may not answer us in the way we desire, but He will sometimes alter the plan He has for us at our request.

In those days Hezekiah was sick and near death. And Isaiah the prophet, the son of Amoz, went to him and said to him, "Thus says the LORD: 'Set your house in order, for you shall die, and not live.'"

Then he turned his face toward the wall, and prayed to the

LORD, saying, "Remember now, O LORD, I pray, how I have walked before You in truth and with a loyal heart, and have done *what was* good in Your sight." And Hezekiah wept bitterly.

And it happened, before Isaiah had gone out into the middle court, that the word of the LORD came to him, saying, **"Return and tell Hezekiah the leader of My people, 'Thus says the LORD, the God of David your father: "I have heard your prayer, I have seen your tears; surely I will heal you. On the third day you shall go up to the house of the LORD. And I will add to your days fifteen years.** I will deliver you and this city from the hand of the king of Assyria; and I will defend this city for My own sake, and for the sake of My servant David."'"

Then Isaiah said, "Take a lump of figs." So they took and laid *it* on the boil, and he recovered. 2 KINGS 20:1–7

While Hezekiah's story focuses on the length of his life, Jeremiah's story goes all the way back before he was born. Jeremiah was a prophet who lived in the time of the divided kingdom. He lived in the southern kingdom of Judah and prophesied to the people there of their coming conquest and exile by the Babylonians. In the lives of both Hezekiah and Jeremiah, God was not distant or ambivalent, but near and loving. Notice how specific and detailed God's warnings were, and yet how He assured Jeremiah of His intervention and protection.

The words of Jeremiah the son of Hilkiah, of the priests who *were* in Anathoth in the land of Benjamin, to whom the word of the LORD came in the days of Josiah the son of Amon, king of Judah, in the thirteenth year of his reign. It came also in the days of Jehoiakim the son of Josiah, king of Judah, until the end of the eleventh year of Zedekiah the son of Josiah, king of Judah, until the carrying away of Jerusalem captive in the fifth month.

Then the word of the LORD came to me, saying:

"Before I formed you in the womb I knew you;
Before you were born I sanctified you;
I ordained you a prophet to the nations."

Then said I:

"Ah, Lord GOD!
Behold, I cannot speak, for I *am* a youth."

But the LORD said to me:

"Do not say, 'I *am* a youth,'
For you shall go to all to whom I send you,
And whatever I command you, you shall speak.
Do not be afraid of their faces,
For I *am* with you to deliver you," says the LORD.

Then the LORD put forth His hand and touched my mouth, and the LORD said to me:

"Behold, I have put My words in your mouth.
See, I have this day set you over the nations and over the kingdoms,
To root out and to pull down,
To destroy and to throw down,
To build and to plant."

Moreover the word of the LORD came to me, saying, "Jeremiah, what do you see?"

And I said, "I see a branch of an almond tree."

Then the LORD said to me, "You have seen well, for I am ready to perform My word."

And the word of the LORD came to me the second time, saying, "What do you see?"

And I said, "I see a boiling pot, and it is facing away from the north."

Then the LORD said to me:

"Out of the north calamity shall break forth
On all the inhabitants of the land.
For behold, I am calling
All the families of the kingdoms of the north," says the LORD;
"They shall come and each one set his throne
At the entrance of the gates of Jerusalem,
Against all its walls all around,
And against all the cities of Judah.

I will utter My judgments
Against them concerning all their wickedness,
Because they have forsaken Me,
Burned incense to other gods,
And worshiped the works of their own hands.

"Therefore prepare yourself and arise,
And speak to them all that I command you.
Do not be dismayed before their faces,
Lest I dismay you before them.
For behold, I have made you this day
A fortified city and an iron pillar,
And bronze walls against the whole land—
Against the kings of Judah,
Against its princes,
Against its priests,
And against the people of the land.
They will fight against you,
But they shall not prevail against you.
For I *am* with you," says the LORD, "to deliver you."

JEREMIAH 1:1–19

Jeremiah's role was to reveal the overall plan God was unfolding through Israel. He warned the southern kingdom of Judah about their unfaithfulness and God's pending discipline. He knew up front that they would not listen, but his task was simply to be faithful and courageous and to deliver the message from God. Three times the dreaded Babylonians attacked Jerusalem and carried away some of the people to Babylon. In 597 BC, after the second deportation, God gave Jeremiah the assignment of writing a letter to those exiles to remind them that, as Jeremiah had experienced personally, God had a grand and good plan for their lives.

Now these *are* the words of the letter that Jeremiah the prophet sent from Jerusalem to the remainder of the elders who were carried away captive—to the priests, the prophets, and all the people whom Nebuchadnezzar had carried away captive from Jerusalem to Babylon. (This happened after Jeconiah the king, the queen mother, the eunuchs, the princes of Judah and Jerusalem, the craftsmen, and the smiths had departed from Jerusalem.) *The letter was sent* by the hand of Elasah the son of Shaphan, and Gemariah the son of Hilkiah, whom Zedekiah king of Judah sent to Babylon, to Nebuchadnezzar king of Babylon, saying,

Thus says the LORD of hosts, the God of Israel, to all who were carried away captive, whom I have caused to be carried away from Jerusalem to Babylon:

Build houses and dwell *in them;* plant gardens and eat their fruit. Take wives and beget sons and daughters; and take wives for your sons and give your daughters to husbands, so that they may bear sons and daughters—that you may be increased there, and not diminished. And seek the peace of the city where I have caused you to be carried away captive, and pray to the LORD for it; for in its peace you will have peace. For thus says the LORD of hosts, the God of Israel: Do not let your prophets and your diviners who are in your midst deceive you, nor listen to your dreams which you cause to be dreamed. For they prophesy falsely to you in My name; I have not sent them, says the LORD.

For thus says the LORD: After seventy years are completed at Babylon, I will visit you and perform My good word toward you, and cause you to return to this place. **For I know the thoughts that I think toward you, says the LORD, thoughts of peace and not of evil, to give you a future and a hope.** Then you will call upon Me and go and pray to Me, and I will listen to you. And you will seek Me and find *Me,* when you search for Me with all your heart. I will be found by you, says the LORD, and I will bring you back from your captivity; I will gather you from all the nations and from all the places where I have driven you, says the LORD, and I will bring you to the place from which I cause you to be carried away captive.

JEREMIAH 29:1–14

How did God show the captives
in Babylon that He still cared for them
and wanted the best for them?

God Cares for Us

Jesus, the Son of God, came to earth. He was born as a human baby and lived among us. His arrival removes any doubt about the nearness of God in our lives. Jesus is Immanuel, "God with us."

When a large crowd assembled on a hillside by the Sea of Galilee, Jesus taught this weary and worn bunch about the intimate involvement of God in their lives.

"Therefore I say to you, do not worry about your life, what you will eat or what you will drink; nor about your body, what you will put on. Is not life more than food and the body more than clothing? Look at the birds of the air, for they neither sow nor reap nor gather into barns; yet your heavenly Father feeds them. Are you not of more value than they? Which of you by worrying can add one cubit to his stature?

"So why do you worry about clothing? Consider the lilies of the field, how they grow: they neither toil nor spin; and yet I say to you that even Solomon in all his glory was not arrayed like one of these. Now if God so clothes the grass of the field, which today is, and tomorrow is thrown into the oven, *will He* not much more *clothe* you, O you of little faith?

"Therefore do not worry, saying, 'What shall we eat?' or 'What shall we drink?' or 'What shall we wear?' For after all these things the Gentiles seek. For your heavenly Father knows that you need all these things. But seek first the kingdom of God and His righteousness, and all these things shall be added to you. Therefore do not worry about tomorrow, for tomorrow will worry about its own things. Sufficient for the day *is* its own trouble."

Matthew 6:25–34

Why does Jesus want us to refrain from worry?
How does freedom from worry demonstrate confidence in God's provision and care?

After Jesus' death on the cross, He ascended back to the Father in heaven. Then God the Holy Spirit descended on all who believed in Jesus. The dwelling place for God was no longer in temples built by human hands but in the spirits of His people. From the inside out the Holy Spirit speaks to us, ministers to us, affirms us, directs us, challenges us and empowers us. With pen in hand, the apostle Paul instructed the church that gathered in Rome of this great truth.

Therefore, brethren, we are debtors—not to the flesh, to live according to the flesh. For if you live according to the flesh you will die; but if by the Spirit you put to death the deeds of the body, you will live.

ROMANS 8:12–13

Likewise the Spirit also helps in our weaknesses. For we do not know what we should pray for as we ought, but the Spirit Himself makes intercession for us with groanings which cannot be uttered. Now He who searches the hearts knows what the mind of the Spirit *is,* because He makes intercession for the saints according to *the will of* God.

And we know that all things work together for good to those who love God, to those who are the called according to *His* purpose. For whom He foreknew, He also predestined *to be* conformed to the image of His Son, that He might be the firstborn among many brethren. Moreover whom He predestined, these He also called; whom He called, these He also justified; and whom He justified, these He also glorified.

What then shall we say to these things? **If God *is* for us, who *can be* against us? He who did not spare His own Son, but delivered Him up for us all, how shall He not with Him also freely give us all things?** Who shall bring a charge against God's elect? *It is* God who justifies. Who *is* he who condemns? *It is* Christ who died, and furthermore is also risen, who is even at the right hand of God, who also makes intercession for us. Who shall separate us from the love of Christ? *Shall* tribulation, or distress, or persecution, or famine, or nakedness, or peril, or sword? As it is written:

"For Your sake we are killed all day long;
We are accounted as sheep for the slaughter."

Yet in all these things we are more than conquerors through Him who loved us. For I am persuaded that neither death nor life, nor angels nor principalities nor powers, nor things present nor things to come, nor height nor depth, nor any other created thing, shall be able to separate us from the love of God which is in Christ Jesus our Lord. ROMANS 8:26–39

What amazing love God has for His people! In the spirit of this love, James, the half brother of Jesus, wrote a practical letter to Jesus' early disciples. He reminded them that God is involved in and cares about their daily lives—although they too had a role to play. As believers, we can acknowledge God's involvement in our lives, even during seasons of trial. We can seek God and ask Him for wisdom. We must also be careful not to blame God for our trials and temptations and realize that every good gift comes from His hands.

As you read the passage below from James 1, ask yourself:
How does God show His care and concern
for us when we go through difficult seasons in life?

James, a bondservant of God and of the Lord Jesus Christ,

To the twelve tribes which are scattered abroad:

Greetings.

My brethren, count it all joy when you fall into various trials, knowing that the testing of your faith produces patience. But let patience have *its* perfect work, that you may be perfect and complete, lacking nothing. If any of you lacks wisdom, let him ask of God, who gives to all liberally and without reproach, and it will be given to him. But let him ask in faith, with no doubting, for he who doubts is like a wave of the sea driven and tossed by the wind. For let not that man suppose that he will receive anything from the Lord; *he is* a double-minded man, unstable in all his ways.

Let the lowly brother glory in his exaltation, but the rich in his humiliation, because as a flower of the field he will pass away. For no sooner has the sun risen with a burning heat than it withers the grass; its flower falls, and its beautiful appearance perishes. So the rich man also will fade away in his pursuits.

Blessed *is* the man who endures temptation; for when he has been approved, he will receive the crown of life which the Lord has promised to those who love Him. Let no one say when he is tempted, "I am tempted by God"; for God cannot be tempted by evil, nor does He Himself tempt anyone. But each one is tempted when he is drawn away by his own desires and enticed. Then, when desire has conceived, it gives birth to sin; and sin, when it is full-grown, brings forth death.

Do not be deceived, my beloved brethren. Every good gift and every perfect gift is from above, and comes down from the Father of lights, with whom there is no variation or shadow of turning. Of His own will He brought us forth by the word of truth, that we might be a kind of firstfruits of His creatures.

JAMES 1:1–18

WHAT WE BELIEVE

The God of the Bible is the only true God and is all-powerful and all-knowing. As we read the pages of the Bible we discover over and over again that God is good. His heart and intent toward us is always for what is right, just and good. God also is working out His good and grand plan to restore His original vision to be with us, in community. He is involved in the details of our individual lives. His plan for us offers us hope, prosperity and a future. Bottom line … God cares for us. When we grasp these foundational beliefs, not only in our minds but also in our hearts, we are able to walk through each day with joy, hope and great confidence.

THINK

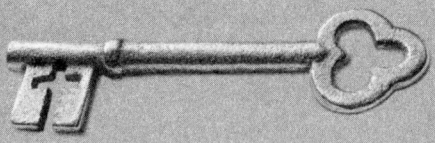

CHAPTER

3

Salvation

KEY QUESTION

How do I have a relationship with God?

KEY IDEA

I believe a person comes into a right relationship with God by God's grace through faith in Jesus Christ.

KEY VERSE

For by grace you have been saved through faith, and that not of yourselves; *it is* the gift of God, not of works, lest anyone should boast.
Ephesians 2:8–9

OUR MAP

We have discovered so far that the God of the Bible is the one true God—Father, Son and Holy Spirit. We have also discovered He is not a distant deity, uninterested in our world and our lives; He is personal and near. He is utterly good. He has a plan and purpose for our lives. He cares deeply for us. Now we turn to what may be the most important question of all, "How do I come into a relationship with God?"

In this chapter we will be reading a collection of Scripture passages about salvation that has all the makings of the greatest love story ever told:

- *The Problem: We Are Not Born Into a Relationship With God*
- *The Solution: There Is Only One Solution and Our Good God Provided It*
- *The Outcome: A Lasting Relationship With Our Loving God*

The Problem: We Are Not Born Into a Relationship With God

Satan, the great deceiver, clothed himself as a serpent, one of God's good creatures, and set out to trick Adam and Eve into disobeying their gracious God. After creating Adam and Eve, God told them not to eat of the fruit of a certain tree in the Garden of Eden. But Satan suggested that God wasn't being honest when He warned of the results of eating the forbidden fruit. The great deceiver's ploy succeeded, and Adam and Eve willfully rejected God and His promise of life together with them in the garden.

The consequences of Adam and Eve's rebellion were passed on to their offspring and then again and again to every generation since. Every human born receives this "virus" at conception and then acts out of this nature throughout their life. The Bible calls it sin. It causes death—both the physical death of our bodies and the spiritual death of separation from God.

The Lord God planted a garden eastward in Eden, and there He put the man whom He had formed. And out of the ground the Lord God made every tree grow that is pleasant to the sight and good for food. The tree of life *was* also in the midst of the garden, and the tree of the knowledge of good and evil. GENESIS 2:8–9

Then the LORD God took the man and put him in the garden of Eden to tend and keep it. And the LORD God commanded the man, saying, "Of every tree of the garden you may freely eat; but of the tree of the knowledge of good and evil you shall not eat, for in the day that you eat of it you shall surely die."

GENESIS 2:15–17

Now the serpent was more cunning than any beast of the field which the LORD God had made. And he said to the woman, "Has God indeed said, 'You shall not eat of every tree of the garden'?"

And the woman said to the serpent, "We may eat the fruit of the trees of the garden; but of the fruit of the tree which *is* in the midst of the garden, God has said, 'You shall not eat it, nor shall you touch it, lest you die.'"

Then the serpent said to the woman, "You will not surely die. For God knows that in the day you eat of it your eyes will be opened, and you will be like God, knowing good and evil."

So when the woman saw that the tree *was* good for food, that it *was* pleasant to the eyes, and a tree desirable to make *one* wise, she took of its fruit and ate. She also gave to her husband with her, and he ate. Then the eyes of both of them were opened, and they knew that they *were* naked; and they sewed fig leaves together and made themselves coverings.

And they heard the sound of the LORD God walking in the garden in the cool of the day, and Adam and his wife hid themselves from the presence of the LORD God among the trees of the garden.

Then the LORD God called to Adam and said to him, "Where *are* you?"

So he said, "I heard Your voice in the garden, and I was afraid because I was naked; and I hid myself."

And He said, "Who told you that you *were* naked? Have you eaten from the tree of which I commanded you that you should not eat?"

Then the man said, "The woman whom You gave *to be* with me, she gave me of the tree, and I ate."

And the LORD God said to the woman, "What *is* this you have done?"

The woman said, "The serpent deceived me, and I ate."

So the LORD God said to the serpent:

"Because you have done this,
You *are* cursed more than all cattle,
And more than every beast of the field;
On your belly you shall go,
And you shall eat dust
All the days of your life.
And I will put enmity
Between you and the woman,
And between your seed and her Seed;
He shall bruise your head,
And you shall bruise His heel."

To the woman He said:

"I will greatly multiply your sorrow and your conception;
In pain you shall bring forth children;
Your desire *shall be* for your husband,
And he shall rule over you."

Then to Adam He said, "Because you have heeded the voice of your wife, and have eaten from the tree of which I commanded you, saying, 'You shall not eat of it':

"Cursed *is* the ground for your sake;
In toil you shall eat *of* it
All the days of your life.
Both thorns and thistles it shall bring forth for you,
And you shall eat the herb of the field.
In the sweat of your face you shall eat bread
Till you return to the ground,
For out of it you were taken;
For dust you *are,*
And to dust you shall return."

And Adam called his wife's name Eve, because she was the mother of all living.

Also for Adam and his wife the LORD God made tunics of skin, and clothed them.

Then the LORD God said, "Behold, the man has become like one of Us, to know good and evil. And now, lest he put out his hand and take also of the tree of life, and eat, and live forever"—**therefore the LORD God sent him out of the garden of Eden to till the ground from which he was taken. So He drove out the man; and He placed cherubim at the east of the garden of Eden, and a flaming sword which turned every way, to guard the way to the tree of life.** GENESIS 3:1–24

How would you describe Adam and Eve's life in the garden with God before they disobeyed Him? What was life with God like for them afterward?

THE SOLUTION: THERE IS ONLY ONE SOLUTION AND OUR GOOD GOD PROVIDED IT

When Adam and Eve sinned, God set into motion His plan to get people back into a relationship with Him. When He replaced their clothes of fig leaves with the skins of animals, He signaled something important—it would take the blood of another to cover the sins of humankind. God began the founding of a brand-new nation through which He would reveal Himself and His plan to restore humankind. For more than 1,600 years, every Biblical story of the chosen people of Israel would point to the coming of the solution.

One of the earliest examples of this "blood covering" took place as God was preparing to deliver Israel from 400 years of captivity in Egypt. God chose Moses as His messenger to Pharaoh to demand that he release God's people from slavery and let them take possession of the promised land. But Pharaoh was hardhearted and would not let the people leave. To make Pharaoh understand and believe in God's power, God issued ten brutal plagues on Egypt and its people. The tenth and final plague foreshadows the ultimate solution of deliverance from humankind's slavery to sin.

And the LORD said to Moses, "I will bring one more plague on Pharaoh and on Egypt. Afterward he will let you go from here. When he lets *you* go, he will surely drive you out of here altogether. Speak now in the hearing of the people, and let every man ask from his neighbor and every woman from her neighbor, articles of silver and articles of gold." And the LORD gave the people favor in the sight of the Egyptians. Moreover the man Moses *was* very great in the land of Egypt, in the sight of Pharaoh's servants and in the sight of the people.

Then Moses said, "Thus says the LORD: 'About midnight I will go out into the midst of Egypt; and all the firstborn in the land of Egypt shall die, from the firstborn of Pharaoh who sits on his throne, even to the firstborn of the female servant who *is* behind the handmill, and all the firstborn of the animals. Then there shall be a great cry throughout all the land of Egypt, such as was not like it *before,* nor shall be like it again. But against none of the children of Israel shall a dog move its tongue, against man or beast, that you may know that the LORD does make a difference between the Egyptians and Israel.' And all these your servants shall come down to me and bow down to me, saying, 'Get out, and all the people who follow you!' After that I will go out." Then he went out from Pharaoh in great anger.

But the LORD said to Moses, "Pharaoh will not heed you, so that My wonders may be multiplied in the land of Egypt." So Moses and Aaron did all these wonders before Pharaoh; and the LORD hardened Pharaoh's heart, and he did not let the children of Israel go out of his land.

Now the LORD spoke to Moses and Aaron in the land of Egypt, saying, "This month *shall be* your beginning of months; it *shall be* the first month of the year to you. Speak to all the congregation of Israel, saying: 'On the tenth of this month every man shall take for himself a lamb, according to the house of *his* father, a lamb for a household. And if the household is too small for the lamb, let him and his neighbor next to his house take *it* according to the number of the persons; according to each man's need you shall make your count for the lamb. Your lamb shall be without blemish, a male of the first year. You may take *it* from the sheep or from the goats. Now you shall keep it until the fourteenth day of the same month.

Then the whole assembly of the congregation of Israel shall kill it at twilight. And they shall take *some* of the blood and put *it* on the two doorposts and on the lintel of the houses where they eat it. Then they shall eat the flesh on that night; roasted in fire, with unleavened bread *and* with bitter *herbs* they shall eat it. Do not eat it raw, nor boiled at all with water, but roasted in fire—its head with its legs and its entrails. You shall let none of it remain until morning, and what remains of it until morning you shall burn with fire. And thus you shall eat it: *with* a belt on your waist, your sandals on your feet, and your staff in your hand. So you shall eat it in haste. It *is* the LORD's Passover.

'For I will pass through the land of Egypt on that night, and will strike all the firstborn in the land of Egypt, both man and beast; and against all the gods of Egypt I will execute judgment: I *am* the LORD. Now the blood shall be a sign for you on the houses where you *are.* And when I see the blood, I will pass over you; and the plague shall not be on you to destroy *you* when I strike the land of Egypt.'"

EXODUS 11:1—12:13

What are the similarities between the sacrificed lamb and the sacrifice of Jesus? What type of "Passover" has been caused by Jesus' blood applied to our lives?

Then Moses called for all the elders of Israel and said to them, "Pick out and take lambs for yourselves according to your families, and kill the Passover *lamb.* And you shall take a bunch of hyssop, dip *it* in the blood that *is* in the basin, and strike the lintel and the two doorposts with the blood that *is* in the basin. And none of you shall go out of the door of his house until morning. For the LORD will pass through to strike the Egyptians; and when He sees the blood on the lintel and on the two doorposts, the LORD will pass over the door and not allow the destroyer to come into your houses to strike *you.* And you shall observe this thing as an ordinance for you and your sons forever. It will come to pass when you come to the land which the LORD will give you, just as He promised, that you shall keep this service. And it shall be, when your children say to you, 'What do you mean by this service?' that you shall say, 'It *is* the Passover sacrifice of the LORD, who passed over the houses of the children of Israel in Egypt when He struck the Egyptians and delivered our households.'" So the people bowed their heads and worshiped. Then the children of Israel went away and did *so;* just as the LORD had commanded Moses and Aaron, so they did.

And it came to pass at midnight that the LORD struck all the firstborn in the land of Egypt, from the firstborn of Pharaoh who sat on his throne to the firstborn of the captive who *was* in the dungeon, and all the firstborn of livestock. So Pharaoh rose in the night, he, all his servants, and all the Egyptians; and there was a great cry in Egypt, for *there was* not a house where *there was* not one dead.

Then he called for Moses and Aaron by night, and said, "Rise, go out from among my people, both you and the children of Israel. And go, serve the LORD as you have said." EXODUS 12:21–31

About 700 years after the exodus and 700 years before the birth of Jesus, God inspired the prophet Isaiah to speak on His behalf. The following prophecy about the Lord's "suffering Servant" takes the concept of blood sacrifice and the Passover lamb to a new level. This Scripture, which is quoted more often in the New Testament than any other Old Testament passage, also foretells the mission of the One who will provide the way for our sins to be forgiven.

Recalling the details of Jesus' time on earth, look for similarities between Jesus' life and Isaiah's prophecy of the "suffering Servant."

Behold, My Servant shall deal prudently;
He shall be exalted and extolled and be very high.
Just as many were astonished at you,
So His visage was marred more than any man,
And His form more than the sons of men;
So shall He sprinkle many nations.
Kings shall shut their mouths at Him;

For what had not been told them they shall see,
And what they had not heard they shall consider.

Who has believed our report?
And to whom has the arm of the LORD been revealed?
For He shall grow up before Him as a tender plant,
And as a root out of dry ground.
He has no form or comeliness;
And when we see Him,
There is no beauty that we should desire Him.
He is despised and rejected by men,
A Man of sorrows and acquainted with grief.
And we hid, as it were, *our* faces from Him;
He was despised, and we did not esteem Him.

Surely He has borne our griefs
And carried our sorrows;
Yet we esteemed Him stricken,
Smitten by God, and afflicted.
But He *was* wounded for our transgressions,
***He was* bruised for our iniquities;**
The chastisement for our peace *was* upon Him,
And by His stripes we are healed.
All we like sheep have gone astray;
We have turned, every one, to his own way;
And the LORD has laid on Him the iniquity of us all.

He was oppressed and He was afflicted,
Yet He opened not His mouth;
He was led as a lamb to the slaughter,
And as a sheep before its shearers is silent,
So He opened not His mouth.
He was taken from prison and from judgment,
And who will declare His generation?
For He was cut off from the land of the living;
For the transgressions of My people He was stricken.
And they made His grave with the wicked—
But with the rich at His death,
Because He had done no violence,
Nor *was any* deceit in His mouth.

Yet it pleased the LORD to bruise Him;
He has put *Him* to grief.
When You make His soul an offering for sin,
He shall see *His* seed, He shall prolong *His* days,
And the pleasure of the LORD shall prosper in His hand.
He shall see the labor of His soul, *and* be satisfied.
By His knowledge My righteous Servant shall justify many,
For He shall bear their iniquities.
Therefore I will divide Him a portion with the great,
And He shall divide the spoil with the strong,
Because He poured out His soul unto death,
And He was numbered with the transgressors,
And He bore the sin of many,
And made intercession for the transgressors.

ISAIAH 52:13—53:12

God's ultimate solution to our problem of separation from Him was poignantly demonstrated and graphically foretold over hundreds of years of Jewish history. When God spared the Israelites through the sacrifice of their Passover lambs, His point was inescapable. When Isaiah foresaw one who would be "wounded for our transgressions and bruised for our iniquities," the identity of the suffering Servant was undeniable. The ritual and the prophecy were fulfilled when the Messiah Jesus was crucified on a cross for the sins of humankind. God's plan, set into motion in the Garden of Eden, was at long last finished.

Now it came to pass, when Jesus had finished all these sayings, *that* He said to His disciples, "You know that after two days is the Passover, and the Son of Man will be delivered up to be crucified."

Then the chief priests, the scribes, and the elders of the people assembled at the palace of the high priest, who was called Caiaphas, and plotted to take Jesus by trickery and kill *Him*.

MATTHEW 26:1–4

Then the soldiers of the governor took Jesus into the Praetorium and gathered the whole garrison around Him. And they stripped Him and put a scarlet robe on Him. When they had twisted a crown of thorns, they put *it* on His head, and a reed in His right hand. And they bowed the knee before Him and mocked Him, saying, "Hail, King of the Jews!" Then they spat on Him, and took the reed and struck Him on the head. And when they had mocked Him, they took the robe off Him, put His *own* clothes on Him, and led Him away to be crucified.

Now as they came out, they found a man of Cyrene, Simon by name. Him they compelled to bear His cross. And when they had come to a place called Golgotha, that is to say, Place of a Skull, they gave Him sour wine mingled with gall to drink. But when He had tasted *it,* He would not drink.

Then they crucified Him, and divided His garments, casting lots, that it might be fulfilled which was spoken by the prophet:

> *"They divided My garments among them,*
> *And for My clothing they cast lots."*

Sitting down, they kept watch over Him there. And they put up over His head the accusation written against Him:

THIS IS JESUS THE KING OF THE JEWS.

Then two robbers were crucified with Him, one on the right and another on the left.

And those who passed by blasphemed Him, wagging their heads and saying, "You who destroy the temple and build *it* in three days, save Yourself! If You are the Son of God, come down from the cross."

Likewise the chief priests also, mocking with the scribes and elders, said, "He saved others; Himself He cannot save. If He is the King of Israel, let Him now come down from the cross, and we will believe Him. He trusted in God; let Him deliver Him now if He will have Him; for He said, 'I am the Son of God.'"

Even the robbers who were crucified with Him reviled Him with the same thing.

Now from the sixth hour until the ninth hour there was darkness over all the land. And about the ninth hour Jesus cried out with a loud voice, saying, "Eli, Eli, lama sabachthani?" that is, *"My God, My God, why have You forsaken Me?"*

Some of those who stood there, when they heard *that,* said,

"This Man is calling for Elijah!" Immediately one of them ran and took a sponge, filled *it* with sour wine and put *it* on a reed, and offered it to Him to drink.

The rest said, "Let Him alone; let us see if Elijah will come to save Him."

And Jesus cried out again with a loud voice, and yielded up His spirit.

Then, behold, the veil of the temple was torn in two from top to bottom; and the earth quaked, and the rocks were split, and the graves were opened; and many bodies of the saints who had fallen asleep were raised; and coming out of the graves after His resurrection, they went into the holy city and appeared to many.

So when the centurion and those with him, who were guarding Jesus, saw the earthquake and the things that had happened, they feared greatly, saying, "Truly this was the Son of God!"

And many women who followed Jesus from Galilee, ministering to Him, were there looking on from afar, among whom were Mary Magdalene, Mary the mother of James and Joses, and the mother of Zebedee's sons.

Now when evening had come, there came a rich man from Arimathea, named Joseph, who himself had also become a disciple of Jesus. This man went to Pilate and asked for the body of Jesus. Then Pilate commanded the body to be given to him. When Joseph had taken the body, he wrapped it in a clean linen cloth, and laid it in his new tomb which he had hewn out of the rock; and he rolled a large stone against the door of the tomb, and departed. And Mary Magdalene was there, and the other Mary, sitting opposite the tomb.

On the next day, which followed the Day of Preparation, the chief priests and Pharisees gathered together to Pilate, saying, "Sir, we remember, while He was still alive, how that deceiver said, 'After three days I will rise.' Therefore command that the tomb be made secure until the third day, lest His disciples come by night and steal Him *away,* and say to the people, 'He has risen from the dead.' So the last deception will be worse than the first."

Pilate said to them, "You have a guard; go your way, make *it* as secure as you know how." So they went and made the tomb secure, sealing the stone and setting the guard.

Now after the Sabbath, as the first *day* of the week began to dawn, Mary Magdalene and the other Mary came to see the tomb. And behold, there was a great earthquake; for an angel of the Lord descended from heaven, and came and rolled back the stone from the door, and sat on it. His countenance was like lightning, and his clothing as white as snow. And the guards shook for fear of him, and became like dead *men.*

But the angel answered and said to the women, "Do not be afraid, for I know that you seek Jesus who was crucified. He is not here; for He is risen, as He said. Come, see the place where the Lord lay. And go quickly and tell His disciples that He is risen from the dead, and indeed He is going before you into Galilee; there you will see Him. Behold, I have told you."

So they went out quickly from the tomb with fear and great joy, and ran to bring His disciples word.

And as they went to tell His disciples, behold, Jesus met them, saying, "Rejoice!" So they came and held Him by the feet and worshiped Him. Then Jesus said to them, "Do not be afraid. Go *and* tell My brethren to go to Galilee, and there they will see Me."

MATTHEW 27:27—28:10

THE OUTCOME: A LASTING RELATIONSHIP WITH OUR LOVING GOD

Even with all the incredible stories connecting the dots from the promised Messiah to the person Jesus, most members of the nation of Israel didn't recognize or accept Jesus as the Savior of the world. They didn't recognize the One who would provide the way for our sin to be forgiven so we could enter into a personal relationship with God, overcome death and have eternal life. John tells the story of one Jewish religious leader who approached Jesus at night to probe His true identity and mission.

There was a man of the Pharisees named Nicodemus, a ruler of the Jews. This man came to Jesus by night and said to Him, "Rabbi, we know that You are a teacher come from God; for no one can do these signs that You do unless God is with him."

Jesus answered and said to him, "Most assuredly, I say to you, unless one is born again, he cannot see the kingdom of God."

Nicodemus said to Him, "How can a man be born when he is old? Can he enter a second time into his mother's womb and be born?"

Jesus answered, "Most assuredly, I say to you, unless one is born of water and the Spirit, he cannot enter the kingdom of God. That which is born of the flesh is flesh, and that which is born of the Spirit is spirit. Do not marvel that I said to you, 'You must be born again.' The wind blows where it wishes, and you hear the sound of it, but cannot tell where it comes from and where it goes. So is everyone who is born of the Spirit."

Nicodemus answered and said to Him, "How can these things be?"

Jesus answered and said to him, "Are you the teacher of Israel, and do not know these things? Most assuredly, I say to you, We speak what We know and testify what We have seen, and you do not receive Our witness. If I have told you earthly things and you do not believe, how will you believe if I tell you heavenly things? No one has ascended to heaven but He who came down from heaven, *that is,* the Son of Man who is in heaven. And as Moses lifted up the serpent in the wilderness, even so must the Son of Man be lifted up, that whoever believes in Him should not perish but have eternal life. **For God so loved the world that He gave His only begotten Son, that whoever believes in Him should not perish but have everlasting life.** For God did not send His Son into the world to condemn the world, but that the world through Him might be saved.

"He who believes in Him is not condemned; but he who does not believe is condemned already, because he has not believed in the name of the only begotten Son of God. And this is the condemnation, that the light has come into the world, and men loved darkness rather than light, because their deeds were evil. For everyone practicing evil hates the light and does not come to the light, lest his deeds should be exposed. But he who does the truth comes to the light, that his deeds may be clearly seen, that they have been done in God."

JOHN 3:1–21

Nicodemus was not the only person who heard and believed Christ's good news. After Jesus ascended back to the Father following His resurrection, the Holy Spirit came down on the disciples as Jesus had promised, and the church was born. Peter exited the Upper Room and gave a powerful sermon to the thousands of people who gathered in Jerusalem for the Pentecost celebration. Read carefully his final challenge and celebrate the outcome.

"Therefore let all the house of Israel know assuredly that God has made this Jesus, whom you crucified, both Lord and Christ."

Now when they heard *this,* they were cut to the heart, and said to Peter and the rest of the apostles, "Men *and* brethren, what shall we do?"

Then Peter said to them, "Repent, and let every one of you be baptized in the name of Jesus Christ for the remission of sins; and you shall receive the gift of the Holy Spirit. For the promise is to you and to your children, and to all who are afar off, as many as the Lord our God will call."

And with many other words he testified and exhorted them, saying, "Be saved from this perverse generation." Then those who gladly received his word were baptized; and that day about three thousand souls were added *to them.* ACTS 2:36–41

In his letter to the church at Rome, the apostle Paul—who was called by God to tell this good news to the rest of the world—further reinforces what we must do to receive this gift of grace.

Therefore, just as through one man sin entered the world, and death through sin, and thus death spread to all men, because all sinned—(For until the law sin was in the world, but sin is not imputed when there is no law. Nevertheless death reigned from Adam to Moses, even over those who had not sinned according to the likeness of the transgression of Adam, who is a type of Him who was to come. But the free gift *is* not like the offense. For if by the one man's offense many died, much more the grace of God and the gift by the grace of the one Man, Jesus Christ, abounded to many. And the gift *is* not like *that which came* through the one who sinned. For the judgment *which came* from one *offense resulted* in condemnation, but the free gift *which came* from many offenses *resulted* in justification. **For if by the one man's offense death reigned through the one, much more those who receive abundance of grace and of the gift of righteousness will reign in life through the One, Jesus Christ.)**

Therefore, as through one man's offense *judgment came* to all men, resulting in condemnation, even so through one Man's righteous act *the free gift came* to all men, resulting in justification of life. For as by one man's disobedience many were made sinners, so also by one Man's obedience many will be made righteous.

Moreover the law entered that the offense might abound. But where sin abounded, grace abounded much more, so that as sin reigned in death, even so grace might reign through righteousness to eternal life through Jesus Christ our Lord. ROMANS 5:12–21

Brethren, my heart's desire and prayer to God for Israel is that they may be saved. For I bear them witness that they have a zeal for God, but not according to knowledge. For they being ignorant of God's righteousness, and seeking to establish their own righteousness, have not submitted to the righteousness of God. For Christ *is* the end of the law for righteousness to everyone who believes.

For Moses writes about the righteousness which is of the law, *"The man who does those things shall live by them."* But the righteousness of faith speaks in this way, *"Do not say in your heart, 'Who will ascend into heaven?'"* (that is, to bring Christ down *from above*) or, *"'Who will descend into the abyss?'"* (that is, to bring Christ up from the dead). But what does it say? *"The word is near you, in your mouth and in your heart"* (that is, the word of faith which we preach): **that if you confess with your mouth the Lord Jesus and believe in your heart that God has raised Him from the dead, you will be saved. For with the heart one believes unto righteousness, and with the mouth confession is made unto salvation.** For the Scripture says, *"Whoever believes on Him will not be put to shame."* For there is no distinction between Jew and Greek, for the same Lord over all is rich to all who call upon Him. For *"whoever calls on the name of the LORD shall be saved."*

ROMANS 10:1–13

Why is it important to both believe in our hearts and profess with our mouths that Jesus is Lord?

The apostle Paul opens his letter to the church at Ephesus with the declaration that God had accomplished His intended outcome of providing to humanity the way of salvation. As you read these beautiful words, celebrate in your heart that the one true personal God of the universe wants to be in a relationship with you.

Blessed *be* the God and Father of our Lord Jesus Christ, who has blessed us with every spiritual blessing in the heavenly *places* in Christ, just as He chose us in Him before the foundation of the world, that we should be holy and without blame before Him in love, having predestined us to adoption as sons by Jesus Christ to Himself, according to the good pleasure of His will, to the praise of the glory of His grace, by which He made us accepted in the Beloved.

In Him we have redemption through His blood, the forgiveness of sins, according to the riches of His grace which He made to abound toward us in all wisdom and prudence, having made known to us the mystery of His will, according to His good pleasure which He purposed in Himself, that in the dispensation of the fullness of the times He might gather together in one all things in Christ, both which are in heaven and which are on earth—in Him. In Him also we have obtained an inheritance, being predestined according to the purpose of Him who works all things according to the counsel of His will, that we who first trusted in Christ should be to the praise of His glory.

In Him you also *trusted,* after you heard the word of truth, the gospel of your salvation; in whom also, having believed, you were sealed with the Holy Spirit of promise, who is the guarantee of our inheritance until the redemption of the purchased possession, to the praise of His glory. EPHESIANS 1:3–14

Can you pinpoint a moment or chart a sequence of moments in time when you realized that Christ died for you? How would you describe that process?

WHAT WE BELIEVE

Before the creation of the world, God had a Plan B in place for humanity to be in relationship with Him. Sure enough, Plan B became necessary when Adam and Eve ate the forbidden fruit, ushering in sin and death to all. But thanks to the sacrifice of the second person of the Trinity—the Son—the way was provided to come back to God through faith in Jesus Christ. If we believe this truth, not only in our heads but also in our hearts, and publicly confess it for the world to hear, we will be saved.

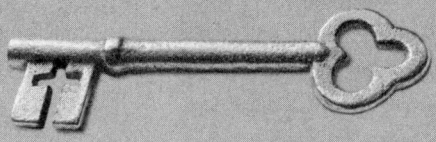

CHAPTER

4

The Bible

KEY QUESTION

How do I know God and His will for my life?

KEY IDEA

I believe the Bible is the inspired Word of God
that guides my beliefs and actions.

KEY VERSE

All Scripture *is* given by inspiration of God, and *is* profitable
for doctrine, for reproof, for correction, for instruction
in righteousness, that the man of God may be complete,
thoroughly equipped for every good work.
2 Timothy 3:16 – 17

OUR MAP

How do we know God? How do we understand and see the world we live in? How do we grasp where we came from and why we are here? How do we know where this story is ultimately heading? The answer is profound—God reveals Himself and His grand plan to us. Our role is to listen and believe.

By simply looking at nature and the world around us we can conclude there is a God. But how do we learn about this God? How do we come into a full relationship with God? What are His plans and purposes for us? What are the principles He wants us to live by to guide us into His truth? The answer to all of these questions is found in God's revelation to us—the Bible.

In this chapter we will read some of God's messages in Scripture that clearly convey His will and discover why the Bible holds such power for the Christian:

- *God Speaks*
- *The Authority of Scripture*
- *The Purpose of Scripture*

God Speaks

The Bible repeatedly records that God communicated to His people at specific times with specific messages. In some cases, such as with Moses at the burning bush, God spoke audibly. In other instances He spoke through dreams, visions or less direct impressions. But the words of the Lord were always given to His people to reveal His plan for them and then recorded in the Scriptures for the benefit of all humanity. God spelled out His story in the Bible because He loves us.

Now Moses was tending the flock of Jethro his father-in-law, the priest of Midian. And he led the flock to the back of the desert, and came to Horeb, the mountain of God. And the Angel of the Lord appeared to him in a flame of fire from the midst of a bush. So he looked, and behold, the bush was burning with fire, but the bush *was* not consumed. Then Moses said, "I will now turn aside and see this great sight, why the bush does not burn."

So when the LORD saw that he turned aside to look, God called to him from the midst of the bush and said, "Moses, Moses!"

And he said, "Here I am."

Then He said, "Do not draw near this place. Take your sandals off your feet, for the place where you stand *is* holy ground." Moreover He said, "I *am* the God of your father—the God of Abraham, the God of Isaac, and the God of Jacob." And Moses hid his face, for he was afraid to look upon God.

And the LORD said: "I have surely seen the oppression of My people who *are* in Egypt, and have heard their cry because of their taskmasters, for I know their sorrows. So I have come down to deliver them out of the hand of the Egyptians, and to bring them up from that land to a good and large land, to a land flowing with milk and honey, to the place of the Canaanites and the Hittites and the Amorites and the Perizzites and the Hivites and the Jebusites. Now therefore, behold, the cry of the children of Israel has come to Me, and I have also seen the oppression with which the Egyptians oppress them. Come now, therefore, and I will send you to Pharaoh that you may bring My people, the children of Israel, out of Egypt."

But Moses said to God, "Who *am* I that I should go to Pharaoh, and that I should bring the children of Israel out of Egypt?"

So He said, "I will certainly be with you. And this *shall be* a sign to you that I have sent you: When you have brought the people out of Egypt, you shall serve God on this mountain."

Then Moses said to God, "Indeed, *when* I come to the children of Israel and say to them, 'The God of your fathers has sent me to you,' and they say to me, 'What *is* His name?' what shall I say to them?"

And God said to Moses, "I AM WHO I AM." And He said, "Thus you shall say to the children of Israel, 'I AM has sent me to you.'" Moreover God said to Moses, "Thus you shall say to the children of Israel: 'The LORD God of your fathers, the God of Abraham, the God of Isaac, and the God of Jacob, has sent me to you. This *is* My name forever, and this *is* My memorial to all generations.' Go and gather the elders of Israel together, and say to them, 'The LORD God of your fathers, the God of Abraham, of Isaac, and of Jacob, appeared to me, saying, "I have surely visited you and *seen* what is done to you in Egypt; and I have said I will bring you up out of the affliction of Egypt to the land of the Canaanites and the Hittites and the Amorites and the Perizzites and the Hivites and the Jebusites, to a land flowing with milk and honey."' Then they will heed your voice; and you shall come, you and the elders of Israel, to the king of Egypt; and you shall say to him, 'The LORD God of the Hebrews has met with us; and now, please, let us go three days' journey into the wilderness, that we may sacrifice to the LORD our God.' But I am sure that the king of Egypt will not let you go, no, not even by a mighty hand. So I will stretch out My hand and strike Egypt with all My wonders which I will do in its midst; and after that he will let you go. And I will give this people favor in the sight of the Egyptians; and it shall be, when you go, that you shall not go empty-handed. But every woman shall ask of her neighbor, namely, of her who dwells near her house, articles of silver, articles of gold, and clothing; and you shall put *them* on your sons and on your daughters. So you shall plunder the Egyptians."

Then Moses answered and said, "But suppose they will not believe me or listen to my voice; suppose they say, 'The LORD has not appeared to you.'"

So the LORD said to him, "What *is* that in your hand?"

He said, "A rod."

And He said, "Cast it on the ground." So he cast it on the ground, and it became a serpent; and Moses fled from it. Then the LORD said to Moses, "Reach out your hand and take *it* by the tail" (and he reached out his hand and caught it, and it became a rod in his hand), "that they may believe that the LORD God of their fathers, the God of Abraham, the God of Isaac, and the God of Jacob, has appeared to you."

Furthermore the LORD said to him, "Now put your hand in your bosom." And he put his hand in his bosom, and when he took it out, behold, his hand *was* leprous, like snow. And He said, "Put your hand in your bosom again." So he put his hand in his bosom again, and drew it out of his bosom, and behold, it was restored like his *other* flesh. "Then it will be, if they do not believe you, nor heed the message of the first sign, that they may believe the message of the latter sign. And it shall be, if they do not believe even these two signs, or listen to your voice, that you shall take water from the river and pour *it* on the dry *land.* The water which you take from the river will become blood on the dry *land.*"

Then Moses said to the LORD, "O my Lord, I *am* not eloquent, neither before nor since You have spoken to Your servant; but I *am* slow of speech and slow of tongue."

So the LORD said to him, "Who has made man's mouth? Or who makes the mute, the deaf, the seeing, or the blind? *Have* not I, the LORD? Now therefore, go, and I will be with your mouth and teach you what you shall say."

But he said, "O my Lord, please send by the hand of whomever *else* You may send."

So the anger of the LORD was kindled against Moses, and He said: "Is not Aaron the Levite your brother? I know that he can speak well. And look, he is also coming out to meet you. When he sees you, he will be glad in his heart. Now you shall speak to him and put the words in his mouth. And I will be with your mouth and with his mouth, and I will teach you what you shall do. So he shall be your spokesman to the people. And he himself shall be as a mouth for you, and you shall be to him as God. And you shall take this rod in your hand, with which you shall do the signs."

EXODUS 3:1—4:17

What can we learn about God's character from the story of Moses and the burning bush? How did Moses react to this direct communication from God? How would you respond in a similar situation?

The Lord spoke mostly through prophets in the Old Testament and through Jesus and the apostles in the New Testament. After Jesus' death on the cross and miraculous resurrection, two of His followers were walking on the road from Jerusalem to Emmaus. Jesus came up and started walking with them and talking about His identity, though they were kept from recognizing Him at first. Soon after, Jesus appeared to them again once they rejoined the disciples. It is significant that to prove to them He was the Mes-

siah, He drew from the Old Testament. Jesus obviously understood these writings to be inspired by God.

And beginning at Moses and all the Prophets, [Jesus] expounded to them in all the Scriptures the things concerning Himself.

Then they drew near to the village where they were going, and He indicated that He would have gone farther. But they constrained Him, saying, "Abide with us, for it is toward evening, and the day is far spent." And He went in to stay with them.

Now it came to pass, as He sat at the table with them, that He took bread, blessed and broke *it,* and gave it to them. Then their eyes were opened and they knew Him; and He vanished from their sight.

And they said to one another, "Did not our heart burn within us while He talked with us on the road, and while He opened the Scriptures to us?" So they rose up that very hour and returned to Jerusalem, and found the eleven and those *who were* with them gathered together, saying, "The Lord is risen indeed, and has appeared to Simon!" And they told about the things *that had happened* on the road, and how He was known to them in the breaking of bread.

Now as they said these things, Jesus Himself stood in the midst of them, and said to them, "Peace to you." But they were terrified and frightened, and supposed they had seen a spirit. And He said to them, "Why are you troubled? And why do doubts arise in your hearts? Behold My hands and My feet, that it is I Myself. Handle Me and see, for a spirit does not have flesh and bones as you see I have."

When He had said this, He showed them His hands and His feet. But while they still did not believe for joy, and marveled, He said to them, "Have you any food here?" So they gave Him a piece of a broiled fish and some honeycomb. And He took *it* and ate in their presence.

Then He said to them, "These *are* the words which I spoke to you while I was still with you, that all things must be fulfilled which were written in the Law of Moses and *the* Prophets

and *the* Psalms concerning Me." And He opened their understanding, that they might comprehend the Scriptures.

Then He said to them, "Thus it is written, and thus it was necessary for the Christ to suffer and to rise from the dead the third day, and that repentance and remission of sins should be preached in His name to all nations, beginning at Jerusalem. And you are witnesses of these things. Behold, I send the Promise of My Father upon you; but tarry in the city of Jerusalem until you are endued with power from on high." LUKE 24:27–49

How did Jesus help His disciples understand who He was and why He came?

Before appearing to the Eleven in Jerusalem, Jesus appeared to Peter, also known as Simon, who, after denying Jesus, went on to become a faithful follower of Christ and a key leader in the early church.

Like other leaders of the church, Peter sent letters to those early believers; those letters are preserved in the Bible in the New Testament. He wrote this letter to one of the churches because false teaching was infiltrating the church and causing followers to stray from God's Word. Peter wrote to them to shepherd them back toward the truth. In the process, he provided insight into the origin of Scripture and how followers can use it to guide their lives.

As you read the passage below from 2 Peter 1, think about how God, through Scripture, built a case for the identity and purpose of Jesus.

Simon Peter, a bondservant and apostle of Jesus Christ,

To those who have obtained like precious faith with us by the righteousness of our God and Savior Jesus Christ:

Grace and peace be multiplied to you in the knowledge of

God and of Jesus our Lord, as His divine power has given to us all things that *pertain* to life and godliness, through the knowledge of Him who called us by glory and virtue, by which have been given to us exceedingly great and precious promises, that through these you may be partakers of the divine nature, having escaped the corruption *that is* in the world through lust.

But also for this very reason, giving all diligence, add to your faith virtue, to virtue knowledge, to knowledge self-control, to self-control perseverance, to perseverance godliness, to godliness brotherly kindness, and to brotherly kindness love. For if these things are yours and abound, *you* will be neither barren nor unfruitful in the knowledge of our Lord Jesus Christ. For he who lacks these things is shortsighted, even to blindness, and has forgotten that he was cleansed from his old sins.

Therefore, brethren, be even more diligent to make your call and election sure, for if you do these things you will never stumble; for so an entrance will be supplied to you abundantly into the everlasting kingdom of our Lord and Savior Jesus Christ.

For this reason I will not be negligent to remind you always of these things, though you know and are established in the present truth. Yes, I think it is right, as long as I am in this tent, to stir you up by reminding *you*, knowing that shortly I *must* put off my tent, just as our Lord Jesus Christ showed me. Moreover I will be careful to ensure that you always have a reminder of these things after my decease.

For we did not follow cunningly devised fables when we made known to you the power and coming of our Lord Jesus Christ, but were eyewitnesses of His majesty. For He received from God the Father honor and glory when such a voice came to Him from the Excellent Glory: "This is My beloved Son, in whom I am well pleased." And we heard this voice which came from heaven when we were with Him on the holy mountain.

And so we have the prophetic word confirmed, which you do well to heed as a light that shines in a dark place, until the day dawns and the morning star rises in your hearts; **knowing this first, that no prophecy of Scripture is of any private interpretation, for prophecy never came by the will of man, but holy men of God spoke as *they were* moved by the Holy Spirit.** 2 PETER 1:1–21

The Authority of Scripture

To understand the power of the authority of Scripture, we must go back to the early days of Israel. With a mighty hand God led the Israelites out of slavery in Egypt. While they were in the wilderness God made preparations for them to enter into the land of Canaan that He had promised to Abraham 600 years earlier. Soon God descended from the heavens to Mount Sinai to meet with His servant Moses and the people and proclaim to them the Ten Commandments. These laws, spoken directly by God to Moses, guided the values and behavior of the Israelites.

In the third month after the children of Israel had gone out of the land of Egypt, on the same day, they came *to* the Wilderness of Sinai. For they had departed from Rephidim, had come *to* the Wilderness of Sinai, and camped in the wilderness. So Israel camped there before the mountain.

And Moses went up to God, and the LORD called to him from the mountain, saying, "Thus you shall say to the house of Jacob, and tell the children of Israel: 'You have seen what I did to the Egyptians, and *how* I bore you on eagles' wings and brought you to Myself. Now therefore, if you will indeed obey My voice and keep My covenant, then you shall be a special treasure to Me above all people; for all the earth *is* Mine. And you shall be to Me a kingdom of priests and a holy nation.' These *are* the words which you shall speak to the children of Israel."

So Moses came and called for the elders of the people, and laid before them all these words which the LORD commanded him. Then all the people answered together and said, "All that the LORD has spoken we will do." So Moses brought back the words of the people to the LORD. And the LORD said to Moses, "Behold, I come to you in the thick cloud, that the people may hear when I speak with you, and believe you forever."

So Moses told the words of the people to the LORD. EXODUS 19:1–9

Then it came to pass on the third day, in the morning, that there were thunderings and lightnings, and a thick cloud on the mountain; and the sound of the trumpet was very loud, so that all the people who *were* in the camp trembled. And Moses brought the people out of the camp to meet with God, and they stood at the foot of the mountain. **Now Mount Sinai *was* completely in smoke, because the LORD descended upon it in fire. Its smoke ascended like the smoke of a furnace, and the whole mountain quaked greatly. And when the blast of the trumpet sounded long and became louder and louder, Moses spoke, and God answered him by voice.** EXODUS 19:16–19

And God spoke all these words, saying:

"I *am* the LORD your God, who brought you out of the land of Egypt, out of the house of bondage.

"You shall have no other gods before Me.

"You shall not make for yourself a carved image—any likeness *of anything* that *is* in heaven above, or that *is* in the earth beneath, or that *is* in the water under the earth; you shall not bow down to them nor serve them. For I, the LORD your God, *am* a jealous God, visiting the iniquity of the fathers upon the children to the third and fourth *generations* of those who hate Me, but showing mercy to thousands, to those who love Me and keep My commandments.

"You shall not take the name of the LORD your God in vain, for the LORD will not hold *him* guiltless who takes His name in vain.

"Remember the Sabbath day, to keep it holy. Six days you shall labor and do all your work, but the seventh day *is* the Sabbath of the LORD your God. *In it* you shall do no work: you, nor your son, nor your daughter, nor your male servant, nor your female servant, nor your cattle, nor your stranger who *is* within your gates. For *in* six days the LORD made the heavens and the earth, the sea, and all that *is* in them, and rested the seventh day. Therefore the LORD blessed the Sabbath day and hallowed it.

"Honor your father and your mother, that your days may be long upon the land which the LORD your God is giving you.

"You shall not murder.

"You shall not commit adultery.

"You shall not steal.

"You shall not bear false witness against your neighbor.

"You shall not covet your neighbor's house; you shall not covet your neighbor's wife, nor his male servant, nor his female servant, nor his ox, nor his donkey, nor anything that *is* your neighbor's."

Now all the people witnessed the thunderings, the lightning flashes, the sound of the trumpet, and the mountain smoking; and when the people saw *it,* they trembled and stood afar off. Then they said to Moses, "You speak with us, and we will hear; but let not God speak with us, lest we die."

And Moses said to the people, "Do not fear; for God has come to test you, and that His fear may be before you, so that you may not sin." So the people stood afar off, but Moses drew near the thick darkness where God *was.* EXODUS 20:1–21

Are the Ten Commandments as relevant today as they were when Moses delivered them to the Israelites? How?

God's words carry the authority of the One who speaks them. Examples of the authority of Scripture are found throughout the Bible—in both the Old and New Testaments. For instance, immediately after John baptized Jesus, the Spirit led Jesus into the wilderness where Satan sought to take advantage of Jesus' isolation, hunger and physical exhaustion. But God's power was revealed in Jesus' interactions with Satan; Jesus quoted Scripture three times—twice from Deuteronomy and once from Psalms—as His authority to overcome each temptation. Despite facing genuine temptations at a time when He was vulnerable, Jesus remained rooted in the principles recorded in God's Word.

Then Jesus was led up by the Spirit into the wilderness to be tempted by the devil. And when He had fasted forty days and forty nights, afterward He was hungry. Now when the tempter came to Him, he said, "If You are the Son of God, command that these stones become bread."

But He answered and said, "It is written, *'Man shall not live by bread alone, but by every word that proceeds from the mouth of God.'*"

Then the devil took Him up into the holy city, set Him on the pinnacle of the temple, and said to Him, "If You are the Son of God, throw Yourself down. For it is written:

'He shall give His angels charge over you,'

and,

'In their hands they shall bear you up,
Lest you dash your foot against a stone.'"

Jesus said to him, "It is written again, *'You shall not tempt the Lord your God.'*"

Again, the devil took Him up on an exceedingly high mountain, and showed Him all the kingdoms of the world and their glory. And he said to Him, "All these things I will give You if You will fall down and worship me."

Then Jesus said to him, "Away with you, Satan! For it is written, *'You shall worship the LORD your God, and Him only you shall serve.'*"

Then the devil left Him, and behold, angels came and ministered to Him.

MATTHEW 4:1–11

Jesus Himself relied on Scripture, and He passed on His reverence for the authority of God's word to His followers. One faithful follower, the apostle Paul, was languishing near death in a dungeon in Rome. Despite his suffering, one of his main priorities was passing the mantle of leadership to young pastors like Timothy. In his final charge to Timothy, Paul encouraged him to continue to follow Scripture, God's Word.

But you have carefully followed my doctrine, manner of life, purpose, faith, longsuffering, love, perseverance, persecutions, afflictions, which happened to me at Antioch, at Iconium, at Lystra—what persecutions I endured. And out of *them* all the Lord delivered me. Yes, and all who desire to live godly in Christ Jesus will suffer persecution. But evil men and impostors will grow worse and worse, deceiving and being deceived. But you must continue in the things which you have learned and been assured of, knowing from whom you have learned *them,* and that from childhood you have known the Holy Scriptures, which are able to make you wise for salvation through faith which is in Christ Jesus.

All Scripture *is* given by inspiration of God, and *is* profitable

for doctrine, for reproof, for correction, for instruction in righteousness, that the man of God may be complete, thoroughly equipped for every good work. 2 Timothy 3:10–17

The Purpose of Scripture

Because the collection of sacred writings, or Scriptures, came from God, it is referred to as the Word of God. In the Old Testament, Isaiah spoke for the Lord during a difficult season in Israel's history. Because the people of the northern kingdom of Israel had perpetually disregarded God and His Word, the nation was destroyed by the Assyrians. The Lord revealed to Isaiah that his own nation, the southern kingdom of Judah, would likewise be conquered—by the Babylonians. But God's prophet, under the inspiration of the Holy Spirit, also looked many years ahead and foretold Judah's restoration following the Babylonian exile. He reminded the Israelites that God's Word is eternal, and that God always accomplishes His purposes.

The voice said, "Cry out!"
And he said, "What shall I cry?"

"All flesh *is* grass,
And all its loveliness *is* like the flower of the field.
The grass withers, the flower fades,
Because the breath of the Lord blows upon it;
Surely the people *are* grass.
The grass withers, the flower fades,
But the word of our God stands forever." Isaiah 40:6–8

Seek the Lord while He may be found,
Call upon Him while He is near.
Let the wicked forsake his way,
And the unrighteous man his thoughts;
Let him return to the Lord,
And He will have mercy on him;
And to our God,
For He will abundantly pardon.

"For My thoughts *are* not your thoughts,
Nor *are* your ways My ways," says the Lord.

"For *as* the heavens are higher than the earth,
So are My ways higher than your ways,
And My thoughts than your thoughts.

"For as the rain comes down, and the snow from heaven,
And do not return there,
But water the earth,
And make it bring forth and bud,
That it may give seed to the sower
And bread to the eater,
So shall My word be that goes forth from My mouth;
It shall not return to Me void,
But it shall accomplish what I please,
And it shall prosper *in the thing* for which I sent it.

"For you shall go out with joy,
And be led out with peace;
The mountains and the hills
Shall break forth into singing before you,
And all the trees of the field shall clap *their* hands.
Instead of the thorn shall come up the cypress tree,
And instead of the brier shall come up the myrtle tree;
And it shall be to the LORD for a name,
For an everlasting sign *that* shall not be cut off."

ISAIAH 55:6–13

The writer of the book of Hebrews builds on the idea that God breathed life into things—including the words of the Bible. Scripture is dynamic and alive and that has a way of "getting under our skin."

For the word of God *is* living and powerful, and sharper than any two-edged sword, piercing even to the division of soul and spirit, and of joints and marrow, and is a discerner of the thoughts and intents of the heart. And there is no creature hidden from His sight, but all things *are* naked and open to the eyes of Him to whom we *must give* account.

HEBREWS 4:12–13

In what ways have you experienced the Word of God as "living and powerful" in your own spiritual life?

Throughout the Bible the writers warned readers that they should not add or take away from God's Word. God has given and preserved His Word for us so we can rely on it to guide our lives into all truth and according to God's good plan. Therefore, Christians revere the Bible and affirm its right to command our beliefs and actions.

Moses writes,

"Now, O Israel, listen to the statutes and the judgments which I teach you to observe, that you may live, and go in and possess the land which the LORD God of your fathers is giving you. You shall not add to the word which I command you, nor take from it, that you may keep the commandments of the LORD your God which I command you." DEUTERONOMY 4:1–2

In the book of Proverbs, Agur declares,

Every word of God *is* pure;
He *is* a shield to those who put their trust in Him.
Do not add to His words,
Lest He rebuke you, and you be found a liar. PROVERBS 30:5–6

John, the author of Revelation, writes,

For I testify to everyone who hears the words of the prophecy of this book: If anyone adds to these things, God will add to him the plagues that are written in this book; and if anyone takes away from the words of the book of this prophecy, God shall take away his part from the Book of Life, from the holy city, and *from* the things which are written in this book. REVELATION 22:18–19

WHAT WE BELIEVE

How do we know God and His will for our lives? The loving, personal, one true God speaks to us. Throughout history God has spoken through dreams, visions and even burning bushes. The primary way God reveals Himself and His truth to us today is through the Bible. Because these words are from God, we can give it the rightful authority to guide our lives. Whatever God promises in His Word will come to pass and accomplish His purposes. Do you believe the Bible is the Word of God and has the right to command your beliefs and actions?

THINK

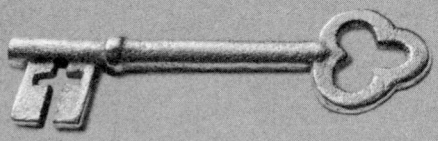

CHAPTER

5

Identity in Christ

KEY IDEA

Who am I?

KEY IDEA

I believe I am significant because of
my position as a child of God.

KEY VERSE

But as many as received Him, to them
He gave the right to become children of God,
to those who believe in His name.
John 1:12

OUR MAP

When we open the pages of the Bible, God's trusted revelation to us, we discover that the one true God—Father, Son and Holy Spirit—is involved in and cares about our daily lives. We also learn that He has provided the way for us to come into a personal relationship with Him through faith in Jesus Christ. When we believe and receive this gift of grace, we become a new person with a new identity and a new outlook on life. Our worth is no longer defined by what we do, but by who we know. We are significant because we are children of God.

Who am I? In the following pages, soak in God's truth about:

- *Our New Name*
- *A New Covenant*
- *Our Adoption*
- *Being an Heir of God*

Our New Name

During Bible times, a person's name was more than simply a reference to one's family or a way to uniquely identify someone; typically it characterized something about them. There are several instances recorded in the Bible of God giving a person a new name. When God renamed a person, He was establishing for them a new identity and marking that He was changing their mission or place in life. This was the case with Abram (meaning "exalted father"), whose name God changed to Abraham (meaning "father of many"). The meaning of the name "Abraham" represented God's plan to make Abraham's offspring into the great nation of Israel—and eventually into the body of Christ through Abraham's spiritual descendants.

When Abram was ninety-nine years old, the Lord appeared to Abram and said to him, "I *am* Almighty God; walk before Me and be blameless. And I will make My covenant between Me and you, and will multiply you exceedingly." Then Abram fell on his face, and God talked with him, saying: "As for Me, behold, My covenant is with you, and you shall be a father of many nations. No longer shall your name be called Abram, but your name shall be Abraham; for I have made you a father of many nations. I will make you exceedingly fruitful; and I will make nations of you, and kings shall come from you. And I will establish My covenant between Me and you and your descendants after you in their generations, for an everlasting covenant, to be God to you and your descendants after you."

GENESIS 17:1–7

God's promise to make Abraham a great nation seemed laughable, given the ages of Abraham and Sarah. But God followed through on His promise and gave them a son when Abraham was one hundred years old and Sarah was ninety. God gave him the name Isaac, which means "he laughs."

Then Abraham fell on his face and laughed, and said in his heart, "Shall *a child* be born to a man who is one hundred years old? And shall Sarah, who is ninety years old, bear *a child?*"

GENESIS 17:17

Then God said: "No, Sarah your wife shall bear you a son, and you shall call his name Isaac; I will establish My covenant with him for an everlasting covenant, *and* with his descendants after him."

GENESIS 17:19

And the LORD visited Sarah as He had said, and the LORD did for Sarah as He had spoken. For Sarah conceived and bore Abraham a son in his old age, at the set time of which God had spoken to him. And Abraham called the name of his son who was born to him—whom Sarah bore to him—Isaac. Then Abraham circumcised his son Isaac when he was eight days old, as God had commanded him. Now Abraham was one hundred years old when his son Isaac was born to him. And Sarah said, "God has made me laugh, *and* all who hear will laugh with me." She also said, "Who would have said to Abraham that Sarah would nurse children? For I have borne *him* a son in his old age."

GENESIS 21:1–7

God gave Abraham and Sarah new names to represent their new identities and their covenant with God. Looking back on the time since you first encountered God, what would your new name be if you could pick one? Why?

A New Covenant

In Old Testament times, God provided His people with a promise termed the old covenant, which included His directions to His people under Moses' leadership. A covenant is a binding agreement between two parties, in this case God and Israel, that lays out what each side promises to do. The prophet Jeremiah, however, foretold of a new covenant—a new deal God had in the works—that would redefine the identity of God's people. This time it involved more than just a name change. The old covenant changed God's people from the outside in; the new covenant changes us from the inside out.

"Behold, the days are coming, says the Lord, when I will make a new covenant with the house of Israel and with the house of Judah—not according to the covenant that I made with their fathers in the day *that* I took them by the hand to lead them out of the land of Egypt, My covenant which they broke, though I was a husband to them, says the Lord. But this *is* the covenant that I will make with the house of Israel after those days, says the Lord: I will put My law in their minds, and write it on their hearts; and I will be their God, and they shall be My people. No more shall every man teach his neighbor, and every man his brother, saying, 'Know the Lord,' for they all shall know Me, from the least of them to the greatest of them, says the Lord. **For I will forgive their iniquity, and their sin I will remember no more."**

Jeremiah 31:31–34

What are the main points of God's new covenant? What effect does the new covenant have on our identity?

Jesus Christ fulfilled the requirements of the old covenant God made with Moses and ushered in a new season of amazing grace. Those who embrace this new covenant and turn from their sins will have their sins wiped away and will receive a new identity.

That was the true Light which gives light to every man coming into the world.

He was in the world, and the world was made through Him, and the world did not know Him. He came to His own, and His own did not receive Him. But as many as received Him, to them He gave the right to become children of God, to those who believe in His name: who were born, not of blood, nor of the will of the flesh, nor of the will of man, but of God. JOHN 1:9–13

As you read the passage below from Hebrews 10, compare and contrast the sacrifices made to fulfill the requirements of the old covenant with the sacrifice of Jesus that sealed the new covenant.

For the law, having a shadow of the good things to come, *and* not the very image of the things, can never with these same sacrifices, which they offer continually year by year, make those who approach perfect. For then would they not have ceased to be offered? For the worshipers, once purified, would have had no more consciousness of sins. But in those *sacrifices there is* a reminder of sins every year. For *it is* not possible that the blood of bulls and goats could take away sins.

Therefore, when He came into the world, He said:

"Sacrifice and offering You did not desire,
But a body You have prepared for Me.
In burnt offerings and sacrifices for sin
You had no pleasure.
Then I said, 'Behold, I have come—
In the volume of the book it is written of Me—
To do Your will, O God.'"

Previously saying, *"Sacrifice and offering, burnt offerings, and offerings for sin You did not desire, nor had pleasure in them"* (which are offered according to the law), then He said, *"Behold, I have come to do Your will, O God."* He takes away the first that He may establish the second. By that will we have been sanctified through the offering of the body of Jesus Christ once *for all.*

And every priest stands ministering daily and offering repeatedly the same sacrifices, which can never take away sins. But this Man, after He had offered one sacrifice for sins forever, sat down at the right hand of God, from that time waiting till His enemies are made His footstool. For by one offering He has perfected forever those who are being sanctified.

But the Holy Spirit also witnesses to us; for after He had said before,

***"This is the covenant that I will make with them after those days, says the LORD: I will put My laws into their hearts, and in their minds I will write them," then He adds, "Their sins and their lawless deeds I will remember no more."* Now where there is remission of these, there is no longer an offering for sin.**

HEBREWS 10:1–18

OUR ADOPTION

The beautiful thing about God's kingdom is that all those who welcome Jesus as their Lord are given the opportunity to accept a new identity through Him. This is illustrated poignantly through the story of a crooked tax collector named Zacchaeus. Tax collectors were among the most despised people in Israel because they chose to work for Rome and were making themselves rich by gouging their fellow Jews. But the story of Zacchaeus shows that even the outcast can be adopted by God and made new.

Then *Jesus* entered and passed through Jericho. Now behold, *there was* a man named Zacchaeus who was a chief tax collector, and he was rich. And he sought to see who Jesus was, but could not because of the crowd, for he was of short stature. So he ran ahead and climbed up into a sycamore tree to see Him, for He was going to pass that *way.* And when Jesus came to the place, He looked up and saw him, and said to him, "Zacchaeus, make haste and come down, for today I must stay at your house." So he made haste and came down, and received Him joyfully. But when they saw *it,* they all complained, saying, "He has gone to be a guest with a man who is a sinner."

Then Zacchaeus stood and said to the Lord, "Look, Lord, I give half of my goods to the poor; and if I have taken anything from anyone by false accusation, I restore fourfold."

And Jesus said to him, "Today salvation has come to this house, because he also is a son of Abraham." LUKE 19:1–9

The people in the early church were living examples of the changes that resulted from following Jesus. The letter to the Romans was written by the apostle Paul to present the full picture of the new covenant—its cost, the payment exacted for it and the promise it holds for those who agree to it. Follow along as Paul starts with our position in sin and the payment required to release us from its power; he finishes with a glorious description of how our adoption into God's family gives us a new identity.

As it is written:

"There is none righteous, no, not one;
There is none who understands;
There is none who seeks after God.
They have all turned aside;
They have together become unprofitable;
There is none who does good, no, not one."
"Their throat is an open tomb;
With their tongues they have practiced deceit";
"The poison of asps is under their lips";
"Whose mouth is full of cursing and bitterness."
"Their feet are swift to shed blood;
Destruction and misery are in their ways;
And the way of peace they have not known."
"There is no fear of God before their eyes."

Now we know that whatever the law says, it says to those who are under the law, that every mouth may be stopped, and all the world may become guilty before God. Therefore by the deeds of the law no flesh will be justified in His sight, for by the law *is* the knowledge of sin.

But now the righteousness of God apart from the law is revealed, being witnessed by the Law and the Prophets, even the righteousness of God, through faith in Jesus Christ, to all and on all who believe. For there is no difference; for all have sinned and fall short of the glory of God, being justified freely by His grace through the redemption that is in Christ Jesus, whom God set forth *as* a propitiation by His blood, through faith, to demonstrate His righteousness, because in His forbearance God had passed over the sins that were previously committed, to demonstrate at the present time His righteousness, that He might be just and the justifier of the one who has faith in Jesus. ROMANS 3:10–26

Therefore, having been justified by faith, we have peace with God through our Lord Jesus Christ, through whom also we have access by faith into this grace in which we stand, and rejoice in hope of the glory of God. ROMANS 5:1–2

For when we were still without strength, in due time Christ died for the ungodly. For scarcely for a righteous man will one die; yet perhaps for a good man someone would even dare to die. But God demonstrates His own love toward us, in that while we were still sinners, Christ died for us. Much more then, having now been justified by His blood, we shall be saved from wrath through Him. For if when we were enemies we were reconciled to God through the death of His Son, much more, having been reconciled, we shall be saved by His life. And not only *that,* but we also rejoice in God through our Lord Jesus Christ, through whom we have now received the reconciliation. ROMANS 5:6–11

What shall we say then? Shall we continue in sin that grace may abound? Certainly not! How shall we who died to sin live any longer in it? Or do you not know that as many of us as were baptized into Christ Jesus were baptized into His death? Therefore we were buried with Him through baptism into death, that just as Christ was raised from the dead by the glory of the Father, even so we also should walk in newness of life.

For if we have been united together in the likeness of His death, certainly we also shall be *in the likeness* of *His* resurrection, **knowing this, that our old man was crucified with *Him*, that the body of sin might be done away with, that we should no longer be slaves of sin. For he who has died has been freed from sin.**

ROMANS 6:1–7

As you read Romans 8:1–25 below, look for what God gives to those who find their identity in Jesus Christ.

There is therefore now no condemnation to those who are in Christ Jesus, who do not walk according to the flesh, but according to the Spirit. For the law of the Spirit of life in Christ Jesus has made me free from the law of sin and death. For what the law could not do in that it was weak through the flesh, God *did* by sending His own Son in the likeness of sinful flesh, on account of sin: He condemned sin in the flesh, that the righteous requirement of the law might be fulfilled in us who do not walk according to the flesh but according to the Spirit. For those who live according to the flesh set their minds on the things of the flesh, but those *who live* according to the Spirit, the things of the Spirit. For to be carnally minded *is* death, but to be spiritually minded *is* life and peace. Because the carnal mind *is* enmity against God; for it is not subject to the law of God, nor indeed can be. So then, those who are in the flesh cannot please God.

But you are not in the flesh but in the Spirit, if indeed the Spirit of God dwells in you. Now if anyone does not have the Spirit of Christ, he is not His. And if Christ *is* in you, the body *is* dead because of sin, but the Spirit *is* life because of righteousness. But if the Spirit of Him who raised Jesus from the dead dwells in you, He who raised Christ from the dead will also give life to your mortal bodies through His Spirit who dwells in you.

Therefore, brethren, we are debtors—not to the flesh, to live according to the flesh. For if you live according to the flesh you will die; but if by the Spirit you put to death the deeds of the body, you will live. For as many as are led by the Spirit of God, these are sons of God. **For you did not receive the spirit of bondage again**

to fear, but you received the Spirit of adoption by whom we cry out, "Abba, Father." The Spirit Himself bears witness with our spirit that we are children of God, and if children, then heirs—heirs of God and joint heirs with Christ, if indeed we suffer with *Him*, that we may also be glorified together.

For I consider that the sufferings of this present time are not worthy *to be compared* with the glory which shall be revealed in us. For the earnest expectation of the creation eagerly waits for the revealing of the sons of God. For the creation was subjected to futility, not willingly, but because of Him who subjected *it* in hope; because the creation itself also will be delivered from the bondage of corruption into the glorious liberty of the children of God. **For we know that the whole creation groans and labors with birth pangs together until now. Not only *that*, but we also who have the firstfruits of the Spirit, even we ourselves groan within ourselves, eagerly waiting for the adoption, the redemption of our body.** For we were saved in this hope, but hope that is seen is not hope; for why does one still hope for what he sees? But if we hope for what we do not see, we eagerly wait for *it* with perseverance.

ROMANS 8:1–25

BEING AN HEIR OF GOD

One of Paul's favorite themes throughout his writings is our identity in Christ. He writes in Romans 8:1–25 about how we need to live by the Spirit in order to fully experience our new identity. When he wrote to the believers in Ephesus, he eloquently laid out the incredible reality of our magnificent heritage, made possible by God's great love.

You *He made alive,* who were dead in trespasses and sins, in which you once walked according to the course of this world, according to the prince of the power of the air, the spirit who now works in the sons of disobedience, among whom also we all once conducted ourselves in the lusts of our flesh, fulfilling the desires of the flesh and of the mind, and were by nature children of wrath, just as the others.

But God, who is rich in mercy, because of His great love with which He loved us, even when we were dead in trespasses, made us alive together with Christ (by grace you have been saved), and raised *us* up together, and made *us* sit together in the heavenly *places* in Christ Jesus, that in the ages to come He might show the exceeding riches of His grace in *His* kindness toward us in Christ Jesus. For by grace you have been saved through faith, and that not of yourselves; *it is* the gift of God, not of works, lest anyone should boast. For we are His workmanship, created in Christ Jesus for good works, which God prepared beforehand that we should walk in them.

Therefore remember that you, once Gentiles in the flesh—who are called Uncircumcision by what is called the Circumcision made in the flesh by hands—that at that time you were without Christ, being aliens from the commonwealth of Israel and strangers from the covenants of promise, having no hope and without God in the world. But now in Christ Jesus you who once were far off have been brought near by the blood of Christ.

For He Himself is our peace, who has made both one, and has broken down the middle wall of separation, having abolished in His flesh the enmity, *that is,* the law of commandments *contained* in ordinances, so as to create in Himself one new man *from* the two, *thus* making peace, and that He might reconcile them both to God in one body through the cross, thereby putting to death the enmity. And He came and preached peace to you who were afar off and to those who were near. For through Him we both have access by one Spirit to the Father.

Now, therefore, you are no longer strangers and foreigners, but fellow citizens with the saints and members of the household of God, having been built on the foundation of the apostles and prophets, Jesus Christ Himself being the chief corner*stone*, in whom the whole building, being fitted together, grows into a holy temple in the Lord, in whom you also are being built together for a dwelling place of God in the Spirit.

For this reason I, Paul, the prisoner of Christ Jesus for you Gentiles—if indeed you have heard of the dispensation of the grace of God which was given to me for you, how that by revelation He made known to me the mystery (as I have briefly written already, by which, when you read, you may understand my knowledge in the mystery of Christ), which in other ages was not made known to the sons of men, as it has now been revealed by the Spirit to His holy apostles and prophets: that the Gentiles should be fellow heirs, of the same body, and partakers of His promise in Christ through the gospel, of which I became a minister according to the gift of the grace of God given to me by the effective working of His power.

To me, who am less than the least of all the saints, this grace was given, that I should preach among the Gentiles the unsearchable riches of Christ, and to make all see what *is* the fellowship of the mystery, which from the beginning of the ages has been hidden in God who created all things through Jesus Christ; to the intent that now the manifold wisdom of God might be made known by the church to the principalities and powers in the heavenly *places,* according to the eternal purpose which He accomplished in Christ Jesus our Lord, in whom we have boldness and access with confidence through faith in Him. Therefore I ask that you do not lose heart at my tribulations for you, which is your glory.

For this reason I bow my knees to the Father of our Lord Jesus Christ, from whom the whole family in heaven and earth is named, that He would grant you, according to the riches of His glory, to be strengthened with might through His Spirit in the inner man, that Christ may dwell in your hearts through faith; that you, being rooted and grounded in love, may be able to comprehend with all the saints what *is* the width and length and depth and height—to know the love of Christ which passes knowledge; that you may be filled with all the fullness of God.

Now to Him who is able to do exceedingly abundantly above all that we ask or think, according to the power that works in us, to Him *be* glory in the church by Christ Jesus to all generations, forever and ever. Amen.

EPHESIANS 2:1—3:21

The church at Corinth in Greece was blessed with spiritual gifts but struggled to grasp the full meaning and freedom of being heirs with Christ. Paul wrote passionately to help them understand their new identity and to call them to live up to it in their daily lives. And as he did in his letter to the Ephesians, he also exalted the reality and importance of their life together as the body of Christ.

Do you not know that you are the temple of God and *that* the Spirit of God dwells in you? If anyone defiles the temple of God, God will destroy him. For the temple of God is holy, which *temple* you are. 1 CORINTHIANS 3:16–17

Or do you not know that your body is the temple of the Holy Spirit *who is* in you, whom you have from God, and you are not your own? 1 CORINTHIANS 6:19

For as the body is one and has many members, but all the members of that one body, being many, are one body, so also *is* Christ. For by one Spirit we were all baptized into one body—whether Jews or Greeks, whether slaves or free—and have all been made to drink into one Spirit. For in fact the body is not one member but many. 1 CORINTHIANS 12:12–14

The apostle Peter felt as deeply about these new realities as the apostle Paul. He wrote to believers scattered throughout Asia Minor (in modern-day Turkey), reinforcing the new identity they had in Christ. Though his readers consisted of both Jewish and Gentile Christians, Peter used lofty words like "chosen" and "holy" that previously had been reserved for the people of Israel.

Peter, an apostle of Jesus Christ,

To the pilgrims of the Dispersion in Pontus, Galatia, Cappadocia, Asia, and Bithynia, elect according to the foreknowledge of God the Father, in sanctification of the Spirit, for obedience and sprinkling of the blood of Jesus Christ:

Grace to you and peace be multiplied.

Blessed *be* the God and Father of our Lord Jesus Christ, who according to His abundant mercy has begotten us again to a living hope through the resurrection of Jesus Christ from the dead, to an inheritance incorruptible and undefiled and that does not fade away, reserved in heaven for you, who are kept by the power of God through faith for salvation ready to be revealed in the last time.

1 PETER 1:1–5

Since you have purified your souls in obeying the truth through the Spirit in sincere love of the brethren, love one another fervently with a pure heart, having been born again, not of corruptible seed but incorruptible, through the word of God which lives and abides forever. 1 PETER 1:22–23

Coming to Him *as to* a living stone, rejected indeed by men, but chosen by God *and* precious, you also, as living stones, are being built up a spiritual house, a holy priesthood, to offer up spiritual sacrifices acceptable to God through Jesus Christ. Therefore it is also contained in the Scripture,

> *"Behold, I lay in Zion*
> *A chief cornerstone, elect, precious,*
> *And he who believes on Him will by no means be put to shame."*

Therefore, to you who believe, *He is* precious; but to those who are disobedient,

> *"The stone which the builders rejected*
> *Has become the chief cornerstone,"*

and

> *"A stone of stumbling*
> *And a rock of offense."*

They stumble, being disobedient to the word, to which they also were appointed.

But you *are* a chosen generation, a royal priesthood, a holy nation, His own special people, that you may proclaim the praises of Him who called you out of darkness into His marvelous light; who once *were* not a people but *are* now the people of God, who had not obtained mercy but now have obtained mercy. 1 PETER 2:4–10

Highlight or underline all the phrases that speak to our new identity in Christ.

WHAT WE BELIEVE

Who am I? As the key verse declares in John 1:12, when we believe and receive Jesus Christ as our Savior, we are given a new name, a new unconditional covenant. We are adopted. We become heirs of all that belongs to God—and so much more. As we face each day, our worth is not up for grabs. Our identity is rooted firmly and permanently in our honored position as children of God. We do not live our lives to prove who we are but to express who we are in Christ.

THINK

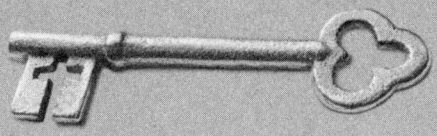

CHAPTER

6

Church

KEY QUESTION

How will God accomplish His plan?

KEY IDEA

I believe the church is God's primary way to accomplish His purposes on earth.

KEY VERSE

But, speaking the truth in love,
[we] may grow up in all things into Him
who is the head—Christ.
Ephesians 4:15

OUR MAP

The first five key beliefs we have read so far are mostly vertical in nature—they deal with our relationships with God. The God of the Bible is the one true God who is involved in and cares about our daily lives. This God has provided the way for us to come into a relationship with Him through faith in Jesus Christ. God revealed this to us along with a roadmap (the Bible) for our lives. This special book is from God and therefore has the right to command our beliefs and actions. We who embrace these beliefs and receive Jesus as our Savior from sin are given a new identity. From that moment on we can find our significance not in our performance but in our position as children of God.

The final set of five beliefs is more horizontal in nature—they deal with our relationship with others. Out of our relationship with God we engage our world in a purposeful and fruitful way. How will God accomplish the plan for humanity He has laid out in the Bible? God has chosen to use two communities He created—the ancient nation of Israel and the church—to accomplish His purposes on earth. If you are a Christian, you are a part of this community.

In this chapter we will explore the following regarding the church:

- *Founding*
- *Expansion*
- *Plan and Purpose*

Founding

From the very beginning God had a vision to be with His people in perfect community. When the first two humans—Adam and Eve—rejected this vision and were escorted from the Garden of Eden, God began to unveil a plan to provide the way back to Him.

God's plan consisted of making Abraham's offspring into a great nation. From this single nation would come the solution for all people of all nations to come back into a relationship with the one true God. Thus the story of Israel pointed people of all nations to Abraham's descendant Jesus and was part of God's plan to restore a relationship with His people.

Again we return to the story of Abraham (Abram) where we can see the beginnings of God's covenant with a people who came to be known as Israel. It starts with God's call to Abram and Abram's amazing response of complete faith and trust.

Now the LORD had said to Abram:

"Get out of your country,
From your family
And from your father's house,
To a land that I will show you.
I will make you a great nation;
I will bless you
And make your name great;
And you shall be a blessing.
I will bless those who bless you,
And I will curse him who curses you;
And in you all the families of the earth shall be blessed."

So Abram departed as the LORD had spoken to him, and Lot went with him. And Abram *was* seventy-five years old when he departed from Haran. Then Abram took Sarai his wife and Lot his brother's son, and all their possessions that they had gathered, and the people whom they had acquired in Haran, and they departed to go to the land of Canaan. So they came to the land of Canaan. Abram passed through the land to the place of Shechem, as far as the terebinth tree of Moreh. And the Canaanites *were* then in the land.

Then the LORD appeared to Abram and said, "To your descendants I will give this land." And there he built an altar to the LORD, who had appeared to him. And he moved from there to the mountain east of Bethel, and he pitched his tent *with* Bethel on the west and Ai on the east; there he built an altar to the LORD and called on the name of the LORD. So Abram journeyed, going on still toward the South.

GENESIS 12:1–9

After these things the word of the LORD came to Abram in a vision, saying, "Do not be afraid, Abram. I *am* your shield, your exceedingly great reward."

But Abram said, "Lord GOD, what will You give me, seeing I go childless, and the heir of my house *is* Eliezer of Damascus?" Then Abram said, "Look, You have given me no offspring; indeed one born in my house is my heir!"

And behold, the word of the LORD *came* to him, saying, "This one shall not be your heir, but one who will come from your own body shall be your heir." Then He brought him outside and said, "Look now toward heaven, and count the stars if you are able to number them." And He said to him, "So shall your descendants be."

And he believed in the LORD, and He accounted it to him for righteousness. GENESIS 15:1–6

At this time and place in history, a covenant was a type of promise. The covenant described in the following verses is a covenant that would have been made between a king and a subject. The narrative describes the establishment of a covenant between God and Abram, initiated by God Himself. God was making an unconditional promise (not dependent on Israel's obedience). By God's mighty hand the descendants of Abram survived and God accomplished His plan through them.

Then He said to him, "I *am* the LORD, who brought you out of Ur of the Chaldeans, to give you this land to inherit it."

And he said, "Lord GOD, how shall I know that I will inherit it?"

So He said to him, "Bring Me a three-year-old heifer, a three-year-old female goat, a three-year-old ram, a turtledove, and a young pigeon." Then he brought all these to Him and cut them in two, down the middle, and placed each piece opposite the other; but he did not cut the birds in two. And when the vultures came down on the carcasses, Abram drove them away.

Now when the sun was going down, a deep sleep fell upon Abram; and behold, horror *and* great darkness fell upon him. Then He said to Abram: "Know certainly that your descendants will be strangers in a land *that is* not theirs, and will serve them, and they will afflict them four hundred years. And also the nation whom they serve I will judge; afterward they shall come out with great possessions. Now as for you, you shall go to your fathers in peace; you shall be buried at a good old age. But in the fourth generation they shall return here, for the iniquity of the Amorites *is* not yet complete."

And it came to pass, when the sun went down and it was dark, that behold, there appeared a smoking oven and a burning torch that passed between those pieces. On the same day the LORD made a covenant with Abram, saying:

"To your descendants I have given this land, from the river of Egypt to the great river, the River Euphrates—the Kenites, the Kenezzites, the Kadmonites, the Hittites, the Perizzites, the Rephaim, the Amorites, the Canaanites, the Girgashites, and the Jebusites."

GENESIS 15:7–21

The covenant with Abram was the beginning of God's long and complicated relationship with the nation of Israel. The Old Testament of the Bible contains the details of this relationship, but as we have read in previous chapters, a new covenant was instituted. In the end, God's plan was accomplished through Israel and the new covenant was ushered in when the Messiah was born.

As Jesus was nearing His crucifixion, He told the disciples what was ahead and explained their role in accomplishing God's ultimate vision for the coming kingdom. This exchange highlights that God's plan for believers is still in force; the vision is for believers to come together in a new community that continues to this day. And here Jesus speaks of the founding of that community—the church.

When Jesus came into the region of Caesarea Philippi, He asked His disciples, saying, "Who do men say that I, the Son of Man, am?"

So they said, "Some *say* John the Baptist, some Elijah, and others Jeremiah or one of the prophets."

He said to them, "But who do you say that I am?"

Simon Peter answered and said, "You are the Christ, the Son of the living God."

Jesus answered and said to him, "Blessed are you, Simon Bar-Jonah, for flesh and blood has not revealed *this* to you, but My Father who is in heaven. And I also say to you that you are Peter, and on this rock I will build My church, and the gates of

Hades shall not prevail against it. And I will give you the keys of the kingdom of heaven, and whatever you bind on earth will be bound in heaven, and whatever you loose on earth will be loosed in heaven."

MATTHEW 16:13–19

Look back over the last two stories of Abraham (see Genesis 12:1–9; 15:1–6,7–21) and Peter (see Matthew 16:13–19). What was Abraham's response that was "accounted it to him for righteousness"? How did Peter respond when Jesus asked, "Who do you say that I am?" How are these responses related?

After the resurrection and ascension of Jesus, God formed this community, called the church, led by His disciples. The story of the church points people of all nations to the second coming of Christ when He will fully restore God's original vision.

Forty days after Jesus' resurrection and just before His ascension back to the Father, Jesus visited with His disciples and gave them His final instructions. Luke, who also wrote the Gospel bearing his name, recorded the incident in the book of Acts. The result? The church was born!

The former account I made, O Theophilus, of all that Jesus began both to do and teach, until the day in which He was taken up, after He through the Holy Spirit had given commandments to the apostles whom He had chosen, to whom He also presented Himself alive after His suffering by many infallible proofs, being seen by them during forty days and speaking of the things pertaining to the kingdom of God.

And being assembled together with *them,* He commanded them not to depart from Jerusalem, but to wait for the Promise of the Father, "which," *He said,* "you have heard from Me; for John truly baptized with water, but you shall be baptized with the Holy Spirit not many days from now." Therefore, when they had come together, they asked Him, saying, "Lord, will You at this time restore the kingdom to Israel?" **And He said to them, "It is not for you to know times or seasons which the Father has put in His own authority. But you shall receive power when the Holy**

Spirit has come upon you; and you shall be witnesses to Me in Jerusalem, and in all Judea and Samaria, and to the end of the earth."

Now when He had spoken these things, while they watched, He was taken up, and a cloud received Him out of their sight. And while they looked steadfastly toward heaven as He went up, behold, two men stood by them in white apparel, who also said, "Men of Galilee, why do you stand gazing up into heaven? This *same* Jesus, who was taken up from you into heaven, will so come in like manner as you saw Him go into heaven."

ACTS 1:1–11

How did God equip the people of the early church to carry out their mission to spread the gospel of Jesus Christ?

For the next ten days, Jesus' followers—about 120 men and women—met together. They joined together continually in prayer in anticipation of what was about to happen. After they became filled with the Holy Spirit, Peter used the "keys of the kingdom" that Jesus had mentioned earlier. Peter announced that the door of the kingdom had been unlocked.

When the Day of Pentecost had fully come, they were all with one accord in one place. And suddenly there came a sound from heaven, as of a rushing mighty wind, and it filled the whole house where they were sitting. Then there appeared to them divided tongues, as of fire, and *one* sat upon each of them. And they were all filled with the Holy Spirit and began to speak with other tongues, as the Spirit gave them utterance.

And there were dwelling in Jerusalem Jews, devout men, from every nation under heaven. And when this sound occurred, the multitude came together, and were confused, because everyone heard them speak in his own language. Then they were all amazed and marveled, saying to one another, "Look, are not all these who speak Galileans? And how *is it that* we hear, each in our own language in which we were born? Parthians and Medes and Elamites, those dwelling in Mesopotamia, Judea and Cappadocia, Pontus and Asia, Phrygia and Pamphylia, Egypt and the parts of Libya adjoining Cyrene, visitors from Rome, both Jews and proselytes, Cretans and Arabs—we hear them speaking in our own tongues the wonderful works of God." So they were all amazed and perplexed, saying to one another, "Whatever could this mean?"

Others mocking said, "They are full of new wine."

But Peter, standing up with the eleven, raised his voice and said to them, "Men of Judea and all who dwell in Jerusalem, let this be known to you, and heed my words. For these are not drunk, as you suppose, since it is *only* the third hour of the day. But this is what was spoken by the prophet Joel:

> *'And it shall come to pass in the last days, says God,*
> *That I will pour out of My Spirit on all flesh;*
> *Your sons and your daughters shall prophesy,*
> *Your young men shall see visions,*
> *Your old men shall dream dreams.*
> *And on My menservants and on My maidservants*
> *I will pour out My Spirit in those days;*
> *And they shall prophesy.*
> *I will show wonders in heaven above*
> *And signs in the earth beneath:*
> *Blood and fire and vapor of smoke.*
> *The sun shall be turned into darkness,*
> *And the moon into blood,*
> *Before the coming of the great and awesome day*
> *of the* LORD.
> *And it shall come to pass*
> *That whoever calls on the name of the* LORD
> *Shall be saved.'*

"Men of Israel, hear these words: Jesus of Nazareth, a Man attested by God to you by miracles, wonders, and signs which God did through Him in your midst, as you yourselves also know—Him, being delivered by the determined purpose and foreknowledge of God, you have taken by lawless hands, have crucified, and put to death; whom God raised up, having loosed the pains of death, because it was not possible that He should be held by it. For David says concerning Him:

'I foresaw the LORD *always before my face,*
For He is at my right hand, that I may not be shaken.
Therefore my heart rejoiced, and my tongue was glad;
Moreover my flesh also will rest in hope.
For You will not leave my soul in Hades,
Nor will You allow Your Holy One to see corruption.
You have made known to me the ways of life;
You will make me full of joy in Your presence.'

"Men *and* brethren, let *me* speak freely to you of the patriarch David, that he is both dead and buried, and his tomb is with us to this day. Therefore, being a prophet, and knowing that God had sworn with an oath to him that of the fruit of his body, according to the flesh, He would raise up the Christ to sit on his throne, he, foreseeing this, spoke concerning the resurrection of the Christ, that His soul was not left in Hades, nor did His flesh see corruption. This Jesus God has raised up, of which we are all witnesses. Therefore being exalted to the right hand of God, and having received from the Father the promise of the Holy Spirit, He poured out this which you now see and hear.

"For David did not ascend into the heavens, but he says himself:

'The LORD *said to my Lord,*
"Sit at My right hand,
Till I make Your enemies Your footstool."'

"Therefore let all the house of Israel know assuredly that God has made this Jesus, whom you crucified, both Lord and Christ."

Now when they heard *this,* they were cut to the heart, and said to Peter and the rest of the apostles, "Men *and* brethren, what shall we do?"

Then Peter said to them, "Repent, and let every one of you be baptized in the name of Jesus Christ for the remission of sins; and you shall receive the gift of the Holy Spirit. For the promise is to you and to your children, and to all who are afar off, as many as the Lord our God will call."

And with many other words he testified and exhorted them, saying, "Be saved from this perverse generation." Then those who gladly received his word were baptized; and that day about three thousand souls were added *to them.* ACTS 2:1–41

The thread from here back to where we started is undeniable. The church was born out of a supernatural movement of the Holy Spirit. The Holy Spirit was given to the followers of Jesus. Jesus the Messiah, long promised to the Jewish nation, was born through a lineage that traced back to Abraham. Abraham believed God's original promise to make of him a great nation, and it was upon his faith that the seeds of the church were planted.

EXPANSION

Jesus' commission to the first disciples in AD 30 was to spread the good news and to build His church beyond Jerusalem to all of Judea and Samaria and ultimately, to the ends of the earth. The book of Acts records the fulfillment of that mission by chronicling the miraculous journey and exponential development of the church community. The story of the expansion of the church beyond Jerusalem comes on the heels of the stoning of the disciple Stephen for his bold faith amid a hostile crowd of Jews.

As you read the following story from Acts 8 about the expansion of the church, note some of the events that show the transformation of a small group of Jesus' Jewish followers into a universal Christian church.

At that time a great persecution arose against the church which was at Jerusalem; and they were all scattered throughout the regions of Judea and Samaria, except the apostles. And devout men carried Stephen *to his burial,* and made great lamentation over him.

As for Saul, he made havoc of the church, entering every house, and dragging off men and women, committing *them* to prison.

Therefore those who were scattered went everywhere preaching the word. Then Philip went down to the city of Samaria and preached Christ to them. And the multitudes with one accord heeded the things spoken by Philip, hearing and seeing the miracles which he did. For unclean spirits, crying with a loud voice, came out of many who were possessed; and many who were paralyzed and lame were healed. And there was great joy in that city.

ACTS 8:1–8

Now when the apostles who were at Jerusalem heard that Samaria had received the word of God, they sent Peter and John to them, who, when they had come down, prayed for them that they might receive the Holy Spirit. For as yet He had fallen upon none of them. They had only been baptized in the name of the Lord Jesus. Then they laid hands on them, and they received the Holy Spirit.

ACTS 8:14–17

So when they had testified and preached the word of the Lord, they returned to Jerusalem, preaching the gospel in many villages of the Samaritans.

ACTS 8:25

Then the churches throughout all Judea, Galilee, and Samaria had peace and were edified. And walking in the fear of the Lord and in the comfort of the Holy Spirit, they were multiplied.

ACTS 9:31

Identify some of the ways in which persecution helped the early church in its mission to share the gospel.

Just as Peter had used the "keys of the kingdom" on the day of Pentecost to announce to the Jews in Jerusalem that the door of the kingdom had been unlocked, he also used those keys to open the door to the Gentiles. God supernaturally led Peter and a Roman centurion named Cornelius to meet each other. When Peter told Cornelius and his relatives and close friends the good news about Jesus, they believed, were filled with the Holy Spirit and were baptized.

Now the apostles and brethren who were in Judea heard that the Gentiles had also received the word of God. And when Peter came up to Jerusalem, those of the circumcision contended with him, saying, "You went in to uncircumcised men and ate with them!"

But Peter explained *it* to them in order from the beginning, saying: "I was in the city of Joppa praying; and in a trance I saw a vision, an object descending like a great sheet, let down from heaven by four corners; and it came to me. When I observed it intently and considered, I saw four-footed animals of the earth, wild beasts, creeping things, and birds of the air. And I heard a voice saying to me, 'Rise, Peter; kill and eat.' But I said, 'Not so, Lord! For nothing common or unclean has at any time entered my mouth.' But the voice answered me again from heaven, 'What God has cleansed you must not call common.' Now this was done three times, and all were drawn up again into heaven. At that very moment, three men stood before the house where I was, having been sent to me from Caesarea. Then the Spirit told me to go with them, doubting nothing. Moreover these six brethren accompanied me, and we entered the man's house. And he told us how he had seen an angel standing in his house, who said to him, 'Send men to Joppa, and call for Simon whose surname is Peter, who will tell you words by which you and all your household will be saved.' And as I began to speak, the Holy Spirit fell upon them, as upon us at the beginning. Then I remembered the word of the Lord, how He said, 'John indeed baptized with water, but you shall be baptized with the Holy Spirit.' If therefore God gave them the same gift as *He gave* us when we believed on the Lord Jesus Christ, who was I that I could withstand God?"

When they heard these things they became silent; and they glorified God, saying, "Then God has also granted to the Gentiles repentance to life." ACTS 11:1–18

In an unlikely turn of events, the persecution of the church caused it to spread. Believers fled from Jerusalem where they were in danger, taking refuge in far-flung cities in the Gentile world. And as improbable as it sounds, it is Saul, one of the chief persecutors of the church, who God would use to take the gospel and the church to the Gentiles. Around AD 35, Saul personally encountered the risen Jesus in a vision while on the road to Damascus. Saul surrendered his life to Christ and devoted the rest of his days on earth to building Christ's church. His home base was the church at Antioch.

Now those who were scattered after the persecution that arose over Stephen traveled as far as Phoenicia, Cyprus, and Antioch, preaching the word to no one but the Jews only. But some of them were men from Cyprus and Cyrene, who, when they had come to Antioch, spoke to the Hellenists, preaching the Lord Jesus. And the hand of the Lord was with them, and a great number believed and turned to the Lord.

Then news of these things came to the ears of the church in Jerusalem, and they sent out Barnabas to go as far as Antioch. When he came and had seen the grace of God, he was glad, and encouraged them all that with purpose of heart they should continue with the Lord. For he was a good man, full of the Holy Spirit and of faith. And a great many people were added to the Lord.

Then Barnabas departed for Tarsus to seek Saul. And when he had found him, he brought him to Antioch. So it was that for a whole year they assembled with the church and taught a great many people. And the disciples were first called Christians in Antioch.

ACTS 11:19–26

Now in the church that was at Antioch there were certain prophets and teachers: Barnabas, Simeon who was called Niger, Lucius of Cyrene, Manaen who had been brought up with Herod the tetrarch, and Saul. As they ministered to the Lord and fasted, the Holy Spirit said, "Now separate to Me Barnabas and Saul for the work to which I have called them." Then, having fasted and prayed, and laid hands on them, they sent *them* away.

ACTS 13:1–3

Saul, soon to be known as Paul for approximately the next 20 years, would embark on numerous journeys to spread the gospel and strengthen and build the church as it stretched toward the ends of the earth, just as Jesus had envisioned. Paul's first missionary trip began around AD 46, and in each city he visited, he used a skillful blend of history, theology and philosophy to declare the good news to both Jews and Gentiles, who responded and joined the expanding church.

When Paul and his companions came to Antioch, Paul stood up in the synagogue to a predominantly Jewish audience and gave a powerful sermon similar to Peter's on the day of Pentecost. He told them the story of the Jews in chronological order beginning with Israel of the Old Testament. We pick up at the end of his message, where Paul boldly extends an invitation to them to receive this good news. Notice then the shift in focus away from the Jews, based on their rejection.

"Therefore let it be known to you, brethren, that through this Man is preached to you the forgiveness of sins; and by Him everyone who believes is justified from all things from which you could not be justified by the law of Moses. Beware therefore, lest what has been spoken in the prophets come upon you:

> *'Behold, you despisers,*
> *Marvel and perish!*
> *For I work a work in your days,*
> *A work which you will by no means believe,*
> *Though one were to declare it to you.'"*

So when the Jews went out of the synagogue, the Gentiles begged that these words might be preached to them the next Sabbath. Now when the congregation had broken up, many of the Jews and devout proselytes followed Paul and Barnabas, who, speaking to them, persuaded them to continue in the grace of God.

On the next Sabbath almost the whole city came together to hear the word of God. But when the Jews saw the multitudes, they were filled with envy; and contradicting and blaspheming, they opposed the things spoken by Paul. **Then Paul and Barnabas grew bold and said, "It was necessary that the word of God should be spoken to you first; but since you reject it, and judge yourselves unworthy of everlasting life, behold, we turn to the Gentiles. For so the Lord has commanded us:**

> ***'I have set you as a light to the Gentiles,***
> ***That you should be for salvation to the ends of the earth.'"***

Now when the Gentiles heard this, they were glad and glorified the word of the Lord. And as many as had been appointed to eternal life believed.

And the word of the Lord was being spread throughout all the region. But the Jews stirred up the devout and prominent women and the chief men of the city, raised up persecution against Paul and Barnabas, and expelled them from their region. But they shook off the dust from their feet against them, and came to Iconium. And the disciples were filled with joy and with the Holy Spirit.

ACTS 13:38–52

Paul's attention turned to spreading the gospel and building the church in a world dominated by Gentiles. One of the churches dear to Paul's heart was at Ephesus. During his third missionary journey, he spent between two and three years there building the church and its leadership. A couple of years later, around AD 57, Paul was in a hurry to get to Jerusalem before Pentecost. Concerned that he might never return to Ephesus, he called for the elders of the church to meet him on his way to Jerusalem. He wanted to have one last meeting with them to build them up and stabilize the fledgling church he had sacrificed so much to launch.

From Miletus he sent to Ephesus and called for the elders of the church. And when they had come to him, he said to them: "You know, from the first day that I came to Asia, in what manner I always lived among you, serving the Lord with all humility, with many tears and trials which happened to me by the plotting of the Jews; how I kept back nothing that was helpful, but proclaimed it to you, and taught you publicly and from house to house, testifying to Jews, and also to Greeks, repentance toward God and faith toward our Lord Jesus Christ. And see, now I go bound in the spirit to Jerusalem, not knowing the things that will happen to me there, except that the Holy Spirit testifies in every city, saying that chains and tribulations await me. **But none of these things move me; nor do I count my life dear to myself, so that I may finish my race with joy, and the ministry which I received from the Lord Jesus, to testify to the gospel of the grace of God.**

"And indeed, now I know that you all, among whom I have gone preaching the kingdom of God, will see my face no more. Therefore I testify to you this day that I *am* innocent of the blood of all *men.* For I have not shunned to declare to you the whole counsel of God. **Therefore take heed to yourselves and to all the flock, among which the Holy Spirit has made you overseers, to shepherd the church of God which He purchased with His own blood.** For I know this, that after my departure savage wolves will come in among you, not sparing the flock. Also from among yourselves men will rise up, speaking perverse things, to draw away the disciples after themselves. Therefore watch, and remember that for three years I did not cease to warn everyone night and day with tears.

"So now, brethren, I commend you to God and to the word of His grace, which is able to build you up and give you an inheritance among all those who are sanctified. I have coveted no one's silver or gold or apparel. Yes, you yourselves know that these hands have provided for my necessities, and for those who were with me. I have shown you in every way, by laboring like this, that you must support the weak. And remember the words of the Lord Jesus, that He said, 'It is more blessed to give than to receive.'"

And when he had said these things, he knelt down and prayed with them all. Then they all wept freely, and fell on Paul's neck and kissed him, sorrowing most of all for the words which he spoke, that they would see his face no more. And they accompanied him to the ship.

Now it came to pass, that when we had departed from them and set sail, running a straight course we came to Cos, the following *day* to Rhodes, and from there to Patara. ACTS 20:17—21:1

PLAN AND PURPOSE

As Paul had anticipated, prison and hardships awaited him when he arrived in Jerusalem. While under house arrest in Rome a few years later, around AD 60, Paul penned a letter to the church at Ephesus. Paul explained God's great plan for the church, the new community of Christ. Along with reconciling individuals to Himself, God has reconciled them to one another. Through His death, Christ has broken down the barriers, uniting believers in one body—the church. The church community is now invited to live up to the calling they have in Jesus Christ.

As you read the passages below from Ephesians 4 and Revelation 2, identify the key phrases that define the purpose of the Christian church in the world.

I, therefore, the prisoner of the Lord, beseech you to walk worthy of the calling with which you were called, with all lowliness and gentleness, with longsuffering, bearing with one another in love, endeavoring to keep the unity of the Spirit in the bond of peace. *There is* one body and one Spirit, just as you were called in one hope of your calling; one Lord, one faith, one baptism; one God and Father of all, who *is* above all, and through all, and in you all.

But to each one of us grace was given according to the measure of Christ's gift. Therefore He says:

> *"When He ascended on high,*
> *He led captivity captive,*
> *And gave gifts to men."*

(Now this, *"He ascended"*—what does it mean but that He also first descended into the lower parts of the earth? He who descended is also the One who ascended far above all the heavens, that He might fill all things.)

And He Himself gave some *to be* apostles, some prophets, some evangelists, and some pastors and teachers, for the equipping of the saints for the work of ministry, for the edifying of the body of Christ, till we all come to the unity of the faith and of the knowledge of the Son of God, to a perfect man, to the measure of the stature of the fullness of Christ; that we should no longer be children, tossed to and fro and carried about with every wind of doctrine, by the trickery of men, in the cunning craftiness of deceitful plotting, but, speaking the truth in love, may grow up in all things into Him who is the head—Christ—from whom the whole body, joined and knit together by what every joint supplies, according to the effective working by which every part does its share, causes growth of the body for the edifying of itself in love.

EPHESIANS 4:1–16

Near the end of the first century, around AD 95, the apostle John received amazing visions from God that are contained in the book of Revelation. He addresses the book to seven churches in the Roman province of Asia (in modern-day Turkey); one of them was the church in Ephesus. As part of the book, John records letters from the risen Christ to those seven churches, in which He typically issues words of commendation, complaint and correction. Some 45 years after Paul penned his letter to the church in Ephesus, Christ's message to them represents a report card on their progress. It is both a word of encouragement and a challenge to the church today.

"To the angel of the church of Ephesus write,

'These things says He who holds the seven stars in His right hand, who walks in the midst of the seven golden lampstands: "I know your works, your labor, your patience, and that you cannot bear those who are evil. And you have tested those who say they are apostles and are not, and have found them liars; and you have persevered and have patience, and have labored for My name's sake and have not become weary. **Nevertheless I have *this* against you, that you have left your first love.** Remember therefore from where you have fallen; repent and do the first works, or else I will come to you quickly and remove your lampstand from its place—unless you repent. But this you have, that you hate the deeds of the Nicolaitans, which I also hate.

"He who has an ear, let him hear what the Spirit says to the churches. To him who overcomes I will give to eat from the tree of life, which is in the midst of the Paradise of God."'" REVELATION 2:1–7

WHAT WE BELIEVE

God used both Israel and the church to accomplish His grand plan to redeem and restore us to a right relationship with Him. God's plan for Israel was to bring us Jesus, who would provide the only way back to God. It took a little more than 2,000 years for this divine plan to be fulfilled.

After Jesus' resurrection and ascension back to the Father, God created the church. Empowered by the Holy Spirit, the church has existed for approximately 2,000 years. God's primary plan for the church is to spread the good news of Jesus Christ to all nations until Jesus comes again. Today there are an estimated 2.2 billion Christians in the world. If you have received and accepted the grace of Christ, then you are a member of the body of Christ. And remember you are an integral part of His plan—God wants you to be fully vested in His church to accomplish His great and wonderful purposes!

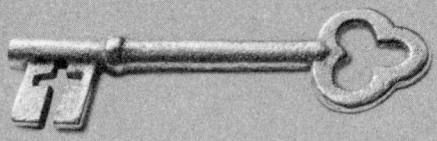

CHAPTER

7

Humanity

KEY QUESTION

How does God see us?

KEY IDEA

I believe all people are loved by God
and need Jesus Christ as their Savior.

KEY VERSE

For God so loved the world
that He gave His only begotten Son,
that whoever believes in Him should not perish
but have everlasting life.
John 3:16

OUR MAP

God created everything, but the pinnacle of creation was the making of human beings—creatures crafted in the image of God. Humanity is special, and the Bible is the record of the love story between Creator and created, between God and humans. From the very beginning of time to the era of the modern-day church, God has loved and pursued His people in order to restore His image within and among them.

In this chapter we will read Scripture passages on:

- *Origins*
- *The Devastating Human Condition*
- *God's Love*
- *All and Whoever*
- *Seeing People as God Sees Them*

This chapter will come to a close with Scripture that invites us to embrace every believer as a precious family member.

Origins

God is the origin of all life.

In the beginning God created the heavens and the earth. The earth was without form, and void; and darkness *was* on the face of the deep. And the Spirit of God was hovering over the face of the waters.

Then God said, "Let there be light"; and there was light. And God saw the light, that *it was* good; and God divided the light from the darkness. God called the light Day, and the darkness He called Night. So the evening and the morning were the first day.

Then God said, "Let there be a firmament in the midst of the waters, and let it divide the waters from the waters." Thus God made the firmament, and divided the waters which *were* under the firmament from the waters which *were* above the firmament; and it was so. And God called the firmament Heaven. So the evening and the morning were the second day.

Then God said, "Let the waters under the heavens be gathered together into one place, and let the dry *land* appear"; and it was so.

And God called the dry *land* Earth, and the gathering together of the waters He called Seas. And God saw that *it was* good.

Then God said, "Let the earth bring forth grass, the herb *that* yields seed, *and* the fruit tree *that* yields fruit according to its kind, whose seed *is* in itself, on the earth"; and it was so. And the earth brought forth grass, the herb *that* yields seed according to its kind, and the tree *that* yields fruit, whose seed *is* in itself according to its kind. And God saw that *it was* good. So the evening and the morning were the third day.

Then God said, "Let there be lights in the firmament of the heavens to divide the day from the night; and let them be for signs and seasons, and for days and years; and let them be for lights in the firmament of the heavens to give light on the earth"; and it was so. Then God made two great lights: the greater light to rule the day, and the lesser light to rule the night. *He made* the stars also. God set them in the firmament of the heavens to give light on the earth, and to rule over the day and over the night, and to divide the light from the darkness. And God saw that *it was* good. So the evening and the morning were the fourth day.

Then God said, "Let the waters abound with an abundance of living creatures, and let birds fly above the earth across the face of the firmament of the heavens." So God created great sea creatures and every living thing that moves, with which the waters abounded, according to their kind, and every winged bird according to its kind. And God saw that *it was* good. And God blessed them, saying, "Be fruitful and multiply, and fill the waters in the seas, and let birds multiply on the earth." So the evening and the morning were the fifth day.

Then God said, "Let the earth bring forth the living creature according to its kind: cattle and creeping thing and beast of the earth, *each* according to its kind"; and it was so. And God made the beast of the earth according to its kind, cattle according to its kind, and everything that creeps on the earth according to its kind. And God saw that *it was* good.

Then God said, "Let Us make man in Our image, according to Our likeness; let them have dominion over the fish of the sea, over the birds of the air, and over the cattle, over all the earth and over every creeping thing that creeps on the earth."

So God created man in His *own* image; in the image of God He created him; male and female He created them. Then God blessed them, and God said to them, "Be fruitful and multiply; fill the earth and subdue it; have dominion over the fish of the sea, over the birds of the air, and over every living thing that moves on the earth."

And God said, "See, I have given you every herb *that* yields seed which *is* on the face of all the earth, and every tree whose fruit yields seed; to you it shall be for food. Also, to every beast of the earth, to every bird of the air, and to everything that creeps on the earth, in which *there is* life, *I have given* every green herb for food"; and it was so. Then God saw everything that He had made, and indeed *it was* very good. So the evening and the morning were the sixth day.

GENESIS 1:1–31

Describe in your own words God's original intent for the human race.

THE DEVASTATING HUMAN CONDITION

God created the cosmos and everything in it. He created the earth so that He could be with the people He created. Unfortunately, the first two people—Adam and Eve—rejected God's vision for His creation, causing sin to enter into their nature and thereby making them unfit for community with a holy God. The greatest pandemic ever experienced by humanity is the transference of this sin "DNA" to every generation.

What are some of the results of human sin reflected below in the story of Cain and Abel in Genesis 4?

Now Adam knew Eve his wife, and she conceived and bore Cain, and said, "I have acquired a man from the LORD." Then she bore again, this time his brother Abel. Now Abel was a keeper of sheep, but Cain was a tiller of the ground. And in the process of time it came to pass that Cain brought an offering of the fruit of the ground to the LORD. Abel also brought of the firstborn of his flock and of their fat. And the LORD respected Abel and his offering, but He did not respect Cain and his offering. And Cain was very angry, and his countenance fell. GENESIS 4:1–5

Here we see the results of Adam and Eve's choices. We know from other Scriptures that God rejected Cain's offering and accepted Abel's offering because of what He saw in the faith of the two men. The Bible doesn't explicitly tell us why God rejected Cain's offering, but it involved Cain's attitude toward God.

Abel brought the first of his harvest and the best of his flock, while Cain brought "an offering of the fruit of the ground." We learn throughout the Old Testament that it pleases God when we bring Him our first and best, not our leftovers.

So the LORD said to Cain, "Why are you angry? And why has your countenance fallen? If you do well, will you not be accepted? And if you do not do well, sin lies at the door. And its desire *is* for you, but you should rule over it."

Now Cain talked with Abel his brother; and it came to pass, when they were in the field, that Cain rose up against Abel his brother and killed him.

Then the LORD said to Cain, "Where *is* Abel your brother?"

He said, "I do not know. *Am* I my brother's keeper?"

And He said, "What have you done? The voice of your brother's blood cries out to Me from the ground. So now you *are* cursed from the earth, which has opened its mouth to receive your brother's blood from your hand. When you till the ground, it shall no longer yield its strength to you. A fugitive and a vagabond you shall be on the earth."

And Cain said to the LORD, "My punishment *is* greater than I can bear! Surely You have driven me out this day from the face of the ground; I shall be hidden from Your face; I shall be a fugitive and a vagabond on the earth, and it will happen *that* anyone who finds me will kill me."

And the LORD said to him, "Therefore, whoever kills Cain, vengeance shall be taken on him sevenfold." And the LORD set a mark on Cain, lest anyone finding him should kill him.

Then Cain went out from the presence of the LORD and dwelt in the land of Nod on the east of Eden. GENESIS 4:6–16

Adam and Eve had more children, but their offspring continued inheriting and passing on a fallen, sinful nature. In the New Testament era, Jude, who was both a half brother and a follower of Jesus, wrote a letter to warn Christians about false teachers who were trying to convince believers that salvation by grace gave them license to sin. Jude notes that these dangerous teachers had "gone in the way of Cain," meaning the way of selfishness and greed—demonstrated by Cain's careless, thoughtless offering—and the way of hatred and murder—demonstrated by Cain's slaying of Abel.

Jude, a bondservant of Jesus Christ, and brother of James,

To those who are called, sanctified by God the Father, and preserved in Jesus Christ:

Mercy, peace, and love be multiplied to you.

Beloved, while I was very diligent to write to you concerning our common salvation, I found it necessary to write to you exhorting you to contend earnestly for the faith which was once for all delivered to the saints. For certain men have crept in unnoticed, who long ago were marked out for this condemnation, ungodly men, who turn the grace of our God into lewdness and deny the only Lord God and our Lord Jesus Christ.

But I want to remind you, though you once knew this, that the Lord, having saved the people out of the land of Egypt, afterward destroyed those who did not believe. And the angels who did not keep their proper domain, but left their own abode, He has reserved in everlasting chains under darkness for the judgment of the great day; as Sodom and Gomorrah, and the cities around them in a similar manner to these, having given themselves over to sexual immorality and gone after strange flesh, are set forth as an example, suffering the vengeance of eternal fire.

Likewise also these dreamers defile the flesh, reject authority, and speak evil of dignitaries. Yet Michael the archangel, in contending with the devil, when he disputed about the body of

Moses, dared not bring against him a reviling accusation, but said, "The Lord rebuke you!" But these speak evil of whatever they do not know; and whatever they know naturally, like brute beasts, in these things they corrupt themselves. **Woe to them! For they have gone in the way of Cain,** have run greedily in the error of Balaam for profit, and perished in the rebellion of Korah.

These are spots in your love feasts, while they feast with you without fear, serving *only* themselves. *They are* clouds without water, carried about by the winds; late autumn trees without fruit, twice dead, pulled up by the roots; raging waves of the sea, foaming up their own shame; wandering stars for whom is reserved the blackness of darkness forever.

Now Enoch, the seventh from Adam, prophesied about these men also, saying, "Behold, the Lord comes with ten thousands of His saints, to execute judgment on all, to convict all who are ungodly among them of all their ungodly deeds which they have committed in an ungodly way, and of all the harsh things which ungodly sinners have spoken against Him."

These are grumblers, complainers, walking according to their own lusts; and they mouth great swelling *words*, flattering people to gain advantage. JUDE 1–16

Paul's letter to the Christians in Rome contains a chilling declaration of the extent and consequences of the sin nature that has permeated the entire human race, beginning with Adam and Eve and their offspring. First, Paul indicts the sinfulness of the Gentiles and then, perhaps surprising his readers, shows the sinfulness of the Jews. He makes it clear that no one is righteous.

For the wrath of God is revealed from heaven against all ungodliness and unrighteousness of men, who suppress the truth in unrighteousness, because what may be known of God is manifest in them, for God has shown *it* to them. For since the creation of the world His invisible *attributes* are clearly seen, being understood by the things that are made, *even* His eternal power and Godhead, so that they are without excuse, because, although they knew God, they did not glorify *Him* as God, nor were thankful, but became futile in their thoughts, and their foolish hearts were darkened. Professing to be wise, they became fools, and changed the glory of the incorruptible God into an image made like corruptible man—and birds and four-footed animals and creeping things.

Therefore God also gave them up to uncleanness, in the lusts of their hearts, to dishonor their bodies among themselves, who exchanged the truth of God for the lie, and worshiped and served the creature rather than the Creator, who is blessed forever. Amen.

For this reason God gave them up to vile passions. For even their women exchanged the natural use for what is against nature. Likewise also the men, leaving the natural use of the woman, burned in their lust for one another, men with men committing what is shameful, and receiving in themselves the penalty of their error which was due.

And even as they did not like to retain God in *their* knowledge, God gave them over to a debased mind, to do those things which are not fitting; being filled with all unrighteousness, sexual immorality, wickedness, covetousness, maliciousness; full of envy, murder, strife, deceit, evil-mindedness; *they are* whisperers, backbiters, haters of God, violent, proud, boasters, inventors of evil things, disobedient to parents, undiscerning, untrustworthy, unloving, unforgiving, unmerciful; who, knowing the righteous judgment of God, that those who practice such things are deserving of death, not only do the same but also approve of those who practice them.

ROMANS 1:18–32

Indeed you are called a Jew, and rest on the law, and make your boast in God, and know *His* will, and approve the things that are excellent, being instructed out of the law, and are confident that you yourself are a guide to the blind, a light to those who are in darkness, an instructor of the foolish, a teacher of babes, having the form of knowledge and truth in the law. You, therefore, who teach another, do you not teach yourself? You who preach that a man should not steal, do you steal? You who say, "Do not commit adultery," do you commit adultery? You who abhor idols, do you rob temples? You who make your boast in the law, do you dishonor God through breaking the law? For *"the name of God is blasphemed among the Gentiles because of you,"* as it is written.

ROMANS 2:17–24

What then? Are we better *than they?* Not at all. For we have previously charged both Jews and Greeks that they are all under sin.

As it is written:

> ***"There is none righteous, no, not one;***
> ***There is none who understands;***
> ***There is none who seeks after God.***
> *They have all turned aside;*
> *They have together become unprofitable;*
> *There is none who does good, no, not one."*
> *"Their throat is an open tomb;*
> *With their tongues they have practiced deceit";*
> *"The poison of asps is under their lips";*
> *"Whose mouth is full of cursing and bitterness."*
> *"Their feet are swift to shed blood;*
> *Destruction and misery are in their ways;*
> *And the way of peace they have not known."*
> *"There is no fear of God before their eyes."*

Now we know that whatever the law says, it says to those who are under the law, that every mouth may be stopped, and all the world may become guilty before God. Therefore by the deeds of the law no flesh will be justified in His sight, for by the law *is* the knowledge of sin.

ROMANS 3:9–20

How is God our best defense against false teachers?

GOD'S LOVE

Despite the sin that has permeated His creation, God remains faithful to His people. In the Old Testament, God modeled His love for humankind through His special relationship with Israel. God used a profound and unusual object lesson to illustrate how much He loved the Israelites despite their unfaithfulness.

He asked Hosea, a prophet to the northern kingdom of Israel, to marry an immoral woman named Gomer. Hosea would play the part of God; Gomer would play the part of Israel.

The word of the LORD that came to Hosea the son of Beeri, in the days of Uzziah, Jotham, Ahaz, *and* Hezekiah, kings of Judah, and in the days of Jeroboam the son of Joash, king of Israel.

When the LORD began to speak by Hosea, the LORD said to Hosea:

"Go, take yourself a wife of harlotry
And children of harlotry,
For the land has committed great harlotry
By departing from the LORD."

So he went and took Gomer the daughter of Diblaim, and she conceived and bore him a son. HOSEA 1:1–3

Hosea provided Gomer with a wonderful life of love and provision. But she chose to spurn his love; Gomer left Hosea and returned to her immoral lifestyle. Evidently she became a slave. God told Hosea to track down his wife, purchase her, take her back in and love her. What Hosea did for Gomer, God did for the Israelites.

Then the LORD said to me, "Go again, love a woman *who is* loved by a lover and is committing adultery, just like the love of the LORD for the children of Israel, who look to other gods and love *the* raisin cakes *of the pagans.*"

So I bought her for myself for fifteen *shekels* of silver, and one and one-half homers of barley. And I said to her, "You shall stay with me many days; you shall not play the harlot, nor shall you have a man—so, too, *will* I *be* toward you." HOSEA 3:1–3

In the book of Hosea, God reflected on His relationship with Israel in terms of a wayward son as well as an unfaithful wife. He intervened for the Israelites even when they didn't recognize His presence. Out of love He had rescued them from slavery in Egypt. Now Israel, referred to as Ephraim after Israel's largest tribe, was about to go into slavery again. This time the mighty nation of Assyria was going to take the people captive. They would experience the blows of God's discipline for walking away from Him, but He declared yet again that He would redeem them. This is the same kind of unending, undeserved love God has for us.

"When Israel *was* a child, I loved him,
And out of Egypt I called My son.
As they called them,
So they went from them;
They sacrificed to the Baals,
And burned incense to carved images.

"I taught Ephraim to walk,
Taking them by their arms;
But they did not know that I healed them.
I drew them with gentle cords,
With bands of love,
And I was to them as those who take the yoke
from their neck.
I stooped *and* fed them.

"He shall not return to the land of Egypt;
But the Assyrian shall be his king,
Because they refused to repent.
And the sword shall slash in his cities,
Devour his districts,
And consume *them,*
Because of their own counsels.
My people are bent on backsliding from Me.
Though they call to the Most High,
None at all exalt *Him.*

"How can I give you up, Ephraim?
***How* can I hand you over, Israel?**
How can I make you like Admah?
***How* can I set you like Zeboiim?**
My heart churns within Me;
My sympathy is stirred.

I will not execute the fierceness of My anger;
I will not again destroy Ephraim.
For I *am* God, and not man,
The Holy One in your midst;
And I will not come with terror.

"They shall walk after the LORD.
He will roar like a lion.
When He roars,
Then *His* sons shall come trembling from the west;
They shall come trembling like a bird from Egypt,
Like a dove from the land of Assyria.
And I will let them dwell in their houses,"
Says the LORD. HOSEA 11:1–11

How does the book of Hosea show God's discipline and punishment as well as His compassion and redemption? How do you see His discipline and punishment fitting in with your concept of God as a God of love?

ALL AND WHOEVER

One of the special assignments John took on in his Gospel was to share that Jesus' offer of forgiveness and restoration to God for eternity is for everyone. As you read this collection of powerful declarations, keep in mind that we are included in every statement; therefore God extends His offer of love to us. He "so loves us."

In Him was life, and the life was the light of men. JOHN 1:4

[John the Baptist] came for a witness, to bear witness of the Light, that all through him might believe. JOHN 1:7

He came to His own, and His own did not receive Him. But as many as received Him, to them He gave the right to become children of God, to those who believe in His name. JOHN 1:11–12

"For God so loved the world that He gave His only begotten Son, that whoever believes in Him should not perish but have everlasting life." JOHN 3:16

"He who believes in the Son has everlasting life; and he who does not believe the Son shall not see life, but the wrath of God abides on him." JOHN 3:36

"Whoever drinks of the water that I shall give him will never thirst. But the water that I shall give him will become in him a fountain of water springing up into everlasting life." JOHN 4:14

"Most assuredly, I say to you, he who hears My word and believes in Him who sent Me has everlasting life, and shall not come into judgment, but has passed from death into life." JOHN 5:24

And Jesus said to them, "I am the bread of life. He who comes to Me shall never hunger, and he who believes in Me shall never thirst." JOHN 6:35

"All that the Father gives Me will come to Me, and the one who comes to Me I will by no means cast out." JOHN 6:37

"I am the living bread which came down from heaven. If anyone eats of this bread, he will live forever; and the bread that I shall give is My flesh, which I shall give for the life of the world." JOHN 6:51

"Whoever eats My flesh and drinks My blood has eternal life, and I will raise him up at the last day." JOHN 6:54

"He who believes in Me, as the Scripture has said, out of his heart will flow rivers of living water." JOHN 7:38

Then Jesus spoke to them again, saying, "I am the light of the world. He who follows Me shall not walk in darkness, but have the light of life." JOHN 8:12

"Most assuredly, I say to you, if anyone keeps My word he shall never see death."

JOHN 8:51

"I am the door. If anyone enters by Me, he will be saved, and will go in and out and find pasture."

JOHN 10:9

"And whoever lives and believes in Me shall never die. Do you believe this?"

JOHN 11:26

"Now is the judgment of this world; now the ruler of this world will be cast out. And I, if I am lifted up from the earth, will draw all *peoples* to Myself."

JOHN 12:31–32

SEEING PEOPLE AS GOD SEES THEM

As the parable of the wandering sheep illustrates, God loves us deeply. He also wants us to follow His example in how we treat one another.

At that time the disciples came to Jesus, saying, "Who then is greatest in the kingdom of heaven?"

Then Jesus called a little child to Him, set him in the midst of them, and said, "Assuredly, I say to you, unless you are converted and become as little children, you will by no means enter the kingdom of heaven. Therefore whoever humbles himself as this little child is the greatest in the kingdom of heaven. Whoever receives one little child like this in My name receives Me.

"Whoever causes one of these little ones who believe in Me to sin, it would be better for him if a millstone were hung around his neck, and he were drowned in the depth of the sea. Woe to the world because of offenses! For offenses must come, but woe to that man by whom the offense comes!

"If your hand or foot causes you to sin, cut it off and cast *it* from you. It is better for you to enter into life lame or maimed, rather than having two hands or two feet, to be cast into the everlasting fire. And if your eye causes you to sin, pluck it out and cast *it* from you. It is better for you to enter into life with one eye, rather than having two eyes, to be cast into hell fire.

"Take heed that you do not despise one of these little ones, for

I say to you that in heaven their angels always see the face of My Father who is in heaven. For the Son of Man has come to save that which was lost.

"What do you think? If a man has a hundred sheep, and one of them goes astray, does he not leave the ninety-nine and go to the mountains to seek the one that is straying? And if he should find it, assuredly, I say to you, he rejoices more over that *sheep* than over the ninety-nine that did not go astray. Even so it is not the will of your Father who is in heaven that one of these little ones should perish." MATTHEW 18:1–14

In the early season of His ministry, Jesus spoke to a large crowd of people who gathered to be healed by Him and to hear what He had to say. Jesus taught that we are to see and treat people the way God sees and treats us. Our heavenly Father provides the supreme example that we are to follow.

"But I say to you who hear: Love your enemies, do good to those who hate you, bless those who curse you, and pray for those who spitefully use you. To him who strikes you on the *one* cheek, offer the other also. And from him who takes away your cloak, do not withhold *your* tunic either. Give to everyone who asks of you. And from him who takes away your goods do not ask *them* back. And just as you want men to do to you, you also do to them likewise.

"But if you love those who love you, what credit is that to you? For even sinners love those who love them. And if you do good to those who do good to you, what credit is that to you? For even sinners do the same. And if you lend *to those* from whom you hope to receive back, what credit is that to you? For even sinners lend to sinners to receive as much back. **But love your enemies, do good, and lend, hoping for nothing in return; and your reward will be great, and you will be sons of the Most High. For He is kind to the unthankful and evil. Therefore be merciful, just as your Father also is merciful."** LUKE 6:27–36

The new reality in Christ is this: There is no more division between Jews and Gentiles, men and women, masters and slaves. We all belong to Christ equally. The apostle Paul had a grand oppor-

tunity to demonstrate this in the latter years of his life. His good friend Philemon had a slave—Onesimus—who may have stolen from Philemon and then ran away (a crime punishable by death). Amazingly, while Paul was in Rome he met Onesimus, and Onesimus became a Christian. Paul wrote Philemon a letter with the personal appeal to welcome Onesimus back, not as a slave but as a brother in Christ. God lays before us today the same challenge—to embrace every believer as a precious family member.

Paul, a prisoner of Christ Jesus, and Timothy *our* brother,

To Philemon our beloved *friend* and fellow laborer, to the beloved Apphia, Archippus our fellow soldier, and to the church in your house:

Grace to you and peace from God our Father and the Lord Jesus Christ.

I thank my God, making mention of you always in my prayers, hearing of your love and faith which you have toward the Lord Jesus and toward all the saints, that the sharing of your faith may become effective by the acknowledgment of every good thing which is in you in Christ Jesus. For we have great joy and consolation in your love, because the hearts of the saints have been refreshed by you, brother.

Therefore, though I might be very bold in Christ to command you what is fitting, *yet* for love's sake I rather appeal *to you*—being such a one as Paul, the aged, and now also a prisoner of Jesus Christ—I appeal to you for my son Onesimus, whom I have begotten *while* in my chains, who once was unprofitable to you, but now is profitable to you and to me.

I am sending him back. You therefore receive him, that is, my own heart, whom I wished to keep with me, that on your behalf he might minister to me in my chains for the gospel. But without your consent I wanted to do nothing, that your good deed might not be by compulsion, as it were, but voluntary.

For perhaps he departed for a while for this *purpose*, that you might receive him forever, no longer as a slave but more than a slave—a beloved brother, especially to me but how much more to you, both in the flesh and in the Lord.

If then you count me as a partner, receive him as *you would* me. But if he has wronged you or owes anything, put that on my account. I, Paul, am writing with my own hand. I will repay—not to mention to you that you owe me even your own self besides. Yes, brother, let me have joy from you in the Lord; refresh my heart in the Lord.

Having confidence in your obedience, I write to you, knowing that you will do even more than I say. But, meanwhile, also prepare a guest room for me, for I trust that through your prayers I shall be granted to you.

Epaphras, my fellow prisoner in Christ Jesus, greets you, *as do* Mark, Aristarchus, Demas, Luke, my fellow laborers.

The grace of our Lord Jesus Christ *be* with your spirit.

PHILEMON 1–25

How do the stories in this chapter highlight God's persistence and compassion in bringing people into a right relationship with one another? Which phrases speak to you personally?

WHAT WE BELIEVE

It cannot be denied. We are the crowning achievement of God's creation. We were made in the very image of God with the express purpose of living in perfect community with God on earth. But the first two people rejected God's vision, introducing death and separation from God into the human race. We see clearly in the story of Cain and Abel, throughout human history and even in our own stories that this sin nature has been passed down and all people fall victim to it. But God loves us and wants us back. Like Hosea pursued his unfaithful wife, Gomer, so God pursues us. All His "sympathy is stirred" (see Hosea 11:8) when He thinks of us. God's love knows no boundaries. Forgiveness and salvation are available to everyone who will receive them in Christ Jesus. God calls all Christians to see people the same way He does. What would happen in our world if we would do just that?

THINK

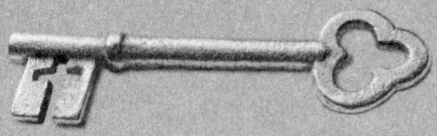

CHAPTER

8

Compassion

KEY QUESTION

What about the poor and injustice?

KEY IDEA

I believe God calls all Christians to show compassion to people in need.

KEY VERSE

Defend the poor and fatherless;
Do justice to the afflicted and needy.
Deliver the poor and needy;
Free *them* from the hand of the wicked.
Psalm 82:3–4

OUR MAP

All human beings are valuable to God, and He calls us to see people as He sees them. Compassion goes a step further by compelling us to feel their pain. Compassion literally means "suffer with." God calls us to come alongside people who are suffering. It doesn't mean we can fix their problems, but it does mean we can enter into their pain. Before we act or practice this belief, we must believe it is God's call on the life of all Christ followers. When we believe this in our hearts, we will show compassion to all people, especially to those in need. This is not a "do as I say, not as I do" command from the Lord. God Himself is merciful and full of compassion. This is where our journey into compassion starts.

In this chapter we will read about:

- *God: Full of Justice and Compassion*
- *Israel: Called to Compassion*
- *Jesus: Model of Compassion*
- *Believers: The Ongoing Call to Compassion*

God: Full of Justice and Compassion

Throughout their history, the Israelites struggled to stay true to God. Sometimes they followed God, but those periods of faithfulness were followed by times of sin and rebellion. But God's love for His people was always evident. His compassion was constant as He offered the people relief from the misery caused by their sin. In this passage, the Israelites are back in the promised land after suffering years of exile and hardship. The Levites invited the people to stand to their feet as they rehearsed together the history of God's compassion toward them, from the very beginning of time until that very moment.

As you read this account from Nehemiah 9,
look for some of the ways God showed compassion
and justice to the Israelites.

Now on the twenty-fourth day of this month the children of Israel were assembled with fasting, in sackcloth, and with dust on their heads. Then those of Israelite lineage separated themselves from all foreigners; and they stood and confessed their sins and the iniquities of their fathers. And they stood up in their place and read from the Book of the Law of the LORD their God *for one-fourth* of the day; and *for another* fourth they confessed and worshiped the LORD their God.

Then Jeshua, Bani, Kadmiel, Shebaniah, Bunni, Sherebiah, Bani, *and* Chenani stood on the stairs of the Levites and cried out with a loud voice to the LORD their God. And the Levites, Jeshua, Kadmiel, Bani, Hashabniah, Sherebiah, Hodijah, Shebaniah, *and* Pethahiah, said:

"Stand up *and* bless the LORD your God
Forever and ever!

"Blessed be Your glorious name,
Which is exalted above all blessing and praise!
You alone *are* the LORD;
You have made heaven,
The heaven of heavens, with all their host,
The earth and everything on it,
The seas and all that is in them,
And You preserve them all.
The host of heaven worships You.

"You *are* the LORD God,
Who chose Abram,
And brought him out of Ur of the Chaldeans,
And gave him the name Abraham;
You found his heart faithful before You,
And made a covenant with him
To give the land of the Canaanites,
The Hittites, the Amorites,
The Perizzites, the Jebusites,
And the Girgashites—
To give *it* to his descendants.
You have performed Your words,
For You *are* righteous.

"You saw the affliction of our fathers in Egypt,
And heard their cry by the Red Sea.
You showed signs and wonders against Pharaoh,
Against all his servants,
And against all the people of his land.
For You knew that they acted proudly against them.
So You made a name for Yourself, as *it is* this day.
And You divided the sea before them,
So that they went through the midst of the sea on the
dry land;
And their persecutors You threw into the deep,
As a stone into the mighty waters.
Moreover You led them by day with a cloudy pillar,
And by night with a pillar of fire,
To give them light on the road
Which they should travel.

"You came down also on Mount Sinai,
And spoke with them from heaven,
And gave them just ordinances and true laws,
Good statutes and commandments.
You made known to them Your holy Sabbath,
And commanded them precepts, statutes and laws,
By the hand of Moses Your servant.
You gave them bread from heaven for their hunger,
And brought them water out of the rock for their thirst,
And told them to go in to possess the land
Which You had sworn to give them.

"But they and our fathers acted proudly,
Hardened their necks,
And did not heed Your commandments.
They refused to obey,
And they were not mindful of Your wonders
That You did among them.
But they hardened their necks,
And in their rebellion
They appointed a leader
To return to their bondage.

But You *are* God,
Ready to pardon,
Gracious and merciful,
Slow to anger,
Abundant in kindness,
And did not forsake them.

"Even when they made a molded calf for themselves,
And said, 'This *is* your god
That brought you up out of Egypt,'
And worked great provocations,
Yet in Your manifold mercies
You did not forsake them in the wilderness.
The pillar of the cloud did not depart from them by day,
To lead them on the road;
Nor the pillar of fire by night,
To show them light,
And the way they should go.
You also gave Your good Spirit to instruct them,
And did not withhold Your manna from their mouth,
And gave them water for their thirst.
Forty years You sustained them in the wilderness;
They lacked nothing;
Their clothes did not wear out
And their feet did not swell.

"Moreover You gave them kingdoms and nations,
And divided them into districts.
So they took possession of the land of Sihon,
The land of the king of Heshbon,
And the land of Og king of Bashan.
You also multiplied their children as the stars of heaven,
And brought them into the land
Which You had told their fathers
To go in and possess.
So the people went in
And possessed the land;
You subdued before them the inhabitants of the land,
The Canaanites,

And gave them into their hands,
With their kings
And the people of the land,
That they might do with them as they wished.
And they took strong cities and a rich land,
And possessed houses full of all goods,
Cisterns *already* dug, vineyards, olive groves,
And fruit trees in abundance.
So they ate and were filled and grew fat,
And delighted themselves in Your great goodness.

"Nevertheless they were disobedient
And rebelled against You,
Cast Your law behind their backs
And killed Your prophets, who testified against them
To turn them to Yourself;
And they worked great provocations.
Therefore You delivered them into the hand of their
enemies,
Who oppressed them;
And in the time of their trouble,
When they cried to You,
You heard from heaven;
And according to Your abundant mercies
You gave them deliverers who saved them
From the hand of their enemies.

"But after they had rest,
They again did evil before You.
Therefore You left them in the hand of their enemies,
So that they had dominion over them;
Yet when they returned and cried out to You,
You heard from heaven;
And many times You delivered them according
to Your mercies,
And testified against them,
That You might bring them back to Your law.
Yet they acted proudly,
And did not heed Your commandments,

But sinned against Your judgments,
'Which if a man does, he shall live by them.'
And they shrugged their shoulders,
Stiffened their necks,
And would not hear.
Yet for many years You had patience with them,
And testified against them by Your Spirit in Your
prophets.
Yet they would not listen;
Therefore You gave them into the hand of the peoples
of the lands.
Nevertheless in Your great mercy
You did not utterly consume them nor forsake them;
For You *are* God, gracious and merciful.

"Now therefore, our God,
The great, the mighty, and awesome God,
Who keeps covenant and mercy:
Do not let all the trouble seem small before You
That has come upon us,
Our kings and our princes,
Our priests and our prophets,
Our fathers and on all Your people,
From the days of the kings of Assyria until this day.
However You *are* just in all that has befallen us;
For You have dealt faithfully,
But we have done wickedly.
Neither our kings nor our princes,
Our priests nor our fathers,
Have kept Your law,
Nor heeded Your commandments and Your testimonies,
With which You testified against them.
For they have not served You in their kingdom,
Or in the many good *things* that You gave them,
Or in the large and rich land which You set before them;
Nor did they turn from their wicked works.

"Here we *are,* servants today!
And the land that You gave to our fathers,

To eat its fruit and its bounty,
Here we *are,* servants in it!
And it yields much increase to the kings
You have set over us,
Because of our sins;
Also they have dominion over our bodies and our cattle
At their pleasure;
And we *are* in great distress.

"And because of all this,
We make a sure *covenant* and write *it;*
Our leaders, our Levites, *and* our priests seal *it.*"

NEHEMIAH 9:1–38

From the beginning God has graciously shown compassion for His people, with the ultimate demonstration being the sacrifice of His only Son, Jesus Christ. Because the only just response to the sins of humankind was death, our just God, according to His righteousness, issued the death penalty on us. Then, out of His limitless compassion, He offered Jesus as a "substitutionary atonement"—that is, Jesus took humanity's place. Through this act God demonstrated His complete compassion without budging an inch on His complete justice. We who are guilty are made righteous by the sacrifice of the only person who was completely righteous.

But now the righteousness of God apart from the law is revealed, being witnessed by the Law and the Prophets, even the righteousness of God, through faith in Jesus Christ, to all and on all who believe. **For there is no difference; for all have sinned and fall short of the glory of God, being justified freely by His grace through the redemption that is in Christ Jesus, whom God set forth *as* a propitiation by His blood, through faith, to demonstrate His righteousness, because in His forbearance God had passed over the sins that were previously committed, to demonstrate at the present time His righteousness, that He might be just and the justifier of the one who has faith in Jesus.**

ROMANS 3:21–26

Beloved, let us love one another, for love is of God; and everyone who loves is born of God and knows God. He who does not love does not know God, for God is love. In this the love of God was manifested toward us, that God has sent His only begotten Son into the world, that we might live through Him. **In this is love, not that we loved God, but that He loved us and sent His Son *to be* the propitiation for our sins.** 1 JOHN 4:7–10

ISRAEL: CALLED TO COMPASSION

Compassion was an important aspect of the testimony of the people of Israel to the world. When God set up the foundational laws for His people, He revealed through Moses specific guidelines for helping the poor and those in need.

As you read the selected passages below from Deuteronomy 24 and 25, look for some of the principles behind the laws Moses gave to govern how the Israelites were to treat others.

"When you lend your brother anything, you shall not go into his house to get his pledge. You shall stand outside, and the man to whom you lend shall bring the pledge out to you. And if the man *is* poor, you shall not keep his pledge overnight. You shall in any case return the pledge to him again when the sun goes down, that he may sleep in his own garment and bless you; and it shall be righteousness to you before the LORD your God.

"You shall not oppress a hired servant *who is* poor and needy, *whether* one of your brethren or one of the aliens who *is* in your land within your gates. Each day you shall give *him* his wages, and not let the sun go down on it, for he *is* poor and has set his heart on it; lest he cry out against you to the LORD, and it be sin to you."

DEUTERONOMY 24:10–15

"You shall not pervert justice due the stranger or the fatherless, nor take a widow's garment as a pledge. But you shall remember that you were a slave in Egypt, and the LORD your God redeemed you from there; therefore I command you to do this thing.

"When you reap your harvest in your field, and forget a

sheaf in the field, you shall not go back to get it; it shall be for the stranger, the fatherless, and the widow, that the LORD your God may bless you in all the work of your hands. When you beat your olive trees, you shall not go over the boughs again; it shall be for the stranger, the fatherless, and the widow. When you gather the grapes of your vineyard, you shall not glean *it* afterward; it shall be for the stranger, the fatherless, and the widow. And you shall remember that you were a slave in the land of Egypt; therefore I command you to do this thing." DEUTERONOMY 24:17–22

In the promised land, the continuity of each family and its allotment of land was of considerable importance. Though it may seem strange to us today, God led Moses to lay out for Israel the custom known as "levirate marriage," by which a brother (or nearest relative by marriage) would marry a widow without children and produce descendants in the dead relative's name. This ensured a lineage and inheritance for that family. Although the brother-in-law (or "a close relative") wasn't strictly obligated to marry his brother's wife, social shame would have discouraged him from failing to do so.

"If brothers dwell together, and one of them dies and has no son, the widow of the dead man shall not be *married* to a stranger outside *the family;* her husband's brother shall go in to her, take her as his wife, and perform the duty of a husband's brother to her. And it shall be *that* the firstborn son which she bears will succeed to the name of his dead brother, that his name may not be blotted out of Israel. But if the man does not want to take his brother's wife, then let his brother's wife go up to the gate to the elders, and say, 'My husband's brother refuses to raise up a name to his brother in Israel; he will not perform the duty of my husband's brother.' Then the elders of his city shall call him and speak to him. But *if* he stands firm and says, 'I do not want to take her,' then his brother's wife shall come to him in the presence of the elders, remove his sandal from his foot, spit in his face, and answer and say, 'So shall it be done to the man who will not build up his brother's house.' And his name shall be called in Israel, 'The house of him who had his sandal removed.'" DEUTERONOMY 25:5–10

Moses issued the above laws in the 1400s BC while the Israelites were wandering in the wilderness. A couple of hundred years later, during the time of the judges, a beautiful application of the principle of levirate marriage unfolded. Because of famine, Naomi and Elimelech and their two children left for the land of Moab. While there, the two sons married Moabite women, but over the years the father and the sons died. Naomi and one of her daughters-in-law, Ruth, made their way back to Naomi's hometown of Bethlehem. Without husbands or children, Naomi and Ruth were forced to live a life of poverty.

One day, Ruth decided to go out and glean after the harvesters in order to provide food for herself and Naomi. When Ruth came home after a successful day of gleaning, her mother-in-law asked her in whose field she had gleaned. The rest of the story shows the power and provision of the principle of gleaning and the role of the close relative Moses put in place years earlier.

There was a relative of Naomi's husband, a man of great wealth, of the family of Elimelech. His name *was* Boaz. So Ruth the Moabitess said to Naomi, "Please let me go to the field, and glean heads of grain after *him* in whose sight I may find favor."

And she said to her, "Go, my daughter."

Then she left, and went and gleaned in the field after the reapers. And she happened to come to the part of the field *belonging* to Boaz, who *was* of the family of Elimelech.

Now behold, Boaz came from Bethlehem, and said to the reapers, "The LORD *be* with you!"

And they answered him, "The LORD bless you!"

Then Boaz said to his servant who was in charge of the reapers, "Whose young woman *is* this?"

So the servant who was in charge of the reapers answered and said, "It *is* the young Moabite woman who came back with Naomi from the country of Moab. And she said, 'Please let me glean and gather after the reapers among the sheaves.' So she came and has continued from morning until now, though she rested a little in the house."

Then Boaz said to Ruth, "You will listen, my daughter, will you not? Do not go to glean in another field, nor go from here, but stay close by my young women. *Let* your eyes *be* on the field which they reap, and go after them. Have I not commanded the young men not to touch you? And when you are thirsty, go to the vessels and drink from what the young men have drawn."

So she fell on her face, bowed down to the ground, and said to him, "Why have I found favor in your eyes, that you should take notice of me, since I *am* a foreigner?"

And Boaz answered and said to her, "It has been fully reported to me, all that you have done for your mother-in-law since the death of your husband, and *how* you have left your father and your mother and the land of your birth, and have come to a people whom you did not know before. The LORD repay your work, and a full reward be given you by the LORD God of Israel, under whose wings you have come for refuge."

Then she said, "Let me find favor in your sight, my lord; for you have comforted me, and have spoken kindly to your maidservant, though I am not like one of your maidservants."

Now Boaz said to her at mealtime, "Come here, and eat of the bread, and dip your piece of bread in the vinegar." So she sat beside the reapers, and he passed parched *grain* to her; and she ate and was satisfied, and kept some back. And when she rose up to glean, Boaz commanded his young men, saying, "Let her glean even among the sheaves, and do not reproach her. Also let *grain* from the bundles fall purposely for her; leave *it* that she may glean, and do not rebuke her."

So she gleaned in the field until evening, and beat out what she had gleaned, and it was about an ephah of barley. Then she took *it* up and went into the city, and her mother-in-law saw what she had gleaned. So she brought out and gave to her what she had kept back after she had been satisfied.

And her mother-in-law said to her, "Where have you gleaned today? And where did you work? Blessed be the one who took notice of you."

So she told her mother-in-law with whom she had worked, and said, "The man's name with whom I worked today *is* Boaz."

Then Naomi said to her daughter-in-law, "Blessed *be* he of the LORD, who has not forsaken His kindness to the living and

the dead!" And Naomi said to her, "This man *is* a relation of ours, one of our close relatives."

Ruth the Moabitess said, "He also said to me, 'You shall stay close by my young men until they have finished all my harvest.'"

And Naomi said to Ruth her daughter-in-law, "*It is* good, my daughter, that you go out with his young women, and that people do not meet you in any other field." So she stayed close by the young women of Boaz, to glean until the end of barley harvest and wheat harvest; and she dwelt with her mother-in-law. RUTH 2:1–23

The principle of gleaning worked. By gathering the extra grain left behind by the harvesters (and helped along by the kind protection of Boaz), Ruth's gleaning helped to sustain these two poor women—one an Israelite, the other a foreigner from a group of people who in the past had caused the Israelites much heartache. Yet the extent of Boaz's compassion didn't stop there. Through a series of events he exercised his right and obligation as a close relative.

So Boaz took Ruth and she became his wife; and when he went in to her, the LORD gave her conception, and she bore a son. Then the women said to Naomi, "Blessed *be* the LORD, who has not left you this day without a close relative; and may his name be famous in Israel! And may he be to you a restorer of life and a nourisher of your old age; for your daughter-in-law, who loves you, who is better to you than seven sons, has borne him." Then Naomi took the child and laid him on her bosom, and became a nurse to him. Also the neighbor women gave him a name, saying, "There is a son born to Naomi." And they called his name Obed. He *is* the father of Jesse, the father of David. RUTH 4:13–17

When Obed came of age he didn't carry on the name of Boaz but of Elimelech, Naomi's deceased husband, and Mahlon, Ruth's deceased husband. In addition, all the land and property Boaz purchased was kept in Naomi's family line when Obed became heir to it. What an amazing story of human compassion! But the blessings did not stop with Naomi and her family. Through Boaz's act of compassion a child was born. From this child would come David and from David would ultimately come Jesus, our Savior. A single act of compassion can live on for generations to come!

How did Boaz express his faith when he helped Ruth and Naomi? What was the motive behind his acts of compassion?

Jesus: Model of Compassion

Jesus, the very model of compassion, told a beautiful story we call The Parable of the Good Samaritan. The telling of the story was prompted by an exchange that zeroed in on one of two chief laws of the Old Testament: to love our neighbor as ourselves. Through this classic story, Jesus made the startling point that His most mature follower is not necessarily the priest or the pastor but the one who actually lives out the commandment.

And behold, a certain lawyer stood up and tested Him, saying, "Teacher, what shall I do to inherit eternal life?"

He said to him, "What is written in the law? What is your reading *of it?*"

So he answered and said, " *'You shall love the* LORD *your God with all your heart, with all your soul, with all your strength, and with all your mind,'* and *'your neighbor as yourself.'"*

And He said to him, "You have answered rightly; do this and you will live."

But he, wanting to justify himself, said to Jesus, "And who is my neighbor?"

Then Jesus answered and said: "A certain *man* went down from Jerusalem to Jericho, and fell among thieves, who stripped him of his clothing, wounded *him,* and departed, leaving *him* half dead. Now by chance a certain priest came down that road. And when he saw him, he passed by on the other side. Likewise a Levite, when he arrived at the place, came and looked, and passed by on the other side. But a certain Samaritan, as he journeyed, came where he was. And when he saw him, he had compassion. So he went to *him* and bandaged his wounds, pouring on oil and wine; and he set him on his own animal, brought him to an inn, and took care of him. On the next day, when he departed, he took out two denarii, gave *them* to the innkeeper, and said to him, 'Take care of him; and whatever more you spend, when I come again, I will repay you.' **So which of these three do you think was neighbor to him who fell among the thieves?"**

And he said, "He who showed mercy on him."

Then Jesus said to him, "Go and do likewise." LUKE 10:25–37

Throughout His teaching ministry, Jesus frequently and masterfully instructed His followers to show compassion to people in need as the ultimate fulfillment of the Law of Moses. Toward the very end of His life on earth, Jesus provided His disciples with divine insight into the ministry of compassion to the poor and needy. He told them their acts of compassion would have eternal consequences. When Jesus returns He will separate the obedient followers from the unbelievers. How we treat others should make it clear into which of the two groups we fall. After all, our behavior has results that reach far beyond our time on this earth.

"When the Son of Man comes in His glory, and all the holy angels with Him, then He will sit on the throne of His glory. All the nations will be gathered before Him, and He will separate them one from another, as a shepherd divides *his* sheep from the goats. And He will set the sheep on His right hand, but the goats on the left. Then the King will say to those on His right hand, 'Come, you blessed of My Father, inherit the kingdom prepared for you from the foundation of the world: for I was hungry and you gave Me food; I was thirsty and you gave Me drink; I was a stranger and you took Me in; I *was* naked and you clothed Me; I was sick and you visited Me; I was in prison and you came to Me.'

"Then the righteous will answer Him, saying, 'Lord, when did we see You hungry and feed *You,* or thirsty and give *You* drink? When did we see You a stranger and take *You* in, or naked and clothe *You?* Or when did we see You sick, or in prison, and come to You?' **And the King will answer and say to them, 'Assuredly, I say to you, inasmuch as you did *it* to one of the least of these My brethren, you did *it* to Me.'**

"Then He will also say to those on the left hand, 'Depart from

Me, you cursed, into the everlasting fire prepared for the devil and his angels: for I was hungry and you gave Me no food; I was thirsty and you gave Me no drink; I was a stranger and you did not take Me in, naked and you did not clothe Me, sick and in prison and you did not visit Me.'

"Then they also will answer Him, saying, 'Lord, when did we see You hungry or thirsty or a stranger or naked or sick or in prison, and did not minister to You?' Then He will answer them, saying, 'Assuredly, I say to you, inasmuch as you did not do *it* to one of the least of these, you did not do *it* to Me.' And these will go away into everlasting punishment, but the righteous into eternal life."

MATTHEW 25:31–46

In your own words, describe how love for God and love for others are related.

BELIEVERS: THE ONGOING CALL TO COMPASSION

The same challenge given to the people of Israel to live a life of compassion was also issued to the newly formed Christian church after Jesus' death and resurrection. James, who became the leader of the church in Jerusalem and was likely the half brother of Jesus, wrote what may have been the first book of the New Testament. In his letter, James instructs new believers on the practical how-tos of living this new life in Christ. These same charges apply to believers today.

So then, my beloved brethren, let every man be swift to hear, slow to speak, slow to wrath; for the wrath of man does not produce the righteousness of God.

Therefore lay aside all filthiness and overflow of wickedness, and receive with meekness the implanted word, which is able to save your souls.

But be doers of the word, and not hearers only, deceiving yourselves. For if anyone is a hearer of the word and not a doer, he is like a man observing his natural face in a mirror; for he observes himself, goes away, and immediately forgets what kind of man he was. But he who looks into the perfect law of liberty and continues *in it,* and is not a forgetful hearer but a doer of the work, this one will be blessed in what he does.

If anyone among you thinks he is religious, and does not bridle his tongue but deceives his own heart, this one's religion *is* useless. **Pure and undefiled religion before God and the Father is this: to visit orphans and widows in their trouble, *and* to keep oneself unspotted from the world.**

My brethren, do not hold the faith of our Lord Jesus Christ, *the Lord* of glory, with partiality. For if there should come into your assembly a man with gold rings, in fine apparel, and there should also come in a poor man in filthy clothes, and you pay attention to the one wearing the fine clothes and say to him, "You sit here in a good place," and say to the poor man, "You stand there," or, "Sit here at my footstool," have you not shown partiality among yourselves, and become judges with evil thoughts?

Listen, my beloved brethren: Has God not chosen the poor of this world *to be* rich in faith and heirs of the kingdom which He promised to those who love Him? But you have dishonored the poor man. Do not the rich oppress you and drag you into the courts? Do they not blaspheme that noble name by which you are called?

If you really fulfill *the* royal law according to the Scripture, *"You shall love your neighbor as yourself,"* you do well; but if you show partiality, you commit sin, and are convicted by the law as transgressors. For whoever shall keep the whole law, and yet stumble in one *point,* he is guilty of all. For He who said, *"Do not commit adultery,"* also said, *"Do not murder."* Now if you do not commit adultery, but you do murder, you have become a transgressor of the law. So speak and so do as those who will be judged by the law of liberty. For judgment is without mercy to the one who has shown no mercy. Mercy triumphs over judgment. JAMES 1:19—2:13

What are the attitudes that James advocates?
How can you adopt those same attitudes?

WHAT WE BELIEVE

What about the poor and injustice? We begin by taking our cue from God Himself. He showed the ultimate compassion toward humanity by sending Jesus as a sacrifice for sin when we did not deserve it. Throughout Israel's history, time and time again, God showed amazing compassion to rescue His people and provide for their needs. When we look back on our own lives, we will see the same pattern.

Israel was given laws to govern them regarding how to show compassion to each other and to strangers. The story of Ruth provides a beautiful example of the spirit of these laws lived out. And Jesus, the ultimate example of one who suffered for our sake, calls believers to a life of compassion, not because the law demands it but because God's love in us compels us. Living such a life begins when we embrace the belief in our heads and our hearts that God calls all Christians to show compassion to those in need.

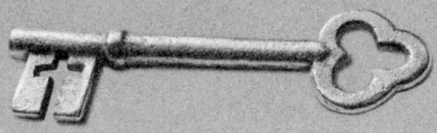

CHAPTER

9

Stewardship

KEY QUESTION

What is God's call on my life?

KEY IDEA

I believe everything I am and
everything I own belongs to God.

KEY VERSE

The earth *is* the LORD's, and all its fullness,
The world and those who dwell therein.
For He has founded it upon the seas,
And established it upon the waters.
Psalm 24:1–2

OUR MAP

In Chapter 7 we learned to see humanity the way God does—through eyes of love. Then, in Chapter 8 we were challenged to treat people the way God does—with compassion. And now Chapter 9 declares that everything we are and everything we own belongs to God. The three beliefs are linked together. People devoted to thinking like Jesus believe they are to take the resources they are given, even their very lives, and use them to meet the needs of others. Because we believe the God of the Bible is the one true God who has a good plan revealed in His Word for all people to come into a relationship with Him, the church offers a resounding "yes" to this key belief called stewardship.

In this chapter we will learn:

- *God Is Owner*
- *God's People Are Managers*
  - *... of God's Creation*
  - *... of Their Children*
  - *... of Their Money*
  - *... of Their Homes*
  - *... of Their Bodies*
  - *... Over All They Do*

God Is Owner

Psalm 24 was a processional psalm used by the ancient Israelites to celebrate the entrance of the ark of the covenant, the symbol of the Lord's presence, into Jerusalem and into God's sanctuary. Whether or not the psalm was written for the occasion when King David brought the ark to Jerusalem, it was likely used at later commemorations of that event. The psalm begins by praising God as the owner of the earth and everything in it—a reality that consequently makes us, in turn, the stewards of the world and its resources.

> The earth *is* the Lord's, and all its fullness,
> The world and those who dwell therein.
> For He has founded it upon the seas,
> And established it upon the waters.

Who may ascend into the hill of the LORD?
Or who may stand in His holy place?
He who has clean hands and a pure heart,
Who has not lifted up his soul to an idol,
Nor sworn deceitfully.
He shall receive blessing from the LORD,
And righteousness from the God of his salvation.
This *is* Jacob, the generation of those who seek Him,
Who seek Your face.

Lift up your heads, O you gates!
And be lifted up, you everlasting doors!
And the King of glory shall come in.
Who *is* this King of glory?
The LORD strong and mighty,
The LORD mighty in battle.
Lift up your heads, O you gates!
Lift up, you everlasting doors!
And the King of glory shall come in.
Who is this King of glory?
The LORD of hosts,
He *is* the King of glory.

PSALM 24:1–10

One way that the Lord wanted His people to honor Him was through thank offerings, overflowing out of a heart of gratitude for all God has given. But too often the Israelites offered sacrifices but then lived however they wanted, with no sincere thanksgiving behind their actions. They were just going through the motions—like a person today who goes to church on Sunday and then ignores God's commands for living on the other six days of the week. Though God commanded His people to offer sacrifices, and their offerings were pleasing to Him, what He was most looking for was their wholehearted obedience in every aspect of their lives.

As you read the passage below from Psalm 50, ponder this question: if God is self-sufficient, why are we asked to return a portion of our wealth to Him?

The Mighty One, God the LORD,
Has spoken and called the earth
From the rising of the sun to its going down.
Out of Zion, the perfection of beauty,
God will shine forth.
Our God shall come, and shall not keep silent;
A fire shall devour before Him,
And it shall be very tempestuous all around Him.

He shall call to the heavens from above,
And to the earth, that He may judge His people:
"Gather My saints together to Me,
Those who have made a covenant with Me by sacrifice."
Let the heavens declare His righteousness,
For God Himself *is* Judge.

"Hear, O My people, and I will speak,
O Israel, and I will testify against you;
I *am* God, your God!
I will not rebuke you for your sacrifices
Or your burnt offerings,
Which are continually before Me.
I will not take a bull from your house,
***Nor* goats out of your folds.**
For every beast of the forest is Mine,
***And* the cattle on a thousand hills.**
I know all the birds of the mountains,
And the wild beasts of the field *are* Mine.

"If I were hungry, I would not tell you;
For the world *is* Mine, and all its fullness.
Will I eat the flesh of bulls,
Or drink the blood of goats?
Offer to God thanksgiving,
And pay your vows to the Most High.
Call upon Me in the day of trouble;
I will deliver you, and you shall glorify Me."

But to the wicked God says:
"What *right* have you to declare My statutes,

Or take My covenant in your mouth,
Seeing you hate instruction
And cast My words behind you?
When you saw a thief, you consented with him,
And have been a partaker with adulterers.
You give your mouth to evil,
And your tongue frames deceit.
You sit *and* speak against your brother;
You slander your own mother's son.
These *things* you have done, and I kept silent;
You thought that I was altogether like you;
But I will rebuke you,
And set *them* in order before your eyes.

"Now consider this, you who forget God,
Lest I tear *you* in pieces,
And *there be* none to deliver:
Whoever offers praise glorifies Me;
And to him who orders *his* conduct *aright*
I will show the salvation of God." PSALM 50:1–23

God's People Are Managers

Since God created everything, including humans, how do we fit into the created order? What is our role in this reality? The parable below instructs us on the importance of seeing ourselves not as owners but as managers of our lives and gifts. The talents represent any resource God, the Master, gives us. He ultimately owns the resource, but we are charged with caring for it and investing it in ways that yield results for the sake of the kingdom of God.

"For *the kingdom of heaven is* like a man traveling to a far country, *who* called his own servants and delivered his goods to them. And to one he gave five talents, to another two, and to another one, to each according to his own ability; and immediately he went on a journey. Then he who had received the five talents went and traded with them, and made another five talents. And likewise he who *had received* two gained two more also. But he who had received one went and dug in the ground, and hid his lord's money.

After a long time the lord of those servants came and settled accounts with them.

"So he who had received five talents came and brought five other talents, saying, 'Lord, you delivered to me five talents; look, I have gained five more talents besides them.' **His lord said to him, 'Well *done*, good and faithful servant; you were faithful over a few things, I will make you ruler over many things. Enter into the joy of your lord.'** He also who had received two talents came and said, 'Lord, you delivered to me two talents; look, I have gained two more talents besides them.' His lord said to him, 'Well *done*, good and faithful servant; you have been faithful over a few things, I will make you ruler over many things. Enter into the joy of your lord.'

"Then he who had received the one talent came and said, 'Lord, I knew you to be a hard man, reaping where you have not sown, and gathering where you have not scattered seed. And I was afraid, and went and hid your talent in the ground. Look, *there* you have *what is* yours.'

"But his lord answered and said to him, 'You wicked and lazy servant, you knew that I reap where I have not sown, and gather where I have not scattered seed. So you ought to have deposited my money with the bankers, and at my coming I would have received back my own with interest. So take the talent from him, and give *it* to him who has ten talents.

'For to everyone who has, more will be given, and he will have abundance; but from him who does not have, even what he has will be taken away. And cast the unprofitable servant into the outer darkness. There will be weeping and gnashing of teeth.'"

MATTHEW 25:14–30

... OF GOD'S CREATION

God showed great attentiveness in creating the earth, which He entrusted to humankind to care for. Being created in His likeness, we are responsible to be respectful stewards of His precious design and the creatures that are a part of it.

Then God said, "Let Us make man in Our image, according to Our likeness; let them have dominion over the fish of the sea, over the birds of the air, and over the cattle, over all the earth and over every creeping thing that creeps on the earth." So God created man in His *own* image; in the image of God He created him; male and female He created them. **Then God blessed them, and God said to them, "Be fruitful and multiply; fill the earth and subdue it; have dominion over the fish of the sea, over the birds of the air, and over every living thing that moves on the earth."**

And God said, "See, I have given you every herb *that* yields seed which *is* on the face of all the earth, and every tree whose fruit yields seed; to you it shall be for food. Also, to every beast of the earth, to every bird of the air, and to everything that creeps on the earth, in which *there is* life, *I have given* every green herb for food"; and it was so.

GENESIS 1:26–30

... OF THEIR CHILDREN

The book of 1 Samuel tells the story of a woman named Hannah who could not have children. She pleaded earnestly with the Lord for a child, and He granted her request. Hannah's story highlights that the Lord gives our children to us to raise according to His instructions and purposes, but ultimately, they belong to Him.

Now there was a certain man of Ramathaim Zophim, of the mountains of Ephraim, and his name *was* Elkanah the son of Jeroham, the son of Elihu, the son of Tohu, the son of Zuph, an Ephraimite. And he had two wives: the name of one *was* Hannah, and the name of the other Peninnah. Peninnah had children, but Hannah had no children. This man went up from his city yearly to worship and sacrifice to the LORD of hosts in Shiloh. Also the two sons of Eli, Hophni and Phinehas, the priests of the LORD, *were* there. And whenever the time came for Elkanah to make an offering, he would give portions to Peninnah his wife and to all her sons and daughters. But to Hannah he would give a double portion, for he loved Hannah, although the LORD had closed her womb. And her rival also provoked her severely, to make her miserable, because the LORD had closed her womb. So it was, year by year, when she went up to the house of the LORD, that she provoked her; therefore she wept and did not eat.

Then Elkanah her husband said to her, "Hannah, why do you

weep? Why do you not eat? And why is your heart grieved? *Am* I not better to you than ten sons?"

So Hannah arose after they had finished eating and drinking in Shiloh. Now Eli the priest was sitting on the seat by the doorpost of the tabernacle of the LORD. And she *was* in bitterness of soul, and prayed to the LORD and wept in anguish. Then she made a vow and said, "O LORD of hosts, if You will indeed look on the affliction of Your maidservant and remember me, and not forget Your maidservant, but will give Your maidservant a male child, then I will give him to the LORD all the days of his life, and no razor shall come upon his head."

And it happened, as she continued praying before the LORD, that Eli watched her mouth. Now Hannah spoke in her heart; only her lips moved, but her voice was not heard. Therefore Eli thought she was drunk. So Eli said to her, "How long will you be drunk? Put your wine away from you!"

But Hannah answered and said, "No, my lord, I *am* a woman of sorrowful spirit. I have drunk neither wine nor intoxicating drink, but have poured out my soul before the LORD. Do not consider your maidservant a wicked woman, for out of the abundance of my complaint and grief I have spoken until now."

Then Eli answered and said, "Go in peace, and the God of Israel grant your petition which you have asked of Him."

And she said, "Let your maidservant find favor in your sight." So the woman went her way and ate, and her face was no longer *sad.*

Then they rose early in the morning and worshiped before the LORD, and returned and came to their house at Ramah. And Elkanah knew Hannah his wife, and the LORD remembered her. So it came to pass in the process of time that Hannah conceived and bore a son, and called his name Samuel, *saying,* "Because I have asked for him from the LORD."

Now the man Elkanah and all his house went up to offer to the LORD the yearly sacrifice and his vow. But Hannah did not go up, for she said to her husband, "*Not* until the child is weaned; then I will take him, that he may appear before the LORD and remain there forever."

So Elkanah her husband said to her, "Do what seems best to

you; wait until you have weaned him. Only let the LORD establish His word." Then the woman stayed and nursed her son until she had weaned him.

Now when she had weaned him, she took him up with her, with three bulls, one ephah of flour, and a skin of wine, and brought him to the house of the LORD in Shiloh. And the child *was* young. **Then they slaughtered a bull, and brought the child to Eli. And she said, "O my lord! As your soul lives, my lord, I *am* the woman who stood by you here, praying to the LORD. For this child I prayed, and the LORD has granted me my petition which I asked of Him. Therefore I also have lent him to the LORD; as long as he lives he shall be lent to the LORD." So they worshiped the LORD there.**

1 SAMUEL 1:1–28

But Samuel ministered before the LORD, *even as* a child, wearing a linen ephod. Moreover his mother used to make him a little robe, and bring *it* to him year by year when she came up with her husband to offer the yearly sacrifice. And Eli would bless Elkanah and his wife, and say, "The LORD give you descendants from this woman for the loan that was given to the LORD." Then they would go to their own home.

And the LORD visited Hannah, so that she conceived and bore three sons and two daughters. Meanwhile the child Samuel grew before the LORD.

1 SAMUEL 2:18–21

... OF THEIR MONEY

In several places in the Old Testament law, the Israelites were instructed to bring the first portion of the resources and other offerings God provided back to Him. If they did, they would be blessed.

"But you shall seek the place where the LORD your God chooses, out of all your tribes, to put His name for His dwelling place; and there you shall go. There you shall take your burnt offerings, your sacrifices, your tithes, the heave offerings of your hand, your vowed offerings, your freewill offerings, and the firstborn of your herds and flocks. And there you shall eat before the LORD your God, and you shall rejoice in all to which you have put your hand, you and your households, in which the LORD your God has blessed you."

DEUTERONOMY 12:5–7

For some people today, money is the hardest thing to let go of. But holding tightly to what we have earned is not just a modern-day problem.

During the prophet Malachi's day, at the end of the Old Testament era, the Israelites were failing to follow the requirements for offerings and gifts outlined for them. God, through Malachi, challenged the people to honor Him with their material resources as they had been commanded to do.

"For I *am* the LORD, I do not change;
Therefore you are not consumed, O sons of Jacob.
Yet from the days of your fathers
You have gone away from My ordinances
And have not kept *them*.
Return to Me, and I will return to you,"
Says the LORD of hosts.
"But you said,
'In what way shall we return?'
"Will a man rob God?
Yet you have robbed Me!
But you say,
'In what way have we robbed You?'
In tithes and offerings.
You are cursed with a curse,
For you have robbed Me,
Even this whole nation.
Bring all the tithes into the storehouse,
That there may be food in My house,
And try Me now in this,"
Says the LORD of hosts,
"If I will not open for you the windows of heaven
And pour out for you *such* blessing
That *there will* not *be room* enough *to receive it.*

"And I will rebuke the devourer for your sakes,
So that he will not destroy the fruit of your ground,
Nor shall the vine fail to bear fruit for you in the field,"
Says the LORD of hosts;
"And all nations will call you blessed,
For you will be a delightful land,"
Says the LORD of hosts.

MALACHI 3:6–12

What are the key identifiers of "good stewardship"? How does God reward good stewardship of His resources?

Because everything we have is ultimately from the Lord, when we fail to return to Him a portion of what He has provided for us, we rob Him. In a rather unusual parable, Jesus explained a powerful principle regarding how we are to manage the money God has entrusted to us. Money has a lot of power and can be used for good or for evil. We are to look for "shrewd" ways to use God's resources, not to help ourselves, but to help others and serve God.

[Jesus] also said to His disciples: "There was a certain rich man who had a steward, and an accusation was brought to him that this man was wasting his goods. So he called him and said to him, 'What is this I hear about you? Give an account of your stewardship, for you can no longer be steward.'

"Then the steward said within himself, 'What shall I do? For my master is taking the stewardship away from me. I cannot dig; I am ashamed to beg. I have resolved what to do, that when I am put out of the stewardship, they may receive me into their houses.'

"So he called every one of his master's debtors to *him,* and said to the first, 'How much do you owe my master?' And he said, 'A hundred measures of oil.' So he said to him, 'Take your bill, and sit down quickly and write fifty.' Then he said to another, 'And how much do you owe?' So he said, 'A hundred measures of wheat.' And he said to him, 'Take your bill, and write eighty.' So the master commended the unjust steward because he had dealt shrewdly.

For the sons of this world are more shrewd in their generation than the sons of light.

"And I say to you, make friends for yourselves by unrighteous mammon, that when you fail, they may receive you into an everlasting home. He who *is* faithful in *what is* least is faithful also in much; and he who is unjust in *what is* least is unjust also in much. Therefore if you have not been faithful in the unrighteous mammon, who will commit to your trust the true *riches?* And if you have not been faithful in what is another man's, who will give you what is your own?

"No servant can serve two masters; for either he will hate the one and love the other, or else he will be loyal to the one and despise the other. You cannot serve God and mammon."

Now the Pharisees, who were lovers of money, also heard all these things, and they derided Him. And He said to them, "You are those who justify yourselves before men, but God knows your hearts. For what is highly esteemed among men is an abomination in the sight of God." LUKE 16:1–15

Contrast the lifestyle of someone who loves money with that of someone who loves God.

In sharp contrast to the Pharisees, one poor widow Jesus encountered outside the temple used the money in her possession, though it was very little, not for herself but for God's kingdom. Unlike many others, she gave not to be noticed but to give back to God.

Now Jesus sat opposite the treasury and saw how the people put money into the treasury. And many *who were* rich put in much. Then one poor widow came and threw in two mites, which make a quadrans. So He called His disciples to *Himself* and said to them, "Assuredly, I say to you that this poor widow has put in more than all those who have given to the treasury; for they all put in out of their abundance, but she out of her poverty put in all that she had, her whole livelihood." MARK 12:41–44

... of Their Homes

Hospitality was highly valued during Old Testament times, by the Israelites as well as by other peoples. Elijah was a mighty prophet of God who announced an impending drought in Israel brought on by the spiritual unfaithfulness of the king and the people. God sent Elijah outside Israel's borders, to the home of a destitute Gentile widow, who seemed to be the least likely person to be able to provide hospitality. Their story exemplifies the power of both human hospitality and divine provision.

And Elijah the Tishbite, of the inhabitants of Gilead, said to Ahab, "*As* the LORD God of Israel lives, before whom I stand, there shall not be dew nor rain these years, except at my word."

Then the word of the LORD came to him, saying, "Get away from here and turn eastward, and hide by the Brook Cherith, which flows into the Jordan. And it will be *that* you shall drink from the brook, and I have commanded the ravens to feed you there."

So he went and did according to the word of the LORD, for he went and stayed by the Brook Cherith, which flows into the Jordan. The ravens brought him bread and meat in the morning, and bread and meat in the evening; and he drank from the brook. And it happened after a while that the brook dried up, because there had been no rain in the land.

Then the word of the LORD came to him, saying, "Arise, go to Zarephath, which *belongs* to Sidon, and dwell there. See, I have commanded a widow there to provide for you." So he arose and went to Zarephath. And when he came to the gate of the city, indeed a widow *was* there gathering sticks. And he called to her and said, "Please bring me a little water in a cup, that I may drink." And as she was going to get *it,* he called to her and said, "Please bring me a morsel of bread in your hand."

So she said, "As the LORD your God lives, I do not have bread, only a handful of flour in a bin, and a little oil in a jar; and see, I *am* gathering a couple of sticks that I may go in and prepare it for myself and my son, that we may eat it, and die."

And Elijah said to her, "Do not fear; go *and* do as you have said, but make me a small cake from it first, and bring *it* to me; and afterward make *some* for yourself and your son. For thus says the LORD God of Israel: 'The bin of flour shall not be used up, nor shall the jar of oil run dry, until the day the LORD sends rain on the earth.'"

So she went away and did according to the word of Elijah; and she and he and her household ate for *many* days. The bin of flour was not used up, nor did the jar of oil run dry, according to the word of the LORD which He spoke by Elijah.

Now it happened after these things *that* the son of the woman who owned the house became sick. And his sickness was so serious that there was no breath left in him. So she said to Elijah, "What have I to do with you, O man of God? Have you come to me to bring my sin to remembrance, and to kill my son?"

And he said to her, "Give me your son." So he took him out of her arms and carried him to the upper room where he was staying, and laid him on his own bed. Then he cried out to the LORD and said, "O LORD my God, have You also brought tragedy on the widow with whom I lodge, by killing her son?" And he stretched himself out on the child three times, and cried out to the LORD and said, "O LORD my God, I pray, let this child's soul come back to him." Then the LORD heard the voice of Elijah; and the soul of the child came back to him, and he revived.

And Elijah took the child and brought him down from the upper room into the house, and gave him to his mother. And Elijah said, "See, your son lives!"

Then the woman said to Elijah, "Now by this I know that you *are* a man of God, *and* that the word of the LORD in your mouth *is* the truth." 1 KINGS 17:1–24

Our homes—no matter how large or small, how simple or fancy—belong to God and we can use them to accomplish His purposes. The importance of hospitality portrayed in the Old Testament is intensified in the New Testament, as believers are instructed, commanded and commended in regard to practicing hospitality.

Paul's challenge:

Be kindly affectionate to one another with brotherly love, in honor giving preference to one another; not lagging in diligence, fervent in spirit, serving the Lord; rejoicing in hope, patient in tribulation, continuing steadfastly in prayer; distributing to the needs of the saints, given to hospitality. ROMANS 12:10–13

Instructions from the writer of Hebrews:

Do not forget to entertain strangers, for by so *doing* some have unwittingly entertained angels. HEBREWS 13:2

Peter's charge:

Be hospitable to one another without grumbling. 1 PETER 4:9

John's commendation:

Beloved, I pray that you may prosper in all things and be in health, just as your soul prospers. For I rejoiced greatly when brethren came and testified of the truth *that is* in you, just as you walk in the truth. I have no greater joy than to hear that my children walk in truth.

Beloved, you do faithfully whatever you do for the brethren and for strangers, who have borne witness of your love before the church. *If* you send them forward on their journey in a manner worthy of God, you will do well, because they went forth for His name's sake, taking nothing from the Gentiles. **We therefore ought to receive such, that we may become fellow workers for the truth.** 3 JOHN 2–8

Why are we encouraged to practice hospitality?
Why is hospitality important to God?

. . . OF THEIR BODIES

Paul challenged the members of the church at Corinth to honor God with their bodies. Why? Because, like our resources, our bodies belong to God. We are mere caretakers.

All things are lawful for me, but all things are not helpful. All things are lawful for me, but I will not be brought under the power of any. Foods for the stomach and the stomach for foods, but God will destroy both it and them. Now the body *is* not for sexual immorality but for the Lord, and the Lord for the body. And God both raised up the Lord and will also raise us up by His power.

Do you not know that your bodies are members of Christ? Shall I then take the members of Christ and make *them* members of a harlot? Certainly not! Or do you not know that he who is joined to a harlot is one body *with her?* For *"the two,"* He says, *"shall become one flesh."* But he who is joined to the Lord is one spirit *with Him.*

Flee sexual immorality. Every sin that a man does is outside the body, but he who commits sexual immorality sins against his own body. **Or do you not know that your body is the temple of the Holy Spirit *who is* in you, whom you have from God, and you are not your own? For you were bought at a price; therefore glorify God in your body and in your spirit, which are God's.**

1 Corinthians 6:12–20

... Over All They Do

Paul brings us full circle by quoting from Psalm 24, which declares God's ownership over everything. We, however, are not owners, but managers—of the earth, our families, our money, our homes and our bodies. Everything we do, we are to do for His glory.

All things are lawful for me, but not all things are helpful; all things are lawful for me, but not all things edify. Let no one seek his own, but each one the other's *well-being.*

Eat whatever is sold in the meat market, asking no questions for conscience' sake; for *"the earth is the Lord's, and all its fullness."*

If any of those who do not believe invites you *to dinner,* and you desire to go, eat whatever is set before you, asking no question for conscience' sake. But if anyone says to you, "This was offered to idols," do not eat it for the sake of the one who told you, and for conscience' sake; for *"the earth is the Lord's, and all its fullness."* "Conscience," I say, not your own, but that of the other. For why is my liberty judged by another *man's* conscience? But if I partake with thanks, why am I evil spoken of for *the food* over which I give thanks?

Therefore, whether you eat or drink, or whatever you do, do all to the glory of God. Give no offense, either to the Jews or to the Greeks or to the church of God, just as I also please all *men* in all *things,* not seeking my own profit, but the *profit* of many, that they may be saved.

Imitate me, just as I also *imitate* Christ. 1 CORINTHIANS 10:23—11:1

List some of the things God has entrusted to you to manage. How are you doing in each of these areas? How can you improve your stewardship of them?

WHAT WE BELIEVE

Stewardship can make a major difference in our lives when we move from simply understanding it in our heads to fully embracing it in our hearts. God is the owner of everything we have and everything we are. When we come to faith in Christ, we turn over the "deed" of everything—our children, our money, our homes, our bodies, our very breath—to Him. God then turns to us and invites us to manage all these things according to His purposes. When we do, we are freed from the hassles of ownership and enter into a life of reward and blessing.

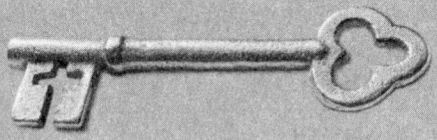

CHAPTER

10

Eternity

KEY QUESTION

What happens next?

KEY IDEA

I believe there is a heaven and a hell and that Jesus will return to judge all people and to establish His eternal kingdom.

KEY VERSE

Let not your heart be troubled; you believe in God, believe also in Me. In My Father's house are many mansions; if *it were* not *so*, I would have told you. I go to prepare a place for you.
John 14:1–2

OUR MAP

Embracing the first nine beliefs of the Christian faith in our minds and hearts dramatically enhances our own quality of life, as well as the quality of life for the community around us. But there is something more—and it is huge. There is life after death. Eternal life with God. God wants to restore His original vision of life with us in the garden. The only way back into the garden (which can be called heaven or God's kingdom) is through faith in Jesus Christ. Those who embrace Christ in this life are reconciled to God and become a new creation with a new identity. For the Christian, not only can life be abundant today, but anticipating what is in store for us when we are reunited with God in the new heaven and new earth is simply breathtaking.

The Scripture in this chapter will unfold the journey to that place:

- *The Ending of a Life*
- *The Intermediate State*
- *The Resurrection*
- *The Return of Christ*
- *A New Heaven and a New Earth*

The Ending of a Life

While the Old Testament writers don't address the afterlife in as much detail as the New Testament writers, the Old Testament does contain the magnificent description of the prophet Elijah being taken up to heaven without dying. Elijah is one of only three people taken to heaven in bodily form, the other two being Enoch (you can read about him in Genesis 5:21–24) and, of course, Jesus. While our experience will be quite different at the end of our lives in these bodies, we bask in the promise of what awaits us on the other side.

And it came to pass, when the LORD was about to take up Elijah into heaven by a whirlwind, that Elijah went with Elisha from Gilgal. Then Elijah said to Elisha, "Stay here, please, for the LORD has sent me on to Bethel."

But Elisha said, "*As* the LORD lives, and *as* your soul lives, I will not leave you!" So they went down to Bethel.

Now the sons of the prophets who *were* at Bethel came out to Elisha, and said to him, "Do you know that the LORD will take away your master from over you today?"

And he said, "Yes, I know; keep silent!"

Then Elijah said to him, "Elisha, stay here, please, for the LORD has sent me on to Jericho."

But he said, "*As* the LORD lives, and *as* your soul lives, I will not leave you!" So they came to Jericho.

Now the sons of the prophets who *were* at Jericho came to Elisha and said to him, "Do you know that the LORD will take away your master from over you today?"

So he answered, "Yes, I know; keep silent!"

Then Elijah said to him, "Stay here, please, for the LORD has sent me on to the Jordan."

But he said, "*As* the LORD lives, and *as* your soul lives, I will not leave you!" So the two of them went on. And fifty men of the sons of the prophets went and stood facing *them* at a distance, while the two of them stood by the Jordan. Now Elijah took his mantle, rolled *it* up, and struck the water; and it was divided this way and that, so that the two of them crossed over on dry ground.

And so it was, when they had crossed over, that Elijah said to Elisha, "Ask! What may I do for you, before I am taken away from you?"

Elisha said, "Please let a double portion of your spirit be upon me."

So he said, "You have asked a hard thing. *Nevertheless,* if you see me *when I am* taken from you, it shall be so for you; but if not, it shall not be *so.*" **Then it happened, as they continued on and talked, that suddenly a chariot of fire *appeared* with horses of fire, and separated the two of them; and Elijah went up by a whirlwind into heaven.**

And Elisha saw *it,* and he cried out, "My father, my father, the chariot of Israel and its horsemen!" So he saw him no more. And he took hold of his own clothes and tore them into two pieces. He also took up the mantle of Elijah that had fallen from him, and went back and stood by the bank of the Jordan. Then he took the mantle of Elijah that had fallen from him, and struck the water, and said, "Where *is* the LORD God of Elijah?" And when he also had struck the water, it was divided this way and that; and Elisha crossed over.

Now when the sons of the prophets who *were* from Jericho saw him, they said, "The spirit of Elijah rests on Elisha." And they came to meet him, and bowed to the ground before him. Then they said to him, "Look now, there are fifty strong men with your servants. Please let them go and search for your master, lest perhaps the Spirit of the LORD has taken him up and cast him upon some mountain or into some valley."

And he said, "You shall not send anyone."

But when they urged him till he was ashamed, he said, "Send *them!*" Therefore they sent fifty men, and they searched for three days but did not find him. And when they came back to him, for he had stayed in Jericho, he said to them, "Did I not say to you, 'Do not go'?"

2 KINGS 2:1–18

Given that the afterlife was not talked about much in the Old Testament, why do you think the prophets insisted on looking for Elijah? How would you have responded if you were there?

THE INTERMEDIATE STATE

What happens when we die? The New Testament indicates that people experience an "intermediate state," which refers to a person's existence between their time of death and the promised resurrection of their new body. Their earthly body goes into the grave; their spirit lives on in one of two places—in God's presence where they enjoy a time of peace until they receive their resurrected bodies or in a place of torment where they await final judgment. Jesus talked about this vividly in the story about a rich man and Lazarus (not the Lazarus Jesus raised from the dead). Jesus described the place of blessedness for the righteous as Abraham's bosom and the place of torment for the wicked as Hades.

"There was a certain rich man who was clothed in purple and fine linen and fared sumptuously every day. But there was a certain beggar named Lazarus, full of sores, who was laid at his gate, desiring to be fed with the crumbs which fell from the rich man's table. Moreover the dogs came and licked his sores. So it was that the beggar died, and was carried by the angels to Abraham's bosom. The rich man also died and was buried. And being in torments in Hades, he lifted up his eyes and saw Abraham afar off, and Lazarus in his bosom.

"Then he cried and said, 'Father Abraham, have mercy on me, and send Lazarus that he may dip the tip of his finger in water and cool my tongue; for I am tormented in this flame.' But Abraham said, 'Son, remember that in your lifetime you received your good things, and likewise Lazarus evil things; but now he is comforted and you are tormented. And besides all this, between us and you there is a great gulf fixed, so that those who want to pass from here to you cannot, nor can those from there pass to us.'

"Then he said, 'I beg you therefore, father, that you would send him to my father's house, for I have five brothers, that he may testify to them, lest they also come to this place of torment.' Abraham said to him, 'They have Moses and the prophets; let them hear them.' And he said, 'No, father Abraham; but if one goes to them from the dead, they will repent.' But he said to him, 'If they do not hear Moses and the prophets, neither will they be persuaded though one rise from the dead.'" LUKE 16:19–31

Having a person come back from the dead to tell you what they experienced on the other side would seem rather compelling. Why did Abraham disagree?

THE RESURRECTION

There is more to come after we die than our spirits going to be with God while our bodies remain in the grave. The grand promise of God and the ultimate hope for all Christians is the resurrection. Just as Christ was raised from the dead and received an imperishable body, so will all those who believe in Christ. Paul, writing to the church at Corinth, details this major truth.

Moreover, brethren, I declare to you the gospel which I preached to you, which also you received and in which you stand, by which also you are saved, if you hold fast that word which I preached to you—unless you believed in vain.

For I delivered to you first of all that which I also received: that Christ died for our sins according to the Scriptures, and that He was buried, and that He rose again the third day according to the Scriptures, and that He was seen by Cephas, then by the twelve. After that He was seen by over five hundred brethren at once, of whom the greater part remain to the present, but some have fallen asleep. After that He was seen by James, then by all the apostles. Then last of all He was seen by me also, as by one born out of due time.

For I am the least of the apostles, who am not worthy to be called an apostle, because I persecuted the church of God. But by the grace of God I am what I am, and His grace toward me was not in vain; but I labored more abundantly than they all, yet not I, but the grace of God *which was* with me. Therefore, whether *it was* I or they, so we preach and so you believed.

Now if Christ is preached that He has been raised from the dead, how do some among you say that there is no resurrection of the dead? But if there is no resurrection of the dead, then Christ is not risen. And if Christ is not risen, then our preaching *is* empty and your faith *is* also empty. Yes, and we are found false witnesses of God, because we have testified of God that He raised up Christ, whom He did not raise up—if in fact the dead do not rise. For if *the* dead do not rise, then Christ is not risen. And if Christ is not risen, your faith *is* futile; you are still in your sins! Then also those who have fallen asleep in Christ have perished. If in this life only we have hope in Christ, we are of all men the most pitiable.

But now Christ is risen from the dead, *and* has become the firstfruits of those who have fallen asleep. For since by man *came* death, by Man also *came* the resurrection of the dead. For as in Adam all die, even so in Christ all shall be made alive. But each one in his own order: Christ the firstfruits, afterward those *who are* Christ's at His coming. Then *comes* the end, when He delivers the kingdom to God the Father, when He puts an end to all rule and all authority and power. For He must reign till He has put all enemies under His feet. The last enemy *that* will be destroyed *is* death. For *"He has put all things under His feet."* But when He says "all things are put under *Him," it is* evident that He who put all things under Him is excepted. Now when all things are made subject to Him, then the Son Himself will also be subject to Him who put all things under Him, that God may be all in all.

1 Corinthians 15:1–28

But someone will say, "How are the dead raised up? And with what body do they come?" Foolish one, what you sow is not made alive unless it dies. And what you sow, you do not sow that body that shall be, but mere grain—perhaps wheat or some other *grain.* But God gives it a body as He pleases, and to each seed its own body.

All flesh *is* not the same flesh, but *there is* one *kind of* flesh of men, another flesh of animals, another of fish, *and* another of birds.

There are also celestial bodies and terrestrial bodies; but the glory of the celestial *is* one, and the *glory* of the terrestrial *is* another. *There is* one glory of the sun, another glory of the moon, and another glory of the stars; for *one* star differs from *another* star in glory.

So also *is* the resurrection of the dead. *The body* is sown in corruption, it is raised in incorruption. It is sown in dishonor, it is raised in glory. It is sown in weakness, it is raised in power. It is sown a natural body, it is raised a spiritual body. There is a natural body, and there is a spiritual body. And so it is written, *"The first man Adam became a living being."* The last Adam *became* a life-giving spirit.

However, the spiritual is not first, but the natural, and afterward the spiritual. The first man *was* of the earth, *made* of dust; the second Man *is* the Lord from heaven. As *was* the *man* of dust, so also *are* those *who are made* of dust; and as *is* the heavenly *Man,* so also *are* those *who are* heavenly. And as we have borne the image of the *man* of dust, we shall also bear the image of the heavenly *Man.*

Now this I say, brethren, that flesh and blood cannot inherit the kingdom of God; nor does corruption inherit incorruption. **Behold, I tell you a mystery: We shall not all sleep, but we shall all be changed—in a moment, in the twinkling of an eye, at the last trumpet. For the trumpet will sound, and the dead will be raised incorruptible, and we shall be changed.** For this corruptible must put on incorruption, and this mortal *must* put on immortality. So when this corruptible has put on incorruption, and this mortal has put on immortality, then shall be brought to pass the saying that is written: *"Death is swallowed up in victory."*

> *"O Death, where is your sting?*
> *O Hades, where is your victory?"*

The sting of death *is* sin, and the strength of sin *is* the law. But thanks *be* to God, who gives us the victory through our Lord Jesus Christ.

Therefore, my beloved brethren, be steadfast, immovable, always abounding in the work of the Lord, knowing that your labor is not in vain in the Lord.

1 Corinthians 15:35–58

How will our resurrected bodies be different from our earthly bodies? How does what the Bible says compare with some of our culture's popular notions of what we'll be like in heaven?

The Return of Christ

The event that will trigger this promised resurrection is the second coming of Christ. There are varied beliefs about the details leading up to this momentous occasion, but all followers of Jesus embrace its truth and significance. Often the Bible refers to the return of Christ as the "day of the Lord." Paul uses this phrase in an important letter addressed to the church at Thessalonica. Some of the believers there thought all Christians would be alive at the return of Christ, causing the Thessalonians to be concerned about fellow believers who had died. Paul explains that on the great day of Christ's return, God will resurrect those who have died. Then all believers will be brought together and will be with the Lord Jesus forever.

As you read the passages below from
1 Thessalonians 4–5 and 2 Peter 3,
look for ways we are encouraged to live
our lives today considering Christ's imminent return.

But I do not want you to be ignorant, brethren, concerning those who have fallen asleep, lest you sorrow as others who have no hope. For if we believe that Jesus died and rose again, even so God will bring with Him those who sleep in Jesus.

For this we say to you by the word of the Lord, that we who are alive *and* remain until the coming of the Lord will by no means precede those who are asleep. **For the Lord Himself will descend from heaven with a shout, with the voice of an archangel, and with the trumpet of God. And the dead in Christ will rise first. Then we who are alive *and* remain shall be caught up together with them in the clouds to meet the Lord in the air. And thus we shall always be with the Lord. Therefore comfort one another with these words.**

But concerning the times and the seasons, brethren, you have no need that I should write to you. For you yourselves know perfectly that the day of the Lord so comes as a thief in the night. For when they say, "Peace and safety!" then sudden destruction comes upon them, as labor pains upon a pregnant woman. And they shall not escape. But you, brethren, are not in darkness, so that this Day should overtake you as a thief. You are all sons of light and sons of the day. We are not of the night nor of darkness. Therefore let us not sleep, as others *do,* but let us watch and be sober. For those who sleep, sleep at night, and those who get drunk are drunk at night. But let us who are of the day be sober, putting on the breastplate of faith and love, and *as* a helmet the hope of salvation. For God did not appoint us to wrath, but to obtain salvation through our Lord Jesus Christ, who died for us, that whether we wake or sleep, we should live together with Him.

Therefore comfort each other and edify one another, just as you also are doing.

1 Thessalonians 4:13—5:11

The apostle Peter also writes in great detail about "the day of the Lord," adding further clarification and admonition regarding how believers should live their lives in light of this future reality.

Beloved, I now write to you this second epistle (in *both of* which I stir up your pure minds by way of reminder), that you may be mindful of the words which were spoken before by the holy prophets, and of the commandment of us, the apostles of the Lord and Savior, knowing this first: that scoffers will come in the last days, walking according to their own lusts, and saying, "Where is the promise of His coming? For since the fathers fell asleep, all things continue as *they were* from the beginning of creation." For this they willfully forget: that by the word of God the heavens were of old, and the earth standing out of water and in the water, by which the world *that* then existed perished, being flooded with water. But the heavens and the earth *which* are now preserved by the same word, are reserved for fire until the day of judgment and perdition of ungodly men.

But, beloved, do not forget this one thing, that with the Lord one day *is* as a thousand years, and a thousand years as one day. The Lord is not slack concerning *His* promise, as some count slackness, but is longsuffering toward us, not willing that any should perish but that all should come to repentance.

But the day of the Lord will come as a thief in the night, in which the heavens will pass away with a great noise, and the elements will melt with fervent heat; both the earth and the works that are in it will be burned up. Therefore, since all these things will be dissolved, what manner *of persons* ought you to be in holy conduct and godliness, looking for and hastening the coming of the day of God, because of which the heavens will be dissolved, being on fire, and the elements will melt with fervent heat? Nevertheless we, according to His promise, look for new heavens and a new earth in which righteousness dwells.

Therefore, beloved, looking forward to these things, be diligent to be found by Him in peace, without spot and blameless; and consider *that* the longsuffering of our Lord *is* salvation—as also our beloved brother Paul, according to the wisdom given to him, has written to you, as also in all his epistles, speaking in them of these things, in which are some things hard to understand, which untaught and unstable *people* twist to their own destruction, as *they do* also the rest of the Scriptures.

You therefore, beloved, since you know *this* beforehand, beware lest you also fall from your own steadfastness, being led away with the error of the wicked; but grow in the grace and knowledge of our Lord and Savior Jesus Christ.

To Him *be* the glory both now and forever. Amen. 2 Peter 3:1–18

A New Heaven and a New Earth

After Jesus returns and we are resurrected into our imperishable bodies, there will be a final judgment by God of every nation. John saw and recorded a vision from God about what will happen at this time of judgment. John wrote down the final movement in God's grand story—the restoration of what was lost in the beginning. What we read in the opening creation story of Genesis we see again in Revelation, a re-creation, but on a grander scale to accommodate all the people over the centuries who have embraced Christ and received eternal life.

Then I saw a great white throne and Him who sat on it, from whose face the earth and the heaven fled away. And there was found no place for them. And I saw the dead, small and great, standing before God, and books were opened. And another book was opened, which is *the Book* of Life. And the dead were judged according to their works, by the things which were written in the books. The sea gave up the dead who were in it, and Death and Hades delivered up the dead who were in them. And they were judged, each one according to his works. Then Death and Hades were cast into the lake of fire. This is the second death. And anyone not found written in the Book of Life was cast into the lake of fire.

Now I saw a new heaven and a new earth, for the first heaven and the first earth had passed away. Also there was no more sea. Then I, John, saw the holy city, New Jerusalem, coming down out of heaven from God, prepared as a bride adorned for her husband. And I heard a loud voice from heaven saying, "Behold, the tabernacle of God *is* with men, and He will dwell

with them, and they shall be His people. God Himself will be with them *and be* their God. And God will wipe away every tear from their eyes; there shall be no more death, nor sorrow, nor crying. There shall be no more pain, for the former things have passed away."

Then He who sat on the throne said, "Behold, I make all things new." And He said to me, "Write, for these words are true and faithful."

And He said to me, "It is done! I am the Alpha and the Omega, the Beginning and the End. I will give of the fountain of the water of life freely to him who thirsts. He who overcomes shall inherit all things, and I will be his God and he shall be My son. But the cowardly, unbelieving, abominable, murderers, sexually immoral, sorcerers, idolaters, and all liars shall have their part in the lake which burns with fire and brimstone, which is the second death."

Then one of the seven angels who had the seven bowls filled with the seven last plagues came to me and talked with me, saying, "Come, I will show you the bride, the Lamb's wife." And he carried me away in the Spirit to a great and high mountain, and showed me the great city, the holy Jerusalem, descending out of heaven from God, having the glory of God. Her light *was* like a most precious stone, like a jasper stone, clear as crystal. Also she had a great and high wall with twelve gates, and twelve angels at the gates, and names written on them, which are *the names* of the twelve tribes of the children of Israel: three gates on the east, three gates on the north, three gates on the south, and three gates on the west.

Now the wall of the city had twelve foundations, and on them were the names of the twelve apostles of the Lamb. And he who talked with me had a gold reed to measure the city, its gates, and its wall. The city is laid out as a square; its length is as great as its breadth. And he measured the city with the reed: twelve thousand furlongs. Its length, breadth, and height are equal. Then he measured its wall: one hundred *and* forty-four cubits, *according* to the measure of a man, that is, of an angel. The construction of its wall was *of* jasper; and the city *was* pure gold, like clear glass. The foundations of the wall of the city *were* adorned with all kinds of precious stones: the first foundation *was* jasper, the second sapphire, the third chalcedony, the fourth emerald, the fifth sardonyx, the sixth sardius, the seventh chrysolite, the eighth beryl, the ninth topaz, the tenth chrysoprase, the eleventh jacinth, and the twelfth amethyst. The twelve gates *were* twelve pearls: each individual gate was of one pearl. And the street of the city *was* pure gold, like transparent glass.

But I saw no temple in it, for the Lord God Almighty and the Lamb are its temple. The city had no need of the sun or of the moon to shine in it, for the glory of God illuminated it. The Lamb *is* its light. And the nations of those who are saved shall walk in its light, and the kings of the earth bring their glory and honor into it. Its gates shall not be shut at all by day (there shall be no night there). And they shall bring the glory and the honor of the nations into it. But there shall by no means enter it anything that defiles, or causes an abomination or a lie, but only those who are written in the Lamb's Book of Life.

And he showed me a pure river of water of life, clear as crystal, proceeding from the throne of God and of the Lamb. In the middle of its street, and on either side of the river, *was* the tree of life, which bore twelve fruits, each *tree* yielding its fruit every month. The leaves of the tree *were* for the healing of the nations. And there shall be no more curse, but the throne of God and of the Lamb shall be in it, and His servants shall serve Him. They shall see His face, and His name *shall be* on their foreheads. There shall be no night there: They need no lamp nor light of the sun, for the Lord God gives them light. And they shall reign forever and ever.

Then he said to me, "These words *are* faithful and true." And the Lord God of the holy prophets sent His angel to show His servants the things which must shortly take place.

"Behold, I am coming quickly! Blessed *is* he who keeps the words of the prophecy of this book."

Now I, John, saw and heard these things. And when I heard and saw, I fell down to worship before the feet of the angel who showed me these things.

Then he said to me, "See *that you do* not *do that.* For I am your fellow servant, and of your brethren the prophets, and of those who keep the words of this book. Worship God." And he said to me, "Do not seal the words of the prophecy of this book, for the time is at hand. He who is unjust, let him be unjust still; he who is filthy, let him be filthy still; he who is righteous, let him be righteous still; he who is holy, let him be holy still."

"And behold, I am coming quickly, and My reward *is* with Me, to give to every one according to his work. I am the Alpha and the Omega, *the* Beginning and *the* End, the First and the Last."

Blessed *are* those who do His commandments, that they may have the right to the tree of life, and may enter through the gates into the city. But outside *are* dogs and sorcerers and sexually immoral and murderers and idolaters, and whoever loves and practices a lie.

"I, Jesus, have sent My angel to testify to you these things in the churches. I am the Root and the Offspring of David, the Bright and Morning Star."

And the Spirit and the bride say, "Come!" And let him who hears say, "Come!" And let him who thirsts come. Whoever desires, let him take the water of life freely.

For I testify to everyone who hears the words of the prophecy of this book: If anyone adds to these things, God will add to him the plagues that are written in this book; and if anyone takes away from the words of the book of this prophecy, God shall take away his part from the Book of Life, from the holy city, and *from* the things which are written in this book.

He who testifies to these things says, "Surely I am coming quickly."

Amen. Even so, come, Lord Jesus!

The grace of our Lord Jesus Christ *be* with you all. Amen.

REVELATION 20:11—22:21

In Jesus' last week on earth before He returned to the Father, He comforted the disciples concerning the future. He informed them that He was leaving, but He also promised that He would be overseeing the construction of a place for each of them in heaven—the new Jerusalem that John saw and described. As you read these words, know that Jesus' message to the disciples applies to you as well. He has prepared an eternal home for all those who believe.

"Let not your heart be troubled; you believe in God, believe also in Me. In My Father's house are many mansions; if *it were* not *so,* I would have told you. I go to prepare a place for you. **And if I go and prepare a place for you, I will come again and receive you to Myself; that where I am, *there* you may be also.** And where I go you know, and the way you know."

Thomas said to Him, "Lord, we do not know where You are going, and how can we know the way?"

Jesus said to him, "I am the way, the truth, and the life. No one comes to the Father except through Me.

"If you had known Me, you would have known My Father also; and from now on you know Him and have seen Him." JOHN 14:1–7

As you ponder eternal life in the garden on the new earth without the presence of sin, hatred, strife, war or death, what do you most look forward to?

WHAT WE BELIEVE

When we die our bodies go into the ground and our spirits go to be with the Lord as we await the return of Christ. When He comes to establish the new heaven and the new earth, our spirits will receive the tent of a new, imperishable, resurrected body just as Jesus did. In these bodies we will live forever in the new garden with God and all those who believed in Jesus. And it is with this exciting reality that we conclude our journey through the ten key beliefs of the Christian life. As followers of God we are invited to ponder and understand these profound concepts in our minds. Yet, to really think like Jesus and experience the full life Christ has given us, we must embrace these beliefs in our hearts—where real decisions are made. So how do we move these fantastic ideas from simply being the right answer to a way of life? We do so through the ten key practices of the Christian life, which are highlighted in the next section. Engaging in these activities (in partnership with God) will enable you to express your beliefs while reinforcing them in your heart. Turn the page with the anticipation of actually becoming more like Jesus!

ACT

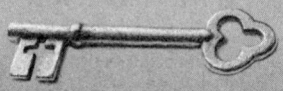

What Should I Do?

Do you not know that those who run in a race all run, but one receives the prize? Run in such a way that you may obtain *it*. And everyone who competes *for the prize* is temperate in all things. Now they *do it* to obtain a perishable crown, but we *for* an imperishable *crown*. Therefore I run thus: not with uncertainty. Thus I fight: not as *one who* beats the air. But I discipline my body and bring *it* into subjection, lest, when I have preached to others, I myself should become disqualified.
1 Corinthians 9:24–27

When you study the life of Jesus you will notice a distinct pattern. Jesus faithfully lived in a purposeful way. Once again, Jesus was modeling for us the Christian life. We would do well to simply follow His pattern — to *act* like Jesus.

The following ten chapters are going to introduce you to the key spiritual practices of the Christian life. You will encounter axioms to guide you and real-life stories to inspire you.

As you read each chapter and come to understand what God wants you to do, prayerfully ask yourself, "Will I do what God is inviting me to do?" In the passage above, the apostle Paul invites us to think of the Christian life like an athlete. If an Olympic runner wants to cross the finish line first, they must commit to a life of strict training. Essentially, Paul is saying that if we want to win at life, we too need to be disciplined in the way we approach each day.

If you resolve to practice what you are about to learn, remember you will not be alone. God's Spirit can give you the internal strength, silence the voices of dissenters and blow wind at your back.

These practices will not only aid you in understanding the key beliefs, they will also catalyze you in fulfilling your mission to love God and to let His love flow through you to your neighbors, so all people will know God and know you are His disciple.

On your mark … get set … GO!

ACT

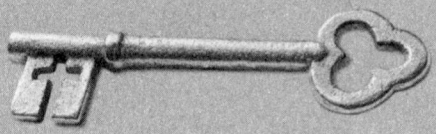

CHAPTER 11

Worship

KEY QUESTION

How do I honor God in the way He deserves?

KEY IDEA

I worship God for who He is
and what He has done for me.

KEY VERSE

Oh come, let us sing to the LORD!
Let us shout joyfully to the Rock of our salvation.
Let us come before His presence with thanksgiving;
Let us shout joyfully to Him with psalms.
Psalm 95:1–2

OUR MAP

As we read in Chapter 1, the first key belief in the Christian life begins with God. It is only logical that the first key practice in the Christian life is worshiping God. When we worship we are taking the revelation about the one true God—Father, Son and Holy Spirit—and reaffirming our belief that He is involved in our lives and wants to be in a relationship with us. As we do this, the amazing truths about God move from concepts in our heads to cries of our hearts. When we worship God for who He is and what He has done for us, it not only cements our confidence in God as we approach each day and each situation, but it also enables us to receive His love. When we receive God's love in our hearts, we begin to see the world differently—as people made in God's image.

So we can read this chapter with great anticipation as we explore the different aspects of worship, including:

- *The Heart's Intent*
- *Unashamed Worshipers*
- *Worshiping Together*

The Heart's Intent

Worshiping God for who He is and what He has done for us can be expressed in many different forms and diverse environments, but it's what we believe in our hearts that matters to God. Throughout Scripture we see how God's people worshiped Him on towering mountaintops, inside homes with dirt floors, at a lavishly adorned temple and in dark prisons. They demonstrated their devotion to God with singing, dancing, sacrifices and public and private prayer. What's most important to God is not the way that we choose to worship Him, but the motivation that directs our actions.

What does the following passage from Psalm 95 tell us about how and why we should worship God?

Oh come, let us sing to the Lord!
Let us shout joyfully to the Rock of our salvation.

Let us come before His presence with thanksgiving;
Let us shout joyfully to Him with psalms.
For the LORD *is* the great God,
And the great King above all gods.
In His hand *are* the deep places of the earth;
The heights of the hills *are* His also.
The sea *is* His, for He made it;
And His hands formed the dry *land.*

Oh come, let us worship and bow down;
Let us kneel before the LORD our Maker.
For He *is* our God,
And we *are* the people of His pasture,
And the sheep of His hand. PSALM 95:1–7

During Old Testament times, worship involved animal sacrifices. Instead of leaving His people with no recourse except to face their punishment for sin, God, in His mercy, allowed His people to sacrifice the best animals from their herd as a payment for their disobedience. The animal had to be without defect, since a defective sacrifice could not be a substitute for a defective people. This practice was intended to be accompanied by repentance. The worshiper confessed their sin and laid hands on the animal; then the sin was symbolically transferred away from the sinner to the sacrifice.

Unfortunately, over time the Israelites' sacrifices became meaningless rituals. God was angry and heartbroken. The people brought Him an abundance of sacrifices, yet their character and conduct were anything but pleasing to Him. God doesn't want us to simply go through the motions; He wants us to change in our hearts.

"To what purpose *is* the multitude of your sacrifices
to Me?"
Says the LORD.
"I have had enough of burnt offerings of rams
And the fat of fed cattle.
I do not delight in the blood of bulls,
Or of lambs or goats.

"When you come to appear before Me,
Who has required this from your hand,
To trample My courts?
Bring no more futile sacrifices;
Incense is an abomination to Me.
The New Moons, the Sabbaths, and the calling of
assemblies—
I cannot endure iniquity and the sacred meeting.
Your New Moons and your appointed feasts
My soul hates;
They are a trouble to Me,
I am weary of bearing *them.*
When you spread out your hands,
I will hide My eyes from you;
Even though you make many prayers,
I will not hear.
Your hands are full of blood.

"Wash yourselves, make yourselves clean;
Put away the evil of your doings from before My eyes.
Cease to do evil,
Learn to do good;
Seek justice,
Rebuke the oppressor;
Defend the fatherless,
Plead for the widow.

"Come now, and let us reason together,"
Says the LORD,
"Though your sins are like scarlet,
They shall be as white as snow;
Though they are red like crimson,
They shall be as wool.
If you are willing and obedient,
You shall eat the good of the land;
But if you refuse and rebel,
You shall be devoured by the sword";
For the mouth of the LORD has spoken. ISAIAH 1:11–20

Despite knowing better, God's people throughout history failed Him in their worship practices. In the New Testament, those who neglected to worship and honor God properly received some harsh words from Jesus. This was especially true for the religious leaders whose layers of religious exercises and rituals hid a weak and shallow faith. As a crowd gathered to listen to Jesus as He taught, He warned them about the influence of these hollow religious leaders.

As you read the passage below from Matthew 23, ponder this question: With what behaviors and attitudes of the Pharisees did Jesus take issue? (Hint: Jesus introduced each one with "woe to you.")

Then Jesus spoke to the multitudes and to His disciples, saying: "The scribes and the Pharisees sit in Moses' seat. Therefore whatever they tell you to observe, *that* observe and do, but do not do according to their works; for they say, and do not do. For they bind heavy burdens, hard to bear, and lay *them* on men's shoulders; but they *themselves* will not move them with one of their fingers. But all their works they do to be seen by men. They make their phylacteries broad and enlarge the borders of their garments. They love the best places at feasts, the best seats in the synagogues, greetings in the marketplaces, and to be called by men, 'Rabbi, Rabbi.' But you, do not be called 'Rabbi'; for One is your Teacher, the Christ, and you are all brethren. Do not call anyone on earth your father; for One is your Father, He who is in heaven. And do not be called teachers; for One is your Teacher, the Christ. But he who is greatest among you shall be your servant. And whoever exalts himself will be humbled, and he who humbles himself will be exalted.

"But **woe to you**, scribes and Pharisees, hypocrites! For you shut up the kingdom of heaven against men; for you neither go in *yourselves,* nor do you allow those who are entering to go in. Woe to you, scribes and Pharisees, hypocrites! For you devour widows' houses, and for a pretense make long prayers. Therefore you will receive greater condemnation.

"Woe to you, scribes and Pharisees, hypocrites! For you travel land and sea to win one proselyte, and when he is won, you make him twice as much a son of hell as yourselves.

"**Woe to you,** blind guides, who say, 'Whoever swears by the temple, it is nothing; but whoever swears by the gold of the temple, he is obliged *to perform it.*' Fools and blind! For which is greater, the gold or the temple that sanctifies the gold? And, 'Whoever swears by the altar, it is nothing; but whoever swears by the gift that is on it, he is obliged *to perform it.*' Fools and blind! For which is greater, the gift or the altar that sanctifies the gift? Therefore he who swears by the altar, swears by it and by all things on it. He who swears by the temple, swears by it and by Him who dwells in it. And he who swears by heaven, swears by the throne of God and by Him who sits on it.

"**Woe to you,** scribes and Pharisees, hypocrites! For you pay tithe of mint and anise and cummin, and have neglected the weightier *matters* of the law: justice and mercy and faith. These you ought to have done, without leaving the others undone. Blind guides, who strain out a gnat and swallow a camel!

"**Woe to you,** scribes and Pharisees, hypocrites! For you cleanse the outside of the cup and dish, but inside they are full of extortion and self-indulgence. Blind Pharisee, first cleanse the inside of the cup and dish, that the outside of them may be clean also.

"**Woe to you,** scribes and Pharisees, hypocrites! For you are like whitewashed tombs which indeed appear beautiful outwardly, but inside are full of dead *men's* bones and all uncleanness. Even so you also outwardly appear righteous to men, but inside you are full of hypocrisy and lawlessness."

MATTHEW 23:1–28

UNASHAMED WORSHIPERS

When God calls us to love Him with all our hearts, souls, minds and strength, He is demanding that we hold nothing back from Him. A commitment to worship God is a vow to be bold and unashamed of our love and devotion to Him. With great power, God rescued the Israelites when the army of Egypt had them backed against the Red Sea. After their escape, Moses and his sister, Miriam, led the Israelites in an unapologetic song of celebration and blessing, praising God for who He is and what He had done for them.

Then Moses and the children of Israel sang this song to the LORD, and spoke, saying:

"I will sing to the LORD,
For He has triumphed gloriously!
The horse and its rider
He has thrown into the sea!
The LORD *is* my strength and song,
And He has become my salvation;
He *is* my God, and I will praise Him;
My father's God, and I will exalt Him.
The LORD *is* a man of war;
The LORD *is* His name.
Pharaoh's chariots and his army He has cast into the sea;
His chosen captains also are drowned in the Red Sea.
The depths have covered them;
They sank to the bottom like a stone.

"Your right hand, O LORD, has become glorious
in power;
Your right hand, O LORD, has dashed the enemy
in pieces.
And in the greatness of Your excellence
You have overthrown those who rose against You;
You sent forth Your wrath;
It consumed them like stubble.
And with the blast of Your nostrils
The waters were gathered together;
The floods stood upright like a heap;
The depths congealed in the heart of the sea.
The enemy said, 'I will pursue,
I will overtake,
I will divide the spoil;
My desire shall be satisfied on them.
I will draw my sword,
My hand shall destroy them.'
You blew with Your wind,
The sea covered them;
They sank like lead in the mighty waters.

"Who *is* like You, O LORD, among the gods?
Who *is* like You, glorious in holiness,
Fearful in praises, doing wonders?
You stretched out Your right hand;
The earth swallowed them.
You in Your mercy have led forth
The people whom You have redeemed;
You have guided *them* in Your strength
To Your holy habitation.

"The people will hear *and* be afraid;
Sorrow will take hold of the inhabitants of Philistia.
Then the chiefs of Edom will be dismayed;
The mighty men of Moab,
Trembling will take hold of them;
All the inhabitants of Canaan will melt away.
Fear and dread will fall on them;
By the greatness of Your arm
They will be *as* still as a stone,
Till Your people pass over, O LORD,
Till the people pass over
Whom You have purchased.
You will bring them in and plant them
In the mountain of Your inheritance,
In the place, O LORD, *which* You have made
For Your own dwelling,
The sanctuary, O Lord, *which* Your hands have
established.

"The LORD shall reign forever and ever."

For the horses of Pharaoh went with his chariots and his horsemen into the sea, and the LORD brought back the waters of the sea upon them. But the children of Israel went on dry *land* in the midst of the sea.

Then Miriam the prophetess, the sister of Aaron, took the timbrel in her hand; and all the women went out after her with timbrels and with dances. And Miriam answered them:

"Sing to the LORD,
For He has triumphed gloriously!
The horse and its rider
He has thrown into the sea!" EXODUS 15:1–21

While Moses and Miriam expressed their praise vocally, bold worship can also be displayed with very few words. Take Daniel, for example. His quiet refusal to worship anyone or anything but the one true God was risky because King Darius dealt harshly with disobedience in his kingdom. Unlike the songs of Moses and Miriam, it was Daniel's actions that did all the talking.

It pleased Darius to set over the kingdom one hundred and twenty satraps, to be over the whole kingdom; and over these, three governors, of whom Daniel *was* one, that the satraps might give account to them, so that the king would suffer no loss. Then this Daniel distinguished himself above the governors and satraps, because an excellent spirit *was* in him; and the king gave thought to setting him over the whole realm. So the governors and satraps sought to find *some* charge against Daniel concerning the kingdom; but they could find no charge or fault, because he *was* faithful; nor was there any error or fault found in him. Then these men said, "We shall not find any charge against this Daniel unless we find *it* against him concerning the law of his God."

So these governors and satraps thronged before the king, and said thus to him: "King Darius, live forever! All the governors of the kingdom, the administrators and satraps, the counselors and advisors, have consulted together to establish a royal statute and to make a firm decree, that whoever petitions any god or man for thirty days, except you, O king, shall be cast into the den of lions. Now, O king, establish the decree and sign the writing, so that it cannot be changed, according to the law of the Medes and Persians, which does not alter." Therefore King Darius signed the written decree.

Now when Daniel knew that the writing was signed, he went home. And in his upper room, with his windows open toward Jerusalem, he knelt down on his knees three times that day,

and prayed and gave thanks before his God, as was his custom since early days.

Then these men assembled and found Daniel praying and making supplication before his God. And they went before the king, and spoke concerning the king's decree: "Have you not signed a decree that every man who petitions any god or man within thirty days, except you, O king, shall be cast into the den of lions?"

The king answered and said, "The thing *is* true, according to the law of the Medes and Persians, which does not alter."

So they answered and said before the king, "That Daniel, who is one of the captives from Judah, does not show due regard for you, O king, or for the decree that you have signed, but makes his petition three times a day."

And the king, when he heard *these* words, was greatly displeased with himself, and set *his* heart on Daniel to deliver him; and he labored till the going down of the sun to deliver him. Then these men approached the king, and said to the king, "Know, O king, that *it is* the law of the Medes and Persians that no decree or statute which the king establishes may be changed."

So the king gave the command, and they brought Daniel and cast *him* into the den of lions. *But* the king spoke, saying to Daniel, "Your God, whom you serve continually, He will deliver you." Then a stone was brought and laid on the mouth of the den, and the king sealed it with his own signet ring and with the signets of his lords, that the purpose concerning Daniel might not be changed.

Now the king went to his palace and spent the night fasting; and no musicians were brought before him. Also his sleep went from him. Then the king arose very early in the morning and went in haste to the den of lions. And when he came to the den, he cried out with a lamenting voice to Daniel. The king spoke, saying to Daniel, "Daniel, servant of the living God, has your God, whom you serve continually, been able to deliver you from the lions?"

Then Daniel said to the king, "O king, live forever! My God sent His angel and shut the lions' mouths, so that they have not hurt me, because I was found innocent before Him; and also, O king, I have done no wrong before you."

Now the king was exceedingly glad for him, and commanded that they should take Daniel up out of the den. So Daniel was taken up out of the den, and no injury whatever was found on him, because he believed in his God.

And the king gave the command, and they brought those men who had accused Daniel, and they cast *them* into the den of lions—them, their children, and their wives; and the lions overpowered them, and broke all their bones in pieces before they ever came to the bottom of the den.

Then King Darius wrote:

To all peoples, nations, and languages that dwell in all the earth:

Peace be multiplied to you.

I make a decree that in every dominion of my kingdom *men must* tremble and fear before the God of Daniel.

For He *is* the living God,
And steadfast forever;
His kingdom *is the one* which shall not be destroyed,
And His dominion *shall endure* to the end.
He delivers and rescues,
And He works signs and wonders
In heaven and on earth,
Who has delivered Daniel from the power of the lions.

DANIEL 6:1–27

What effect did Daniel's bold worship have on the unbelieving King Darius? In what ways do you think our modern-day worship could have that same effect?

God's rescue of Daniel from the lions is just one example of His power and greatness.

God's signs and wonders are undeniably awe-inspiring. In the book of Acts, Paul's and Silas' boldness got them thrown into jail; then as they prayed and sang hymns of worship during the night, a sudden earthquake resulted in their release.

Now it happened, as we went to prayer, that a certain slave girl possessed with a spirit of divination met us, who brought her masters much profit by fortune-telling. This girl followed Paul and us, and cried out, saying, "These men are the servants of the Most High God, who proclaim to us the way of salvation." And this she did for many days.

But Paul, greatly annoyed, turned and said to the spirit, "I command you in the name of Jesus Christ to come out of her." And he came out that very hour. But when her masters saw that their hope of profit was gone, they seized Paul and Silas and dragged *them* into the marketplace to the authorities.

And they brought them to the magistrates, and said, "These men, being Jews, exceedingly trouble our city; and they teach customs which are not lawful for us, being Romans, to receive or observe." Then the multitude rose up together against them; and the magistrates tore off their clothes and commanded *them* to be beaten with rods. And when they had laid many stripes on them, they threw *them* into prison, commanding the jailer to keep them securely. Having received such a charge, he put them into the inner prison and fastened their feet in the stocks.

But at midnight Paul and Silas were praying and singing hymns to God, and the prisoners were listening to them. Suddenly there was a great earthquake, so that the foundations of the prison were shaken; and immediately all the doors were opened and everyone's chains were loosed. And the keeper of the prison, awaking from sleep and seeing the prison doors open, supposing the prisoners had fled, drew his sword and was about to kill himself. But Paul called with a loud voice, saying, "Do yourself no harm, for we are all here."

Then he called for a light, ran in, and fell down trembling before Paul and Silas. And he brought them out and said, "Sirs, what must I do to be saved?"

So they said, "Believe on the Lord Jesus Christ, and you will be saved, you and your household." Then they spoke the word of the Lord to him and to all who were in his house. And he took them the same hour of the night and washed *their* stripes. And immediately he and all his *family* were baptized. Now when he had brought them into his house, he set food before them; and he rejoiced, having believed in God with all his household.

And when it was day, the magistrates sent the officers, saying, "Let those men go."

ACTS 16:16–35

Why do you think God desires that we worship Him when we are in a difficult situation? When was the last time you worshiped God when it might not have immediately made sense to do so?

Worshiping Together

A relationship with God can be a private and personal experience, but much of worship is meant to be practiced in community. God is a community within Himself (Father, Son and Holy Spirit), and His Word encourages us to gather with other believers to encourage one another, pray together and remember God's love for us. Since the crucifixion, death and resurrection of Jesus, the dynamics of communal worship have changed drastically. Animal sacrifices are no longer required to restore a relationship with God. Instead, through Jesus' blood, shed as a voluntary sacrifice, those who repent and accept Jesus as their Savior will have their sins forgiven.

For the law, having a shadow of the good things to come, *and* not the very image of the things, can never with these same sacrifices, which they offer continually year by year, make those who approach perfect. For then would they not have ceased to be offered? For the worshipers, once purified, would have had no more consciousness of sins. But in those *sacrifices there is* a reminder of sins every year. For *it is* not possible that the blood of bulls and goats could take away sins.

Therefore, when He came into the world, He said:

> *"Sacrifice and offering You did not desire,*
> *But a body You have prepared for Me.*
> *In burnt offerings and sacrifices for sin*
> *You had no pleasure.*
> *Then I said, 'Behold, I have come—*
> *In the volume of the book it is written of Me—*
> *To do Your will, O God.'"*

Previously saying, *"Sacrifice and offering, burnt offerings, and offerings for sin You did not desire, nor had pleasure in them"* (which are offered according to the law), then He said, *"Behold, I have come to do Your will, O God."* He takes away the first that He may establish the second. By that will we have been sanctified through the offering of the body of Jesus Christ once *for all.*

And every priest stands ministering daily and offering repeatedly the same sacrifices, which can never take away sins. But this Man, after He had offered one sacrifice for sins forever, sat down at the right hand of God, from that time waiting till His enemies are made His footstool. For by one offering He has perfected forever those who are being sanctified.

But the Holy Spirit also witnesses to us; for after He had said before,

"This is the covenant that I will make with them after those days, says the LORD*: I will put My laws into their hearts, and in their minds I will write them," then He adds, "Their sins and their lawless deeds I will remember no more."* Now where there is remission of these, *there is* no longer an offering for sin.

Therefore, brethren, having boldness to enter the Holiest by the blood of Jesus, by a new and living way which He consecrated for us, through the veil, that is, His flesh, and *having* a High Priest over the house of God, let us draw near with a true heart in full assurance of faith, having our hearts sprinkled from an evil conscience and our bodies washed with pure water. Let us hold fast the confession of *our* hope without wavering, for He who promised *is* faithful. And let us consider one another in order to stir up love and good works, not forsaking the assembling of ourselves together, as *is* the manner of some, but exhorting *one another,* and so much the more as you see the Day approaching.

HEBREWS 10:1–25

The Lord's Supper essentially replaced the practice of animal sacrifice for sin in the New Testament church. When believers gather to pray, sing and learn, they break bread and share a cup of wine as a way of remembering Christ's love for them. Jesus introduced this new practice to His disciples the night before His crucifixion.

Then came the Day of Unleavened Bread, when the Passover must be killed. And He sent Peter and John, saying, "Go and prepare the Passover for us, that we may eat."

So they said to Him, "Where do You want us to prepare?"

And He said to them, "Behold, when you have entered the city, a man will meet you carrying a pitcher of water; follow him into the house which he enters. Then you shall say to the master of the house, 'The Teacher says to you, "Where is the guest room where I may eat the Passover with My disciples?"' Then he will show you a large, furnished upper room; there make ready."

So they went and found it just as He had said to them, and they prepared the Passover.

When the hour had come, He sat down, and the twelve apostles with Him. Then He said to them, "With *fervent* desire I have desired to eat this Passover with you before I suffer; for I say to you, I will no longer eat of it until it is fulfilled in the kingdom of God."

Then He took the cup, and gave thanks, and said, "Take this and divide *it* among yourselves; for I say to you, I will not drink of the fruit of the vine until the kingdom of God comes."

And He took bread, gave thanks and broke *it*, and gave *it* to them, saying, "This is My body which is given for you; do this in remembrance of Me."

Likewise He also *took* the cup after supper, saying, "This cup *is* the new covenant in My blood, which is shed for you. But behold, the hand of My betrayer *is* with Me on the table. And truly the Son of Man goes as it has been determined, but woe to that man by whom He is betrayed!"

Then they began to question among themselves, which of them it was who would do this thing.

Now there was also a dispute among them, as to which of them should be considered the greatest. And He said to them, "The kings of the Gentiles exercise lordship over them, and those who exercise authority over them are called 'benefactors.' But not so *among* you; on the contrary, he who is greatest among you, let him be as the younger, and he who governs as he who serves. For who *is* greater, he who sits at the table, or he who serves? *Is* it not he who sits at the table? Yet I am among you as the One who serves.

"But you are those who have continued with Me in My trials. And I bestow upon you a kingdom, just as My Father bestowed *one* upon Me, that you may eat and drink at My table in My kingdom, and sit on thrones judging the twelve tribes of Israel." LUKE 22:7–30

Of course, believers can also honor Jesus' sacrifice every day in the way that they choose to live. No one emphasized this more consistently than the apostle Paul. While under house arrest in Rome, Paul wrote to the Christians in the city of Colosse. He encouraged them to throw off their old, self-centered way of living and commit to live solely for the purpose of worshiping and serving God. Paul's instructions were not addressed to individual worshipers, but to the worship community as a whole.

If then you were raised with Christ, seek those things which are above, where Christ is, sitting at the right hand of God. Set your mind on things above, not on things on the earth. For you died, and your life is hidden with Christ in God. When Christ *who is* our life appears, then you also will appear with Him in glory.

Therefore put to death your members which are on the earth: fornication, uncleanness, passion, evil desire, and covetousness, which is idolatry. Because of these things the wrath of God is coming upon the sons of disobedience, in which you yourselves once walked when you lived in them.

But now you yourselves are to put off all these: anger, wrath, malice, blasphemy, filthy language out of your mouth. Do not lie to one another, since you have put off the old man with his deeds, and have put on the new *man* who is renewed in knowledge according to the image of Him who created him, where there is neither Greek nor Jew, circumcised nor uncircumcised, barbarian, Scythian, slave *nor* free, but Christ *is* all and in all.

Therefore, as *the* elect of God, holy and beloved, put on tender mercies, kindness, humility, meekness, longsuffering; bearing with one another, and forgiving one another, if anyone has a complaint against another; even as Christ forgave you, so you also *must do.* But above all these things put on love, which is the bond of perfection. **And let the peace of God rule in your hearts, to which also you were called in one body; and be thankful. Let the word of Christ dwell in you richly in all wisdom, teaching and admonishing one another in psalms and hymns and spiritual songs, singing with grace in your hearts to the Lord. And whatever you do in word or deed, *do* all in the name of the Lord Jesus, giving thanks to God the Father through Him.** COLOSSIANS 3:1–17

According to the apostle Paul, what was the centerpiece of New Testament worship? What attitudes and actions constituted proper worship?

WHAT WE BELIEVE

Throughout Scripture, believers in God are instructed to worship Him. We are not called to merely go through the motions but instead we are encouraged to authentically worship God from our very hearts—as broken as they may be. While worshiping God for who He is and what He has done for us can be a private and personal practice, we can also feel free to share our worship of the one true God with the world. Finally, the practice of worship should also be expressed in community with others. This pleases God and encourages us. We can worship God from our hearts through every single breath, expression, thought and activity of our lives. Doing this habitually will surely lead us closer to the great and gracious God of the universe. So, "Oh come, let us sing to the LORD*! Let us shout joyfully to the Rock of our salvation. Let us come before His presence with thanksgiving; Let us shout joyfully to Him with psalms" (Psalm 95:1–2).*

ACT

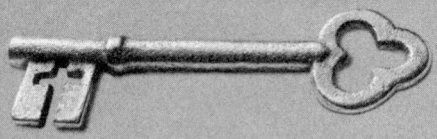

CHAPTER

12

Prayer

KEY QUESTION

How do I grow by communicating with God?

KEY IDEA

I pray to God to know Him, to find direction for my life and to lay my requests before Him.

KEY VERSE

If I regard iniquity in my heart, the Lord will not hear. *But* certainly God has heard *me*; he has attended to the voice of my prayer. Blessed *be* God, who has not turned away my prayer, nor His mercy from me!
Psalm 66:18 – 20

OUR MAP

The key beliefs of the Christian faith we studied in the first ten chapters emphasize that the one true God is a personal God who desires a real relationship with us. He provided the only way to this relationship through the sacrifice of His Son, Jesus Christ. When we embrace and receive Christ's forgiveness, we become children of God and gain access to Him. He is not a distant, cosmic being, but a good Father who longs to interact with His children. Prayer is the spiritual practice through which we take God up on His "open door" policy. Prayer is a conversation between God and His people. What an amazing privilege!

In this chapter we will find examples of those who model a vibrant prayer life, as well as information about how to use prayer to make the most of our relationship with God:

- *The Model Prayer Life*
- *A Way to Know God*
- *A Way to Find the Direction We Need*
- *A Way to Lay Our Requests Before God*

We serve a God who is not threatened by our questions and doubts. We don't have to put on a false persona to please Him. He permits us to be honest about our fears, our feelings of isolation and our disappointments. When we rehearse our story before Him, we see His personal involvement in our lives.

Come *and* hear, all you who fear God,
And I will declare what He has done for my soul.
I cried to Him with my mouth,
And He was extolled with my tongue.
If I regard iniquity in my heart,
The Lord will not hear.
But certainly God has heard *me;*
He has attended to the voice of my prayer.

Blessed *be* God,
Who has not turned away my prayer,
Nor His mercy from me! PSALM 66:16–20

The Model Prayer Life

Scripture contains many examples of men and women who demonstrated a dynamic prayer life, but there is a no more perfect model than Jesus. Spending time in prayer with the Father gave Him the strength and guidance He needed to fulfill His purpose in coming to earth. Jesus consistently sought direction and support from His Father, as we see on two occasions from early in His ministry.

Notice how Jesus prayed before and after each major event in His life. What can we learn from this pattern of prayer Jesus demonstrated throughout His life?

At evening, when the sun had set, they brought to Him all who were sick and those who were demon-possessed. And the whole city was gathered together at the door. Then He healed many who were sick with various diseases, and cast out many demons; and He did not allow the demons to speak, because they knew Him.

Now in the morning, having risen a long while before daylight, He went out and departed to a solitary place; and there He prayed. Mark 1:32–35

And also . . .

Now it came to pass in those days that He went out to the mountain to pray, and continued all night in prayer to God. And when it was day, He called His disciples to *Himself;* and from them He chose twelve whom He also named apostles: Simon, whom He also named Peter, and Andrew his brother; James and John; Philip and Bartholomew; Matthew and Thomas; James the *son* of Alphaeus, and Simon called the Zealot; Judas *the son* of James, and Judas Iscariot who also became a traitor. Luke 6:12–16

Sometime after choosing His disciples, Jesus received news that Herod had cruelly beheaded Jesus' cousin John the Baptist. Upon hearing the news and to avoid the threat of Herod, Jesus went by boat with His disciples to a solitary place. However, thou-

sands of followers got ahead of the group and met them when they landed on shore. Despite the interruption to His plans, Jesus took pity on the people and taught them about the kingdom of God. At the end of the day, when the people were hungry, the disciples told Jesus to send them away. But Jesus miraculously turned five loaves and two fish into a meal that would feed five thousand people. After the emotion of losing his cousin John and a long day of ministering, Jesus retreated to a secluded place to spend time with the Father.

Then [Jesus] commanded [the disciples] to make them all sit down in groups on the green grass. So they sat down in ranks, in hundreds and in fifties. And when He had taken the five loaves and the two fish, He looked up to heaven, blessed and broke the loaves, and gave *them* to His disciples to set before them; and the two fish He divided among *them* all. So they all ate and were filled. And they took up twelve baskets full of fragments and of the fish. Now those who had eaten the loaves were about five thousand men.

Immediately He made His disciples get into the boat and go before Him to the other side, to Bethsaida, while He sent the multitude away. And when He had sent them away, He departed to the mountain to pray. MARK 6:39–46

Prayer never ceased to be part of Jesus' life. As Jesus approached the conclusion of His ministry, He knew it would culminate on a cross, which typically meant a slow and excruciatingly painful death. Knowing what He was about to endure, Jesus took refuge in an extended time of prayer. He appealed to God for a way around the torture, though He remained unflinching in His resolve to accomplish His Father's will.

Then Jesus came with them to a place called Gethsemane, and said to the disciples, "Sit here while I go and pray over there." And He took with Him Peter and the two sons of Zebedee, and He began to be sorrowful and deeply distressed. Then He said to them, "My soul is exceedingly sorrowful, even to death. Stay here and watch with Me."

He went a little farther and fell on His face, and prayed,

saying, "O My Father, if it is possible, let this cup pass from Me; nevertheless, not as I will, but as You *will*."

Then He came to the disciples and found them sleeping, and said to Peter, "What! Could you not watch with Me one hour? Watch and pray, lest you enter into temptation. The spirit indeed *is* willing, but the flesh *is* weak."

Again, a second time, He went away and prayed, saying, "O My Father, if this cup cannot pass away from Me unless I drink it, Your will be done." And He came and found them asleep again, for their eyes were heavy.

So He left them, went away again, and prayed the third time, saying the same words. Then He came to His disciples and said to them, "Are *you* still sleeping and resting? Behold, the hour is at hand, and the Son of Man is being betrayed into the hands of sinners. Rise, let us be going. See, My betrayer is at hand."

MATTHEW 26:36–46

A WAY TO KNOW GOD

As Jesus modeled, prayer is the best way to become closer to God. The authors of the psalms seemed to understand this. The prayers in this book reveal that people in Bible times were very much like people today: they had hopes, fears, joy and pain. These writers spilled out to the powerful God of the universe what was on their hearts. They believed God wanted to know what they were experiencing and feeling. God longs to hear from us today as well.

I cried out to God with my voice—
To God with my voice;
And He gave ear to me.
In the day of my trouble I sought the Lord;
My hand was stretched out in the night without ceasing;
My soul refused to be comforted.
I remembered God, and was troubled;
I complained, and my spirit was overwhelmed.

You hold my eyelids *open;*
I am so troubled that I cannot speak.

I have considered the days of old,
The years of ancient times.
I call to remembrance my song in the night;
I meditate within my heart,
And my spirit makes diligent search.

Will the Lord cast off forever?
And will He be favorable no more?
Has His mercy ceased forever?
Has *His* promise failed forevermore?
Has God forgotten to be gracious?
Has He in anger shut up His tender mercies?

And I said, "This *is* my anguish;
***But I will remember* the years of the right hand of the Most High."**
I will remember the works of the LORD;
Surely I will remember Your wonders of old.
I will also meditate on all Your work,
And talk of Your deeds.
Your way, O God, *is* in the sanctuary;
Who *is* so great a God as *our* God?
You *are* the God who does wonders;
You have declared Your strength among the peoples.
You have with *Your* arm redeemed Your people,
The sons of Jacob and Joseph.

The waters saw You, O God;
The waters saw You, they were afraid;
The depths also trembled.
The clouds poured out water;
The skies sent out a sound;
Your arrows also flashed about.
The voice of Your thunder *was* in the whirlwind;
The lightnings lit up the world;
The earth trembled and shook.
Your way *was* in the sea,
Your path in the great waters,
And Your footsteps were not known.

You led Your people like a flock
By the hand of Moses and Aaron. PSALM 77:1–20

It's possible that Solomon was familiar with the psalmist's lyrics that ended with "You led Your people like a flock." The imagery of a flock of sheep who know the shepherd's voice is a repeated theme in Scripture. Perhaps that's why Solomon wrote in the next passage that we should approach prayer with a priority to listen. Like a shepherd, God makes Himself accessible, but we should not approach Him with hollow words, rote prayers, or promises made lightly. Prayer is an intimate conversation with God and should be treated as such.

Walk prudently when you go to the house of God; and draw near to hear rather than to give the sacrifice of fools, for they do not know that they do evil.

Do not be rash with your mouth,
And let not your heart utter anything hastily before God.
For God *is* in heaven, and you on earth;
Therefore let your words be few.
For a dream comes through much activity,
And a fool's voice *is known* by *his* many words.

ECCLESIASTES 5:1–3

What can we learn about prayer from the psalmist and Solomon?

A Way to Find the Direction We Need

Like a needle on a compass, prayer helps us navigate life's toughest obstacles. Heroes of the faith from the beginning to the end of the Bible used prayer to determine their actions. Often the directions they received seemed a bit odd. For example, Gideon, who was by no means fearless, was asked to lead the Israelites into battle against an army that greatly outnumbered his own. God's clear directions allowed him to triumph. But before he set out, Gideon asked God to give him clarity on this overwhelming assignment. This is a good practice for all of us today. When we take our concerns and questions to God, He will provide the clarity we need.

Then the children of Israel did evil in the sight of the LORD. So the LORD delivered them into the hand of Midian for seven years, and the hand of Midian prevailed against Israel. Because of the Midianites, the children of Israel made for themselves the dens, the caves, and the strongholds which *are* in the mountains. So it was, whenever Israel had sown, Midianites would come up; also Amalekites and the people of the East would come up against them. Then they would encamp against them and destroy the produce of the earth as far as Gaza, and leave no sustenance for Israel, neither sheep nor ox nor donkey. For they would come up with their livestock and their tents, coming in as numerous as locusts; both they and their camels were without number; and they would enter the land to destroy it. So Israel was greatly impoverished because of the Midianites, and the children of Israel cried out to the LORD.

And it came to pass, when the children of Israel cried out to the LORD because of the Midianites, that the LORD sent a prophet to the children of Israel, who said to them, "Thus says the LORD God of Israel: 'I brought you up from Egypt and brought you out of the house of bondage; and I delivered you out of the hand of the Egyptians and out of the hand of all who oppressed you, and drove them out before you and gave you their land. Also I said to you, "I *am* the LORD your God; do not fear the gods of the Amorites, in whose land you dwell." But you have not obeyed My voice.'"

Now the Angel of the LORD came and sat under the terebinth tree which *was* in Ophrah, which *belonged* to Joash the Abiezrite, while his son Gideon threshed wheat in the winepress, in order to hide *it* from the Midianites. And the Angel of the LORD appeared to him, and said to him, "The LORD *is* with you, you mighty man of valor!"

Gideon said to Him, "O my lord, if the LORD is with us, why then has all this happened to us? And where *are* all His miracles which our fathers told us about, saying, 'Did not the LORD bring us up from Egypt?' But now the LORD has forsaken us and delivered us into the hands of the Midianites."

Then the LORD turned to him and said, "Go in this might of yours, and you shall save Israel from the hand of the Midianites. Have I not sent you?"

So he said to Him, "O my Lord, how can I save Israel? Indeed my clan *is* the weakest in Manasseh, and I *am* the least in my father's house."

And the LORD said to him, "Surely I will be with you, and you shall defeat the Midianites as one man."

Then he said to Him, "If now I have found favor in Your sight, then show me a sign that it is You who talk with me. Do not depart from here, I pray, until I come to You and bring out my offering and set *it* before You."

And He said, "I will wait until you come back."

So Gideon went in and prepared a young goat, and unleavened bread from an ephah of flour. The meat he put in a basket, and he put the broth in a pot; and he brought *them* out to Him under the terebinth tree and presented *them.* The Angel of God said to him, "Take the meat and the unleavened bread and lay *them* on this rock, and pour out the broth." And he did so.

Then the Angel of the LORD put out the end of the staff that *was* in His hand, and touched the meat and the unleavened bread; and fire rose out of the rock and consumed the meat and the unleavened bread. And the Angel of the LORD departed out of his sight.

Now Gideon perceived that He *was* the Angel of the LORD. So Gideon said, "Alas, O Lord GOD! For I have seen the Angel of the LORD face to face."

Then the LORD said to him, "Peace *be* with you; do not fear, you shall not die." So Gideon built an altar there to the LORD, and called it The-LORD-*Is*-Peace. To this day it *is* still in Ophrah of the Abiezrites.

Now it came to pass the same night that the LORD said to him, "Take your father's young bull, the second bull of seven years old, and tear down the altar of Baal that your father has, and cut down the wooden image that *is* beside it; and build an altar to the LORD your God on top of this rock in the proper arrangement, and take the second bull and offer a burnt sacrifice with the wood of the image which you shall cut down." So Gideon took ten men from among his servants and did as the LORD had said to him. But because he feared his father's household and the men of the city too much to do *it* by day, he did *it* by night.

And when the men of the city arose early in the morning, there was the altar of Baal, torn down; and the wooden image that *was* beside it was cut down, and the second bull was being offered on the altar *which had been* built. So they said to one another, "Who has done this thing?" And when they had inquired and asked, they said, "Gideon the son of Joash has done this thing." Then the men of the city said to Joash, "Bring out your son, that he may die, because he has torn down the altar of Baal, and because he has cut down the wooden image that *was* beside it."

But Joash said to all who stood against him, "Would you plead for Baal? Would you save him? Let the one who would plead for him be put to death by morning! If he *is* a god, let him plead for himself, because his altar has been torn down!" Therefore on that day he called him Jerubbaal, saying, "Let Baal plead against him, because he has torn down his altar."

Then all the Midianites and Amalekites, the people of the East, gathered together; and they crossed over and encamped in the Valley of Jezreel. But the Spirit of the LORD came upon Gideon; then he blew the trumpet, and the Abiezrites gathered behind him. And he sent messengers throughout all Manasseh, who also gathered behind him. He also sent messengers to Asher, Zebulun, and Naphtali; and they came up to meet them.

So Gideon said to God, "If You will save Israel by my hand as You have said—look, I shall put a fleece of wool on the threshing floor; if there is dew on the fleece only, and *it is* dry on all the ground, then I shall know that You will save Israel by my hand, as You have said." And it was so. When he rose early the next morning and squeezed the fleece together, he wrung the dew out of the fleece, a bowlful of water. Then Gideon said to God, "Do not be angry with me, but let me speak just once more: Let me test, I pray, just once more with the fleece; let it now be dry only on the fleece, but on all the ground let there be dew." And God did so that night. It was dry on the fleece only, but there was dew on all the ground.

Then Jerubbaal (that *is,* Gideon) and all the people who *were* with him rose early and encamped beside the well of Harod, so that the camp of the Midianites was on the north side of them by the hill of Moreh in the valley.

And the LORD said to Gideon, "The people who *are* with you *are* too many for Me to give the Midianites into their hands, lest Israel claim glory for itself against Me, saying, 'My own hand has saved me.' Now therefore, proclaim in the hearing of the people, saying, 'Whoever *is* fearful and afraid, let him turn and depart at once from Mount Gilead.'" And twenty-two thousand of the people returned, and ten thousand remained.

But the LORD said to Gideon, "The people *are* still *too* many; bring them down to the water, and I will test them for you there. Then it will be, *that* of whom I say to you, 'This one shall go with you,' the same shall go with you; and of whomever I say to you, 'This one shall not go with you,' the same shall not go." So he brought the people down to the water. And the LORD said to Gideon, "Everyone who laps from the water with his tongue, as a dog laps, you shall set apart by himself; likewise everyone who gets down on his knees to drink." And the number of those who lapped, *putting* their hand to their mouth, was three hundred men; but all the rest of the people got down on their knees to drink water. Then the LORD said to Gideon, "By the three hundred men who lapped I will save you, and deliver the Midianites into your hand. Let all the *other* people go, every man to his place." So the people took provisions and their trumpets in their hands. And he sent away all *the rest of* Israel, every man to his tent, and retained those three hundred men. Now the camp of Midian was below him in the valley.

It happened on the same night that the LORD said to him, "Arise, go down against the camp, for I have delivered it into your hand. But if you are afraid to go down, go down to the camp with Purah your servant, and you shall hear what they say; and afterward your hands shall be strengthened to go down against the camp." Then he went down with Purah his servant to the outpost of the armed men who *were* in the camp. Now the Midianites and Amalekites, all the people of the East, were lying in the valley as numerous as locusts; and their camels *were* without number, as the sand by the seashore in multitude.

And when Gideon had come, there was a man telling a dream to his companion. He said, "I have had a dream: *To my* surprise, a loaf of barley bread tumbled into the camp of Midian; it came to a tent and struck it so that it fell and overturned, and the tent collapsed."

Then his companion answered and said, "This *is* nothing else but the sword of Gideon the son of Joash, a man of Israel! Into his hand God has delivered Midian and the whole camp."

And so it was, when Gideon heard the telling of the dream and its interpretation, that he worshiped. He returned to the camp of Israel, and said, "Arise, for the LORD has delivered the camp of Midian into your hand." Then he divided the three hundred men *into* three companies, and he put a trumpet into every man's hand, with empty pitchers, and torches inside the pitchers. And he said to them, "Look at me and do likewise; watch, and when I come to the edge of the camp you shall do as I do: When I blow the trumpet, I and all who *are* with me, then you also blow the trumpets on every side of the whole camp, and say, '*The sword of* the LORD and of Gideon!'"

So Gideon and the hundred men who *were* with him came to the outpost of the camp at the beginning of the middle watch, just as they had posted the watch; and they blew the trumpets and broke the pitchers that *were* in their hands. Then the three companies blew the trumpets and broke the pitchers—they held the torches in their left hands and the trumpets in their right hands for blowing—and they cried, "The sword of the LORD and of Gideon!" And every man stood in his place all around the camp; and the whole army ran and cried out and fled. When the three hundred blew the trumpets, the LORD set every man's sword against his companion throughout the whole camp; and the army fled to Beth Acacia, toward Zererah, as far as the border of Abel Meholah, by Tabbath.

JUDGES 6:1—7:22

What do Gideon's interactions with God teach us about God's character?

Like Gideon, shepherd-turned-king David experienced God's leading throughout his life. Psalm 25 captures David's passion for his Lord. Notice how David sought to know God personally by truthfully laying out his requests and seeking God's direction.

To You, O LORD, I lift up my soul.
O my God, I trust in You;
Let me not be ashamed;
Let not my enemies triumph over me.
Indeed, let no one who waits on You be ashamed;
Let those be ashamed who deal treacherously without cause.

Show me Your ways, O LORD;
Teach me Your paths.
Lead me in Your truth and teach me,
For You *are* the God of my salvation;
On You I wait all the day.

Remember, O LORD, Your tender mercies and Your lovingkindnesses,
For they *are* from of old.
Do not remember the sins of my youth, nor my transgressions;
According to Your mercy remember me,
For Your goodness' sake, O LORD.

Good and upright *is* the LORD;
Therefore He teaches sinners in the way.
The humble He guides in justice,
And the humble He teaches His way.
All the paths of the LORD *are* mercy and truth,
To such as keep His covenant and His testimonies.
For Your name's sake, O LORD,
Pardon my iniquity, for it *is* great.

Who *is* the man that fears the LORD?
Him shall He teach in the way He chooses.
He himself shall dwell in prosperity,
And his descendants shall inherit the earth.

The secret of the LORD *is* with those who fear Him,
And He will show them His covenant.
My eyes *are* ever toward the LORD,
For He shall pluck my feet out of the net. PSALM 25:1–15

A WAY TO LAY OUR REQUESTS BEFORE GOD

Because we are God's most prized creations, He wants to know the desires of our hearts. Scripture encourages us to lay our requests before Him without hesitation. The Bible includes many stories in which God's people express their needs, wants and desires to God. For example, after God issued the order to destroy the sin-filled cities of Sodom and Gomorrah, where Abraham's nephew Lot and his family lived, Abraham engaged in a conversation with God that displays the freedom we have to talk honestly with Him.

And the LORD said, "Because the outcry against Sodom and Gomorrah is great, and because their sin is very grave, I will go down now and see whether they have done altogether according to the outcry against it that has come to Me; and if not, I will know."

Then the men turned away from there and went toward Sodom, but Abraham still stood before the LORD. And Abraham came near and said, "Would You also destroy the righteous with the wicked? Suppose there were fifty righteous within the city; would You also destroy the place and not spare *it* for the fifty righteous that were in it? Far be it from You to do such a thing as this, to slay the righteous with the wicked, so that the righteous should be as the wicked; far be it from You! Shall not the Judge of all the earth do right?"

So the LORD said, "If I find in Sodom fifty righteous within the city, then I will spare all the place for their sakes."

Then Abraham answered and said, "Indeed now, I who *am but* dust and ashes have taken it upon myself to speak to the Lord: Suppose there were five less than the fifty righteous; would You destroy all of the city for *lack of* five?"

So He said, "If I find there forty-five, I will not destroy *it*."

And he spoke to Him yet again and said, "Suppose there should be forty found there?"

So He said, "I will not do *it* for the sake of forty."

Then he said, "Let not the Lord be angry, and I will speak: Suppose thirty should be found there?"

So He said, "I will not do *it* if I find thirty there."

And he said, "Indeed now, I have taken it upon myself to speak to the Lord: Suppose twenty should be found there?"

So He said, "I will not destroy *it* for the sake of twenty."

Then he said, "Let not the Lord be angry, and I will speak but once more: Suppose ten should be found there?"

And He said, "I will not destroy *it* for the sake of ten." So the LORD went His way as soon as He had finished speaking with Abraham; and Abraham returned to his place. GENESIS 18:20–33

King Hezekiah is another ancient leader who had the boldness to speak honestly before the Lord. Hezekiah was one of the few good kings in Judah during the era of the divided kingdom. He laid a daring personal request before God, and God answered with a powerful "yes."

In those days Hezekiah was sick and near death. And Isaiah the prophet, the son of Amoz, went to him and said to him, "Thus says the LORD: 'Set your house in order, for you shall die, and not live.'"

Then he turned his face toward the wall, and prayed to the LORD, saying, "Remember now, O LORD, I pray, how I have walked before You in truth and with a loyal heart, and have done *what was* good in Your sight." And Hezekiah wept bitterly.

And it happened, before Isaiah had gone out into the middle court, that the word of the LORD came to him, saying, "Return and tell Hezekiah the leader of My people, 'Thus says the LORD, the God of David your father: "I have heard your prayer, I have seen your tears; surely I will heal you. On the third day you shall go up to the house of the LORD. And I will add to your days fifteen years. I will deliver you and this city from the hand of the king of Assyria; and I will defend this city for My own sake, and for the sake of My servant David."'"

Then Isaiah said, "Take a lump of figs." So they took and laid *it* on the boil, and he recovered.

And Hezekiah said to Isaiah, "What *is* the sign that the LORD will heal me, and that I shall go up to the house of the LORD the third day?"

Then Isaiah said, "This is the sign to you from the LORD, that the LORD will do the thing which He has spoken: *shall* the shadow go forward ten degrees or go backward ten degrees?"

And Hezekiah answered, "It is an easy thing for the shadow to go down ten degrees; no, but let the shadow go backward ten degrees."

So Isaiah the prophet cried out to the LORD, and He brought the shadow ten degrees backward, by which it had gone down on the sundial of Ahaz. 2 KINGS 20:1–11

Our ultimate prayer model, Jesus, using tangible illustrations, encouraged His followers to be bold in their prayers.

In the following passage from Luke 11, what are the main points of Jesus' teaching about prayer?

Now it came to pass, as [Jesus] was praying in a certain place, when He ceased, *that* one of His disciples said to Him, "Lord, teach us to pray, as John also taught his disciples."

So He said to them, "When you pray, say:

Our Father in heaven,
Hallowed be Your name.
Your kingdom come.
Your will be done
On earth as *it is* in heaven.
Give us day by day our daily bread.
And forgive us our sins,
For we also forgive everyone who is indebted to us.
And do not lead us into temptation,
But deliver us from the evil one."

And He said to them, "Which of you shall have a friend, and go to him at midnight and say to him, 'Friend, lend me three loaves; for a friend of mine has come to me on his journey, and I have nothing to set before him'; and he will answer from within and say, 'Do not trouble me; the door is now shut, and my children are with me in bed; I cannot rise and give to you'? I say to you, though he will not rise and give to him because he is his friend, yet because of his persistence he will rise and give him as many as he needs.

"So I say to you, ask, and it will be given to you; seek, and you will find; knock, and it will be opened to you. For everyone who asks receives, and he who seeks finds, and to him who knocks it will be opened. If a son asks for bread from any father among you, will he give him a stone? Or if *he asks* for a fish, will he give him a serpent instead of a fish? Or if he asks for an egg, will he offer him a scorpion? If you then, being evil, know how to give good gifts to your children, how much more will *your* heavenly Father give the Holy Spirit to those who ask Him!"

LUKE 11:1–13

The result of prayerfully laying our requests before God is peace. The apostle Paul experienced this firsthand. He endured incredible hardships, including religious persecution, wrongful imprisonment and a catastrophic shipwreck. Yet in the letters he wrote to the churches he had started throughout the Mediterranean (letters to the Galatians, Ephesians, Philippians, Colossians, etc.), he encouraged the people to do something he was obviously modeling himself: despite circumstances, finding peace in God through prayer.

Be anxious for nothing, but in everything by prayer and supplication, with thanksgiving, let your requests be made known to God; and the peace of God, which surpasses all understanding, will guard your hearts and minds through Christ Jesus.

Finally, brethren, whatever things are true, whatever things *are* noble, whatever things *are* just, whatever things *are* pure, whatever things *are* lovely, whatever things *are* of good report, if *there is* any virtue and if *there is* anything praiseworthy—meditate on these things. The things which you learned and received and heard and saw in me, these do, and the God of peace will be with you.

PHILIPPIANS 4:6–9

How do Paul's words about prayer encourage you?
How do they challenge you?

WHAT WE BELIEVE

Prayer is not only a practice; it is a privilege! To have direct access to the one true God 24/7 proves He is a personal God who wants to be in a relationship with us. Each time we pray we affirm our identity as children of God. He not only gives us the right to come to Him, but He also longs for us to come to Him. Jesus modeled the life of prayer during His stay on earth. Prayer (talking, listening and resting in God's presence) is an effective way to know Him better and find direction for our lives. Why carry life's burdens alone when God invites us to lay them before Him? When we do, we find a peace "which surpasses all understanding."

ACT

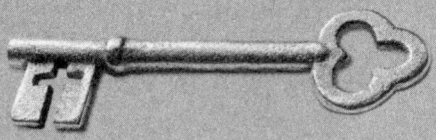

CHAPTER

13

Bible Study

KEY QUESTION

How do I study God's Word?

KEY IDEA

I study the Bible to know God and His truth
and to find direction for my daily life.

KEY VERSE

For the word of God *is* living and powerful, and sharper than any two-edged sword, piercing even to the division of soul and spirit, and of joints and marrow, and is a discerner of the thoughts and intents of the heart.
Hebrews 4:12

OUR MAP

The key idea highlighted in Chapter 4—the Bible is the Word of God and has the right to command our beliefs and actions—is a key belief for every Christian. Over many years God superintended the process to bring us His Word, His revelation. It is through the Bible that we learn how to think, act and become like Jesus. The ancient stories and words are "living and powerful" and totally capable of leading us along the right path. But like a trustworthy map, it must be used for it to be effective. Making Bible study a key practice can help us get to where God wants to take us.

In this chapter we will be reading about:

- *The First Scriptures*
- *The Road Map for Living*
- *Aids to Understanding*
- *A Transformed Life*

Each of these topics, supported with text from the Bible, is crafted to inspire and guide us to access the Bible for ourselves. So we read with great eagerness to learn from God's good Word and apply it to our lives!

The First Scriptures

Both Jews and Christians have traditionally regarded Moses as the author of the first five books of the Old Testament. Until the time of Moses, the words of God and the stories of His people were communicated orally from generation to generation. And even after Moses wrote these first portions of Scripture, the people didn't have access to their own complete copy. Before Moses died, the Lord led him to deliver farewell messages to the people, which are recorded in Deuteronomy. Parents were charged with the responsibility to share with their children God's principles and commandments. Moses also made a provision to ensure that everyone living in Israel would regularly and faithfully hear God's Word.

"You shall fear the LORD your God and serve Him, and shall take oaths in His name. You shall not go after other gods, the gods of the peoples who *are* all around you (for the LORD your God *is* a jealous God among you), lest the anger of the LORD your God be aroused against you and destroy you from the face of the earth.

"You shall not tempt the LORD your God as you tempted *Him* in Massah. You shall diligently keep the commandments of the LORD your God, His testimonies, and His statutes which He has commanded you. And you shall do *what is* right and good in the sight of the LORD, that it may be well with you, and that you may go in and possess the good land of which the LORD swore to your fathers, to cast out all your enemies from before you, as the LORD has spoken.

"When your son asks you in time to come, saying, 'What *is the meaning of* the testimonies, the statutes, and the judgments which the LORD our God has commanded you?' then you shall say to your son: 'We were slaves of Pharaoh in Egypt, and the LORD brought us out of Egypt with a mighty hand; and the LORD showed signs and wonders before our eyes, great and severe, against Egypt, Pharaoh, and all his household. Then He brought us out from there, that He might bring us in, to give us the land of which He swore to our fathers. And the LORD commanded us to observe all these statutes, to fear the LORD our God, for our good always, that He might preserve us alive, as *it is* this day. Then it will be righteousness for us, if we are careful to observe all these commandments before the LORD our God, as He has commanded us.'" DEUTERONOMY 6:13–25

So Moses wrote this law and delivered it to the priests, the sons of Levi, who bore the ark of the covenant of the LORD, and to all the elders of Israel. **And Moses commanded them, saying: "At the end of *every* seven years, at the appointed time in the year of release, at the Feast of Tabernacles, when all Israel comes to appear before the LORD your God in the place which He chooses, you shall read this law before all Israel in their hearing. Gather the people together, men and women and little ones, and the stranger who *is* within your gates, that they may hear and that they may learn to fear the LORD your God and carefully observe all the words of this law, and *that* their children, who have not known it, may hear and learn to fear the LORD your God as long as you live in the land which you cross the Jordan to possess."** DEUTERONOMY 31:9–13

After Moses' death, the mantle of leadership was passed to Joshua. God visited Joshua to remind him of the importance of following God's laws and commands.

After the death of Moses the servant of the LORD, it came to pass that the LORD spoke to Joshua the son of Nun, Moses' assistant, saying: "Moses My servant is dead. Now therefore, arise, go over this Jordan, you and all this people, to the land which I am giving to them—the children of Israel. Every place that the sole of your foot will tread upon I have given you, as I said to Moses. From the wilderness and this Lebanon as far as the great river, the River Euphrates, all the land of the Hittites, and to the Great Sea toward the going down of the sun, shall be your territory. No man shall *be able to* stand before you all the days of your life; as I was with Moses, *so* I will be with you. I will not leave you nor forsake you. Be strong and of good courage, for to this people you shall divide as an inheritance the land which I swore to their fathers to give them. Only be strong and very courageous, that you may observe to do according to all the law which Moses My servant commanded you; do not turn from it to the right hand or to the left, that you may prosper wherever you go. **This Book of the Law shall not depart from your mouth, but you shall meditate in it day and night, that you may observe to do according to all that is written in it. For then you will make your way prosperous, and then you will have good success.** Have I not commanded you? Be strong and of good courage; do not be afraid, nor be dismayed, for the LORD your God *is* with you wherever you go." JOSHUA 1:1–9

The value of reflecting on God's words was not lost on God's people. In 586 BC, Jerusalem was destroyed and the people of Judah went into exile in Babylon. In 537, the Jews began returning home. In 444, the restored community came together in Jerusalem to hear the reading of the Book of the Law of God. Revival broke out as the people were filled with great emotion and resolve. With an insatiable appetite for Scripture, they discovered the Lord's desire for them to observe the Feast of Tabernacles. The great joy with which the people celebrated had not been seen since the days of Joshua nearly a thousand years earlier.

Below you will read a touching account of Israel's return to God's Word from Nehemiah 7–9. In light of this and your own experiences, what are the benefits of studying God's Word in community?

When the seventh month came, the children of Israel *were* in their cities.

Now all the people gathered together as one man in the open square that *was* in front of the Water Gate; and they told Ezra the scribe to bring the Book of the Law of Moses, which the LORD had commanded Israel. So Ezra the priest brought the Law before the assembly of men and women and all who *could* hear with understanding on the first day of the seventh month. Then he read from it in the open square that *was* in front of the Water Gate from morning until midday, before the men and women and those who could understand; and the ears of all the people *were attentive* to the Book of the Law.

So Ezra the scribe stood on a platform of wood which they had made for the purpose; and beside him, at his right hand, stood Mattithiah, Shema, Anaiah, Urijah, Hilkiah, and Maaseiah; and at his left hand Pedaiah, Mishael, Malchijah, Hashum, Hashbadana, Zechariah, *and* Meshullam. And Ezra opened the book in the sight of all the people, for he was *standing* above all the people; and when he opened it, all the people stood up. And Ezra blessed the LORD, the great God.

Then all the people answered, "Amen, Amen!" while lifting up their hands. And they bowed their heads and worshiped the LORD with *their* faces to the ground.

Also Jeshua, Bani, Sherebiah, Jamin, Akkub, Shabbethai, Hodijah, Maaseiah, Kelita, Azariah, Jozabad, Hanan, Pelaiah, and the Levites, helped the people to understand the Law; and the people *stood* in their place. **So they read distinctly from the book, in the Law of God; and they gave the sense, and helped *them* to understand the reading.**

And Nehemiah, who *was* the governor, Ezra the priest *and* scribe, and the Levites who taught the people said to all the people,

"This day *is* holy to the LORD your God; do not mourn nor weep." For all the people wept, when they heard the words of the Law.

Then he said to them, "Go your way, eat the fat, drink the sweet, and send portions to those for whom nothing is prepared; for *this* day *is* holy to our Lord. Do not sorrow, for the joy of the LORD is your strength."

So the Levites quieted all the people, saying, "Be still, for the day *is* holy; do not be grieved." And all the people went their way to eat and drink, to send portions and rejoice greatly, because they understood the words that were declared to them.

Now on the second day the heads of the fathers' *houses* of all the people, with the priests and Levites, were gathered to Ezra the scribe, in order to understand the words of the Law. And they found written in the Law, which the LORD had commanded by Moses, that the children of Israel should dwell in booths during the feast of the seventh month, and that they should announce and proclaim in all their cities and in Jerusalem, saying, "Go out to the mountain, and bring olive branches, branches of oil trees, myrtle branches, palm branches, and branches of leafy trees, to make booths, as *it is* written."

Then the people went out and brought *them* and made themselves booths, each one on the roof of his house, or in their courtyards or the courts of the house of God, and in the open square of the Water Gate and in the open square of the Gate of Ephraim. So the whole assembly of those who had returned from the captivity made booths and sat under the booths; for since the days of Joshua the son of Nun until that day the children of Israel had not done so. And there was very great gladness. Also day by day, from the first day until the last day, he read from the Book of the Law of God. And they kept the feast seven days; and on the eighth day *there was* a sacred assembly, according to the *prescribed* manner.

Now on the twenty-fourth day of this month the children of Israel were assembled with fasting, in sackcloth, and with dust on their heads. Then those of Israelite lineage separated themselves from all foreigners; and they stood and confessed their sins and the iniquities of their fathers. And they stood up in their place and read from the Book of the Law of the LORD their God *for one*-fourth of the day; and *for another* fourth they confessed and worshiped the LORD their God. NEHEMIAH 7:73—9:3

THE ROAD MAP FOR LIVING

Judging by their reaction when they heard God's Word again after a long hiatus, the Israelites were lost without their road map for living. But there are other examples in the Bible of those who never seemed to lose sight of God's Word. For instance, the author of Psalm 19 relied on it to guide him, to help him in crisis, to gain understanding in confusing times, and to refresh him and give him joy.

The law of the LORD *is* perfect, converting the soul;
The testimony of the LORD *is* sure, making wise the simple;
The statutes of the LORD *are* right, rejoicing the heart;
The commandment of the LORD *is* pure, enlightening the eyes;
The fear of the LORD *is* clean, enduring forever;
The judgments of the LORD *are* true *and* righteous altogether.
More to be desired *are they* than gold,
Yea, than much fine gold;
Sweeter also than honey and the honeycomb.
Moreover by them Your servant is warned,
And in keeping them *there is* great reward.

Who can understand *his* errors?
Cleanse me from secret *faults.*
Keep back Your servant also from presumptuous *sins;*
Let them not have dominion over me.
Then I shall be blameless,
And I shall be innocent of great transgression.

Let the words of my mouth and the meditation of my heart
Be acceptable in Your sight,
O LORD, my strength and my Redeemer. PSALM 19:7–14

The value of reading and studying the Word of our strength and Redeemer is emphasized vividly throughout Psalm 119, the longest chapter in the Bible. In these portions, the passion the psalmist has for the Holy Scriptures is strikingly obvious.

How can a young man cleanse his way?
By taking heed according to Your word.
With my whole heart I have sought You;
Oh, let me not wander from Your commandments!
Your word I have hidden in my heart,
That I might not sin against You.
Blessed *are* You, O LORD!
Teach me Your statutes.
With my lips I have declared
All the judgments of Your mouth.
I have rejoiced in the way of Your testimonies,
As *much as* in all riches.
I will meditate on Your precepts,
And contemplate Your ways.
I will delight myself in Your statutes;
I will not forget Your word.

Deal bountifully with Your servant,
That I may live and keep Your word.
Open my eyes, that I may see
Wondrous things from Your law.
I *am* a stranger in the earth;
Do not hide Your commandments from me.
My soul breaks with longing
For Your judgments at all times.
You rebuke the proud—the cursed,
Who stray from Your commandments.
Remove from me reproach and contempt,
For I have kept Your testimonies.
Princes also sit *and* speak against me,
But Your servant meditates on Your statutes.
Your testimonies also *are* my delight
And my counselors.

PSALM 119:9–24

Teach me, O LORD, the way of Your statutes,
And I shall keep it *to* the end.
Give me understanding, and I shall keep Your law;
Indeed, I shall observe it with *my* whole heart.
Make me walk in the path of Your commandments,
For I delight in it.
Incline my heart to Your testimonies,
And not to covetousness.
Turn away my eyes from looking at worthless things,
And revive me in Your way.
Establish Your word to Your servant,
Who *is devoted* to fearing You.
Turn away my reproach which I dread,
For Your judgments *are* good.
Behold, I long for Your precepts;
Revive me in Your righteousness. PSALM 119:33–40

Oh, how I love Your law!
It *is* my meditation all the day.
You, through Your commandments, make me wiser
than my enemies;
For they *are* ever with me.
I have more understanding than all my teachers,
For Your testimonies *are* my meditation.
I understand more than the ancients,
Because I keep Your precepts.
I have restrained my feet from every evil way,
That I may keep Your word.
I have not departed from Your judgments,
For You Yourself have taught me.
How sweet are Your words to my taste,
Sweeter than honey to my mouth!
Through Your precepts I get understanding;
Therefore I hate every false way.

Your word *is* a lamp to my feet
And a light to my path.
I have sworn and confirmed
That I will keep Your righteous judgments.

I am afflicted very much;
Revive me, O LORD, according to Your word.
Accept, I pray, the freewill offerings of my mouth, O LORD,
And teach me Your judgments.
My life *is* continually in my hand,
Yet I do not forget Your law.
The wicked have laid a snare for me,
Yet I have not strayed from Your precepts.
Your testimonies I have taken as a heritage forever,
For they *are* the rejoicing of my heart.
I have inclined my heart to perform Your statutes
Forever, to the very end. PSALM 119:97–112

What is the difference between studying God's Word and hiding it in our hearts? What is the difference between reading God's Word and meditating on it day and night?

AIDS TO UNDERSTANDING

As you have probably observed, the Bible is unlike any other narrative. It is God's story, chock-full of amazing depth and application for our lives. Jesus reminds us that the condition of our hearts is important when we hear or read God's Word. If we are open and receptive to God's words, they will take root in our lives and transform us.

In the passage below, Jesus refers to four types of soil on which the seed of His Word falls. Which type best describes you right now? Was there a time when you would have answered differently?

Jesus went out of the house and sat by the sea. And great multitudes were gathered together to Him, so that He got into a boat and sat; and the whole multitude stood on the shore.

Then He spoke many things to them in parables, saying: "Behold, a sower went out to sow. And as he sowed, some *seed* fell by the wayside; and the birds came and devoured them. Some fell on stony places, where they did not have much earth; and they immediately sprang up because they had no depth of earth. But when the sun was up they were scorched, and because they had no root they withered away. And some fell among thorns, and the thorns sprang up and choked them. But others fell on good ground and yielded a crop: some a hundredfold, some sixty, some thirty. He who has ears to hear, let him hear!"

And the disciples came and said to Him, "Why do You speak to them in parables?"

He answered and said to them, "Because it has been given to you to know the mysteries of the kingdom of heaven, but to them it has not been given. For whoever has, to him more will be given, and he will have abundance; but whoever does not have, even what he has will be taken away from him. Therefore I speak to them in parables, because seeing they do not see, and hearing they do not hear, nor do they understand. And in them the prophecy of Isaiah is fulfilled, which says:

> *'Hearing you will hear and shall not understand,*
> *And seeing you will see and not perceive;*
> *For the hearts of this people have grown dull.*
> *Their ears are hard of hearing,*
> *And their eyes they have closed,*
> *Lest they should see with their eyes and hear with their ears,*
> *Lest they should understand with their hearts and turn,*
> *So that I should heal them.'*

But blessed *are* your eyes for they see, and your ears for they hear; for assuredly, I say to you that many prophets and righteous *men* desired to see what you see, and did not see *it,* and to hear what you hear, and did not hear *it.*

"Therefore hear the parable of the sower: When anyone hears the word of the kingdom, and does not understand *it,* then the wicked *one* comes and snatches away what was sown in his heart. This is he who received seed by the wayside. But he who received the seed on stony places, this is he who hears the word and immediately receives it with joy; yet he has no root in himself, but endures only for a while. For when tribulation or persecution arises because of the word, immediately he stumbles. Now he who received seed among the thorns is he who hears the word, and the cares of this world and the deceitfulness of riches choke the word, and he becomes unfruitful. **But he who received seed on the good ground is he who hears the word and understands *it*, who indeed bears fruit and produces: some a hundredfold, some sixty, some thirty."**

MATTHEW 13:1–23

But how do our hearts open up to God in order to be receptive to His words? Jesus told His disciples that after He returned to heaven, the Holy Spirit would come to reside in them and to remind them of everything He had said. This same Spirit lives in all believers today.

As you read the following passages from John 14 and 1 Corinthians 2, look for ways in which the Holy Spirit helps us understand Scripture.

"If you love Me, keep My commandments. And I will pray the Father, and He will give you another Helper, that He may abide with you forever—the Spirit of truth, whom the world cannot receive, because it neither sees Him nor knows Him; but you know Him, for He dwells with you and will be in you. I will not leave you orphans; I will come to you.

"A little while longer and the world will see Me no more, but you will see Me. Because I live, you will live also. At that day you will know that I *am* in My Father, and you in Me, and I in you. He who has My commandments and keeps them, it is he who loves Me. And he who loves Me will be loved by My Father, and I will love him and manifest Myself to him."

Judas (not Iscariot) said to Him, "Lord, how is it that You will manifest Yourself to us, and not to the world?"

Jesus answered and said to him, "If anyone loves Me, he will keep My word; and My Father will love him, and We will come to him and make Our home with him. He who does not love Me does not keep My words; and the word which you hear is not Mine but the Father's who sent Me.

"These things I have spoken to you while being present with you. But the Helper, the Holy Spirit, whom the Father will send in My name, He will teach you all things, and bring to your remembrance all things that I said to you. Peace I leave with you, My peace I give to you; not as the world gives do I give to you. Let not your heart be troubled, neither let it be afraid."

JOHN 14:15–27

The early church was devoted to the Word of God. However, at that time people did not have their own personal copies of the books of the Bible, so they had to rely heavily on the public reading of Scripture during their meetings. As promised by Jesus, the Holy Spirit came down to indwell believers.

One of the roles of the Holy Spirit is to illuminate the message of Scripture. It is through the Holy Spirit that we are able to understand the Bible's full meaning, accept it in our hearts and know how to apply it to our lives. The apostle Paul informed the church at Corinth of this truth.

And I, brethren, when I came to you, did not come with excellence of speech or of wisdom declaring to you the testimony of God. For I determined not to know anything among you except Jesus Christ and Him crucified. I was with you in weakness, in fear, and in much trembling. And my speech and my preaching *were* not with persuasive words of human wisdom, but in demonstration of the Spirit and of power, that your faith should not be in the wisdom of men but in the power of God.

However, we speak wisdom among those who are mature, yet not the wisdom of this age, nor of the rulers of this age, who are coming to nothing. But we speak the wisdom of God in a mystery, the hidden *wisdom* which God ordained before the ages for our glory, which none of the rulers of this age knew; for had they known, they would not have crucified the Lord of glory.

But as it is written:

"Eye has not seen, nor ear heard,
Nor have entered into the heart of man
The things which God has prepared for those
who love Him."

But God has revealed *them* to us through His Spirit. For the Spirit searches all things, yes, the deep things of God. For what man knows the things of a man except the spirit of the man which is in him? Even so no one knows the things of God except the Spirit of God. **Now we have received, not the spirit of the world, but the Spirit who is from God, that we might know the things that have been freely given to us by God.**

These things we also speak, not in words which man's wisdom teaches but which the Holy Spirit teaches, comparing spiritual things with spiritual. But the natural man does not receive the things of the Spirit of God, for they are foolishness to him; nor can he know *them,* because they are spiritually discerned. But he who is spiritual judges all things, yet he himself is *rightly* judged by no one. For *"who has known the mind of the* LORD *that he may instruct Him?"* But we have the mind of Christ. 1 CORINTHIANS 2:1–16

Anchoring our beliefs in the truth of God's Word is critical for the believer. Because of this, teachers of God's Word have a special calling to deliver the teachings of God's Word correctly, to call out false teachings and to model the message before the congregation and community.

Now the Spirit expressly says that in latter times some will depart from the faith, giving heed to deceiving spirits and doctrines of demons, speaking lies in hypocrisy, having their own conscience seared with a hot iron, forbidding to marry, *and commanding* to abstain from foods which God created to be received with thanksgiving by those who believe and know the truth. For every creature of God *is* good, and nothing is to be refused if it is received with thanksgiving; for it is sanctified by the word of God and prayer.

If you instruct the brethren in these things, you will be a good minister of Jesus Christ, nourished in the words of faith and of the good doctrine which you have carefully followed. But reject profane and old wives' fables, and exercise yourself toward godliness. For bodily exercise profits a little, but godliness is profitable for all things, having promise of the life that now is and of that which is to come. This *is* a faithful saying and worthy of all acceptance. For to this *end* we both labor and suffer reproach, because we trust in the living God, who is *the* Savior of all men, especially of those who believe. These things command and teach.

Let no one despise your youth, but be an example to the believers in word, in conduct, in love, in spirit, in faith, in purity. Till I come, give attention to reading, to exhortation, to doctrine. Do not neglect the gift that is in you, which was given to you by prophecy with the laying on of the hands of the eldership. Meditate on these things; give yourself entirely to them, that your progress may be evident to all. Take heed to yourself and to the doctrine. Continue in them, for in doing this you will save both yourself and those who hear you. 1 Timothy 4:1–16

Remind *them* of these things, charging *them* before the Lord not to strive about words to no profit, to the ruin of the hearers. **Be diligent to present yourself approved to God, a worker who does not need to be ashamed, rightly dividing the word of truth.** But shun profane *and* idle babblings, for they will increase to more ungodliness. 2 Timothy 2:14–16

A Transformed Life

The desired outcome of studying God's truth is transformation. It guides us along a path of maturity in Christ. We get into the Bible and the Bible turns around and gets into us and changes us for the good.

And having been perfected, He became the author of eternal salvation to all who obey Him, called by God as High Priest *"according to the order of Melchizedek,"* of whom we have much to say, and hard to explain, since you have become dull of hearing.

For though by this time you ought to be teachers, you need *someone* to teach you again the first principles of the oracles of God; and you have come to need milk and not solid food. For everyone who partakes *only* of milk *is* unskilled in the word of righteousness, for he is a babe. **But solid food belongs to those who are of full age, *that is,* those who by reason of use have their senses exercised to discern both good and evil.**

Therefore, leaving the discussion of the elementary *principles* of Christ, let us go on to perfection, not laying again the foundation of repentance from dead works and of faith toward God, of the doctrine of baptisms, of laying on of hands, of resurrection of the dead, and of eternal judgment. And this we will do if God permits.

HEBREWS 5:9—6:3

Reflect on the key verse at the beginning of this chapter. According to the author, the Word of God is like a two-edged sword; it gets under our skins and speaks directly to our hearts. In what ways have you experienced this?

WHAT WE BELIEVE

If we believe the Bible is the Word of God and can be trusted to guide us in the best and right direction, we must gain the skill and discipline to read, study, meditate on and apply it to our lives. God told Joshua that if he did this, he would be successful. God makes the same offer to us. When we open up God's Word, we learn more about the one true God who knows and loves us. The more we know about God's nature, character and movements, the easier it is to discern His will and direction for our lives. But the Bible can be a bit overwhelming, can't it? Remember, you are not alone. You have the Spirit of God within you and a community of believers around you to help you. So please don't give up. Keep reading!

ACT

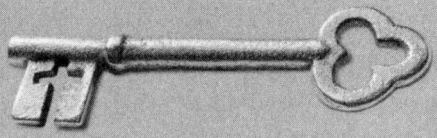

CHAPTER 14

Single-Mindedness

KEY QUESTION

How do I keep my focus on Jesus amidst distractions?

KEY IDEA

I focus on God and His priorities for my life.

KEY VERSE

But seek first the kingdom of God
and His righteousness, and
all these things shall be added to you.
Matthew 6:33

OUR MAP

To be single-minded means to have one desire that trumps all others. One goal. One focus. From the beginning God made clear that He should be His people's main focus. But this is challenging in a hectic, fast-paced world. It's easy for days, months and even years to get away from us. The spiritual practice of single-mindedness is all about determining our priorities to ensure we are practicing our faith, living out our beliefs and accomplishing God's will for our lives.

In this chapter we will be reading Scripture that addresses:

- *Principles of Single-Mindedness*
- *Profiles of Single-Mindedness*
- *Product of Single-Mindedness*

Principles of Single-Mindedness

"I *am* the Lord your God, who brought you out of the land of Egypt, out of the house of bondage.

"You shall have no other gods before Me." Exodus 20:2–3

In the first of the Ten Commandments, God commanded the Israelites to serve Him exclusively because He was worthy of their trust, as He had proved by delivering them from Egypt. Later, just before Moses died and the Israelites entered the promised land, God inspired Moses to remind the people of their single-minded calling.

We read this passage in Chapter 1 to reinforce that the God of the Bible is the one true God. Now we will read this powerful text again and hear the call to prioritize our lives around God.

As you read the passage below from Deuteronomy 6, look for what God promised to the Israelites if they obeyed the first commandment and kept their covenant with Him.

"Now this *is* the commandment, *and these are* the statutes and judgments which the Lord your God has commanded to teach you, that you may observe *them* in the land which you are crossing over to possess, that you may fear the LORD your God, to keep all His statutes and His commandments which I command you, you and your son and your grandson, all the days of your life, and that your days may be prolonged. Therefore hear, O Israel, and be careful to observe *it,* that it may be well with you, and that you may multiply greatly as the LORD God of your fathers has promised you—'a land flowing with milk and honey.'

"Hear, O Israel: The LORD our God, the LORD *is* one! You shall love the LORD your God with all your heart, with all your soul, and with all your strength.

"And these words which I command you today shall be in your heart. You shall teach them diligently to your children, and shall talk of them when you sit in your house, when you walk by the way, when you lie down, and when you rise up. You shall bind them as a sign on your hand, and they shall be as frontlets between your eyes. You shall write them on the doorposts of your house and on your gates." DEUTERONOMY 6:1–9

God's people were given the first commandment because they needed to submit fully to His authority and look to Him and Him only to provide all they needed. In the New Testament, Jesus described the "other gods" we might have in a way that hits close to home.

"Do not lay up for yourselves treasures on earth, where moth and rust destroy and where thieves break in and steal; but lay up for yourselves treasures in heaven, where neither moth nor rust destroys and where thieves do not break in and steal. For where your treasure is, there your heart will be also.

"The lamp of the body is the eye. If therefore your eye is good, your whole body will be full of light. But if your eye is bad, your whole body will be full of darkness. If therefore the light that is in you is darkness, how great *is* that darkness!

"No one can serve two masters; for either he will hate the one and love the other, or else he will be loyal to the one and despise the other. You cannot serve God and mammon."

MATTHEW 6:19–24

What kind of "treasure" keeps us from being single-minded?
How can "bad eyes" keep us from being single-minded?
Why isn't it possible to serve two masters?

Seeking first God's kingdom was the apostle Paul's message as he traveled from city to city teaching people about the gift of salvation and how believers could single-mindedly follow Christ. In many cases, a combative group of religious leaders approached the new churches after Paul had left and tried to undermine his authority and teaching. They boasted about their religious credentials and weighed down Paul's message with Jewish laws and traditions. This infuriated Paul, who then urged the believers to follow his example in keeping their focus steadfastly on Jesus alone.

Finally, my brethren, rejoice in the Lord. For me to write the same things to you *is* not tedious, but for you *it is* safe.

Beware of dogs, beware of evil workers, beware of the mutilation! For we are the circumcision, who worship God in the Spirit, rejoice in Christ Jesus, and have no confidence in the flesh, though I also might have confidence in the flesh. If anyone else thinks he may have confidence in the flesh, I more so: circumcised the eighth day, of the stock of Israel, *of* the tribe of Benjamin, a Hebrew of the Hebrews; concerning the law, a Pharisee; concerning zeal, persecuting the church; concerning the righteousness which is in the law, blameless.

But what things were gain to me, these I have counted loss for Christ. Yet indeed I also count all things loss for the excellence of the knowledge of Christ Jesus my Lord, for whom I have suffered the loss of all things, and count them as rubbish, that I may gain Christ and be found in Him, not having my own righteousness, which *is* from the law, but that which *is* through faith in Christ, the righteousness which is from God by faith; that I may know Him and the power of His resurrection, and the fellowship of His sufferings, being conformed to His death, if, by any means, I may attain to the resurrection from the dead.

Not that I have already attained, or am already perfected; but

I press on, that I may lay hold of that for which Christ Jesus has also laid hold of me. Brethren, I do not count myself to have apprehended; **but one thing *I do*, forgetting those things which are behind and reaching forward to those things which are ahead, I press toward the goal for the prize of the upward call of God in Christ Jesus.**

PHILIPPIANS 3:1–14

PROFILES OF SINGLE-MINDEDNESS

King Jehoshaphat of the southern kingdom of Judah faced a tremendous challenge. His land was threatened by a hostile army. Rather than being overcome by fear, Jehoshaphat led the people to turn to the Lord with single-minded and wholehearted trust.

In the following passage from 2 Chronicles 20, identify the key beliefs in which Jehoshaphat anchors his prayer. How can these key beliefs instill confidence in God's provision and guide our decisions?

The people of Moab with the people of Ammon, and *others* with them besides the Ammonites, came to battle against Jehoshaphat. Then some came and told Jehoshaphat, saying, "A great multitude is coming against you from beyond the sea, from Syria; and they are in Hazazon Tamar" (which *is* En Gedi). And Jehoshaphat feared, and set himself to seek the LORD, and proclaimed a fast throughout all Judah. So Judah gathered together to ask *help* from the LORD; and from all the cities of Judah they came to seek the LORD.

Then Jehoshaphat stood in the assembly of Judah and Jerusalem, in the house of the LORD, before the new court, and said: "O LORD God of our fathers, *are* You not God in heaven, and do You *not* rule over all the kingdoms of the nations, and in Your hand *is there not* power and might, so that no one is able to withstand You? *Are* You not our God, *who* drove out the inhabitants of this land before Your people Israel, and gave it to the descendants of Abraham Your friend forever? And they dwell in it, and have built You a sanctuary in it for Your name, saying, 'If disaster comes upon us—sword, judgment, pestilence, or famine—we will stand before this temple and in Your presence (for Your name *is* in this temple), and cry out to You in our affliction, and You will hear and save.' And now, here are the people of Ammon, Moab, and Mount Seir—whom You would not let Israel invade when they came out of the land of Egypt, but they turned from them and did not destroy them—here they are, rewarding us by coming to throw us out of Your possession which You have given us to inherit. O our God, will You not judge them? For we have no power against this great multitude that is coming against us; **nor do we know what to do, but our eyes *are* upon You."**

Now all Judah, with their little ones, their wives, and their children, stood before the LORD.

Then the Spirit of the LORD came upon Jahaziel the son of Zechariah, the son of Benaiah, the son of Jeiel, the son of Mattaniah, a Levite of the sons of Asaph, in the midst of the assembly. And he said, "Listen, all you of Judah and you inhabitants of Jerusalem, and you, King Jehoshaphat! Thus says the LORD to you: 'Do not be afraid nor dismayed because of this great multitude, for the battle *is* not yours, but God's. Tomorrow go down against them. They will surely come up by the Ascent of Ziz, and you will find them at the end of the brook before the Wilderness of Jeruel. **You will not *need* to fight in this *battle*. Position yourselves, stand still and see the salvation of the LORD, who is with you, O Judah and Jerusalem!' Do not fear or be dismayed; tomorrow go out against them, for the LORD *is* with you."**

And Jehoshaphat bowed his head with *his* face to the ground, and all Judah and the inhabitants of Jerusalem bowed before the LORD, worshiping the LORD. Then the Levites of the children of the Kohathites and of the children of the Korahites stood up to praise the LORD God of Israel with voices loud and high.

So they rose early in the morning and went out into the Wilderness of Tekoa; and as they went out, Jehoshaphat stood and said, "Hear me, O Judah and you inhabitants of Jerusalem: Believe in the LORD your God, and you shall be established; believe His prophets, and you shall prosper." And when he had consulted with the people, he appointed those who should sing to the LORD, and who should praise the beauty of holiness, as they went out before the army and were saying:

"Praise the LORD,
For His mercy *endures* forever."

Now when they began to sing and to praise, the LORD set ambushes against the people of Ammon, Moab, and Mount Seir, who had come against Judah; and they were defeated. For the people of Ammon and Moab stood up against the inhabitants of Mount Seir to utterly kill and destroy *them.* And when they had made an end of the inhabitants of Seir, they helped to destroy one another.

So when Judah came to a place overlooking the wilderness, they looked toward the multitude; and there *were* their dead bodies, fallen on the earth. No one had escaped.

When Jehoshaphat and his people came to take away their spoil, they found among them an abundance of valuables on the dead bodies, and precious jewelry, which they stripped off for themselves, more than they could carry away; and they were three days gathering the spoil because there was so much. And on the fourth day they assembled in the Valley of Berachah, for there they blessed the LORD; therefore the name of that place was called The Valley of Berachah until this day. Then they returned, every man of Judah and Jerusalem, with Jehoshaphat in front of them, to go back to Jerusalem with joy, for the LORD had made them rejoice over their enemies. So they came to Jerusalem, with stringed instruments and harps and trumpets, to the house of the LORD. And the fear of God was on all the kingdoms of *those* countries when they heard that the LORD had fought against the enemies of Israel. Then the realm of Jehoshaphat was quiet, for his God gave him rest all around.

2 CHRONICLES 20:1–30

While Jehoshaphat certainly proved that his focus was on God, Jesus serves as an exemplary model for the type of single-mindedness God had in mind when He announced in the first of His Ten Commandments: "You shall have no other gods before Me." Living out this ancient command, Jesus didn't make choices based on His desires or anyone else's expectations. His sole goal was to live according to His Father's will.

Then Jesus spoke to them again, saying, "I am the light of the world. He who follows Me shall not walk in darkness, but have the light of life."

The Pharisees therefore said to Him, "You bear witness of Yourself; Your witness is not true."

Jesus answered and said to them, "Even if I bear witness of Myself, My witness is true, for I know where I came from and where I am going; but you do not know where I come from and where I am going. You judge according to the flesh; I judge no one. And yet if I do judge, My judgment is true; for I am not alone, but I *am* with the Father who sent Me. It is also written in your law that the testimony of two men is true. I am One who bears witness of Myself, and the Father who sent Me bears witness of Me."

Then they said to Him, "Where is Your Father?"

Jesus answered, "You know neither Me nor My Father. If you had known Me, you would have known My Father also."

These words Jesus spoke in the treasury, as He taught in the temple; and no one laid hands on Him, for His hour had not yet come.

Then Jesus said to them again, "I am going away, and you will seek Me, and will die in your sin. Where I go you cannot come."

So the Jews said, "Will He kill Himself, because He says, 'Where I go you cannot come'?"

And He said to them, "You are from beneath; I am from above. You are of this world; I am not of this world. Therefore I said to you that you will die in your sins; for if you do not believe that I am *He,* you will die in your sins."

Then they said to Him, "Who are You?"

And Jesus said to them, "Just what I have been saying to you from the beginning. I have many things to say and to judge concerning you, but He who sent Me is true; and I speak to the world those things which I heard from Him."

They did not understand that He spoke to them of the Father.

Then Jesus said to them, "When you lift up the Son of Man, then you will know that I am *He,* and *that* I do nothing of Myself; but as My Father taught Me, I speak these things. And He who sent Me is with Me. The Father has not left Me alone, for I always do those things that please Him." As He spoke these words, many believed in Him.

JOHN 8:12–30

Unfortunately, Jesus' disciple Peter had a bit more trouble retaining his single-minded focus when he was distracted. Peter's experience is a good reminder of how we are to think about Jesus, and keep our eyes on Him, even when our thoughts get sidetracked or we feel frightened.

Jesus made His disciples get into the boat and go before Him to the other side, while He sent the multitudes away. And when He had sent the multitudes away, He went up on the mountain by Himself to pray. Now when evening came, He was alone there. But the boat was now in the middle of the sea, tossed by the waves, for the wind was contrary.

Now in the fourth watch of the night Jesus went to them, walking on the sea. And when the disciples saw Him walking on the sea, they were troubled, saying, "It is a ghost!" And they cried out for fear.

But immediately Jesus spoke to them, saying, "Be of good cheer! It is I; do not be afraid."

And Peter answered Him and said, "Lord, if it is You, command me to come to You on the water."

So He said, "Come." **And when Peter had come down out of the boat, he walked on the water to go to Jesus. But when he saw that the wind *was* boisterous, he was afraid; and beginning to sink he cried out, saying, "Lord, save me!"**

And immediately Jesus stretched out *His* hand and caught him, and said to him, "O you of little faith, why did you doubt?" And when they got into the boat, the wind ceased.

Then those who were in the boat came and worshiped Him, saying, "Truly You are the Son of God." MATTHEW 14:22–33

Can you list some of the things that distract you from putting God first in your life? What can you do to become more focused on God?

Ultimately, the disciples adopted Jesus' bold and unwavering devotion to God and His purposes.

And through the hands of the apostles many signs and wonders were done among the people. And they were all with one accord in Solomon's Porch. Yet none of the rest dared join them, but the people esteemed them highly. And believers were increasingly added to the Lord, multitudes of both men and women, so that they brought the sick out into the streets and laid *them* on beds and couches, that at least the shadow of Peter passing by might fall on some of them. Also a multitude gathered from the surrounding cities to Jerusalem, bringing sick people and those who were tormented by unclean spirits, and they were all healed.

Then the high priest rose up, and all those who *were* with him (which is the sect of the Sadducees), and they were filled with indignation, and laid their hands on the apostles and put them in the common prison. But at night an angel of the Lord opened the prison doors and brought them out, and said, "Go, stand in the temple and speak to the people all the words of this life."

And when they heard *that,* they entered the temple early in the morning and taught. But the high priest and those with him came and called the council together, with all the elders of the children of Israel, and sent to the prison to have them brought.

But when the officers came and did not find them in the prison, they returned and reported, saying, "Indeed we found the prison shut securely, and the guards standing outside before the doors; but when we opened them, we found no one inside!" Now when the high priest, the captain of the temple, and the chief priests heard these things, they wondered what the outcome would be. So one came and told them, saying, "Look, the men whom you put in prison are standing in the temple and teaching the people!"

Then the captain went with the officers and brought them without violence, for they feared the people, lest they should be stoned. And when they had brought them, they set *them* before the council. And the high priest asked them, saying, "Did we not strictly command you not to teach in this name? And look, you have filled Jerusalem with your doctrine, and intend to bring this Man's blood on us!"

But Peter and the *other* apostles answered and said: "We ought to obey God rather than men. The God of our fathers raised up Jesus whom you murdered by hanging on a tree. Him

God has exalted to His right hand *to be* Prince and Savior, to give repentance to Israel and forgiveness of sins. And we are His witnesses to these things, and *so* also *is* the Holy Spirit whom God has given to those who obey Him."

When they heard *this,* they were furious and plotted to kill them. Then one in the council stood up, a Pharisee named Gamaliel, a teacher of the law held in respect by all the people, and commanded them to put the apostles outside for a little while. And he said to them: "Men of Israel, take heed to yourselves what you intend to do regarding these men. For some time ago Theudas rose up, claiming to be somebody. A number of men, about four hundred, joined him. He was slain, and all who obeyed him were scattered and came to nothing. After this man, Judas of Galilee rose up in the days of the census, and drew away many people after him. He also perished, and all who obeyed him were dispersed. **And now I say to you, keep away from these men and let them alone; for if this plan or this work is of men, it will come to nothing; but if it is of God, you cannot overthrow it—lest you even be found to fight against God."**

And they agreed with him, and when they had called for the apostles and beaten *them,* they commanded that they should not speak in the name of Jesus, and let them go. So they departed from the presence of the council, rejoicing that they were counted worthy to suffer shame for His name. **And daily in the temple, and in every house, they did not cease teaching and preaching Jesus *as* the Christ.** Acts 5:12–42

Product of Single-Mindedness

Near the end of the book of Deuteronomy—and Moses' life—the Lord called the Israelites to make a choice: trust and obey His commands or go their own way. Speaking through Moses, God gave this message to His people. And what was the result of the people's decision? Because they chose obedience, the following seven years were the most fruitful years in Israel's history—the glory days!

(For you know that we dwelt in the land of Egypt and that we came through the nations which you passed by, and you saw their abominations and their idols which *were* among them—wood and stone and silver and gold); so that there may not be among you man or woman or family or tribe, whose heart turns away today from the LORD our God, to go *and* serve the gods of these nations, and that there may not be among you a root bearing bitterness or wormwood; and so it may not happen, when he hears the words of this curse, that he blesses himself in his heart, saying, 'I shall have peace, even though I follow the dictates of my heart'—as though the drunkard could be included with the sober.

"The LORD would not spare him; for then the anger of the LORD and His jealousy would burn against that man, and every curse that is written in this book would settle on him, and the LORD would blot out his name from under heaven. And the LORD would separate him from all the tribes of Israel for adversity, according to all the curses of the covenant that are written in this Book of the Law, so that the coming generation of your children who rise up after you, and the foreigner who comes from a far land, would say, when they see the plagues of that land and the sicknesses which the LORD has laid on it:

'The whole land *is* brimstone, salt, and burning; it is not sown, nor does it bear, nor does any grass grow there, like the overthrow of Sodom and Gomorrah, Admah, and Zeboiim, which the LORD overthrew in His anger and His wrath.' All nations would say, 'Why has the LORD done so to this land? What does the heat of this great anger mean?' Then *people* would say: 'Because they have forsaken the covenant of the LORD God of their fathers, which He made with them when He brought them out of the land of Egypt; for they went and served other gods and worshiped them, gods that they did not know and that He had not given to them. Then the anger of the LORD was aroused against this land, to bring on it every curse that is written in this book. And the LORD uprooted them from their land in anger, in wrath, and in great indignation, and cast them into another land, as *it is* this day.'

"The secret *things belong* to the LORD our God, but those *things which are* revealed *belong* to us and to our children forever, that *we* may do all the words of this law.

"Now it shall come to pass, when all these things come upon you, the blessing and the curse which I have set before you, and you call *them* to mind among all the nations where the LORD your God drives you, and you return to the LORD your God and obey His voice, according to all that I command you today, you and your children, with all your heart and with all your soul, that the LORD your God will bring you back from captivity, and have compassion on you, and gather you again from all the nations where the LORD your God has scattered you. If *any* of you are driven out to the farthest *parts* under heaven, from there the LORD your God will gather you, and from there He will bring you. Then the LORD your God will bring you to the land which your fathers possessed, and you shall possess it. He will prosper you and multiply you more than your fathers. **And the LORD your God will circumcise your heart and the heart of your descendants, to love the LORD your God with all your heart and with all your soul, that you may live.**

"Also the LORD your God will put all these curses on your enemies and on those who hate you, who persecuted you. And you will again obey the voice of the LORD and do all His commandments which I command you today. The LORD your God will make you abound in all the work of your hand, in the fruit of your body, in the increase of your livestock, and in the produce of your land for good. For the LORD will again rejoice over you for good as He rejoiced over your fathers, if you obey the voice of the LORD your God, to keep His commandments and His statutes which are written in this Book of the Law, *and* if you turn to the LORD your God with all your heart and with all your soul.

"For this commandment which I command you today *is* not *too* mysterious for you, nor *is* it far off. It *is* not in heaven, that you should say, 'Who will ascend into heaven for us and bring it to us, that we may hear it and do it?' Nor *is* it beyond the sea, that you should say, 'Who will go over the sea for us and bring it to us, that we may hear it and do it?' But the word *is* very near you, in your mouth and in your heart, that you may do it.

"See, I have set before you today life and good, death and evil, in that I command you today to love the LORD your God, to walk in His ways, and to keep His commandments, His statutes, and His judgments, that you may live and multiply; and the LORD your God will bless you in the land which you go to possess. But if your heart turns away so that you do not hear, and are drawn away, and worship other gods and serve them, I announce to you today that you shall surely perish; you shall not prolong *your* days in the land which you cross over the Jordan to go in and possess. **I call heaven and earth as witnesses today against you, *that* I have set before you life and death, blessing and cursing; therefore choose life, that both you and your descendants may live; that you may love the LORD your God, that you may obey His voice, and that you may cling to Him, for He *is* your life and the length of your days; and that you may dwell in the land which the LORD swore to your fathers, to Abraham, Isaac, and Jacob, to give them."**

DEUTERONOMY 29:16—30:20

In the New Testament, the apostle Paul also challenged believers to establish a single-minded commitment to God. And with his exhortations came encouraging promises about the fruitful results of such devotion. As it was for the Israelites, so it is with us today: if we single-mindedly focus on Christ and His will for our lives, we will experience our own glory days!

I beseech you therefore, brethren, by the mercies of God, that you present your bodies a living sacrifice, holy, acceptable to God, *which is* your reasonable service. **And do not be conformed to this world, but be transformed by the renewing of your mind, that you may prove what *is* that good and acceptable and perfect will of God.**

ROMANS 12:1–2

If then you were raised with Christ, seek those things which are above, where Christ is, sitting at the right hand of God. **Set your mind on things above, not on things on the earth.** For you died, and your life is hidden with Christ in God. When Christ *who is* our life appears, then you also will appear with Him in glory.

COLOSSIANS 3:1–4

And let the peace of God rule in your hearts, to which also you were called in one body; and be thankful. Let the word of Christ dwell in you richly in all wisdom, teaching and admonishing one another in psalms and hymns and spiritual songs, singing with grace in your hearts to the Lord. **And whatever you do in word or deed, *do* all in the name of the Lord Jesus, giving thanks to God the Father through Him.** COLOSSIANS 3:15–17

Paul writes, "Whatever you do in word or deed, do all in the name of the Lord Jesus." What does this admonishment mean to you? Does it change how you prioritize things in your life?

WHAT WE BELIEVE

The practice of single-mindedness is about setting priorities. This involves putting our past decisions and actions behind us and focusing on God's kingdom with help from the Holy Spirit. The Bible presents us with many inspiring profiles of people who have displayed tremendous single-mindedness for God, including King Jehoshaphat in the Old Testament and Jesus in the New Testament. During his early years Peter struggled to "fix his eyes" on Jesus, but later he and the disciples declared with great conviction in the face of persecution, "We ought to obey God rather than men" (Acts 3:29). The product of a life of single-minded determination and focus is an untouchable peace from the hand of the one true God who loves us deeply. Seek first God's kingdom!

ACT

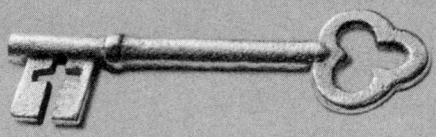

CHAPTER

15

Total Surrender

KEY QUESTION

How do I cultivate a life of sacrificial service?

KEY IDEA

I dedicate my life to God's purposes.

KEY VERSE

I beseech you therefore, brethren,
by the mercies of God, that you present your bodies
a living sacrifice, holy, acceptable to God,
which is your reasonable service.
Romans 12:1

OUR MAP

A genuine decision to follow and obey God is a decision of total surrender. We leave nothing off the negotiation table. We are "all in" as a reasonable response to God being "all in" for us. When God the Father offered up His Son for our redemption, He revealed how valuable we are to Him. The gift of salvation was an act of total surrender by our Savior. Are you willing to return the gesture? Are you prepared to surrender your life for His purposes?

Total surrender does not occur without some sacrifice, which is illustrated poignantly through the people and stories of the Bible:

- *The Expectation: What God Wants From Us*
- *Profiles of Total Surrender*
- *The Cost of Total Surrender*
- *The Inspiration of Martyrs*

Reflect on the key verse. What do you think it means to offer ourselves as "living sacrifices"? Recalling our study of the practice of worship in Chapter 11, why do you think offering ourselves as a living sacrifice is the reasonable way to serve God?

The Expectation: What God Wants From Us

God is often referred to in the Old Testament as "jealous." This passionate description comes out of the language of love, similar to that of a marriage. God is totally committed to us. He, in turn, asks us to be totally committed to Him. He will not share our allegiance with anyone or anything else. He made this very clear to the Israelites when He etched the Ten Commandments on the stone tablets. The first three commandments clearly communicate the exclusivity of our relationship with God.

And God spoke all these words, saying:

"I *am* the Lord your God, who brought you out of the land of Egypt, out of the house of bondage.

"You shall have no other gods before Me.

"You shall not make for yourself a carved image—any likeness *of anything* that *is* in heaven above, or that *is* in the earth beneath, or that *is* in the water under the earth; **you shall not bow down to them nor serve them. For I, the LORD your God, *am* a jealous God, visiting the iniquity of the fathers upon the children to the third and fourth *generations* of those who hate Me, but showing mercy to thousands, to those who love Me and keep My commandments.**

"You shall not take the name of the LORD your God in vain, for the LORD will not hold *him* guiltless who takes His name in vain."

EXODUS 20:1–7

The first three of the Ten Commandments govern our relationship with God. Why do you think it is important to get in a right relationship with God in order to keep the rest of God's commandments?

PROFILES OF TOTAL SURRENDER

Despite having God's expectations written in stone, the Israelites failed to remain faithful. After many years of disobedience, the people suffered when God removed His protection. The northern kingdom of Israel was destroyed by the Assyrians, and the southern kingdom of Judah was conquered by the Babylonians. Before Judah was captured, some of the people were carried off in deportations. Along with Daniel, a small group of bright young men—Shadrach, Meshach and Abed-Nego—were selected from the captives to be trained to serve the king. While in captivity, they were forced to make a crucial choice: worship the one true God or compromise and save their lives. They chose total surrender.

Nebuchadnezzar the king made an image of gold, whose height *was* sixty cubits *and* its width six cubits. He set it up in the plain of Dura, in the province of Babylon. And King Nebuchadnezzar sent *word* to gather together the satraps, the administrators, the governors, the counselors, the treasurers, the judges, the magistrates, and all the officials of the provinces, to come to the dedication of the image which King Nebuchadnezzar had set up. So the satraps, the administrators, the governors, the counselors, the treasurers, the judges, the magistrates, and all the officials of the provinces gathered together for the dedication of the image that King Nebuchadnezzar had set up; and they stood before the image that Nebuchadnezzar had set up. Then a herald cried aloud: "To you it is commanded, O peoples, nations, and languages, *that* at the time you hear the sound of the horn, flute, harp, lyre, *and* psaltery, in symphony with all kinds of music, you shall fall down and worship the gold image that King Nebuchadnezzar has set up; and whoever does not fall down and worship shall be cast immediately into the midst of a burning fiery furnace."

So at that time, when all the people heard the sound of the horn, flute, harp, *and* lyre, in symphony with all kinds of music, all the people, nations, and languages fell down *and* worshiped the gold image which King Nebuchadnezzar had set up.

Therefore at that time certain Chaldeans came forward and accused the Jews. They spoke and said to King Nebuchadnezzar, "O king, live forever! You, O king, have made a decree that everyone who hears the sound of the horn, flute, harp, lyre, *and* psaltery, in symphony with all kinds of music, shall fall down and worship the gold image; and whoever does not fall down and worship shall be cast into the midst of a burning fiery furnace. There are certain Jews whom you have set over the affairs of the province of Babylon: Shadrach, Meshach, and Abed-Nego; these men, O king, have not paid due regard to you. They do not serve your gods or worship the gold image which you have set up."

Then Nebuchadnezzar, in rage and fury, gave the command to bring Shadrach, Meshach, and Abed-Nego. So they brought these men before the king. Nebuchadnezzar spoke, saying to them, "*Is it* true, Shadrach, Meshach, and Abed-Nego, *that* you do not serve my gods or worship the gold image which I have set up? Now if you are ready at the time you hear the sound of the horn, flute, harp, lyre, *and* psaltery, in symphony with all kinds of music, and you fall down and worship the image which I have made, *good!* But if you do not worship, you shall be cast immediately into the midst of a burning fiery furnace. And who *is* the god who will deliver you from my hands?"

Shadrach, Meshach, and Abed-Nego answered and said to

the king, "O Nebuchadnezzar, we have no need to answer you in this matter. If that *is the case,* our God whom we serve is able to deliver *us* from the burning fiery furnace, and He will deliver us from your hand, O king. But if not, let it be known to you, O king, that we do not serve your gods, nor will we worship the gold image which you have set up."

Then Nebuchadnezzar was full of fury, and the expression on his face changed toward Shadrach, Meshach, and Abed-Nego. He spoke and commanded that they heat the furnace seven times more than it was usually heated. And he commanded certain mighty men of valor who *were* in his army to bind Shadrach, Meshach, and Abed-Nego, *and* cast *them* into the burning fiery furnace. Then these men were bound in their coats, their trousers, their turbans, and their *other* garments, and were cast into the midst of the burning fiery furnace. Therefore, because the king's command was urgent, and the furnace exceedingly hot, the flame of the fire killed those men who took up Shadrach, Meshach, and Abed-Nego. And these three men, Shadrach, Meshach, and Abed-Nego, fell down bound into the midst of the burning fiery furnace.

Then King Nebuchadnezzar was astonished; and he rose in haste *and* spoke, saying to his counselors, "Did we not cast three men bound into the midst of the fire?"

They answered and said to the king, "True, O king."

"Look!" he answered, "I see four men loose, walking in the midst of the fire; and they are not hurt, and the form of the fourth is like the Son of God."

Then Nebuchadnezzar went near the mouth of the burning fiery furnace *and* spoke, saying, "Shadrach, Meshach, and Abed-Nego, servants of the Most High God, come out, and come *here.*" Then Shadrach, Meshach, and Abed-Nego came from the midst of the fire. And the satraps, administrators, governors, and the king's counselors gathered together, and they saw these men on whose bodies the fire had no power; the hair of their head was not singed nor were their garments affected, and the smell of fire was not on them.

Nebuchadnezzar spoke, saying, "Blessed be the God of Shadrach, Meshach, and Abed-Nego, who sent His Angel and delivered His servants who trusted in Him, and they have frustrated the king's word, and yielded their bodies, that they should not serve nor worship any god except their own God!" DANIEL 3:1–28

About 70 years after the first deportation of Jews to Babylon, the Babylonians were conquered by the Persians. Although King Cyrus of Persia decreed in 538 BC that the Jews could return to Judah, many of them chose not to go home. We know that Esther and her cousin Mordecai stayed in Susa under the rule of the Persian king, Ahasuerus. When the reigning queen was removed from power, Esther (who kept her Jewish heritage a secret) was selected to replace her. Haman, the king's highest official, hated Mordecai because Mordecai refused to bow down and honor him. As revenge, Haman made plans to kill Mordecai and all the rest of the Jews in Ahasuerus' kingdom. Like Shadrach, Meshach and Abed-Nego, Esther had a difficult decision to make: protect her people or protect her position as queen—and perhaps her own life. She chose total surrender.

After these things King Ahasuerus promoted Haman, the son of Hammedatha the Agagite, and advanced him and set his seat above all the princes who *were* with him. And all the king's servants who *were* within the king's gate bowed and paid homage to Haman, for so the king had commanded concerning him. But Mordecai would not bow or pay homage. Then the king's servants who *were* within the king's gate said to Mordecai, "Why do you transgress the king's command?" Now it happened, when they spoke to him daily and he would not listen to them, that they told *it* to Haman, to see whether Mordecai's words would stand; for *Mordecai* had told them that he *was* a Jew. When Haman saw that Mordecai did not bow or pay him homage, Haman was filled with wrath. But he disdained to lay hands on Mordecai alone, for they had told him of the people of Mordecai. Instead, Haman sought to destroy all the Jews who *were* throughout the whole kingdom of Ahasuerus—the people of Mordecai.

In the first month, which is the month of Nisan, in the twelfth year of King Ahasuerus, they cast Pur (that *is,* the lot), before Haman to determine the day and the month, until *it fell on the* twelfth *month,* which *is* the month of Adar.

Then Haman said to King Ahasuerus, "There is a certain people scattered and dispersed among the people in all the provinces of your kingdom; their laws *are* different from all *other* people's, and they do not keep the king's laws. Therefore it *is* not fitting for the king to let them remain. If it pleases the king, let *a decree* be written that they be destroyed, and I will pay ten thousand talents of silver into the hands of those who do the work, to bring *it* into the king's treasuries."

So the king took his signet ring from his hand and gave it to Haman, the son of Hammedatha the Agagite, the enemy of the Jews. And the king said to Haman, "The money and the people *are* given to you, to do with them as seems good to you."

Then the king's scribes were called on the thirteenth day of the first month, and *a decree* was written according to all that Haman commanded—to the king's satraps, to the governors who *were* over each province, to the officials of all people, to every province according to its script, and to every people in their language. In the name of King Ahasuerus it was written, and sealed with the king's signet ring. And the letters were sent by couriers into all the king's provinces, to destroy, to kill, and to annihilate all the Jews, both young and old, little children and women, in one day, on the thirteenth *day* of the twelfth month, which *is* the month of Adar, and to plunder their possessions. A copy of the document was to be issued as law in every province, being published for all people, that they should be ready for that day. The couriers went out, hastened by the king's command; and the decree was proclaimed in Shushan the citadel. So the king and Haman sat down to drink, but the city of Shushan was perplexed.

When Mordecai learned all that had happened, he tore his clothes and put on sackcloth and ashes, and went out into the midst of the city. He cried out with a loud and bitter cry. He went as far as the front of the king's gate, for no one *might* enter the king's gate clothed with sackcloth. And in every province where the king's command and decree arrived, *there was* great mourning among the Jews, with fasting, weeping, and wailing; and many lay in sackcloth and ashes.

So Esther's maids and eunuchs came and told her, and the queen was deeply distressed. Then she sent garments to clothe

Mordecai and take his sackcloth away from him, but he would not accept *them.* Then Esther called Hathach, *one* of the king's eunuchs whom he had appointed to attend her, and she gave him a command concerning Mordecai, to learn what and why this *was.* So Hathach went out to Mordecai in the city square that *was* in front of the king's gate. And Mordecai told him all that had happened to him, and the sum of money that Haman had promised to pay into the king's treasuries to destroy the Jews. He also gave him a copy of the written decree for their destruction, which was given at Shushan, that he might show it to Esther and explain it to her, and that he might command her to go in to the king to make supplication to him and plead before him for her people. So Hathach returned and told Esther the words of Mordecai.

Then Esther spoke to Hathach, and gave him a command for Mordecai: "All the king's servants and the people of the king's provinces know that any man or woman who goes into the inner court to the king, who has not been called, *he has* but one law: put *all* to death, except the one to whom the king holds out the golden scepter, that he may live. Yet I myself have not been called to go in to the king these thirty days." So they told Mordecai Esther's words.

And Mordecai told *them* to answer Esther: "Do not think in your heart that you will escape in the king's palace any more than all the other Jews. For if you remain completely silent at this time, relief and deliverance will arise for the Jews from another place, but you and your father's house will perish. Yet who knows whether you have come to the kingdom for *such* a time as this?"

Then Esther told *them* to reply to Mordecai: **"Go, gather all the Jews who are present in Shushan, and fast for me; neither eat nor drink for three days, night or day. My maids and I will fast likewise. And so I will go to the king, which *is* against the law; and if I perish, I perish!"** ESTHER 3:1—4:16

THE COST OF TOTAL SURRENDER

A commitment to surrender completely to God's purposes is easy to say but hard to do. Jesus made this clear to His disciples and never masked the harsh reality they would encounter or the impact it would have on their lives. He also never shied away from difficult conversations, as is obvious from His interactions with Peter regarding the disciple's betrayal before Jesus' death. Through Peter's story, we learn that the cost of total surrender can sometimes feel like it's too much to bear.

Then [Jesus] said to *them* all, "If anyone desires to come after Me, let him deny himself, and take up his cross daily, and follow Me. For whoever desires to save his life will lose it, but whoever loses his life for My sake will save it. For what profit is it to a man if he gains the whole world, and is himself destroyed or lost? For whoever is ashamed of Me and My words, of him the Son of Man will be ashamed when He comes in His *own* glory, and *in His* Father's, and of the holy angels." LUKE 9:23–26

Now there was also a dispute among them, as to which of them should be considered the greatest. And He said to them, "The kings of the Gentiles exercise lordship over them, and those who exercise authority over them are called 'benefactors.' But not so *among* you; on the contrary, he who is greatest among you, let him be as the younger, and he who governs as he who serves. For who *is* greater, he who sits at the table, or he who serves? *Is* it not he who sits at the table? Yet I am among you as the One who serves.

"But you are those who have continued with Me in My trials. And I bestow upon you a kingdom, just as My Father bestowed *one* upon Me, that you may eat and drink at My table in My kingdom, and sit on thrones judging the twelve tribes of Israel."

And the Lord said, "Simon, Simon! Indeed, Satan has asked for you, that he may sift *you* as wheat. But I have prayed for you, that your faith should not fail; and when you have returned to *Me,* strengthen your brethren."

But he said to Him, "Lord, I am ready to go with You, both to prison and to death."

Then He said, "I tell you, Peter, the rooster shall not crow this day before you will deny three times that you know Me."

And He said to them, "When I sent you without money bag, knapsack, and sandals, did you lack anything?"

So they said, "Nothing."

Then He said to them, "But now, he who has a money bag, let

him take *it,* and likewise a knapsack; and he who has no sword, let him sell his garment and buy one. For I say to you that this which is written must still be accomplished in Me: *'And He was numbered with the transgressors.'* For the things concerning Me have an end."

So they said, "Lord, look, here *are* two swords."

And He said to them, "It is enough."

Coming out, He went to the Mount of Olives, as He was accustomed, and His disciples also followed Him. When He came to the place, He said to them, "Pray that you may not enter into temptation."

And He was withdrawn from them about a stone's throw, and He knelt down and prayed, saying, "Father, if it is Your will, take this cup away from Me; nevertheless not My will, but Yours, be done." Then an angel appeared to Him from heaven, strengthening Him. And being in agony, He prayed more earnestly. Then His sweat became like great drops of blood falling down to the ground.

When He rose up from prayer, and had come to His disciples, He found them sleeping from sorrow. Then He said to them, "Why do you sleep? Rise and pray, lest you enter into temptation."

And while He was still speaking, behold, a multitude; and he who was called Judas, one of the twelve, went before them and drew near to Jesus to kiss Him. But Jesus said to him, "Judas, are you betraying the Son of Man with a kiss?"

When those around Him saw what was going to happen, they said to Him, "Lord, shall we strike with the sword?" And one of them struck the servant of the high priest and cut off his right ear.

But Jesus answered and said, "Permit even this." And He touched his ear and healed him.

Then Jesus said to the chief priests, captains of the temple, and the elders who had come to Him, "Have you come out, as against a robber, with swords and clubs? When I was with you daily in the temple, you did not try to seize Me. But this is your hour, and the power of darkness."

Having arrested Him, they led *Him* and brought Him into the high priest's house. But Peter followed at a distance. Now when they had kindled a fire in the midst of the courtyard and sat down together, Peter sat among them. And a certain servant girl, seeing him as he sat by the fire, looked intently at him and said, "This man was also with Him."

But he denied Him, saying, "Woman, I do not know Him."

And after a little while another saw him and said, "You also are of them."

But Peter said, "Man, I am not!"

Then after about an hour had passed, another confidently affirmed, saying, "Surely this *fellow* also was with Him, for he is a Galilean."

But Peter said, "Man, I do not know what you are saying!"

Immediately, while he was still speaking, the rooster crowed. And the Lord turned and looked at Peter. Then Peter remembered the word of the Lord, how He had said to him, "Before the rooster crows, you will deny Me three times." So Peter went out and wept bitterly.

LUKE 22:24–62

What did Jesus mean when He instructed the disciples to "take up their cross daily"? Why does Jesus say this is a wise decision to make?

THE INSPIRATION OF MARTYRS

Despite his betrayal, Peter was graciously given a second chance to prove he was totally surrendered to God's purposes. After Jesus' resurrection, Jesus forgave and reinstated Peter to a leadership position. Peter boldly lived out his faith and later in his life, according to ancient tradition, was crucified upside down—perhaps because he didn't feel worthy of dying as Christ had.

Stephen, however, was the first martyr of the Christian church. Although he was not an apostle, he played an important role in the early church by ministering to the widows in Jerusalem and by being a powerful witness for Jesus. His death triggered a tidal wave of persecution in the first century. Stephen was brought before the Sanhedrin where he courageously put his total surrender to God on display.

And Stephen, full of faith and power, did great wonders and signs among the people. Then there arose some from what is called the Synagogue of the Freedmen (Cyrenians, Alexandrians, and those from Cilicia and Asia), disputing with Stephen. And they were not able to resist the wisdom and the Spirit by which he spoke. Then they secretly induced men to say, "We have heard him speak blasphemous words against Moses and God." And they stirred up the people, the elders, and the scribes; and they came upon *him,* seized him, and brought *him* to the council. They also set up false witnesses who said, "This man does not cease to speak blasphemous words against this holy place and the law; for we have heard him say that this Jesus of Nazareth will destroy this place and change the customs which Moses delivered to us." And all who sat in the council, looking steadfastly at him, saw his face as the face of an angel.

Then the high priest said, "Are these things so?"

And he said, "Brethren and fathers, listen: The God of glory appeared to our father Abraham when he was in Mesopotamia, before he dwelt in Haran, and said to him, *'Get out of your country and from your relatives, and come to a land that I will show you.'* Then he came out of the land of the Chaldeans and dwelt in Haran. And from there, when his father was dead, He moved him to this land in which you now dwell. And *God* gave him no inheritance in it, not even *enough* to set his foot on. But even when *Abraham* had no child, He promised to give it to him for a possession, and to his descendants after him. But God spoke in this way: that his descendants would dwell in a foreign land, and that they would bring them into bondage and oppress *them* four hundred years. *'And the nation to whom they will be in bondage I will judge,'* said God, *'and after that they shall come out and serve Me in this place.'* Then He gave him the covenant of circumcision; and so *Abraham* begot Isaac and circumcised him on the eighth day; and Isaac *begot* Jacob, and Jacob *begot* the twelve patriarchs.

"And the patriarchs, becoming envious, sold Joseph into Egypt. But God was with him and delivered him out of all his troubles, and gave him favor and wisdom in the presence of Pharaoh, king of Egypt; and he made him governor over Egypt and all his house. Now a famine and great trouble came over all the land of Egypt and Canaan, and our fathers found no sustenance. But when Jacob heard that there was grain in Egypt, he sent out our fathers first.

And the second *time* Joseph was made known to his brothers, and Joseph's family became known to the Pharaoh. Then Joseph sent and called his father Jacob and all his relatives to *him,* seventy-five people. So Jacob went down to Egypt; and he died, he and our fathers. And they were carried back to Shechem and laid in the tomb that Abraham bought for a sum of money from the sons of Hamor, *the father* of Shechem.

"But when the time of the promise drew near which God had sworn to Abraham, the people grew and multiplied in Egypt till another king arose who did not know Joseph. This man dealt treacherously with our people, and oppressed our forefathers, making them expose their babies, so that they might not live. At this time Moses was born, and was well pleasing to God; and he was brought up in his father's house for three months. But when he was set out, Pharaoh's daughter took him away and brought him up as her own son. And Moses was learned in all the wisdom of the Egyptians, and was mighty in words and deeds.

"Now when he was forty years old, it came into his heart to visit his brethren, the children of Israel. And seeing one of *them* suffer wrong, he defended and avenged him who was oppressed, and struck down the Egyptian. For he supposed that his brethren would have understood that God would deliver them by his hand, but they did not understand. And the next day he appeared to *two of* them as they were fighting, and *tried to* reconcile them, saying, 'Men, you are brethren; why do you wrong one another?' But he who did his neighbor wrong pushed him away, saying, *'Who made you a ruler and a judge over us? Do you want to kill me as you did the Egyptian yesterday?'* Then, at this saying, Moses fled and became a dweller in the land of Midian, where he had two sons.

"And when forty years had passed, an Angel of the Lord appeared to him in a flame of fire in a bush, in the wilderness of Mount Sinai. When Moses saw *it,* he marveled at the sight; and as he drew near to observe, the voice of the Lord came to him, *saying, 'I am the God of your fathers—the God of Abraham, the God of Isaac, and the God of Jacob.'* And Moses trembled and dared not look. *'Then the* LORD *said to him, "Take your sandals off your feet, for the place where you stand is holy ground. I have surely seen the oppression of My people who are in Egypt; I have heard their groaning and have come down to deliver them. And now come, I will send you to Egypt."'*

"This Moses whom they rejected, saying, *'Who made you a ruler and a judge?'* is the one God sent *to be* a ruler and a deliverer by the hand of the Angel who appeared to him in the bush. He brought them out, after he had shown wonders and signs in the land of Egypt, and in the Red Sea, and in the wilderness forty years.

"This is that Moses who said to the children of Israel, *'The LORD your God will raise up for you a Prophet like me from your brethren. Him you shall hear.'*

"This is he who was in the congregation in the wilderness with the Angel who spoke to him on Mount Sinai, and *with* our fathers, the one who received the living oracles to give to us, whom our fathers would not obey, but rejected. And in their hearts they turned back to Egypt, saying to Aaron, *'Make us gods to go before us; as for this Moses who brought us out of the land of Egypt, we do not know what has become of him.'* And they made a calf in those days, offered sacrifices to the idol, and rejoiced in the works of their own hands. Then God turned and gave them up to worship the host of heaven, as it is written in the book of the Prophets:

> *'Did you offer Me slaughtered animals and sacrifices*
> *during forty years in the wilderness,*
> *O house of Israel?*
> *You also took up the tabernacle of Moloch,*
> *And the star of your god Remphan,*
> *Images which you made to worship;*
> *And I will carry you away beyond Babylon.'*

"Our fathers had the tabernacle of witness in the wilderness, as He appointed, instructing Moses to make it according to the pattern that he had seen, which our fathers, having received it in turn, also brought with Joshua into the land possessed by the Gentiles, whom God drove out before the face of our fathers until the days of David, who found favor before God and asked to find a dwelling for the God of Jacob. But Solomon built Him a house.

"However, the Most High does not dwell in temples made with hands, as the prophet says:

'Heaven is My throne,
And earth is My footstool.
What house will you build for Me? says the LORD,
Or what is the place of My rest?
Has My hand not made all these things?'

"*You* stiff-necked and uncircumcised in heart and ears! You always resist the Holy Spirit; as your fathers *did,* so *do* you. Which of the prophets did your fathers not persecute? And they killed those who foretold the coming of the Just One, of whom you now have become the betrayers and murderers, who have received the law by the direction of angels and have not kept *it.*"

When they heard these things they were cut to the heart, and they gnashed at him with *their* teeth. But he, being full of the Holy Spirit, gazed into heaven and saw the glory of God, and Jesus standing at the right hand of God, and said, "Look! I see the heavens opened and the Son of Man standing at the right hand of God!"

Then they cried out with a loud voice, stopped their ears, and ran at him with one accord; and they cast *him* out of the city and stoned *him.* And the witnesses laid down their clothes at the feet of a young man named Saul. **And they stoned Stephen as he was calling on *God* and saying, "Lord Jesus, receive my spirit." Then he knelt down and cried out with a loud voice, "Lord, do not charge them with this sin." And when he had said this, he fell asleep.** ACTS 6:8—7:60

Compare and contrast Stephen's story with the story of Shadrach, Meshach and Abed-Nego. Compare Stephen's death with the death of Christ. Which detail of each story best exemplifies total surrender?

Another martyr of the early church was the apostle Paul. While traveling throughout the Roman Empire on numerous missionary journeys, Paul formed countless close friendships and made some serious enemies. Knowing that severe hardship was in his future, he met with many believers for what he assumed would be one last time.

And finding disciples, we stayed there seven days. They told Paul through the Spirit not to go up to Jerusalem. When we had come to the end of those days, we departed and went on our way; and they all accompanied us, with wives and children, till *we were* out of the city. And we knelt down on the shore and prayed. When we had taken our leave of one another, we boarded the ship, and they returned home.

And when we had finished *our* voyage from Tyre, we came to Ptolemais, greeted the brethren, and stayed with them one day. On the next *day* we who were Paul's companions departed and came to Caesarea, and entered the house of Philip the evangelist, who was *one* of the seven, and stayed with him. Now this man had four virgin daughters who prophesied. And as we stayed many days, a certain prophet named Agabus came down from Judea. When he had come to us, he took Paul's belt, bound his *own* hands and feet, and said, "Thus says the Holy Spirit, 'So shall the Jews at Jerusalem bind the man who owns this belt, and deliver *him* into the hands of the Gentiles.'"

Now when we heard these things, both we and those from that place pleaded with him not to go up to Jerusalem. **Then Paul answered, "What do you mean by weeping and breaking my heart? For I am ready not only to be bound, but also to die at Jerusalem for the name of the Lord Jesus."**

So when he would not be persuaded, we ceased, saying, "The will of the Lord be done." ACTS 21:4–14

The predictions made by Agabus were correct. Paul was arrested in Jerusalem and spent a couple of years imprisoned in Caesarea before finally being shipped to Rome, where he remained under house arrest for a couple more years. Jesus promised that when we lose our life we will truly find it. Surrendering his life for God's purposes was Paul's ultimate goal. Will you make it yours?

But I want you to know, brethren, that the things *which happened* to me have actually turned out for the furtherance of the gospel, so that it has become evident to the whole palace guard, and to all the rest, that my chains are in Christ; and most of the brethren in the Lord, having become confident by my chains, are much more bold to speak the word without fear.

Some indeed preach Christ even from envy and strife, and some also from goodwill: The former preach Christ from selfish ambition, not sincerely, supposing to add affliction to my chains; but the latter out of love, knowing that I am appointed for the defense of the gospel. What then? Only *that* in every way, whether in pretense or in truth, Christ is preached; and in this I rejoice, yes, and will rejoice.

For I know that this will turn out for my deliverance through your prayer and the supply of the Spirit of Jesus Christ, **according to my earnest expectation and hope that in nothing I shall be ashamed, but with all boldness, as always, so now also Christ will be magnified in my body, whether by life or by death. For to me, to live *is* Christ, and to die *is* gain.** PHILIPPIANS 1:12–21

Which of the stories you've read inspires you the most? Why?

WHAT WE BELIEVE

The decision to dedicate our lives to God's purposes is a daily practice. Jesus instructed His disciples to take up their cross daily and follow Him. God expects this kind of dedication from us as well. Part of this dedication includes being a "living sacrifice," which requires a daily decision to crawl up on the altar. Thankfully, we can find inspiration from the stories of many courageous and faithful followers of God, including Shadrach, Meshach, Abed-Nego, Esther, Stephen and Paul. We can also find comfort from the life of Peter, who denied Jesus three times in some of the most critical moments of Jesus' life. Because of the unconditional love He had for him, Jesus restored Peter. And He will do the same for us!

ACT

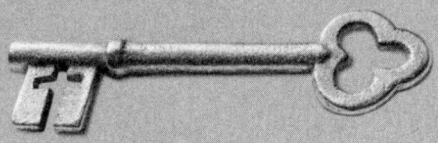

CHAPTER

16

Biblical Community

KEY QUESTION

How do I develop healthy relationships with others?

KEY IDEA

I fellowship with Christians to accomplish God's purposes in my life, in the lives of others and in the world.

KEY VERSE

Now all who believed were together, and had all things in common, and sold their possessions and goods, and divided them among all, as anyone had need. So continuing daily with one accord in the temple, and breaking bread from house to house, they ate their food with gladness and simplicity of heart, praising God and having favor with all the people. And the Lord added to the church daily those who were being saved.
Acts 2:44–47

OUR MAP

We are at the halfway point in our study of the ten key practices. The first five deepen our relationship with God: worship, prayer, Bible study, single-mindedness and total surrender. Now we shift to those that bless our relationships with people around us. The first of these is Biblical community.

We believe the one true God wants to be in a relationship with us for eternity. To make that possible, God provided the way to restore our relationship with Him—through the sacrifice of His Son, Jesus Christ. All those who believe receive a new identity and come together to form a new community called the church. It is through the church that God will accomplish His primary purposes on earth.

Biblical community is essential to the Christian life and a vital aspect of the church. As we engage in this new family under God's leadership, we not only achieve God's purposes in our lives, in the lives of others and in the world, but we also reinforce our belief in God and His church.

Here are the big ideas we will be exploring in this chapter:

- *Created for Community*
- *The Presence of God*
- *The New Community*
- *Marks of Biblical Community*

Created for Community

From the creation account in previous chapters we learned about the Trinity and the origin of sin. Both are necessary to revisit as we talk about how we were created for community. From the beginning, God designed and hardwired us for community. Biblical community is both vertical and horizontal, between God and us, and between us and others. When God planted the garden in Eden, He established one rule that would guard Adam's ability to be in unbroken community with Him—to eat from any tree but the tree of the knowledge of good and evil. Then He created Eve, so that Adam, like God, would not be alone but would have a being out of his own essence with whom to be in community.

This *is* the history of the heavens and the earth when they were created, in the day that the LORD God made the earth and the heavens, before any plant of the field was in the earth and before any herb of the field had grown. For the LORD God had not caused it to rain on the earth, and *there was* no man to till the ground; but a mist went up from the earth and watered the whole face of the ground.

And the LORD God formed man *of* the dust of the ground, and breathed into his nostrils the breath of life; and man became a living being.

The LORD God planted a garden eastward in Eden, and there He put the man whom He had formed. And out of the ground the LORD God made every tree grow that is pleasant to the sight and good for food. The tree of life *was* also in the midst of the garden, and the tree of the knowledge of good and evil.

Now a river went out of Eden to water the garden, and from there it parted and became four riverheads. The name of the first *is* Pishon; it *is* the one which skirts the whole land of Havilah, where *there is* gold. And the gold of that land *is* good. Bdellium and the onyx stone *are* there. The name of the second river *is* Gihon; it *is* the one which goes around the whole land of Cush. The name of the third river *is* Hiddekel; it *is* the one which goes toward the east of Assyria. The fourth river *is* the Euphrates.

Then the LORD God took the man and put him in the garden of Eden to tend and keep it. And the LORD God commanded the man, saying, "Of every tree of the garden you may freely eat; but of the tree of the knowledge of good and evil you shall not eat, for in the day that you eat of it you shall surely die."

And the LORD God said, "*It is* not good that man should be alone; I will make him a helper comparable to him." Out of the ground the LORD God formed every beast of the field and every bird of the air, and brought *them* to Adam to see what he would call them. And whatever Adam called each living creature, that *was* its name. So Adam gave names to all cattle, to the birds of the air, and to every beast of the field. **But for Adam there was not found a helper comparable to him.**

And the LORD God caused a deep sleep to fall on Adam, and he slept; and He took one of his ribs, and closed up the flesh

in its place. Then the rib which the LORD God had taken from man He made into a woman, and He brought her to the man.

And Adam said:

"This *is* now bone of my bones
And flesh of my flesh;
She shall be called Woman,
Because she was taken out of Man."

Therefore a man shall leave his father and mother and be joined to his wife, and they shall become one flesh.

And they were both naked, the man and his wife, and were not ashamed.

GENESIS 2:4–25

Community is not a "nice-to-have" addition, but an essential experience for living a godly and healthy life. God intended for humans to have rich, life-giving relationships with each other; relationships energized and motivated by the actual presence of God among them. Adam and Eve experienced this perfect ideal in the garden. But their rejection of God's vision for their life together caused them to be escorted from the garden and out of community with God. This separation from God and the presence of sin in every human being's nature is a perpetual challenge to creating strong community. But it is clear from God's Word that people were not meant for separation from Him and isolation from one another.

There is one alone, without companion:
He has neither son nor brother.
Yet *there is* no end to all his labors,
Nor is his eye satisfied with riches.
But he never asks,
"For whom do I toil and deprive myself of good?"
This also *is* vanity and a grave misfortune.

Two *are* better than one,
Because they have a good reward for their labor.
For if they fall, one will lift up his companion.
But woe to him *who is* alone when he falls,
For *he has* no one to help him up.

Again, if two lie down together, they will keep warm;
But how can one be warm *alone?*
Though one may be overpowered by another, two can
withstand him.
And a threefold cord is not quickly broken. ECCLESIASTES 4:8–12

The passage above from Ecclesiastes 4 describes a relationship between two people. Why, then, does the Preacher say "a threefold cord" is not quickly broken?

THE PRESENCE OF GOD

In order to sustain life-giving community, God must be at the center of it. But Adam and Eve rejected Him in the garden, so community with God and with each other was difficult to recapture. But God never gave up on us, and the narrative of the Bible traces God's efforts to get back into community with us. After delivering Israel from bondage in Egypt, the Lord informed Moses of His intent to be with His people in a tent known as the tabernacle.

Then the LORD spoke to Moses, saying: "Speak to the children of Israel, that they bring Me an offering. From everyone who gives it willingly with his heart you shall take My offering. And this *is* the offering which you shall take from them: gold, silver, and bronze; blue, purple, and scarlet *thread,* fine linen, and goats' *hair;* ram skins dyed red, badger skins, and acacia wood; oil for the light, and spices for the anointing oil and for the sweet incense; onyx stones, and stones to be set in the ephod and in the breastplate. **And let them make Me a sanctuary, that I may dwell among them. According to all that I show you, *that is,* the pattern of the tabernacle and the pattern of all its furnishings, just so you shall make *it.*"** EXODUS 25:1–9

God's presence would be represented by the ark of the Testimony —an elaborate box containing the Ten Commandments tablets, a gold jar filled with manna, and Aaron's staff. The ark was placed in a special room in the tabernacle called the Most Holy Place, which was sectioned off by a thick curtain. While Moses and the Israelites were camped at the foot of Mount Sinai, they finished the building and preparation necessary to set up the tabernacle.

Then the LORD spoke to Moses, saying: "On the first day of the first month you shall set up the tabernacle of the tent of meeting. You shall put in it the ark of the Testimony, and partition off the ark with the veil. You shall bring in the table and arrange the things that are to be set in order on it; and you shall bring in the lampstand and light its lamps. You shall also set the altar of gold for the incense before the ark of the Testimony, and put up the screen for the door of the tabernacle. Then you shall set the altar of the burnt offering before the door of the tabernacle of the tent of meeting. And you shall set the laver between the tabernacle of meeting and the altar, and put water in it. You shall set up the court all around, and hang up the screen at the court gate.

"And you shall take the anointing oil, and anoint the tabernacle and all that *is* in it; and you shall hallow it and all its utensils, and it shall be holy. You shall anoint the altar of the burnt offering and all its utensils, and consecrate the altar. The altar shall be most holy. And you shall anoint the laver and its base, and consecrate it.

"Then you shall bring Aaron and his sons to the door of the tabernacle of meeting and wash them with water. You shall put the holy garments on Aaron, and anoint him and consecrate him, that he may minister to Me as priest. And you shall bring his sons and clothe them with tunics. You shall anoint them, as you anointed their father, that they may minister to Me as priests; for their anointing shall surely be an everlasting priesthood throughout their generations."

Thus Moses did; according to all that the LORD had commanded him, so he did.

And it came to pass in the first month of the second year, on the first *day* of the month, *that* the tabernacle was raised up.

EXODUS 40:1–17

Then the cloud covered the tabernacle of meeting, and the glory of the LORD filled the tabernacle. And Moses was not able to enter the tabernacle of meeting, because the cloud rested above it, and the glory of the LORD filled the tabernacle. EXODUS 40:34–35

The cloud, symbolic of God's glory that had led the Israelites after their escape from Egypt, covered and filled the newly established tabernacle. About 500 years later, the Israelites built a temple in Jerusalem to replace the tabernacle with a permanent place where they could meet with God. Then God's glory came down after King Solomon's prayer at the dedication of that temple.

When Solomon had finished praying, fire came down from heaven and consumed the burnt offering and the sacrifices; and the glory of the LORD filled the temple. And the priests could not enter the house of the LORD, because the glory of the LORD had filled the LORD's house. When all the children of Israel saw how the fire came down, and the glory of the LORD on the temple, they bowed their faces to the ground on the pavement, and worshiped and praised the LORD, *saying:*

"For *He is* good,
For His mercy *endures* forever." 2 CHRONICLES 7:1–3

In the New Testament, God's presence among His people changed to a new location. Simultaneous with the death of Jesus on the cross, the heavy curtain hanging in front of the Holy Place that quarantined God's people from God's presence was torn from top to bottom. God's presence was no longer isolated to this small room in the temple. Forgiveness of sins was now available to all. Paul instructs us on the new "temple" for God's presence.

As you read the passage below from Ephesians 2, look for the differences between the two dwelling places for God: the temple and the New Testament church. What barriers are there in each of the two places? Who is allowed into each place? What is the cornerstone of each place?

Therefore remember that you, once Gentiles in the flesh—who are called Uncircumcision by what is called the Circumcision made in the flesh by hands—that at that time you were without

Christ, being aliens from the commonwealth of Israel and strangers from the covenants of promise, having no hope and without God in the world. But now in Christ Jesus you who once were far off have been brought near by the blood of Christ.

For He Himself is our peace, who has made both one, and has broken down the middle wall of separation, having abolished in His flesh the enmity, *that is,* the law of commandments *contained* in ordinances, so as to create in Himself one new man *from* the two, *thus* making peace, and that He might reconcile them both to God in one body through the cross, thereby putting to death the enmity. And He came and preached peace to you who were afar off and to those who were near. For through Him we both have access by one Spirit to the Father.

Now, therefore, you are no longer strangers and foreigners, but fellow citizens with the saints and members of the household of God, having been built on the foundation of the apostles and prophets, Jesus Christ Himself being the chief corner*stone*, in whom the whole building, being fitted together, grows into a holy temple in the Lord, in whom you also are being built together for a dwelling place of God in the Spirit.

EPHESIANS 2:11–22

THE NEW COMMUNITY

After the resurrection of Jesus and before His ascension back to the Father, Jesus told the disciples to wait in Jerusalem for the indwelling of the Holy Spirit. As promised, the actual presence of God descended on the believers in Jesus Christ—the new "temple." We read about the arrival of the Holy Spirit on the Day of Pentecost when we studied the birth of the church. Now we read further to discover that with God's presence dwelling in the hearts of believers, their potential for vibrant community with each other escalated.

When the Day of Pentecost had fully come, they were all with one accord in one place. And suddenly there came a sound from heaven, as of a rushing mighty wind, and it filled the whole house where they were sitting. Then there appeared to them divided tongues, as of fire, and *one* sat upon each of them. And they were all filled with the Holy Spirit and began to speak with other tongues, as the Spirit gave them utterance. ACTS 2:1–4

And they continued steadfastly in the apostles' doctrine and fellowship, in the breaking of bread, and in prayers. Then fear came upon every soul, and many wonders and signs were done through the apostles. **Now all who believed were together, and had all things in common,** and sold their possessions and goods, and divided them among all, as anyone had need.

So continuing daily with one accord in the temple, and breaking bread from house to house, they ate their food with gladness and simplicity of heart, praising God and having favor with all the people. And the Lord added to the church daily those who were being saved. ACTS 2:42–47

Now the multitude of those who believed were of one heart and one soul; neither did anyone say that any of the things he possessed was his own, but they had all things in common. And with great power the apostles gave witness to the resurrection of the Lord Jesus. And great grace was upon them all. Nor was there anyone among them who lacked; for all who were possessors of lands or houses sold them, and brought the proceeds of the things that were sold, and laid *them* at the apostles' feet; and they distributed to each as anyone had need.

And Joses, who was also named Barnabas by the apostles (which is translated Son of Encouragement), a Levite of the country of Cyprus, having land, sold *it,* and brought the money and laid *it* at the apostles' feet. ACTS 4:32–37

Imagine what it would have been like to be a member of the early church after Pentecost. Would you have wanted to be a part of that community? Why or why not? In what ways should the early church be a model for churches today?

During the first century, it proved difficult for many Jewish converts to overcome the pressure and persecution they received from other family members who remained in Judaism. The author of Hebrews wrote a letter to these believers to convince them of the superiority of Christ over the law and to encourage them to lean heavily into their new community of faith in order to persevere.

Therefore, brethren, having boldness to enter the Holiest by the blood of Jesus, by a new and living way which He consecrated for us, through the veil, that is, His flesh, and *having* a High Priest over the house of God, let us draw near with a true heart in full assurance of faith, having our hearts sprinkled from an evil conscience and our bodies washed with pure water. Let us hold fast the confession of *our* hope without wavering, for He who promised *is* faithful. **And let us consider one another in order to stir up love and good works, not forsaking the assembling of ourselves together, as *is* the manner of some, but exhorting *one another*, and so much the more as you see the Day approaching.**

HEBREWS 10:19–25

It doesn't take hundreds of people to gather to make a difference and accomplish God's purposes. Jesus said it just takes a few who are committed to gathering around a common purpose.

"For where two or three are gathered together in My name, I am there in the midst of them."

MATTHEW 18:20

MARKS OF BIBLICAL COMMUNITY

Biblical community engages all its members to use their gifts, resources and time in unison to accomplish a task important to the plan of God. The Israelites returned from 70 years of captivity and were rebuilding their lives under the reign of God. Nehemiah returned to spearhead the rebuilding of the wall around the city to protect them from bullying from the surrounding nations. Everyone, including children, was called to help. As you read this story, you might be tempted to quickly skim over the many names. To help you, imagine that your family's name was recorded in connection with this important community project.

So I [Nehemiah] came to Jerusalem and was there three days. Then I arose in the night, I and a few men with me; I told no one what my God had put in my heart to do at Jerusalem; nor was there any animal with me, except the one on which I rode. And I went out by night through the Valley Gate to the Serpent Well and the Refuse Gate, and viewed the walls of Jerusalem which were broken down and its gates which were burned with fire. Then I went on to the Fountain Gate and to the King's Pool, but *there was* no room for the animal under me to pass. So I went up in the night by the valley, and viewed the wall; then I turned back and entered by the Valley Gate, and so returned. And the officials did not know where I had gone or what I had done; I had not yet told the Jews, the priests, the nobles, the officials, or the others who did the work.

Then I said to them, "You see the distress that we *are* in, how Jerusalem *lies* waste, and its gates are burned with fire. Come and let us build the wall of Jerusalem, that we may no longer be a reproach." And I told them of the hand of my God which had been good upon me, and also of the king's words that he had spoken to me.

So they said, "Let us rise up and build." Then they set their hands to *this* good *work*.

But when Sanballat the Horonite, Tobiah the Ammonite official, and Geshem the Arab heard *of it,* they laughed at us and despised us, and said, "What *is* this thing that you are doing? Will you rebel against the king?"

So I answered them, and said to them, "The God of heaven Himself will prosper us; therefore we His servants will arise and build, but you have no heritage or right or memorial in Jerusalem."

Then Eliashib the high priest rose up with his brethren the priests and built the Sheep Gate; they consecrated it and hung its doors. They built as far as the Tower of the Hundred, *and* consecrated it, then as far as the Tower of Hananel. Next to *Eliashib* the men of Jericho built. And next to them Zaccur the son of Imri built.

Also the sons of Hassenaah built the Fish Gate; they laid its beams and hung its doors with its bolts and bars. And next to them Meremoth the son of Urijah, the son of Koz, made repairs. Next to them Meshullam the son of Berechiah, the son of Meshezabel, made repairs. Next to them Zadok the son of Baana made repairs. Next to them the Tekoites made repairs; but their nobles did not put their shoulders to the work of their Lord.

Moreover Jehoiada the son of Paseah and Meshullam the son of Besodeiah repaired the Old Gate; they laid its beams and hung its doors, with its bolts and bars. And next to them Melatiah the Gibeonite, Jadon the Meronothite, the men of Gibeon and Mizpah, repaired the residence of the governor *of the region* beyond the River. Next to him Uzziel the son of Harhaiah, one of the goldsmiths, made repairs. Also next to him Hananiah, one of the perfumers, made repairs; and they fortified Jerusalem as far as the Broad Wall. And next to them Rephaiah the son of Hur, leader of half the district of Jerusalem, made repairs. Next to them Jedaiah the son of Harumaph made repairs in front of his house. And next to him Hattush the son of Hashabniah made repairs.

Malchijah the son of Harim and Hashub the son of Pahath-Moab repaired another section, as well as the Tower of the Ovens. And next to him was Shallum the son of Hallohesh, leader of half the district of Jerusalem; he and his daughters made repairs.

Hanun and the inhabitants of Zanoah repaired the Valley Gate. They built it, hung its doors with its bolts and bars, and *repaired* a thousand cubits of the wall as far as the Refuse Gate.

Malchijah the son of Rechab, leader of the district of Beth Haccerem, repaired the Refuse Gate; he built it and hung its doors with its bolts and bars.

Shallun the son of Col-Hozeh, leader of the district of Mizpah, repaired the Fountain Gate; he built it, covered it, hung its doors with its bolts and bars, and repaired the wall of the Pool of Shelah by the King's Garden, as far as the stairs that go down from the City of David. After him Nehemiah the son of Azbuk, leader of half the district of Beth Zur, made repairs as far as *the place* in front of the tombs of David, to the man-made pool, and as far as the House of the Mighty.

After him the Levites, *under* Rehum the son of Bani, made repairs. Next to him Hashabiah, leader of half the district of Keilah, made repairs for his district. After him their brethren, *under* Bavai the son of Henadad, leader of the *other* half of the district of Keilah, made repairs. And next to him Ezer the son of Jeshua, the leader of Mizpah, repaired another section in front of the Ascent to the Armory at the buttress. After him Baruch the son of Zabbai carefully repaired the other section, from the buttress to the door of the house of Eliashib the high priest. After him Meremoth the son of Urijah, the son of Koz, repaired another section, from the door of the house of Eliashib to the end of the house of Eliashib.

And after him the priests, the men of the plain, made repairs. After him Benjamin and Hasshub made repairs opposite their house. After them Azariah the son of Maaseiah, the son of Ananiah, made repairs by his house. After him Binnui the son of Henadad repaired another section, from the house of Azariah to the buttress, even as far as the corner. Palal the son of Uzai *made repairs* opposite the buttress, and on the tower which projects from the king's upper house that *was* by the court of the prison. After him Pedaiah the son of Parosh *made repairs.*

Moreover the Nethinim who dwelt in Ophel *made repairs* as far as *the place* in front of the Water Gate toward the east, and on the projecting tower. After them the Tekoites repaired another section, next to the great projecting tower, and as far as the wall of Ophel.

Beyond the Horse Gate the priests made repairs, each in front of his *own* house. After them Zadok the son of Immer made repairs in front of his *own* house. After him Shemaiah the son of Shechaniah, the keeper of the East Gate, made repairs. After him Hananiah the son of Shelemiah, and Hanun, the sixth son of Zalaph, repaired another section. After him Meshullam the son of Berechiah made repairs in front of his dwelling. After him Malchijah, one of the goldsmiths, made repairs as far as the house of the Nethinim and of the merchants, in front of the Miphkad Gate, and as far as the upper room at the corner. And between the upper room at the corner, as far as the Sheep Gate, the goldsmiths and the merchants made repairs. NEHEMIAH 2:11—3:32

So the wall was finished on the twenty-fifth *day* of Elul, in fifty-two days. NEHEMIAH 6:15

One of the marked differences between the church and the rest of society is the call to live for others. Throughout the New Testament, Jesus' followers were urged to look out for "one another." When the early Christians did this in faith, it irresistably attracted outsiders to belong to the family of God. The practice of looking out for one another is a hallmark of true Biblical community.

For as we have many members in one body, but all the members do not have the same function, so we, *being* many, are one body in Christ, and individually members of one another.

ROMANS 12:4–5

***Be* kindly affectionate to one another** with brotherly love, in honor giving preference to one another. ROMANS 12:10

Owe no one anything except to **love one another**, for he who loves another has fulfilled the law. ROMANS 13:8

Now may the God of patience and comfort grant you to be like-minded toward one another, according to Christ Jesus, that you may with one mind *and* one mouth glorify the God and Father of our Lord Jesus Christ.

Therefore **receive one another**, just as Christ also received us, to the glory of God. ROMANS 15:5–7

Now I myself am confident concerning you, my brethren, that you also are full of goodness, filled with all knowledge, able also to **admonish one another**. ROMANS 15:14

For you, brethren, have been called to liberty; only do not *use* liberty as an opportunity for the flesh, but through love **serve one another**. GALATIANS 5:13

Bear one another's burdens, and so fulfill the law of Christ.

GALATIANS 6:2

I, therefore, the prisoner of the Lord, beseech you to walk worthy of the calling with which you were called, with all lowliness and gentleness, with longsuffering, **bearing with one another in love.** EPHESIANS 4:1–2

[Submit] to one another in the fear of God. EPHESIANS 5:21

For God did not appoint us to wrath, but to obtain salvation through our Lord Jesus Christ, who died for us, that whether we wake or sleep, we should live together with Him.

Therefore **comfort each other** and edify one another, just as you also are doing. 1 THESSALONIANS 5:9–11

The calling among the early church to care for one another was also demonstrated through simple hospitality. This mandate to show love and demonstrate an open door policy greatly enhanced the quality of community and always left room for new people to belong, regardless of their stations in life.

As you read the passages below from Hebrews 13; Acts 18; 1 Corinthians 16; Romans 16 and 1 John 1–3, ponder the emphasis and importance placed on hospitality. Why do you think it was so important to the early church? Is it still important today? Why or why not?

Let brotherly love continue. **Do not forget to entertain strangers, for by so *doing* some have unwittingly entertained angels.** Remember the prisoners as if chained with them—those who are mistreated—since you yourselves are in the body also.

HEBREWS 13:1–3

Therefore by Him let us continually offer the sacrifice of praise to God, that is, the fruit of *our* lips, giving thanks to His name. **But do not forget to do good and to share, for with such sacrifices God is well pleased.** HEBREWS 13:15–16

A couple named Priscilla and Aquila serve as a beautiful example of how to be hospitable. In the first century, inns were not commonplace, and the early church didn't own buildings. For Biblical community to be experienced, people who owned homes had to open them up for the church to meet in. Paul was on his second missionary journey when he first encountered this warm-hearted couple, who invited him to stay with them.

After these things Paul departed from Athens and went to Corinth. And he found a certain Jew named Aquila, born in Pontus, who had recently come from Italy with his wife Priscilla (because Claudius had commanded all the Jews to depart from Rome); and he came to them. So, because he was of the same trade, he stayed with them and worked; for by occupation they were tent-makers.

ACTS 18:1–3

So Paul still remained a good while. Then he took leave of the brethren and sailed for Syria, and Priscilla and Aquila *were* with him. He had *his* hair cut off at Cenchrea, for he had taken a vow. And he came to Ephesus, and left them there; but he himself entered the synagogue and reasoned with the Jews.

ACTS 18:18–19

Now a certain Jew named Apollos, born at Alexandria, an eloquent man *and* mighty in the Scriptures, came to Ephesus. This man had been instructed in the way of the Lord; and being fervent in spirit, he spoke and taught accurately the things of the Lord, though he knew only the baptism of John. So he began to speak boldly in the synagogue. **When Aquila and Priscilla heard him, they took him aside and explained to him the way of God more accurately.**

ACTS 18:24–26

Paul's admiration for Priscilla and Aquila can be found throughout his letters. Paul wrote 1 Corinthians when he was in Ephesus. He sent greetings on behalf of Aquila and Priscilla, who were hosting the church in their home.

The churches of Asia greet you. Aquila and Priscilla greet you heartily in the Lord, with the church that is in their house.

1 CORINTHIANS 16:19

A couple years later when Paul penned the letter to the Romans, he expressed his gratitude to Priscilla and Aquila, who were now in Rome.

Greet Priscilla and Aquila, my fellow workers in Christ Jesus, who risked their own necks for my life, to whom not only I give thanks, but also all the churches of the Gentiles. ROMANS 16:3–4

In order for the church to accomplish its mission, all believers, looking to the example of Priscilla and Aquila, need to use the gifts God has given them to serve others. In 1 John, the apostle John emphasized the value of Christian fellowship. If we practice this quality and depth of fellowship with other Christians, we will accomplish God's purposes in our lives, in the lives of others and in the world.

That which was from the beginning, which we have heard, which we have seen with our eyes, which we have looked upon, and our hands have handled, concerning the Word of life—the life was manifested, and we have seen, and bear witness, and declare to you that eternal life which was with the Father and was manifested to us—that which we have seen and heard we declare to you, that you also may have fellowship with us; and truly our fellowship *is* with the Father and with His Son Jesus Christ. And these things we write to you that your joy may be full.

This is the message which we have heard from Him and declare to you, that God is light and in Him is no darkness at all. If we say that we have fellowship with Him, and walk in darkness, we lie and do not practice the truth. **But if we walk in the light as He is in the light, we have fellowship with one another, and the blood of Jesus Christ His Son cleanses us from all sin.** 1 JOHN 1:1–7

Brethren, I write no new commandment to you, but an old commandment which you have had from the beginning. The old commandment is the word which you heard from the beginning. Again, a new commandment I write to you, which thing is true in Him and in you, because the darkness is passing away, and the true light is already shining.

He who says he is in the light, and hates his brother, is in darkness until now. He who loves his brother abides in the light, and there is no cause for stumbling in him. But he who hates his brother is in darkness and walks in darkness, and does not know where he is going, because the darkness has blinded his eyes. 1 JOHN 2:7–11

By this we know love, because He laid down His life for us. And we also ought to lay down *our* lives for the brethren. But whoever has this world's goods, and sees his brother in need, and shuts up his heart from him, how does the love of God abide in him?

My little children, let us not love in word or in tongue, but in deed and in truth. 1 JOHN 3:16–18

God's Word places a high value on Christian fellowship.
How important is fellowship to you right now?
What difference is it making in your life?

WHAT WE BELIEVE

We were created by God for community. Given our sinful nature, it is essential for God to be at the center of that community. He was in the garden with Adam and Eve; He dwelled in the tabernacle and temple with Israel; He literally walked among the first disciples for more than 30 years. From the inception of the church until now, God has dwelt not in a temple built by human hands, but in a new temple—the lives of His followers. As we yield to the presence of God's Spirit in and among us, we grow in true Biblical community, marked by caring for one another and open hospitality. As we fellowship with other Christians, it not only becomes the rich experience we were created for, but it also emits an "aroma" that draws others in. So we must make Biblical community a priority in order to accomplish God's purposes in our lives, in the lives of others and in the world.

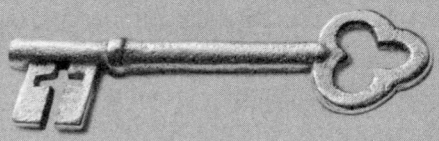

CHAPTER

17

Spiritual Gifts

KEY QUESTION

What gifts and skills has God given me to serve others?

KEY IDEA

I know my spiritual gifts and
use them to fulfill God's purposes.

KEY VERSE

For as we have many members in one body,
but all the members do not have the same function,
so we, *being* many, are one body in Christ, and
individually members of one another. Having then gifts
differing according to the grace that is given to us.
Romans 12:4–6

OUR MAP

God has used two primary communities to accomplish His grand purpose to redeem humanity and restore His vision of being with them forever. In the Old Testament that community was Israel. In the New Testament that community was (and continues to be) the church. God equipped the individual members of these communities with the skills and gifts needed to accomplish His purpose and plan. It is up to each individual to acknowledge and use their gifts for God's intended purposes. Then, collectively, the community must decide to work together in unity. When this happens, amazing things are accomplished. Miracles. Life change.

In this chapter we will be reading Scripture that will help us understand more about spiritual gifts, including:

- *Spiritual Gifts in the Old Testament*
- *The Promised Gift of the Holy Spirit*
- *The Purpose and Function of Spiritual Gifts*
- *Stewardship of Our Gifts*

Spiritual Gifts in the Old Testament

Although the term "spiritual gift" isn't found in the Old Testament, we see clear evidence of the Holy Spirit working through people during this time. The unique empowering of the Spirit was given to individuals (often only temporarily) primarily to enable them to carry out the special responsibilities God had given them. When the Israelites were in the wilderness following the exodus from Egypt, God instructed Moses to build a tabernacle that would be used for God's dwelling place from that day forward. It would take the special gifts and skills of many people to carry out God's intricate plan for building His new sanctuary.

And Moses said to the children of Israel, "See, the Lord has called by name Bezalel the son of Uri, the son of Hur, of the tribe of Judah; and He has filled him with the Spirit of God, in wisdom and understanding, in knowledge and all manner of workmanship, to design artistic works, to work in gold and silver and bronze, in cutting jewels for setting, in carving wood, and to work in all manner of artistic workmanship.

"And He has put in his heart the ability to teach, *in* him and Aholiab the son of Ahisamach, of the tribe of Dan. He has filled them with skill to do all manner of work of the engraver and the designer and the tapestry maker, in blue, purple, and scarlet *thread,* and fine linen, and of the weaver—those who do every work and those who design artistic works.

"And Bezalel and Aholiab, and every gifted artisan in whom the LORD has put wisdom and understanding, to know how to do all manner of work for the service of the sanctuary, shall do according to all that the LORD has commanded." EXODUS 35:30—36:1

God instills in His people the skills needed to accomplish His purposes. This includes not only the work of the priest or pastor but also the swinging of the hammer of the construction worker and the reading of the blueprints of the project manager.

Occasionally in the Old Testament, spiritual gifts were used for the sake of outsiders. In these situations, God used miraculous signs to reveal Himself as the one true God. For instance, while the Israelites were living in exile in Babylon, God empowered Daniel with the ability to interpret a complex dream for King Nebuchadnezzar.

In the second year of Nebuchadnezzar's reign, Nebuchadnezzar had dreams; and his spirit was *so* troubled that his sleep left him. Then the king gave the command to call the magicians, the astrologers, the sorcerers, and the Chaldeans to tell the king his dreams. So they came and stood before the king. And the king said to them, "I have had a dream, and my spirit is anxious to know the dream."

Then the Chaldeans spoke to the king in Aramaic, "O king, live forever! Tell your servants the dream, and we will give the interpretation."

The king answered and said to the Chaldeans, "My decision is firm: if you do not make known the dream to me, and its interpretation, you shall be cut in pieces, and your houses shall be made an ash heap. However, if you tell the dream and its interpretation, you shall receive from me gifts, rewards, and great honor. Therefore tell me the dream and its interpretation."

They answered again and said, "Let the king tell his servants the dream, and we will give its interpretation."

The king answered and said, "I know for certain that you would gain time, because you see that my decision is firm: if you do not make known the dream to me, *there is only* one decree for you! For you have agreed to speak lying and corrupt words before me till the time has changed. Therefore tell me the dream, and I shall know that you can give me its interpretation."

The Chaldeans answered the king, and said, "There is not a man on earth who can tell the king's matter; therefore no king, lord, or ruler has *ever* asked such things of any magician, astrologer, or Chaldean. *It is* a difficult thing that the king requests, and there is no other who can tell it to the king except the gods, whose dwelling is not with flesh."

For this reason the king was angry and very furious, and gave the command to destroy all the wise *men* of Babylon. So the decree went out, and they began killing the wise *men;* and they sought Daniel and his companions, to kill *them.*

Then with counsel and wisdom Daniel answered Arioch, the captain of the king's guard, who had gone out to kill the wise *men* of Babylon; he answered and said to Arioch the king's captain, "Why is the decree from the king so urgent?" Then Arioch made the decision known to Daniel.

So Daniel went in and asked the king to give him time, that he might tell the king the interpretation. Then Daniel went to his house, and made the decision known to Hananiah, Mishael, and Azariah, his companions, that they might seek mercies from the God of heaven concerning this secret, so that Daniel and his companions might not perish with the rest of the wise *men* of Babylon. Then the secret was revealed to Daniel in a night vision. So Daniel blessed the God of heaven.

Daniel answered and said:

"Blessed be the name of God forever and ever,
For wisdom and might are His.
And He changes the times and the seasons;
He removes kings and raises up kings;
He gives wisdom to the wise
And knowledge to those who have understanding.

He reveals deep and secret things;
He knows what *is* in the darkness,
And light dwells with Him.

"I thank You and praise You,
O God of my fathers;
You have given me wisdom and might,
And have now made known to me what we asked of You,
For You have made known to us the king's demand."

Therefore Daniel went to Arioch, whom the king had appointed to destroy the wise *men* of Babylon. He went and said thus to him: "Do not destroy the wise *men* of Babylon; take me before the king, and I will tell the king the interpretation."

Then Arioch quickly brought Daniel before the king, and said thus to him, "I have found a man of the captives of Judah, who will make known to the king the interpretation."

The king answered and said to Daniel, whose name *was* Belteshazzar, "Are you able to make known to me the dream which I have seen, and its interpretation?"

Daniel answered in the presence of the king, and said, "The secret which the king has demanded, the wise *men*, the astrologers, the magicians, and the soothsayers cannot declare to the king. But there is a God in heaven who reveals secrets, and He has made known to King Nebuchadnezzar what will be in the latter days. Your dream, and the visions of your head upon your bed, were these: As for you, O king, thoughts came *to* your *mind while* on your bed, *about* what would come to pass after this; and He who reveals secrets has made known to you what will be. But as for me, this secret has not been revealed to me because I have more wisdom than anyone living, but for *our* sakes who make known the interpretation to the king, and that you may know the thoughts of your heart.

"You, O king, were watching; and behold, a great image! This great image, whose splendor *was* excellent, stood before you; and its form *was* awesome. This image's head *was* of fine gold, its chest and arms of silver, its belly and thighs of bronze, its legs of iron, its feet partly of iron and partly of clay. You watched while a stone was cut out without hands, which struck the image on its feet of iron and clay, and broke them in pieces. Then the iron, the clay, the bronze, the silver, and the gold were crushed together, and became like chaff from the summer threshing floors; the wind carried them away so that no trace of them was found. And the stone that struck the image became a great mountain and filled the whole earth.

"This *is* the dream. Now we will tell the interpretation of it before the king. You, O king, *are* a king of kings. For the God of heaven has given you a kingdom, power, strength, and glory; and wherever the children of men dwell, or the beasts of the field and the birds of the heaven, He has given *them* into your hand, and has made you ruler over them all—you *are* this head of gold. But after you shall arise another kingdom inferior to yours; then another, a third kingdom of bronze, which shall rule over all the earth. And the fourth kingdom shall be as strong as iron, inasmuch as iron breaks in pieces and shatters everything; and like iron that crushes, *that kingdom* will break in pieces and crush all the others. Whereas you saw the feet and toes, partly of potter's clay and partly of iron, the kingdom shall be divided; yet the strength of the iron shall be in it, just as you saw the iron mixed with ceramic clay. And *as* the toes of the feet *were* partly of iron and partly of clay, *so* the kingdom shall be partly strong and partly fragile. As you saw iron mixed with ceramic clay, they will mingle with the seed of men; but they will not adhere to one another, just as iron does not mix with clay. And in the days of these kings the God of heaven will set up a kingdom which shall never be destroyed; and the kingdom shall not be left to other people; it shall break in pieces and consume all these kingdoms, and it shall stand forever. Inasmuch as you saw that the stone was cut out of the mountain without hands, and that it broke in pieces the iron, the bronze, the clay, the silver, and the gold—the great God has made known to the king what will come to pass after this. The dream is certain, and its interpretation is sure."

Then King Nebuchadnezzar fell on his face, prostrate before Daniel, and commanded that they should present an offering and incense to him. **The king answered Daniel, and said, "Truly your God *is* the God of gods, the Lord of kings, and a revealer of secrets, since you could reveal this secret."** DANIEL 2:1–47

What was Daniel's spiritual gift? Why was it important that Daniel acknowledge his gift was from the Lord?

The Promised Gift of the Holy Spirit

In the New Testament, when Jesus ate the Last Supper with His disciples, He knew He would soon be put to death. Wanting them to be encouraged and prepared for life without Him beside them, Jesus promised to send the gift of the Holy Spirit, who would empower them with hope and guidance and the ability to get through the difficult days ahead.

"If you love Me, keep My commandments. And I will pray the Father, and He will give you another Helper, that He may abide with you forever—the Spirit of truth, whom the world cannot receive, because it neither sees Him nor knows Him; but you know Him, for He dwells with you and will be in you. I will not leave you orphans; I will come to you.

"A little while longer and the world will see Me no more, but you will see Me. Because I live, you will live also. At that day you will know that I *am* in My Father, and you in Me, and I in you. He who has My commandments and keeps them, it is he who loves Me. And he who loves Me will be loved by My Father, and I will love him and manifest Myself to him."

Judas (not Iscariot) said to Him, "Lord, how is it that You will manifest Yourself to us, and not to the world?"

Jesus answered and said to him, "If anyone loves Me, he will keep My word; and My Father will love him, and We will come to him and make Our home with him. He who does not love Me does not keep My words; and the word which you hear is not Mine but the Father's who sent Me.

"These things I have spoken to you while being present with you. But the Helper, the Holy Spirit, whom the Father will send in My name, He will teach you all things, and bring to your remembrance all things that I said to you. Peace I leave with you, My peace I give to you; not as the world gives do I give to you. Let not your heart be troubled, neither let it be afraid. You have heard Me say to you, 'I am going away and coming *back* to you.' If you loved Me, you would rejoice because I said, 'I am going to the Father,' for My Father is greater than I.

"And now I have told you before it comes, that when it does come to pass, you may believe. I will no longer talk much with you, for the ruler of this world is coming, and he has nothing in Me. But that the world may know that I love the Father, and as the Father gave Me commandment, so I do."

JOHN 14:15–31

Later, Jesus' last words to His disciples before He ascended to heaven instructed them to wait in Jerusalem for the promised gift of the Holy Spirit. Ten days later, on the Jewish celebration of Pentecost (i.e., 50 days after Passover), the Holy Spirit arrived and the disciples were filled with incredible boldness. The church was born. Jews use this celebration to commemorate the giving of the law. Christians use this day to commemorate the giving of the Spirit.

When the Day of Pentecost had fully come, they were all with one accord in one place. And suddenly there came a sound from heaven, as of a rushing mighty wind, and it filled the whole house where they were sitting. Then there appeared to them divided tongues, as of fire, and *one* sat upon each of them. And they were all filled with the Holy Spirit and began to speak with other tongues, as the Spirit gave them utterance.

And there were dwelling in Jerusalem Jews, devout men, from every nation under heaven. And when this sound occurred, the multitude came together, and were confused, because everyone heard them speak in his own language. Then they were all amazed and marveled, saying to one another, "Look, are not all these who speak Galileans? And how *is it that* we hear, each in our own language in which we were born? Parthians and Medes and Elamites, those dwelling in Mesopotamia, Judea and Cappadocia, Pontus and Asia, Phrygia and Pamphylia, Egypt and the parts of Libya adjoining Cyrene, visitors from Rome, both Jews and proselytes, Cretans and Arabs—we hear them speaking in our own tongues the wonderful works of God." So they were all amazed and perplexed, saying to one another, "Whatever could this mean?"

Others mocking said, "They are full of new wine."

But Peter, standing up with the eleven, raised his voice and said to them, "Men of Judea and all who dwell in Jerusalem, let this be known to you, and heed my words. For these are not drunk, as you suppose, since it is *only* the third hour of the day. But this is what was spoken by the prophet Joel:

> ***'And it shall come to pass in the last days, says God,***
> ***That I will pour out of My Spirit on all flesh;***
> *Your sons and your daughters shall prophesy,*
> *Your young men shall see visions,*
> *Your old men shall dream dreams.*
> *And on My menservants and on My maidservants*
> *I will pour out My Spirit in those days;*
> *And they shall prophesy.*
> *I will show wonders in heaven above*
> *And signs in the earth beneath:*
> *Blood and fire and vapor of smoke.*
> *The sun shall be turned into darkness,*
> *And the moon into blood,*
> *Before the coming of the great and awesome day*
> *of the LORD.*
> *And it shall come to pass*
> *That whoever calls on the name of the LORD*
> *Shall be saved.'"*
>
> ACTS 2:1–21

The Holy Spirit now takes up residence in all who believe in Jesus. We are the new temple of God. In John 14, Jesus called the Holy Spirit our "Helper." What do you think that means?

THE PURPOSE AND FUNCTION OF SPIRITUAL GIFTS

Spiritual gifts are given with a purpose. God wants to redeem this broken world, and He has chosen to use us, the church, to do it. Whereas in the Old Testament the Holy Spirit temporarily came upon followers of God to enable them to fulfill specific tasks, the New Testament clearly indicates that the Holy Spirit indwells all believers and that all believers have spiritual gifts. And since the New Testament refers to specific gifts, it seems safe to assume that God wants us to identify our gifts in order to best use them.

As you read the following passages from Romans 12 and 1 Corinthians 12, highlight or write down which gift(s) you believe you possess. Choose a family member or a friend and do the same for them. Let them know what you think their gifts are and how you have been positively impacted by them.

For as we have many members in one body, but all the members do not have the same function, so we, *being* many, are one body in Christ, and individually members of one another. Having then gifts differing according to the grace that is given to us, *let us use them:* if prophecy, *let us prophesy* in proportion to our faith; or ministry, *let us use it* in *our* ministering; he who teaches, in teaching; he who exhorts, in exhortation; he who gives, with liberality; he who leads, with diligence; he who shows mercy, with cheerfulness.

ROMANS 12:4–8

There are diversities of gifts, but the same Spirit. There are differences of ministries, but the same Lord. And there are diversities of activities, but it is the same God who works all in all. But the manifestation of the Spirit is given to each one for the profit *of all:* for to one is given the word of wisdom through the Spirit, to another the word of knowledge through the same Spirit, to another faith by the same Spirit, to another gifts of healings by the same Spirit, to another the working of miracles, to another prophecy, to another discerning of spirits, to another *different* kinds of tongues, to another the interpretation of tongues. But one and the same Spirit works all these things, distributing to each one individually as He wills.

For as the body is one and has many members, but all the members of that one body, being many, are one body, so also *is* Christ. For by one Spirit we were all baptized into one body—whether Jews or Greeks, whether slaves or free—and have all been made to drink into one Spirit. For in fact the body is not one member but many.

If the foot should say, "Because I am not a hand, I am not of the body," is it therefore not of the body? And if the ear should say, "Because I am not an eye, I am not of the body," is it therefore not of the body? If the whole body *were* an eye, where *would be* the hearing? If the whole *were* hearing, where *would be* the smelling? But now God has set the members, each one of them, in the body just as He pleased. And if they were all one member, where *would* the body *be?*

But now indeed *there are* many members, yet one body. And the eye cannot say to the hand, "I have no need of you"; nor again the head to the feet, "I have no need of you." No, much rather, those members of the body which seem to be weaker are necessary. And those *members* of the body which we think to be less honorable, on these we bestow greater honor; and our unpresentable *parts* have greater modesty, but our presentable *parts* have no need. But God composed the body, having given greater honor to that *part* which lacks it, that there should be no schism in the body, but *that* the members should have the same care for one another. And if one member suffers, all the members suffer with *it;* or if one member is honored, all the members rejoice with *it.*

Now you are the body of Christ, and members individually. And God has appointed these in the church: first apostles, second prophets, third teachers, after that miracles, then gifts of healings, helps, administrations, varieties of tongues. *Are* all apostles? *Are* all prophets? *Are* all teachers? *Are* all workers of miracles? Do all have gifts of healings? Do all speak with tongues? Do all interpret? But earnestly desire the best gifts. And yet I show you a more excellent way.

1 Corinthians 12:4–31

Stewardship of Our Gifts

We are meant to use our spiritual gifts to benefit the body of Christ. Jesus used the unit of money—the "talents" to graphically illustrate this principle for His disciples. Like money that should be invested, our spiritual gifts should be used for the good of others, multiplying the blessing as we share them according to God's purposes.

"For *the kingdom of heaven is* like a man traveling to a far country, *who* called his own servants and delivered his goods to them. And to one he gave five talents, to another two, and to another one, to each according to his own ability; and immediately he went on a journey. Then he who had received the five talents went and traded with them, and made another five talents. And likewise he who *had received* two gained two more also. But he who had received one went and dug in the ground, and hid his lord's money. After a long time the lord of those servants came and settled accounts with them.

"So he who had received five talents came and brought five other talents, saying, 'Lord, you delivered to me five talents; look, I have gained five more talents besides them.' **His lord said to him, 'Well *done*, good and faithful servant; you were faithful over a few things, I will make you ruler over many things. Enter into the joy of your lord.'** He also who had received two talents came and said, 'Lord, you delivered to me two talents; look, I have gained two more talents besides them.' His lord said to him, 'Well *done,* good and faithful servant; you have been faithful over a few things, I will make you ruler over many things. Enter into the joy of your lord.'

"Then he who had received the one talent came and said, 'Lord, I knew you to be a hard man, reaping where you have not sown, and gathering where you have not scattered seed. And I was afraid, and went and hid your talent in the ground. Look, *there* you have *what is* yours.'

"But his lord answered and said to him, 'You wicked and lazy servant, you knew that I reap where I have not sown, and gather where I have not scattered seed. So you ought to have deposited my money with the bankers, and at my coming I would have received back my own with interest. So take the talent from him, and give *it* to him who has ten talents.

'For to everyone who has, more will be given, and he will have abundance; but from him who does not have, even what he has will be taken away. And cast the unprofitable servant into the outer darkness. There will be weeping and gnashing of teeth.'"

MATTHEW 25:14–30

Just as a piston engine requires pure gasoline to run smoothly, our gifts must be fueled with loving intentions. Spiritual gifts that are powered by selfish ambition and pride will sputter and fail.

But the end of all things is at hand; therefore be serious and watchful in your prayers. And above all things have fervent love for one another, for *"love will cover a multitude of sins." Be* hospitable to one another without grumbling. **As each one has received a gift, minister it to one another, as good stewards of the manifold grace of God.** If anyone speaks, *let him speak* as the oracles of God. If anyone ministers, *let him do it* as with the ability which God supplies, that in all things God may be glorified through Jesus Christ, to whom belong the glory and the dominion forever and ever. 1 PETER 4:7–11

What happens when spiritual gifts are exercised without love? Peter cites offering hospitality while grumbling as unacceptable. Why is it so important to be driven by love when using our spiritual gifts?

This final selection from Ephesians 4:1–16 also appeared in Chapter 6 (Church). For the church to accomplish its purpose we must all work together as one unified body. As you reread this passage, note how church leaders are a gift to the church. As they use their spiritual gifts, other believers will be equipped to steward their gifts, resulting in the body of Christ being built up and individual believers becoming mature.

I, therefore, the prisoner of the Lord, beseech you to walk worthy of the calling with which you were called, with all lowliness and gentleness, with longsuffering, bearing with one another in love, endeavoring to keep the unity of the Spirit in the bond of peace. *There is* one body and one Spirit, just as you were called in one hope of your calling; one Lord, one faith, one baptism; one God and Father of all, who *is* above all, and through all, and in you all.

But to each one of us grace was given according to the measure of Christ's gift. Therefore He says:

"When He ascended on high,
He led captivity captive,
And gave gifts to men."

(Now this, *"He ascended"*—what does it mean but that He also first descended into the lower parts of the earth? He who descended is also the One who ascended far above all the heavens, that He might fill all things.)

And He Himself gave some *to be* apostles, some prophets, some evangelists, and some pastors and teachers, for the equipping of the saints for the work of ministry, for the edifying of the body of Christ, till we all come to the unity of the faith and of the knowledge of the Son of God, to a perfect man, to the measure of the stature of the fullness of Christ; that we should no longer be children, tossed to and fro and carried about with every wind of doctrine, by the trickery of men, in the cunning craftiness of deceitful plotting, but, speaking the truth in love, may grow up in all things into Him who is the head—**Christ—from whom the whole body, joined and knit together by what every joint supplies, according to the effective working by which every part does its share, causes growth of the body for the edifying of itself in love.**

EPHESIANS 4:1–16

The Bible compares the church to a body. Collectively, we are the body of Christ. Individual believers are compared to parts of the body that all work together to accomplish what needs to be done. Can you recall a time when one part of your body was injured in some way and how this affected the whole body? How does this analogy work in regard to the church?

WHAT WE BELIEVE

The one true God has partnered with His people to accomplish His purposes on earth. The third person of the Trinity, the Holy Spirit, is the driver of this initiative. In the Old Testament, the Holy Spirit only indwelled select individuals for a period of time to accomplish God's purposes. The Spirit instilled gifts in artisans, architects, builders, priests and prophets. In the New Testament, Jesus promised the indwelling of the Holy Spirit for all believers. That promise was fulfilled on the Day of Pentecost as recorded in Acts 2. The Spirit deposits gifts in every believer for the express purpose of building God's Kingdom. We do not all have the same gift. In unity we are to celebrate the giftedness of others and work together to accomplish God's will in our lives and in the world.

ACT

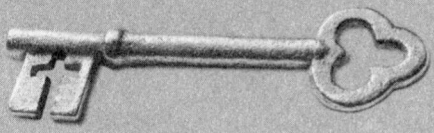

CHAPTER 18

Offering My Time

KEY QUESTION

How do I best use my time to serve God and others?

KEY IDEA

I offer my time to fulfill God's purposes.

KEY VERSE

And *whatever* you do in word or deed,
do all in the name of the Lord Jesus, giving
thanks to God the Father through Him.
Colossians 3:17

OUR MAP

Believe is an action verb. Whatever we believe in our hearts will be expressed in the way we live. Beliefs such as the church, compassion and stewardship naturally lead to the practice of offering our time to God to accomplish His purposes. Every time we act on this key spiritual practice, even if our hearts are not totally committed, it helps to drive these beliefs from our heads to our hearts. So we act out our beliefs in faith.

In this chapter we will be reading Scripture focused on the following key topics:

- *Offering God Our Time*
- *Serving God's Purposes*
- *Managing Our Time*
- *The Rewards of Offering Our Time*

Offering God Our Time

In essence, we cannot talk about "our" time since all time belongs to God. Every moment we have is a gift from Him. It is because of this fact that we are called to use that time to honor our Father. The prophet Jonah learned this the hard way. God called Jonah to redirect his time from the popular job of serving Israel to the unpopular assignment of traveling to Nineveh to give Israel's enemy a chance to repent and be saved by God. Needless to say, Jonah was not committed to the call.

Now the word of the Lord came to Jonah the son of Amittai, saying, "Arise, go to Nineveh, that great city, and cry out against it; for their wickedness has come up before Me." But Jonah arose to flee to Tarshish from the presence of the Lord. He went down to Joppa, and found a ship going to Tarshish; so he paid the fare, and went down into it, to go with them to Tarshish from the presence of the Lord.

But the Lord sent out a great wind on the sea, and there was a mighty tempest on the sea, so that the ship was about to be broken up.

Then the mariners were afraid; and every man cried out to his god, and threw the cargo that *was* in the ship into the sea, to light-en the load. But Jonah had gone down into the lowest parts of the ship, had lain down, and was fast asleep.

So the captain came to him, and said to him, "What do you mean, sleeper? Arise, call on your God; perhaps your God will consider us, so that we may not perish."

And they said to one another, "Come, let us cast lots, that we may know for whose cause this trouble *has come* upon us." So they cast lots, and the lot fell on Jonah. Then they said to him, "Please tell us! For whose cause *is* this trouble upon us? What is your occupation? And where do you come from? What is your country? And of what people are you?"

So he said to them, "I *am* a Hebrew; and I fear the LORD, the God of heaven, who made the sea and the dry *land*."

Then the men were exceedingly afraid, and said to him, "Why have you done this?" For the men knew that he fled from the presence of the LORD, because he had told them. Then they said to him, "What shall we do to you that the sea may be calm for us?"—for the sea was growing more tempestuous.

And he said to them, "Pick me up and throw me into the sea; then the sea will become calm for you. For I know that this great tempest *is* because of me."

Nevertheless the men rowed hard to return to land, but they could not, for the sea continued to grow more tempestuous against them. Therefore they cried out to the LORD and said, "We pray, O LORD, please do not let us perish for this man's life, and do not charge us with innocent blood; for You, O LORD, have done as it pleased You." So they picked up Jonah and threw him into the sea, and the sea ceased from its raging. Then the men feared the LORD exceedingly, and offered a sacrifice to the LORD and took vows.

Now the LORD had prepared a great fish to swallow Jonah. And Jonah was in the belly of the fish three days and three nights.

Then Jonah prayed to the LORD his God from the fish's belly. And he said:

> "I cried out to the LORD because of my affliction,
> And He answered me.
>
> "Out of the belly of Sheol I cried,
> *And* You heard my voice.

For You cast me into the deep,
Into the heart of the seas,
And the floods surrounded me;
All Your billows and Your waves passed over me.
Then I said, 'I have been cast out of Your sight;
Yet I will look again toward Your holy temple.'
The waters surrounded me, *even* to my soul;
The deep closed around me;
Weeds were wrapped around my head.
I went down to the moorings of the mountains;
The earth with its bars *closed* behind me forever;
Yet You have brought up my life from the pit,
O LORD, my God.

"When my soul fainted within me,
I remembered the LORD;
And my prayer went *up* to You,
Into Your holy temple.

"Those who regard worthless idols
Forsake their own Mercy.
But I will sacrifice to You
With the voice of thanksgiving;
I will pay what I have vowed.
Salvation *is* of the LORD."

So the LORD spoke to the fish, and it vomited Jonah onto dry *land.*

JONAH 1:1—2:10

Do you think God still puts people in predicaments such as "the belly of a fish" when they ignore His call?

SERVING GOD'S PURPOSES

Not only are we to give our time to God, but we are also to use that time to serve His purposes, which can mean many different things. Like Jonah, God's people often needed reminders about this. When the first exiles returned to Judah from captivity in Babylon, one of their first priorities was to rebuild the temple and restore worship to the one true God. In 536 BC, under the leadership of Zerubbabel, the building project began. When opposition from the Samaritans and other neighbors intensified, the people got discouraged and the building came to a complete halt. For ten years the project lay dormant. The prophet Haggai delivered a chilling and effective message from God encouraging the people of God to reconsider how they prioritized their time.

In the second year of King Darius, in the sixth month, on the first day of the month, the word of the LORD came by Haggai the prophet to Zerubbabel the son of Shealtiel, governor of Judah, and to Joshua the son of Jehozadak, the high priest, saying, "Thus speaks the LORD of hosts, saying: 'This people says, "The time has not come, the time that the LORD's house should be built."'"

Then the word of the LORD came by Haggai the prophet, saying, "*Is it* time for you yourselves to dwell in your paneled houses, and this temple *to lie* in ruins?" Now therefore, thus says the LORD of hosts: "Consider your ways!

"You have sown much, and bring in little;
You eat, but do not have enough;
You drink, but you are not filled with drink;
You clothe yourselves, but no one is warm;
And he who earns wages,
Earns wages *to put* into a bag with holes."

Thus says the LORD of hosts: "Consider your ways! Go up to the mountains and bring wood and build the temple, that I may take pleasure in it and be glorified," says the LORD. "*You* looked for much, but indeed *it came to* little; and when you brought it home, I blew it away. Why?" says the LORD of hosts. "Because of My house that *is in* ruins, while every one of you runs to his own house. Therefore the heavens above you withhold the dew, and the earth withholds its fruit. For I called for a drought on the land and the mountains, on the grain and the new wine and the oil, on whatever the ground brings forth, on men and livestock, and on all the labor of *your* hands."

Then Zerubbabel the son of Shealtiel, and Joshua the son of

Jehozadak, the high priest, with all the remnant of the people, obeyed the voice of the LORD their God, and the words of Haggai the prophet, as the LORD their God had sent him; and the people feared the presence of the LORD. Then Haggai, the LORD's messenger, spoke the LORD's message to the people, saying, "I *am* with you, says the LORD." So the LORD stirred up the spirit of Zerubbabel the son of Shealtiel, governor of Judah, and the spirit of Joshua the son of Jehozadak, the high priest, and the spirit of all the remnant of the people; and they came and worked on the house of the LORD of hosts, their God, on the twenty-fourth day of the sixth month, in the second year of King Darius. HAGGAI 1:1–15

In light of what we have learned about the Old Testament temple from previous chapters, why did God want the returning captives to build His house before they built their own?

One person who never needed reminding of the fact that His time was to be dedicated to God was God's Son, Jesus. After attending the Feast of the Passover with His earthly parents, Jesus made the decision to stay a little longer and spend some time in the house of His heavenly Father. Even at the young age of twelve, Jesus understood how best to use His time.

[Jesus'] parents went to Jerusalem every year at the Feast of the Passover. And when He was twelve years old, they went up to Jerusalem according to the custom of the feast. When they had finished the days, as they returned, the Boy Jesus lingered behind in Jerusalem. And Joseph and His mother did not know *it;* but supposing Him to have been in the company, they went a day's journey, and sought Him among *their* relatives and acquaintances. So when they did not find Him, they returned to Jerusalem, seeking Him. Now so it was *that* after three days they found Him in the temple, sitting in the midst of the teachers, both listening to them and asking them questions. And all who heard Him were astonished at His understanding and answers. So when they saw Him, they were amazed; and His mother said to Him, "Son, why have You done this to us? Look, Your father and I have sought You anxiously."

And He said to them, "Why did you seek Me? Did you not know that I must be about My Father's business?" But they did not understand the statement which He spoke to them.

Then He went down with them and came to Nazareth, and was subject to them, but His mother kept all these things in her heart. And Jesus increased in wisdom and stature, and in favor with God and men.

LUKE 2:41–52

MANAGING OUR TIME

God desires us to be replenished and renewed to best serve Him and others. But to experience this, we must manage our time according to God's design for the rhythm and balance of life. In the Old Testament, one of the Ten Commandments instructed God's people to set aside the Sabbath as a day of rest. But before God gave the Israelites the Ten Commandments at Mount Sinai, He gave them a command and a lesson regarding the Sabbath and collecting manna. Although Christians today disagree about whether or not Sabbath-keeping is obligatory, God clearly designed people with the need for regular and deliberate rest.

As you read the following passages from Exodus 16; 18 and Proverbs 31, write down any practical principles you find regarding managing time.

And they journeyed from Elim, and all the congregation of the children of Israel came to the Wilderness of Sin, which is between Elim and Sinai, on the fifteenth day of the second month after they departed from the land of Egypt. Then the whole congregation of the children of Israel complained against Moses and Aaron in the wilderness. And the children of Israel said to them, "Oh, that we had died by the hand of the LORD in the land of Egypt, when we sat by the pots of meat *and* when we ate bread to the full! For you have brought us out into this wilderness to kill this whole assembly with hunger."

Then the LORD said to Moses, "Behold, I will rain bread from heaven for you. And the people shall go out and gather a certain quota every day, that I may test them, whether they will walk in My law or not. And it shall be on the sixth day that they shall prepare what they bring in, and it shall be twice as much as they gather daily."

Then Moses and Aaron said to all the children of Israel, "At evening you shall know that the LORD has brought you out of the land of Egypt. And in the morning you shall see the glory of the LORD; for He hears your complaints against the LORD. But what *are* we, that you complain against us?" Also Moses said, "*This shall be seen* when the LORD gives you meat to eat in the evening, and in the morning bread to the full; for the LORD hears your complaints which you make against Him. And what *are* we? Your complaints *are* not against us but against the LORD."

Then Moses spoke to Aaron, "Say to all the congregation of the children of Israel, 'Come near before the LORD, for He has heard your complaints.'" Now it came to pass, as Aaron spoke to the whole congregation of the children of Israel, that they looked toward the wilderness, and behold, the glory of the LORD appeared in the cloud.

And the LORD spoke to Moses, saying, "I have heard the complaints of the children of Israel. Speak to them, saying, 'At twilight you shall eat meat, and in the morning you shall be filled with bread. And you shall know that I *am* the LORD your God.'"

So it was that quails came up at evening and covered the camp, and in the morning the dew lay all around the camp. And when the layer of dew lifted, there, on the surface of the wilderness, was a small round substance, *as* fine as frost on the ground. So when the children of Israel saw *it,* they said to one another, "What is it?" For they did not know what it *was.*

And Moses said to them, "This *is* the bread which the LORD has given you to eat. This is the thing which the LORD has commanded: 'Let every man gather it according to each one's need, one omer for each person, *according to the* number of persons; let every man take for *those* who *are* in his tent.'"

Then the children of Israel did so and gathered, some more, some less. So when they measured *it* by omers, he who gathered much had nothing left over, and he who gathered little

had no lack. Every man had gathered according to each one's need. And Moses said, "Let no one leave any of it till morning." Notwithstanding they did not heed Moses. But some of them left part of it until morning, and it bred worms and stank. And Moses was angry with them. So they gathered it every morning, every man according to his need. And when the sun became hot, it melted.

And so it was, on the sixth day, *that* they gathered twice as much bread, two omers for each one. And all the rulers of the congregation came and told Moses. Then he said to them, "This *is what* the LORD has said: 'Tomorrow *is* a Sabbath rest, a holy Sabbath to the LORD. Bake what you will bake *today,* and boil what you will boil; and lay up for yourselves all that remains, to be kept until morning.'" So they laid it up till morning, as Moses commanded; and it did not stink, nor were there any worms in it. Then Moses said, "Eat that today, for today *is* a Sabbath to the LORD; today you will not find it in the field. Six days you shall gather it, but on the seventh day, the Sabbath, there will be none."

Now it happened *that some* of the people went out on the seventh day to gather, but they found none. And the LORD said to Moses, "How long do you refuse to keep My commandments and My laws? See! For the LORD has given you the Sabbath; therefore He gives you on the sixth day bread for two days. Let every man remain in his place; let no man go out of his place on the seventh day." So the people rested on the seventh day.

EXODUS 16:1–30

Clearly, God's Word, the Bible, contains stories and advice that illustrate healthy and godly time management. For example, the Israelites' needs were daunting after they escaped from Egypt. Living together in the harsh wilderness created conflicts that needed refereeing. As the leader of the community, Moses tried his best to deal with each and every case on his own. Apparently Moses sent his wife, Zipporah, to her father with the news that the Lord had blessed his mission and brought Israel out of Egypt. When his father-in-law came to visit, he was deeply concerned with what he saw and gave Moses a lesson in time management.

Jethro, Moses' father-in-law, came with his sons and his wife to Moses in the wilderness, where he was encamped at the mountain of God. Now he had said to Moses, "I, your father-in-law Jethro, am coming to you with your wife and her two sons with her."

So Moses went out to meet his father-in-law, bowed down, and kissed him. And they asked each other about *their* well-being, and they went into the tent. And Moses told his father-in-law all that the LORD had done to Pharaoh and to the Egyptians for Israel's sake, all the hardship that had come upon them on the way, and *how* the LORD had delivered them. Then Jethro rejoiced for all the good which the LORD had done for Israel, whom He had delivered out of the hand of the Egyptians. And Jethro said, "Blessed *be* the LORD, who has delivered you out of the hand of the Egyptians and out of the hand of Pharaoh, *and* who has delivered the people from under the hand of the Egyptians. Now I know that the LORD *is* greater than all the gods; for in the very thing in which they behaved proudly, *He was* above them." Then Jethro, Moses' father-in-law, took a burnt offering and *other* sacrifices *to offer* to God. And Aaron came with all the elders of Israel to eat bread with Moses' father-in-law before God.

And so it was, on the next day, that Moses sat to judge the people; and the people stood before Moses from morning until evening. So when Moses' father-in-law saw all that he did for the people, he said, "What *is* this thing that you are doing for the people? Why do you alone sit, and all the people stand before you from morning until evening?"

And Moses said to his father-in-law, "Because the people come to me to inquire of God. When they have a difficulty, they come to me, and I judge between one and another; and I make known the statutes of God and His laws."

So Moses' father-in-law said to him, "The thing that you do *is* not good. Both you and these people who *are* with you will surely wear yourselves out. For this thing *is* too much for you; you are not able to perform it by yourself. Listen now to my voice; I will give you counsel, and God will be with you: Stand before God for the people, so that you may bring the difficulties to God. And you shall teach them the statutes and the laws, and show them the way in which they must walk and the work they must do.

Moreover you shall select from all the people able men, such as fear God, men of truth, hating covetousness; and place *such* over them *to be* rulers of thousands, rulers of hundreds, rulers of fifties, and rulers of tens. And let them judge the people at all times. Then it will be *that* every great matter they shall bring to you, but every small matter they themselves shall judge. So it will be easier for you, for they will bear *the burden* with you. If you do this thing, and God *so* commands you, then you will be able to endure, and all this people will also go to their place in peace."

So Moses heeded the voice of his father-in-law and did all that he had said. And Moses chose able men out of all Israel, and made them heads over the people: rulers of thousands, rulers of hundreds, rulers of fifties, and rulers of tens. So they judged the people at all times; the hard cases they brought to Moses, but they judged every small case themselves.

Then Moses let his father-in-law depart, and he went his way to his own land.

EXODUS 18:5–27

The book of Proverbs in the Old Testament is a collection of brief words of wisdom loosely bound together to teach the reader skills for living, including time management. The last chapter in the book is unique. In detail, it describes the day-to-day workings of the "virtuous wife," who is, essentially, a personification of wisdom. The way she juggles her responsibilities while keeping God's purposes at the center of them all is an inspiration to every follower of God.

Who can find a virtuous wife?
For her worth *is* far above rubies.
The heart of her husband safely trusts her;
So he will have no lack of gain.
She does him good and not evil
All the days of her life.
She seeks wool and flax,
And willingly works with her hands.
She is like the merchant ships,
She brings her food from afar.
She also rises while it is yet night,

And provides food for her household,
And a portion for her maidservants.
She considers a field and buys it;
From her profits she plants a vineyard.
She girds herself with strength,
And strengthens her arms.
She perceives that her merchandise *is* good,
And her lamp does not go out by night.
She stretches out her hands to the distaff,
And her hand holds the spindle.
She extends her hand to the poor,
Yes, she reaches out her hands to the needy.
She is not afraid of snow for her household,
For all her household *is* clothed with scarlet.
She makes tapestry for herself;
Her clothing *is* fine linen and purple.
Her husband is known in the gates,
When he sits among the elders of the land.
She makes linen garments and sells *them,*
And supplies sashes for the merchants.
Strength and honor *are* her clothing;
She shall rejoice in time to come.
She opens her mouth with wisdom,
And on her tongue *is* the law of kindness.
She watches over the ways of her household,
And does not eat the bread of idleness.
Her children rise up and call her blessed;
Her husband *also,* and he praises her:
"Many daughters have done well,
But you excel them all."
Charm *is* deceitful and beauty *is* passing,
But a woman *who* fears the LORD, she shall be praised.
Give her of the fruit of her hands,
And let her own works praise her in the gates.

PROVERBS 31:10–31

Like the virtuous wife, Jesus also kept God as His focus in everything He did, including how He managed His time. When Jesus' ministry was in full swing, the demands on His schedule were intense. At this time in His journey, His brothers did not embrace His position as Messiah. With tongues in cheek they suggested Jesus make His way to Judea in time for a major Jewish feast to expedite His "campaign." Jesus informed them of an important principle of His life—He managed His priorities according to the timing of God the Father.

After these things Jesus walked in Galilee; for He did not want to walk in Judea, because the Jews sought to kill Him. Now the Jews' Feast of Tabernacles was at hand. His brothers therefore said to Him, "Depart from here and go into Judea, that Your disciples also may see the works that You are doing. For no one does anything in secret while he himself seeks to be known openly. If You do these things, show Yourself to the world." For even His brothers did not believe in Him.

Then Jesus said to them, "My time has not yet come, but your time is always ready. The world cannot hate you, but it hates Me because I testify of it that its works are evil. You go up to this feast. I am not yet going up to this feast, for My time has not yet fully come." When He had said these things to them, He remained in Galilee.

But when His brothers had gone up, then He also went up to the feast, not openly, but as it were in secret. Then the Jews sought Him at the feast, and said, "Where is He?" And there was much complaining among the people concerning Him. Some said, "He is good"; others said, "No, on the contrary, He deceives the people." However, no one spoke openly of Him for fear of the Jews.

Now about the middle of the feast Jesus went up into the temple and taught. And the Jews marveled, saying, "How does this Man know letters, having never studied?"

Jesus answered them and said, "My doctrine is not Mine, but His who sent Me."

JOHN 7:1–16

THE REWARDS OF OFFERING OUR TIME

When we give our time to others in order to serve the purposes of God, particularly to those who cannot reciprocate, God not only takes notice but may also reward us greatly.

As you read the passages below from
Matthew 25; Ephesians 5 and Galatians 6,
look for the answer to this question:
How does God reward those who do what
He has asked them to do?

"When the Son of Man comes in His glory, and all the holy angels with Him, then He will sit on the throne of His glory. All the nations will be gathered before Him, and He will separate them one from another, as a shepherd divides *his* sheep from the goats. And He will set the sheep on His right hand, but the goats on the left. Then the King will say to those on His right hand, 'Come, you blessed of My Father, inherit the kingdom prepared for you from the foundation of the world: for I was hungry and you gave Me food; I was thirsty and you gave Me drink; I was a stranger and you took Me in; I *was* naked and you clothed Me; I was sick and you visited Me; I was in prison and you came to Me.'

"Then the righteous will answer Him, saying, 'Lord, when did we see You hungry and feed *You,* or thirsty and give *You* drink? When did we see You a stranger and take *You* in, or naked and clothe *You?* Or when did we see You sick, or in prison, and come to You?' **And the King will answer and say to them, 'Assuredly, I say to you, inasmuch as you did *it* to one of the least of these My brethren, you did *it* to Me.'**

"Then He will also say to those on the left hand, 'Depart from Me, you cursed, into the everlasting fire prepared for the devil and his angels: for I was hungry and you gave Me no food; I was thirsty and you gave Me no drink; I was a stranger and you did not take Me in, naked and you did not clothe Me, sick and in prison and you did not visit Me.'

"Then they also will answer Him, saying, 'Lord, when did we see You hungry or thirsty or a stranger or naked or sick or in prison, and did not minister to You?' Then He will answer them, saying, 'Assuredly, I say to you, inasmuch as you did not do *it* to one of the least of these, you did not do *it* to Me.' And these will go away into everlasting punishment, but the righteous into eternal life."

MATTHEW 25:31–46

See then that you walk circumspectly, not as fools but as wise, redeeming the time, because the days are evil.

Therefore do not be unwise, but understand what the will of the Lord *is*. EPHESIANS 5:15–17

Do not be deceived, God is not mocked; for whatever a man sows, that he will also reap. For he who sows to his flesh will of the flesh reap corruption, but he who sows to the Spirit will of the Spirit reap everlasting life. **And let us not grow weary while doing good, for in due season we shall reap if we do not lose heart.** Therefore, as we have opportunity, let us do good to all, especially to those who are of the household of faith. GALATIANS 6:7–10

What one thing can you do to improve in the key practice of offering your time to God?

WHAT WE BELIEVE

Jonah nailed it on the head when confronted by the sailors about the cause of the storm. He answered, "I am a Hebrew; and I fear the LORD, the God of heaven, who made the sea and the dry land" (Jonah 1:9). Jonah worshiped the one true God and knew that God made everything and everything belonged to Him. This belief drives our obedience in offering God our time to accomplish His purposes. As we seek to serve God, we would do well to keep on our minds God's words through the prophet Haggai: "Consider your ways!" (Haggai 1:5). God's Word teaches and encourages us to learn how to manage our time—not for our own sakes, but for the sake of God's kingdom. The goal, reflected in the key verse at the beginning of the chapter, is not only to offer more time to God but to repurpose everything we have, everything we are and everything we do for His glory and honor. The spiritual, physical and relational rewards from God make it worth the effort for those who give themselves faithfully to this godly exercise.

ACT

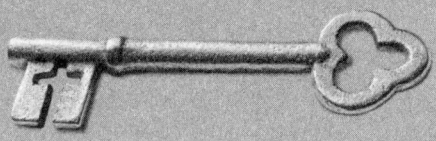

CHAPTER

19

Giving My Resources

KEY QUESTION

How do I best use my resources to serve God and others?

KEY IDEA

I give my resources to fulfill God's purposes.

KEY VERSE

But as you abound in everything—
in faith, in speech, in knowledge,
in all diligence, and in your love for us—
see that you abound in this grace also.
2 Corinthians 8:7

OUR MAP

The key beliefs that compel us to offer our time to God to fulfill His purposes—the church, compassion and stewardship—also drive us to give our resources. Everything we have belongs to God, and we have received clear instruction from the Bible to offer our time and give our resources to help those in need. We also recognize that our God is the one true God who loves us and has provided a way into a relationship with Him as His children now and forever. Because of this, we surrender what rightfully belongs to Him as an act of worship.

In this chapter we will be reading passages from the Old and New Testament that address these topics:

- *Giving Tithes and Offerings*
- *Advice From Wise Men*
- *Teachings From Jesus on Money and Giving*
- *Generosity in Action*

Giving Tithes and Offerings

Throughout the Old Testament, God's people set aside a tenth of their proceeds of land, herds and flocks for God's purposes. This principle is called tithing. Giving a tithe started as a non-religious, political tradition in the ancient world where giving a tribute or tax of a tenth (tithe) to the king was customary. This offering demonstrated allegiance to the monarch's kingdom. When we give the first tenth of our income to God's purposes, we declare our allegiance to God and His kingdom.

Jacob was one of the first followers of God to make a declaration to honor the Lord with a tithe. He was the grandson of Abraham, the son of Isaac and Rebekah, and the twin brother of Esau. Jacob and Esau had a deeply strained relationship. Esau was the firstborn, yet Jacob manipulated him in order to acquire his birthright and then—with the help of his mother—deceived his father in order to receive the firstborn's special blessing. As one might expect, this angered Esau greatly. As a result, Jacob was sent off to live among his relatives in a land far away from Esau.

Now Jacob went out from Beersheba and went toward Haran. So he came to a certain place and stayed there all night, because the sun had set. And he took one of the stones of that place and put it at his head, and he lay down in that place to sleep. Then he dreamed, and behold, a ladder *was* set up on the earth, and its top reached to heaven; and there the angels of God were ascending and descending on it.

And behold, the LORD stood above it and said: "I *am* the LORD God of Abraham your father and the God of Isaac; the land on which you lie I will give to you and your descendants. Also your descendants shall be as the dust of the earth; you shall spread abroad to the west and the east, to the north and the south; and in you and in your seed all the families of the earth shall be blessed. Behold, I *am* with you and will keep you wherever you go, and will bring you back to this land; for I will not leave you until I have done what I have spoken to you."

Then Jacob awoke from his sleep and said, "Surely the LORD is in this place, and I did not know *it*." And he was afraid and said, "How awesome *is* this place! This *is* none other than the house of God, and this *is* the gate of heaven!"

Then Jacob rose early in the morning, and took the stone that he had put at his head, set it up as a pillar, and poured oil on top of it. And he called the name of that place Bethel; but the name of that city had been Luz previously. **Then Jacob made a vow, saying, "If God will be with me, and keep me in this way that I am going, and give me bread to eat and clothing to put on, so that I come back to my father's house in peace, then the LORD shall be my God. And this stone which I have set as a pillar shall be God's house, and of all that You give me I will surely give a tenth to You."** GENESIS 28:10–22

It is evident from many examples in the Bible that our offerings to God need not be confined to our money, but can extend to our possessions, skills, labor, creativity and time. Remarkably, at a point in Israel's history when the Israelites were at their most vulnerable, wandering in the wilderness as nomads, they demonstrated their greatest generosity. God asked Moses to build a place called the tabernacle for Him to dwell with His people. In order for this to happen, God's people needed to contribute their treasures and talents. Their generous response was so over-

whelming that Moses had to tell them to stop bringing their gifts for the tabernacle.

Find all the times the word "willing" is used below
in the passages from Exodus 35 and 36.
Why is a willing heart so important to God?

And Moses spoke to all the congregation of the children of Israel, saying, "This *is* the thing which the LORD commanded, saying: 'Take from among you an offering to the LORD. Whoever *is* of a willing heart, let him bring it as an offering to the LORD: gold, silver, and bronze; blue, purple, and scarlet *thread,* fine linen, and goats' *hair;* ram skins dyed red, badger skins, and acacia wood; oil for the light, and spices for the anointing oil and for the sweet incense; onyx stones, and stones to be set in the ephod and in the breastplate.

'All *who are* gifted artisans among you shall come and make all that the LORD has commanded: the tabernacle, its tent, its covering, its clasps, its boards, its bars, its pillars, and its sockets; the ark and its poles, *with* the mercy seat, and the veil of the covering; the table and its poles, all its utensils, and the showbread; also the lampstand for the light, its utensils, its lamps, and the oil for the light; the incense altar, its poles, the anointing oil, the sweet incense, and the screen for the door at the entrance of the tabernacle; the altar of burnt offering with its bronze grating, its poles, all its utensils, *and* the laver and its base; the hangings of the court, its pillars, their sockets, and the screen for the gate of the court; the pegs of the tabernacle, the pegs of the court, and their cords; the garments of ministry, for ministering in the holy *place*—the holy garments for Aaron the priest and the garments of his sons, to minister as priests.'"

And all the congregation of the children of Israel departed from the presence of Moses. Then everyone came whose heart was stirred, and everyone whose spirit was willing, *and* they brought the LORD's offering for the work of the tabernacle of meeting, for all its service, and for the holy garments. They came, both men and women, as many as had a willing heart, *and* brought earrings and nose rings, rings and necklaces, all jewelry of gold, that is, every man who *made* an offering of gold to the LORD. And every man, with whom was found blue, purple, and scarlet *thread,* fine linen, and goats' *hair,* red skins of rams, and badger skins, brought *them.* Everyone who offered an offering of silver or bronze brought the LORD's offering. And everyone with whom was found acacia wood for any work of the service, brought *it.* All the women *who were* gifted artisans spun yarn with their hands, and brought what they had spun, of blue, purple, *and* scarlet, and fine linen. And all the women whose hearts stirred with wisdom spun yarn of goats' *hair.* The rulers brought onyx stones, and the stones to be set in the ephod and in the breastplate, and spices and oil for the light, for the anointing oil, and for the sweet incense. The children of Israel brought a freewill offering to the LORD, all the men and women whose hearts were willing to bring *material* for all kinds of work which the LORD, by the hand of Moses, had commanded to be done. EXODUS 35:4–29

They received from Moses all the offering which the children of Israel had brought for the work of the service of making the sanctuary. So they continued bringing to him freewill offerings every morning. Then all the craftsmen who were doing all the work of the sanctuary came, each from the work he was doing, and they spoke to Moses, saying, "The people bring much more than enough for the service of the work which the LORD commanded *us* to do."

So Moses gave a commandment, and they caused it to be proclaimed throughout the camp, saying, "Let neither man nor woman do any more work for the offering of the sanctuary." And the people were restrained from bringing, for the material they had was sufficient for all the work to be done—indeed too much. EXODUS 36:3–7

While the Israelites moved from place to place in the wilderness during the time of Moses, they took the tabernacle with them wherever they relocated. Hundreds of years later after Israel had occupied the promised land and become a stable nation, the people once again generously gave from their resources, which they acknowledged had come from God, to build a house worthy of God's presence.

King David said to all the assembly: "My son Solomon, whom alone God has chosen, *is* young and inexperienced; and the work *is* great, because the temple *is* not for man but for the LORD God. Now for the house of my God I have prepared with all my might: gold for *things to be made of* gold, silver for *things of* silver, bronze for *things of* bronze, iron for *things of* iron, wood for *things of* wood, onyx stones, *stones* to be set, glistening stones of various colors, all kinds of precious stones, and marble slabs in abundance. Moreover, because I have set my affection on the house of my God, I have given to the house of my God, over and above all that I have prepared for the holy house, my own special treasure of gold and silver: three thousand talents of gold, of the gold of Ophir, and seven thousand talents of refined silver, to overlay the walls of the houses; the gold for *things of* gold and the silver for *things of* silver, and for all kinds of work *to be done* by the hands of craftsmen. Who *then* is willing to consecrate himself this day to the LORD?"

Then the leaders of the fathers' *houses,* leaders of the tribes of Israel, the captains of thousands and of hundreds, with the officers over the king's work, offered willingly. They gave for the work of the house of God five thousand talents and ten thousand darics of gold, ten thousand talents of silver, eighteen thousand talents of bronze, and one hundred thousand talents of iron. And whoever had *precious* stones gave *them* to the treasury of the house of the LORD, into the hand of Jehiel the Gershonite. Then the people rejoiced, for they had offered willingly, because with a loyal heart they had offered willingly to the LORD; and King David also rejoiced greatly.

Therefore David blessed the LORD before all the assembly; and David said:

"Blessed are You, LORD God of Israel, our Father, forever
and ever.
Yours, O LORD, *is* the greatness,
The power and the glory,
The victory and the majesty;

For all *that is* in heaven and in earth *is Yours;*
Yours *is* the kingdom, O LORD,
And You are exalted as head over all.
Both riches and honor *come* from You,
And You reign over all.
In Your hand *is* power and might;
In Your hand *it is* to make great
And to give strength to all.

"Now therefore, our God,
We thank You
And praise Your glorious name.
But who *am* I, and who *are* my people,
That we should be able to offer so willingly as this?
For all things *come* from You,
And of Your own we have given You.
For we *are* aliens and pilgrims before You,
As *were* all our fathers;
Our days on earth *are* as a shadow,
And without hope.

"O LORD our God, all this abundance that we have prepared to build You a house for Your holy name is from Your hand, and *is* all Your own. I know also, my God, that You test the heart and have pleasure in uprightness. As for me, in the uprightness of my heart I have willingly offered all these *things;* and now with joy I have seen Your people, who are present here to offer willingly to You. O LORD God of Abraham, Isaac, and Israel, our fathers, keep this forever in the intent of the thoughts of the heart of Your people, and fix their heart toward You." 1 CHRONICLES 29:1–18

ADVICE FROM WISE MEN

As you read the following passages
from Proverbs 3 and 11,
identify the one piece of advice that
speaks most clearly to you right now.

Giving away our money and resources is beneficial not only for the recipients but also for us. When we make giving to God's purposes part of our regular spending habits, we honor God and keep greed at bay. The writers of Proverbs offered the following words of wisdom regarding how we should handle what God has given us.

Honor the LORD with your possessions,
And with the firstfruits of all your increase;
So your barns will be filled with plenty,
And your vats will overflow with new wine. PROVERBS 3:9–10

There is *one* who scatters, yet increases more;
And there is *one* who withholds more than is right,
But it *leads* to poverty.
The generous soul will be made rich,
And he who waters will also be watered himself.
PROVERBS 11:24–25

He who trusts in his riches will fall,
But the righteous will flourish like foliage. PROVERBS 11:28

Solomon, one of the writers of Proverbs and the son of King David, accumulated immense wealth during his lifetime. In the book of Ecclesiastes, traditionally considered to be written by Solomon, he reflects on his life and shares his words of wisdom with us regarding the dangers of wealth. Money itself is not evil, but the love of money can lead to sin. More wealth does not mean more satisfaction in life. To avoid falling victim to money's seductive lure, we are to use what we have for the Lord.

He who loves silver will not be satisfied with silver;
Nor he who loves abundance, with increase.
This also *is* vanity.

When goods increase,
They increase who eat them;
So what profit have the owners
Except to see *them* with their eyes?

The sleep of a laboring man *is* sweet,
Whether he eats little or much;
But the abundance of the rich will not permit him
to sleep.

There is a severe evil *which* I have seen under the sun:
Riches kept for their owner to his hurt.
But those riches perish through misfortune;
When he begets a son, *there is* nothing in his hand.
As he came from his mother's womb, naked shall he
return,
To go as he came;
And he shall take nothing from his labor
Which he may carry away in his hand.

And this also *is* a severe evil—
Just exactly as he came, so shall he go.
And what profit has he who has labored for the wind?
All his days he also eats in darkness,
And *he has* much sorrow and sickness and anger.

Here is what I have seen: *It is* good and fitting *for one* to eat and drink, and to enjoy the good of all his labor in which he toils under the sun all the days of his life which God gives him; for it *is* his heritage. **As for every man to whom God has given riches and wealth, and given him power to eat of it, to receive his heritage and rejoice in his labor—this *is* the gift of God. For he will not dwell unduly on the days of his life, because God keeps *him* busy with the joy of his heart.** ECCLESIASTES 5:10–20

At the birth of Jesus, three men came from afar with gifts to visit Him. They were likely astrologers from Persia, southern Arabia or Mesopotamia who had been anticipating the arrival of the "king of the Jews" for some time. Their advice for us doesn't come from their lips as much as from their actions. They gave Him months of their time as they traveled to see Him. They were honored men, yet they humbled themselves and bowed their knees to worship Jesus. They also gave Him costly gifts that were the best they had to give.

Now after Jesus was born in Bethlehem of Judea in the days of Herod the king, behold, wise men from the East came to Jerusalem, saying, "Where is He who has been born King of the Jews? For we have seen His star in the East and have come to worship Him."

When Herod the king heard *this,* he was troubled, and all Jerusalem with him. And when he had gathered all the chief priests and scribes of the people together, he inquired of them where the Christ was to be born.

So they said to him, "In Bethlehem of Judea, for thus it is written by the prophet:

> *'But you, Bethlehem, in the land of Judah,*
> *Are not the least among the rulers of Judah;*
> *For out of you shall come a Ruler*
> *Who will shepherd My people Israel.'"*

Then Herod, when he had secretly called the wise men, determined from them what time the star appeared. And he sent them to Bethlehem and said, "Go and search carefully for the young Child, and when you have found *Him,* bring back word to me, that I may come and worship Him also."

When they heard the king, they departed; and behold, the star which they had seen in the East went before them, till it came and stood over where the young Child was. When they saw the star, they rejoiced with exceedingly great joy. **And when they had come into the house, they saw the young Child with Mary His mother, and fell down and worshiped Him. And when they had opened their treasures, they presented gifts to Him: gold, frankincense, and myrrh.**

Then, being divinely warned in a dream that they should not return to Herod, they departed for their own country another way.

MATTHEW 2:1–12

TEACHINGS FROM JESUS ON MONEY AND GIVING

Jesus said more about money than the topics of heaven and hell combined. Our attitudes toward money and personal resources say so much about our lives. Giving should flow from a pure heart that desires to meet a need. There's a subtle trap to avoid in our giving—it should not be a way to draw attention to ourselves. It is important to think beyond our earthly lives and ask how we can share what we've been given to build God's kingdom.

"Take heed that you do not do your charitable deeds before men, to be seen by them. Otherwise you have no reward from your Father in heaven. Therefore, when you do a charitable deed, do not sound a trumpet before you as the hypocrites do in the synagogues and in the streets, that they may have glory from men. Assuredly, I say to you, they have their reward. **But when you do a charitable deed, do not let your left hand know what your right hand is doing, that your charitable deed may be in secret; and your Father who sees in secret will Himself reward you openly."**

MATTHEW 6:1–4

"Do not lay up for yourselves treasures on earth, where moth and rust destroy and where thieves break in and steal; but lay up for yourselves treasures in heaven, where neither moth nor rust destroys and where thieves do not break in and steal. For where your treasure is, there your heart will be also.

"The lamp of the body is the eye. If therefore your eye is good, your whole body will be full of light. But if your eye is bad, your whole body will be full of darkness. If therefore the light that is in you is darkness, how great *is* that darkness!

"No one can serve two masters; for either he will hate the one and love the other, or else he will be loyal to the one and despise the other. You cannot serve God and mammon."

MATTHEW 6:19–24

Then one from the crowd said to Him, "Teacher, tell my brother to divide the inheritance with me."

But He said to him, "Man, who made Me a judge or an arbitrator over you?" And He said to them, "Take heed and beware of covetousness, for one's life does not consist in the abundance of the things he possesses."

Then He spoke a parable to them, saying: "The ground of a certain rich man yielded plentifully. And he thought within himself, saying, 'What shall I do, since I have no room to store my crops?' So he said, 'I will do this: I will pull down my barns and build greater, and there I will store all my crops and my goods. And I will say to my soul, "Soul, you have many goods laid up for many years; take your ease; eat, drink, *and* be merry."' **But God said to him, 'Fool! This night your soul will be required of you; then whose will those things be which you have provided?'**

"So *is* he who lays up treasure for himself, and is not rich toward God." LUKE 12:13–21

As is evident from the above parable of the rich fool, Jesus had a knack for noticing teachable moments. Everyday encounters with fig trees, water wells and simple dinner parties provided illustrations for Jesus to explain what matters the most to God. In this situation, Jesus was observing the daily activities at the temple when an opportunity arose for Jesus to teach His disciples what type of giving touches God's heart.

Now Jesus sat opposite the treasury and saw how the people put money into the treasury. And many *who were* rich put in much. Then one poor widow came and threw in two mites, which make a quadrans. **So He called His disciples to *Himself* and said to them, "Assuredly, I say to you that this poor widow has put in more than all those who have given to the treasury; for they all put in out of their abundance, but she out of her poverty put in all that she had, her whole livelihood."** MARK 12:41–44

It's easy to give when we know we will receive something in return. Jesus challenges us to remember that true giving has no strings attached.

"But if you love those who love you, what credit is that to you? For even sinners love those who love them. And if you do good to those who do good to you, what credit is that to you? For even sinners do the same. And if you lend *to those* from whom you hope to receive back, what credit is that to you? For even sinners lend to sinners to receive as much back. But love your enemies, do good, and lend, hoping for nothing in return; and your reward will be great, and you will be sons of the Most High. For He is kind to the unthankful and evil. Therefore be merciful, just as your Father also is merciful." LUKE 6:32–36

If someone asked you to summarize what Jesus taught about money and giving, what would you say?

Generosity in Action

After Jesus' death, resurrection and ascension to heaven, His followers committed to give their money generously to help the needy among them and fulfill God's purposes.

Now the multitude of those who believed were of one heart and one soul; neither did anyone say that any of the things he possessed was his own, but they had all things in common. And with great power the apostles gave witness to the resurrection of the Lord Jesus. And great grace was upon them all. Nor was there anyone among them who lacked; for all who were possessors of lands or houses sold them, and brought the proceeds of the things that were sold, and laid *them* at the apostles' feet; and they distributed to each as anyone had need.

And Joses, who was also named Barnabas by the apostles (which is translated Son of Encouragement), a Levite of the country of Cyprus, having land, sold *it,* and brought the money and laid *it* at the apostles' feet. Acts 4:32–37

Evidence of the generosity of the early church can be seen in many circumstances. For instance, Paul encouraged the believers at Corinth to send an offering to their needy fellow believers in Jerusalem, something the Corinthians had intended to do but had not finished.

As you read the Scripture below from 2 Corinthians 8 and 9, look for details concerning how believers can determine what they should give.

Moreover, brethren, we make known to you the grace of God bestowed on the churches of Macedonia: that in a great trial of affliction the abundance of their joy and their deep poverty abounded in the riches of their liberality. For I bear witness that according to *their* ability, yes, and beyond *their* ability, *they were* freely willing, imploring us with much urgency that we would receive the gift and the fellowship of the ministering to the saints. And not *only* as we had hoped, but they first gave themselves to the Lord, and *then* to us by the will of God. So we urged Titus, that as he had begun, so he would also complete this grace in you as well. **But as you abound in everything—in faith, in speech, in knowledge, in all diligence, and in your love for us—*see* that you abound in this grace also.**

I speak not by commandment, but I am testing the sincerity of your love by the diligence of others. For you know the grace of our Lord Jesus Christ, that though He was rich, yet for your sakes He became poor, that you through His poverty might become rich.

And in this I give advice: It is to your advantage not only to be doing what you began and were desiring to do a year ago; but now you also must complete the doing *of it;* that as *there was* a readiness to desire *it,* so *there* also *may be* a completion out of what *you* have. For if there is first a willing mind, *it is* accepted according to what one has, *and* not according to what he does not have.

For *I do* not *mean* that others should be eased and you burdened; but by an equality, *that* now at this time your abundance *may supply* their lack, that their abundance also may *supply* your lack—that there may be equality. As it is written, *"He who gathered much had nothing left over, and he who gathered little had no lack."*

But thanks *be* to God who puts the same earnest care for you into the heart of Titus. For he not only accepted the exhortation, but being more diligent, he went to you of his own accord. And we have sent with him the brother whose praise *is* in the gospel throughout all the churches, and not only *that,* but who was also chosen by the churches to travel with us with this gift, which is administered by us to the glory of the Lord Himself and *to show* your ready mind, avoiding this: that anyone should blame us in this lavish gift which is administered by us—providing honorable things, not only in the sight of the Lord, but also in the sight of men.

And we have sent with them our brother whom we have often proved diligent in many things, but now much more diligent, because of the great confidence which *we have* in you. If *anyone inquires* about Titus, *he is* my partner and fellow worker concerning you. Or if our brethren *are inquired about, they are* messengers of the churches, the glory of Christ. Therefore show to them, and before the churches, the proof of your love and of our boasting on your behalf.

Now concerning the ministering to the saints, it is superfluous for me to write to you; for I know your willingness, about which I boast of you to the Macedonians, that Achaia was ready a year ago; and your zeal has stirred up the majority. Yet I have sent the brethren, lest our boasting of you should be in vain in this respect, that, as I said, you may be ready; lest if *some* Macedonians come with me and find you unprepared, we (not to mention you!) should be ashamed of this confident boasting. Therefore I thought it necessary to exhort the brethren to go to you ahead of time, and prepare your generous gift beforehand, which *you had* previously promised, that it may be ready as *a matter of* generosity and not as a grudging obligation.

But this *I say:* He who sows sparingly will also reap sparingly, and he who sows bountifully will also reap bountifully. *So let* each one *give* as he purposes in his heart, not grudgingly or of necessity; for God loves a cheerful giver. And God *is* able to make all grace abound toward you, that you, always having all sufficiency in all *things,* may have an abundance for every good work. As it is written:

> *"He has dispersed abroad,*
> *He has given to the poor;*
> *His righteousness endures forever."*

Now may He who supplies seed to the sower, and bread for food, supply and multiply the seed you have *sown* and increase the fruits of your righteousness, while *you are* enriched in everything for all liberality, which causes thanksgiving through us to God. For the administration of this service not only supplies the needs of the saints, but also is abounding through many thanksgivings to God, while, through the proof of this ministry, they glorify God for the obedience of your confession to the gospel of Christ, and for *your* liberal sharing with them and all *men,* and by their prayer for you, who long for you because of the exceeding grace of God in you. Thanks *be* to God for His indescribable gift!

2 CORINTHIANS 8:1—9:15

On a scale of 1–10, evaluate your level of generosity.
What has helped you become more generous?
What still causes you to hold back?

WHAT WE BELIEVE

Many people see giving as an obligation, but it is really an act of worship from someone who has embraced in their heart the key beliefs of the Christian faith. The one true God is good and has provided the way to eternal salvation. When we accept this gift of life we are given a new identity and called to a new purpose to fulfill God's mission on earth until He returns. We give away our resources with that motivation and purpose in mind. The people of the Old Testament gave the first 10 percent to God as a declaration of their allegiance to Him. But they gave beyond the tithe out of a willing heart because of God's great love for them. The words of the wisdom writers and the lives of the wise men who visited Jesus at His birth illustrate the importance and benefits of being content and generous with our resources. Jesus reminds us that we should strive to think bigger than our earthly lives and use our resources to strengthen God's kingdom. God is more concerned about the reasons we give than about the size of our gift.

ACT

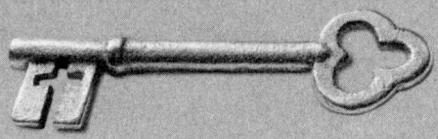

CHAPTER

20

Sharing My Faith

KEY QUESTION

How do I share my faith with those who don't know God?

KEY IDEA

I share my faith with others to fulfill God's purposes.

KEY VERSE

And for me, that utterance may be given to me,
that I may open my mouth boldly to make
known the mystery of the gospel,
for which I am an ambassador in chains;
that in it I may speak boldly, as I ought to speak.
Ephesians 6:19–20

OUR MAP

We believe the one true God has unfolded His grand plan to provide salvation through Jesus Christ. We believe God loves all people and extends an invitation to everyone to receive eternal life. We believe there is a heaven and a hell and that Jesus is returning to judge the earth and establish His eternal kingdom. Only those who receive salvation by faith in Christ in this life will be a part of the eternal life to come. We believe God has purposed the church to be the primary ambassador to spread this message, this good news to the world. Because of these values we commit ourselves to sharing our faith. So how do we share our faith with those who don't know God?

In this chapter we will read Scripture passages that answer that question. Here are the main topics of this chapter:

- *The Call to Share Our Faith*
- *Sharing Our Faith Through Our Lives*
- *Sharing Our Faith Through Our Words*
- *Sharing Our Faith With All*

The Call to Share Our Faith

Catastrophically, the fall of humankind in the Garden of Eden shattered humanity's connection with God—the connection He originally intended when He created people. So God unfolded a plan to provide the way for all people to come back into a relationship with Him. His grand plan included the founding of a brand-new nation. Two thousand years before the arrival of Jesus, God called Abram (later renamed Abraham) to start this new nation, eventually known as Israel. People from all nations would come to know God through Abraham's offspring.

Now the Lord had said to Abram:

"Get out of your country,
From your family
And from your father's house,
To a land that I will show you.
I will make you a great nation;

I will bless you
And make your name great;
And you shall be a blessing.
I will bless those who bless you,
And I will curse him who curses you;
And in you all the families of the earth shall be blessed."

So Abram departed as the LORD had spoken to him, and Lot went with him. And Abram *was* seventy-five years old when he departed from Haran. GENESIS 12:1–4

In the 2,000 years that followed, Israel was a living demonstration to the world of the lengths to which God would go to reestablish His relationship with His people. Then, with the ultimate sacrifice of His Son, the reconciliation with God that was formerly confined to Israel now became available to all humankind. What's remarkable is that we can play a pivotal role in God's restoration plan. By responding to the call to share our faith, we partner with God in His divine pursuit of broken souls.

For the love of Christ compels us, because we judge thus: that if One died for all, then all died; and He died for all, that those who live should live no longer for themselves, but for Him who died for them and rose again.

Therefore, from now on, we regard no one according to the flesh. Even though we have known Christ according to the flesh, yet now we know *Him thus* no longer. Therefore, if anyone *is* in Christ, *he is* a new creation; old things have passed away; behold, all things have become new. Now all things *are* of God, who has reconciled us to Himself through Jesus Christ, and has given us the ministry of reconciliation, that is, that **God was in Christ reconciling the world to Himself, not imputing their trespasses to them, and has committed to us the word of reconciliation.**

Now then, we are ambassadors for Christ, as though God were pleading through us: we implore *you* on Christ's behalf, be reconciled to God. For He made Him who knew no sin *to be* sin for us, that we might become the righteousness of God in Him.

2 CORINTHIANS 5:14–21

What are some ways in which we can be God's "ambassadors" to the world?

Sharing Our Faith Through Our Lives

The most powerful way to share our faith in God is through our lives—being a positive example to all in how we live every day. When others see the faith, hope and love in our lives, they are drawn to live the same way. After paying attention over time, they will notice our confidence in and relationship with the one true God. In 2 Kings we find a story in which a young girl from Israel who had been taken captive speaks up because of her faith and her noble concern for her master, the commander of the army of Syria—Israel's enemy. The girl's words eventually led to the healing of this foreign soldier and inspired his belief in the one true God.

Now Naaman, commander of the army of the king of Syria, was a great and honorable man in the eyes of his master, because by him the LORD had given victory to Syria. He was also a mighty man of valor, *but* a leper. **And the Syrians had gone out on raids, and had brought back captive a young girl from the land of Israel. She waited on Naaman's wife. Then she said to her mistress, "If only my master *were* with the prophet who *is* in Samaria! For he would heal him of his leprosy."** And *Naaman* went in and told his master, saying, "Thus and thus said the girl who *is* from the land of Israel."

Then the king of Syria said, "Go now, and I will send a letter to the king of Israel."

So he departed and took with him ten talents of silver, six thousand *shekels* of gold, and ten changes of clothing. Then he brought the letter to the king of Israel, which said,

Now be advised, when this letter comes to you, that I have sent Naaman my servant to you, that you may heal him of his leprosy.

And it happened, when the king of Israel read the letter, that he tore his clothes and said, "*Am* I God, to kill and make alive, that this man sends a man to me to heal him of his leprosy? Therefore please consider, and see how he seeks a quarrel with me."

So it was, when Elisha the man of God heard that the king of Israel had torn his clothes, that he sent to the king, saying, "Why have you torn your clothes? Please let him come to me, and he shall know that there is a prophet in Israel."

Then Naaman went with his horses and chariot, and he stood at the door of Elisha's house. And Elisha sent a messenger to him, saying, "Go and wash in the Jordan seven times, and your flesh shall be restored to you, and *you shall* be clean." But Naaman became furious, and went away and said, "Indeed, I said to myself, 'He will surely come out *to me,* and stand and call on the name of the LORD his God, and wave his hand over the place, and heal the leprosy.' *Are* not the Abanah and the Pharpar, the rivers of Damascus, better than all the waters of Israel? Could I not wash in them and be clean?" So he turned and went away in a rage. And his servants came near and spoke to him, and said, "My father, *if* the prophet had told you *to do* something great, would you not have done *it?* How much more then, when he says to you, 'Wash, and be clean'?" So he went down and dipped seven times in the Jordan, according to the saying of the man of God; and his flesh was restored like the flesh of a little child, and he was clean.

And [Naaman] returned to the man of God, he and all his aides, and came and stood before him; and he said, "Indeed, now I know that *there is* no God in all the earth, except in Israel." 2 KINGS 5:1–15

The one true God wants us to be a reflection of His image to the world. In His famous Sermon on the Mount, Jesus used the metaphor of "salt and light" to express the power of a life lived in faith and obedience to God.

"You are the salt of the earth; but if the salt loses its flavor, how shall it be seasoned? It is then good for nothing but to be thrown out and trampled underfoot by men.

"You are the light of the world. A city that is set on a hill cannot be hidden. Nor do they light a lamp and put it under a basket, but on a lampstand, and it gives light to all *who are* in the house.

Let your light so shine before men, that they may see your good works and glorify your Father in heaven." MATTHEW 5:13–16

Being the light of the world requires the attitude of a humble servant. Sometimes we must adapt our approach in order to meet the needs of the people we are trying to reach with the gospel. Many new believers in the early church were drawn to the Christian faith by the way the people of the church served one another.

And they continued steadfastly in the apostles' doctrine and fellowship, in the breaking of bread, and in prayers. Then fear came upon every soul, and many wonders and signs were done through the apostles. Now all who believed were together, and had all things in common, and sold their possessions and goods, and divided them among all, as anyone had need.

So continuing daily with one accord in the temple, and breaking bread from house to house, they ate their food with gladness and simplicity of heart, praising God and having favor with all the people. And the Lord added to the church daily those who were being saved. ACTS 2:42–47

The apostle Paul was very aware that his life was to be the light of Christ and the good flavor of salt to his world. He consciously did whatever it took to make sure he was putting others' needs before his own so they would have no reason to reject the good news.

For though I am free from all *men,* I have made myself a servant to all, that I might win the more; and to the Jews I became as a Jew, that I might win Jews; to those *who are* under the law, as under the law, that I might win those *who are* under the law; to those *who are* without law, as without law (not being without law toward God, but under law toward Christ), that I might win those *who are* without law; to the weak I became as weak, that I might win the weak. **I have become all things to all *men,* that I might by all means save some. Now this I do for the gospel's sake, that I may be partaker of it with *you.*** 1 CORINTHIANS 9:19–23

What does Paul mean when he writes, "I have become all things to all *men*, that I might by all means save some"? What do you think this does not mean?

Sharing Our Faith Through Our Words

In addition to sharing our faith by the way we live our lives, we are also called to share through our words who God is and what great things He has done for us. David, overwhelmed with God's involvement in his life, was a strong witness through his words to God's character and acts.

I waited patiently for the Lord;
And He inclined to me,
And heard my cry.
He also brought me up out of a horrible pit,
Out of the miry clay,
And set my feet upon a rock,
And established my steps.
He has put a new song in my mouth—
Praise to our God;
Many will see *it* and fear,
And will trust in the Lord.

Blessed *is* that man who makes the Lord his trust,
And does not respect the proud, nor such as turn aside
to lies.
Many, O Lord my God, *are* Your wonderful works
Which You have done;
And Your thoughts toward us
Cannot be recounted to You in order;
If I would declare and speak *of them,*
They are more than can be numbered.

Sacrifice and offering You did not desire;
My ears You have opened.
Burnt offering and sin offering You did not require.
Then I said, "Behold, I come;
In the scroll of the book *it is* written of me.

I delight to do Your will, O my God,
And Your law *is* within my heart."

I have proclaimed the good news of righteousness
In the great assembly;
Indeed, I do not restrain my lips,
O LORD, You Yourself know.
I have not hidden Your righteousness within my heart;
I have declared Your faithfulness and Your salvation;
I have not concealed Your lovingkindness and Your truth
From the great assembly. PSALM 40:1–10

The entire early church had a mission to share the truth about God's love and faithfulness, which they accomplished by testifying about the resurrected Christ. Although we may feel we are not as eloquent as David or as knowledgeable as Paul, like the early church members, we all have a mission to share our faith with others. It is through God that we have been given the power to carry out that assignment.

The former account I [Luke] made, O Theophilus, of all that Jesus began both to do and teach, until the day in which He was taken up, after He through the Holy Spirit had given commandments to the apostles whom He had chosen, to whom He also presented Himself alive after His suffering by many infallible proofs, being seen by them during forty days and speaking of the things pertaining to the kingdom of God.

And being assembled together with *them,* He commanded them not to depart from Jerusalem, but to wait for the Promise of the Father, "which," *He said,* "you have heard from Me; for John truly baptized with water, but you shall be baptized with the Holy Spirit not many days from now." Therefore, when they had come together, they asked Him, saying, "Lord, will You at this time restore the kingdom to Israel?" And He said to them, "It is not for you to know times or seasons which the Father has put in His own authority. **But you shall receive power when the Holy Spirit has come upon you; and you shall be witnesses to Me in Jerusalem, and in all Judea and Samaria, and to the end of the earth."**

ACTS 1:1–8

The people of the early church had a mission to share the truth about God's love and faithfulness, which they accomplished by testifying about the resurrected Christ. But when it comes to actually using words, we may be afraid we won't know what to say. God promised us the Holy Spirit to give us words when we need them, just as Paul prays in the key verse at the beginning of the chapter. As we see with Philip, the Holy Spirit even makes sure we meet people at just the right time—when they are ready to hear the good news.

As you read about Philip's divine encounter with the Ethiopian in Acts 8, identify Philip's effective strategies for sharing his faith that you can emulate.

At that time a great persecution arose against the church which was at Jerusalem; and they were all scattered throughout the regions of Judea and Samaria, except the apostles. And devout men carried Stephen *to his burial,* and made great lamentation over him.

As for Saul, he made havoc of the church, entering every house, and dragging off men and women, committing *them* to prison.

Therefore those who were scattered went everywhere preaching the word. Then Philip went down to the city of Samaria and preached Christ to them. And the multitudes with one accord heeded the things spoken by Philip, hearing and seeing the miracles which he did. For unclean spirits, crying with a loud voice, came out of many who were possessed; and many who were paralyzed and lame were healed. And there was great joy in that city.

ACTS 8:1–8

Now an angel of the Lord spoke to Philip, saying, "Arise and go toward the south along the road which goes down from Jerusalem to Gaza." This is desert. So he arose and went. And behold, a man of Ethiopia, a eunuch of great authority under Candace the queen of the Ethiopians, who had charge of all her treasury, and had come to Jerusalem to worship, was returning. And sitting in his chariot, he was reading Isaiah the prophet. Then the Spirit said to Philip, "Go near and overtake this chariot."

So Philip ran to him, and heard him reading the prophet Isaiah, and said, "Do you understand what you are reading?"

And he said, "How can I, unless someone guides me?" And he asked Philip to come up and sit with him. The place in the Scripture which he read was this:

> *"He was led as a sheep to the slaughter;*
> *And as a lamb before its shearer is silent,*
> *So He opened not His mouth.*
> *In His humiliation His justice was taken away,*
> *And who will declare His generation?*
> *For His life is taken from the earth."*

So the eunuch answered Philip and said, "I ask you, of whom does the prophet say this, of himself or of some other man?" **Then Philip opened his mouth, and beginning at this Scripture, preached Jesus to him.** Now as they went down the road, they came to some water. And the eunuch said, "See, *here is* water. What hinders me from being baptized?"

Then Philip said, "If you believe with all your heart, you may."

And he answered and said, "I believe that Jesus Christ is the Son of God."

So he commanded the chariot to stand still. And both Philip and the eunuch went down into the water, and he baptized him. Now when they came up out of the water, the Spirit of the Lord caught Philip away, so that the eunuch saw him no more; and he went on his way rejoicing. But Philip was found at Azotus. And passing through, he preached in all the cities till he came to Caesarea.

ACTS 8:26–40

Like Philip illustrated by following the leading of the Holy Spirit, when we partner with God in His plan to piece together this broken world, we become His ambassadors, His representatives on earth. Being an ambassador of Christ is not easy. The apostle Paul, who suffered greatly for sharing his faith, understood this well. Despite the persecution, he was passionate about spreading the good news. While headed to Jerusalem during his third missionary journey, he requested a meeting with his good friends from Ephesus, since he knew there was a chance he'd never see them again. At the meeting, Paul declared his passion for sharing his faith.

From Miletus he sent to Ephesus and called for the elders of the church. And when they had come to him, he said to them: "You know, from the first day that I came to Asia, in what manner I always lived among you, serving the Lord with all humility, with many tears and trials which happened to me by the plotting of the Jews; how I kept back nothing that was helpful, but proclaimed it to you, and taught you publicly and from house to house, testifying to Jews, and also to Greeks, repentance toward God and faith toward our Lord Jesus Christ. And see, now I go bound in the spirit to Jerusalem, not knowing the things that will happen to me there, except that the Holy Spirit testifies in every city, saying that chains and tribulations await me. **But none of these things move me; nor do I count my life dear to myself, so that I may finish my race with joy, and the ministry which I received from the Lord Jesus, to testify to the gospel of the grace of God."** ACTS 20:17–24

In his letters, Paul asked fellow believers to pray for him as he shared his faith. And he called them to make the most of every opportunity to share the message of the good news. Paul's words are precious to us today as we share our faith with those God brings across our paths.

And [pray] for me, that utterance may be given to me, that I may open my mouth boldly to make known the mystery of the gospel, for which I am an ambassador in chains; that in it I may speak boldly, as I ought to speak. EPHESIANS 6:19–20

Continue earnestly in prayer, being vigilant in it with thanksgiving; meanwhile praying also for us, that God would open to us a door for the word, to speak the mystery of Christ, for which I am also in chains, that I may make it manifest, as I ought to speak.

Walk in wisdom toward those *who are* outside, redeeming the time. *Let* your speech always *be* with grace, seasoned with salt, that you may know how you ought to answer each one.

COLOSSIANS 4:2–6

What does it mean to "walk in wisdom toward those who are outside"? What does it mean to have our conversation "be with grace" and "seasoned with salt"?

Sharing Our Faith With All

From the very beginning God anticipated that all nations and all people would be a part of His plan of redemption and restoration. The Israelites resisted God's call to be the channel of His redemptive purposes for the people of the world. This sentiment was demonstrated in the story of Jonah, whom God called to take His message to the Assyrian people in the great city of Nineveh. The Assyrians, a major enemy of Israel, were wicked people with wicked practices. As we read in Chapter 18 (Offering My Time), when God gave Jonah this assignment, Jonah ran away in the opposite direction; he thought the people in Nineveh were beyond saving. He had time to rethink his decision when God placed him in the belly of a giant fish for three days. After God had the fish vomit Jonah onto dry land, God offered Jonah an opportunity to obey, even though Jonah still did not think the people would respond.

Now the word of the Lord came to Jonah the second time, saying, "Arise, go to Nineveh, that great city, and preach to it the message that I tell you." So Jonah arose and went to Nineveh, according to the word of the Lord. Now Nineveh was an exceedingly great city, a three-day journey *in extent.* And Jonah began to enter the city on the first day's walk. Then he cried out and said, "Yet forty days, and Nineveh shall be overthrown!"

So the people of Nineveh believed God, proclaimed a fast, and put on sackcloth, from the greatest to the least of them. Then word came to the king of Nineveh; and he arose from his throne and laid aside his robe, covered *himself* with sackcloth and sat in ashes. And he caused *it* to be proclaimed and published throughout Nineveh by the decree of the king and his nobles, saying,

Let neither man nor beast, herd nor flock, taste anything; do not let them eat, or drink water. But let man and beast be covered with sackcloth, and cry mightily to God; yes, let every one turn from his evil way and from the violence that is in his hands. Who can tell *if* God will turn and relent, and turn away from His fierce anger, so that we may not perish?

Then God saw their works, that they turned from their evil way; and God relented from the disaster that He had said He would bring upon them, and He did not do it.

But it displeased Jonah exceedingly, and he became angry. So he prayed to the LORD, and said, "Ah, LORD, was not this what I said when I was still in my country? Therefore I fled previously to Tarshish; for I know that You *are* a gracious and merciful God, slow to anger and abundant in lovingkindness, One who relents from doing harm. Therefore now, O LORD, please take my life from me, for *it is* better for me to die than to live!"

Then the LORD said, "*Is it* right for you to be angry?"

So Jonah went out of the city and sat on the east side of the city. There he made himself a shelter and sat under it in the shade, till he might see what would become of the city. And the LORD God prepared a plant and made it come up over Jonah, that it might be shade for his head to deliver him from his misery. So Jonah was very grateful for the plant. But as morning dawned the next day God prepared a worm, and it *so* damaged the plant that it withered. And it happened, when the sun arose, that God prepared a vehement east wind; and the sun beat on Jonah's head, so that he grew faint. Then he wished death for himself, and said, "*It is* better for me to die than to live."

Then God said to Jonah, "*Is it* right for you to be angry about the plant?"

And he said, "*It is* right for me to be angry, even to death!"

But the LORD said, "You have had pity on the plant for which you have not labored, nor made it grow, which came up in a night and perished in a night. And should I not pity Nineveh, that great city, in which are more than one hundred and twenty thousand persons who cannot discern between their right hand and their left—and much livestock?" JONAH 3:1—4:11

The resistance of the Jews to sharing their faith with outsiders carried over into the time of Jesus. The Samaritans were a mixed-blood race resulting from the intermarriage of Israelites who were left behind when the people of the northern kingdom were exiled and Gentiles who were brought into the land by the Assyrians. Resentful hostility existed between Jews and Samaritans in Jesus' day. To avoid these people, who lived in the large region between Judea and Galilee, Jews would often go out of their way to cross over the Jordan River and travel on the east side. Modeling the value of inclusivity to His disciples, Jesus traveled directly through Samaria and went out of His way to talk to a Samaritan woman.

[Jesus] left Judea and departed again to Galilee. But He needed to go through Samaria.

So He came to a city of Samaria which is called Sychar, near the plot of ground that Jacob gave to his son Joseph. Now Jacob's well was there. Jesus therefore, being wearied from *His* journey, sat thus by the well. It was about the sixth hour.

A woman of Samaria came to draw water. Jesus said to her, "Give Me a drink." For His disciples had gone away into the city to buy food.

Then the woman of Samaria said to Him, "How is it that You, being a Jew, ask a drink from me, a Samaritan woman?" For Jews have no dealings with Samaritans.

Jesus answered and said to her, "If you knew the gift of God, and who it is who says to you, 'Give Me a drink,' you would have asked Him, and He would have given you living water."

The woman said to Him, "Sir, You have nothing to draw with, and the well is deep. Where then do You get that living water? Are You greater than our father Jacob, who gave us the well, and drank from it himself, as well as his sons and his livestock?"

Jesus answered and said to her, "Whoever drinks of this water will thirst again, but whoever drinks of the water that I shall give him will never thirst. But the water that I shall give him will become in him a fountain of water springing up into everlasting life."

The woman said to Him, "Sir, give me this water, that I may not thirst, nor come here to draw."

Jesus said to her, "Go, call your husband, and come here."

The woman answered and said, "I have no husband."

Jesus said to her, "You have well said, 'I have no husband,' for you have had five husbands, and the one whom you now have is not your husband; in that you spoke truly."

The woman said to Him, "Sir, I perceive that You are a prophet. Our fathers worshiped on this mountain, and you *Jews* say that in Jerusalem is the place where one ought to worship."

Jesus said to her, "Woman, believe Me, the hour is coming when you will neither on this mountain, nor in Jerusalem, worship the Father. You worship what you do not know; we know what we worship, for salvation is of the Jews. But the hour is coming, and now is, when the true worshipers will worship the Father in spirit and truth; for the Father is seeking such to worship Him. God *is* Spirit, and those who worship Him must worship in spirit and truth."

The woman said to Him, "I know that Messiah is coming" (who is called Christ). "When He comes, He will tell us all things."

Jesus said to her, "I who speak to you am *He.*"

And at this *point* His disciples came, and they marveled that He talked with a woman; yet no one said, "What do You seek?" or, "Why are You talking with her?"

The woman then left her waterpot, went her way into the city, and said to the men, "Come, see a Man who told me all things that I ever did. Could this be the Christ?" Then they went out of the city and came to Him.

In the meantime His disciples urged Him, saying, "Rabbi, eat."

But He said to them, "I have food to eat of which you do not know."

Therefore the disciples said to one another, "Has anyone brought Him *anything* to eat?"

Jesus said to them, "My food is to do the will of Him who sent Me, and to finish His work. Do you not say, 'There are still four months and *then* comes the harvest'? **Behold, I say to you, lift up your eyes and look at the fields, for they are already white for harvest! And he who reaps receives wages, and gathers fruit for eternal life, that both he who sows and he who reaps may rejoice together. For in this the saying is true: 'One sows and another reaps.' I sent you to reap that for which you have not labored; others have labored, and you have entered into their labors."**

And many of the Samaritans of that city believed in Him because of the word of the woman who testified, "He told me all that I *ever* did." So when the Samaritans had come to Him, they urged Him to stay with them; and He stayed there two days. And many more believed because of His own word.

Then they said to the woman, "Now we believe, not because of what you said, for we ourselves have heard *Him* and we know that this is indeed the Christ, the Savior of the world." JOHN 4:3–42

In regard to sharing our faith, what did Jesus mean that some will "sow" the seed and others will "reap" the harvest? Why should we share our faith, even if we think our message could be rejected?

Although Paul was known as the apostle to the Gentiles, his heart longed for his fellow Jews to respond to the message about Jesus. In his letter to the Romans, Paul declares God's plan and desire for both Jew and Gentile—all people—to hear the gospel and know Jesus as Lord. We also read this passage in Chapter 3 (Salvation). This time read it with our responsibility to share our faith in mind.

Brethren, my heart's desire and prayer to God for Israel is that they may be saved. For I bear them witness that they have a zeal for God, but not according to knowledge. For they being ignorant of God's righteousness, and seeking to establish their own righteousness, have not submitted to the righteousness of God. For Christ *is* the end of the law for righteousness to everyone who believes.

For Moses writes about the righteousness which is of the law, *"The man who does those things shall live by them."* But the righteousness of faith speaks in this way, *"Do not say in your heart, 'Who will ascend into heaven?'"* (that is, to bring Christ down *from above*) or, *"'Who will descend into the abyss?'"* (that is, to bring Christ up from the dead). But what does it say? *"The word is near you, in your mouth and in your heart"* (that is, the word of faith which we preach): that if you confess with your mouth the Lord Jesus and believe in your heart that God has raised Him from the dead, you will be saved. For with the heart one believes unto righteousness, and with the mouth confession is made unto salvation. For the Scripture says, *"Whoever believes on Him will not be put to shame."* For there is no distinction between Jew and Greek, for the same Lord over all is rich to all who call upon Him. For *"whoever calls on the name of the LORD shall be saved."*

How then shall they call on Him in whom they have not believed? And how shall they believe in Him of whom they have not heard? And how shall they hear without a preacher? And how shall they preach unless they are sent? As it is written:

> ***"How beautiful are the feet of those who preach the gospel of peace,***
> ***Who bring glad tidings of good things!"*** ROMANS 10:1–15

WHAT WE BELIEVE

All believers are called to share their faith with others. We have been given the "ministry of reconciliation"; we are God's "ambassadors" in the world. We are called to share our faith through the way we live our lives. We are to be "salt and light" to the people God has placed in our sphere of influence. The mere beauty of how Christians treat each other is an aroma that draws outsiders to want to know God and be in a relationship with Him. We are also called to share our faith through our words. Like David, our relationship with God is so meaningful to us that we will have a hard time "restraining our lips." Like Philip, we will look for divine appointments to share the gospel with people who are genuinely seeking. God's grace and love know no boundaries. He desires for all people to come into a saving relationship with Him. Therefore, we will share our faith with our enemies, people of different races or religions or sometimes even people in our own family. Let's pray, like Paul, that we "may speak boldly."

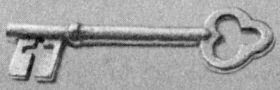

Who Am I Becoming?

I am the vine, you *are* the branches.
He who abides in Me, and I in him, bears much fruit;
for without Me you can do nothing.
John 15:5

In the passage above Jesus compares the Christian life to a vine. He is the vine; we are the branches. If we remain in the vine of Christ, over time we will produce amazing and scrumptious fruit at the end of our branches for all to see and taste.

People love ripe, delicious-tasting fruit but grimace at green, rotten or artificial fruit. Jesus wants to produce in us fruit that brings great joy to us and to others. For this to happen, we must remain in Christ. To remain simply means to "stay put." Becoming like Jesus is a journey. Spiritual growth is compounding. The longer we remain consistent with Christ, the better it gets.

Nurturing the passion and discipline to *think* and *act* like Jesus is our proactive part in remaining in the vine of Christ, but we are not alone. The Father is the gardener. He waters, tills the soil, makes sure we have the proper exposure to the sun and prunes us.

As we remain in Christ and the Gardener does His work, eventually the bud of fruit appears on the end of our branches. With more time the fruit grows and ripens. Mature fruit on the outside gives evidence to the health of the branch on the inside. Mature fruit on the outside ministers to the people God has put in our life. It draws them to us; it nurtures them and gives them refreshment. This pleases God when we "pay forward" the love He first deposited in us.

The final ten chapters lay out the ten key virtues God desires to see developed in your life. As you read, pray, "This is who I want to become!" And with God's help, you will.

I can do all things through Christ who strengthens me.
Philippians 4:13

BE

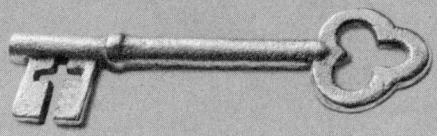

CHAPTER

21

Love

KEY QUESTION

What does it mean to sacrificially and unconditionally love others?

KEY IDEA

I am committed to loving God and loving others.

KEY VERSE

In this is love, not that we loved God, but that He loved us and sent His Son *to be* the propitiation for our sins. Beloved, if God so loved us, we also ought to love one another. No one has seen God at any time. If we love one another, God abides in us, and His love has been perfected in us.
1 John 4:10 – 12

OUR MAP

We believe to become. The ten key beliefs of the Christian life are not an end in themselves. They are to be understood in our minds (a renewal from the fall) and then accepted in our hearts by engaging in the ten spiritual practices. We are now moving to the ten key virtues of the Christian life. As the beliefs are embraced and owned in our hearts, "buds" of the virtues, or the fruit of the Spirit, appear on the external branches of our lives for others to see and taste. The ultimate fruit, the essential virtue, the most important expression of being like Jesus, is LOVE. What does it mean to sacrificially and unconditionally love and forgive others?

The Scripture passages included in this chapter will provide the answer under the following topics:

- *Love Defined*
- *The Greatest Commandment*
- *A New Command*
- *Loving Examples*

Love Defined

The Bible is a complex narrative. But what is the big—yet simple—idea behind all the stories and teachings contained in this ancient book? Love. Love dominates God's story. First Corinthians 13 provides us with an earnest description of love that resonates throughout Scripture.

As you read 1 Corinthians 13 below, make two lists. What are the characteristics of love in the positive sense (all that love is). What characteristics does love not have?

Though I speak with the tongues of men and of angels, but have not love, I have become sounding brass or a clanging cymbal. And though I have *the gift of* prophecy, and understand all mysteries and all knowledge, and though I have all faith, so that I could remove mountains, but have not love, I am nothing. And though I bestow all my goods to feed *the poor,* and though I give my body to be burned, but have not love, it profits me nothing.

Love suffers long *and* is kind; love does not envy; love does not parade itself, is not puffed up; does not behave rudely, does not seek its own, is not provoked, thinks no evil; does not rejoice in iniquity, but rejoices in the truth; bears all things, believes all things, hopes all things, endures all things.

Love never fails. But whether *there are* prophecies, they will fail; whether *there are* tongues, they will cease; whether *there is* knowledge, it will vanish away. For we know in part and we prophesy in part. But when that which is perfect has come, then that which is in part will be done away.

When I was a child, I spoke as a child, I understood as a child, I thought as a child; but when I became a man, I put away childish things. For now we see in a mirror, dimly, but then face to face. Now I know in part, but then I shall know just as I also am known.

And now abide faith, hope, love, these three; but the greatest of these *is* love. 1 Corinthians 13:1–13

The Greatest Commandment

Love as the greatest commandment can be found early in God's story with His people. For example, near the end of his life, Moses gathered the Israelites together to remind them of what truly mattered as they readied themselves to enter the promised land. His words, recorded in the book of Deuteronomy, include a passage known as the Shema (Hebrew for "hear"), which later became the Jewish confession of faith, recited twice daily at the morning and evening prayer services. As the Shema beautifully articulates, the love between God and His people has always been the driver behind a life of faith.

"Hear, O Israel: The Lord our God, the Lord *is* one! **You shall love the Lord your God with all your heart, with all your soul, and with all your strength.**

"And these words which I command you today shall be in your heart. You shall teach them diligently to your children, and shall talk of them when you sit in your house, when you walk by the way, when you lie down, and when you rise up. You shall bind them as a sign on your hand, and they shall be as frontlets between your eyes. You shall write them on the doorposts of your house and on your gates." Deuteronomy 6:4–9

Flowing from the priority to love God with our whole hearts, souls and strength is the command to love our neighbor as ourselves.

"'You shall not hate your brother in your heart. You shall surely rebuke your neighbor, and not bear sin because of him. **You shall not take vengeance, nor bear any grudge against the children of your people, but you shall love your neighbor as yourself: I *am* the LORD.'"** LEVITICUS 19:17–18

Jesus confirmed these two commands from the Old Testament —love God and love others—as the greatest of all the commandments during an encounter recorded in the New Testament between Jesus and the religious leaders.

Then one of the scribes came, and having heard them reasoning together, perceiving that He had answered them well, asked Him, "Which is the first commandment of all?"

Jesus answered him, "The first of all the commandments *is: 'Hear, O Israel, the LORD our God, the LORD is one. And you shall love the LORD your God with all your heart, with all your soul, with all your mind, and with all your strength.'* This *is* the first commandment. And the second, like *it, is* this: *'You shall love your neighbor as yourself.'* There is no other commandment greater than these."

So the scribe said to Him, "Well *said,* Teacher. You have spoken the truth, for there is one God, and there is no other but He. And to love Him with all the heart, with all the understanding, with all the soul, and with all the strength, and to love one's neighbor as oneself, is more than all the whole burnt offerings and sacrifices."

Now when Jesus saw that he answered wisely, He said to him, "You are not far from the kingdom of God."

But after that no one dared question Him. MARK 12:28–34

Do you love the Lord your God with all your heart, soul, mind and strength? How would you describe the amount of love you show for others? Are you satisfied with your answers?

A New Command

Every moral law of the Old Testament fits under one of these two greater commands—love God and love others. The Law was given to express God's high standards for community in His kingdom and to demonstrate legally that people were incapable of keeping God's perfect commands and requirements and needed a savior. Jesus came to fulfill the Law and offered us a new commandment. Interestingly, it was after Judas left the gathering with the disciples at the Last Supper to betray Jesus that Jesus changed the formula for love and issued a new command.

So, when he had gone out, Jesus said, "Now the Son of Man is glorified, and God is glorified in Him. If God is glorified in Him, God will also glorify Him in Himself, and glorify Him immediately. Little children, I shall be with you a little while longer. You will seek Me; and as I said to the Jews, 'Where I am going, you cannot come,' so now I say to you. A new commandment I give to you, that you love one another; as I have loved you, that you also love one another. By this all will know that you are My disciples, if you have love for one another."

John 13:31–35

From this point on the commandment to love is never referred to again in the same way. Instead of us trying hard to love God and others, we receive Christ's love for us and then pass it on to others. This is what Jesus did as our example. He received the love of the Father and passed it on to us. It is God's love in us that gives us the capacity to love others.

Put into your own words what happened in the shift from the Great Commandment of the Old Testament to the new command of Jesus.

Left to our own sinful nature, or flesh, we move away from unconditional and sacrificial love and instead crave to satisfy our own wants over the needs and interests of others. Living a life of love requires the presence of God's love and power within us. When we yield to this presence in our lives, it produces within us love for others. The Law provides some instruction regarding how to live a life of love; the Spirit empowers us to actually do it.

For you, brethren, have been called to liberty; only do not *use* liberty as an opportunity for the flesh, but through love serve one another. For all the law is fulfilled in one word, *even* in this: *"You shall love your neighbor as yourself."* But if you bite and devour one another, beware lest you be consumed by one another!

I say then: Walk in the Spirit, and you shall not fulfill the lust of the flesh. For the flesh lusts against the Spirit, and the Spirit against the flesh; and these are contrary to one another, so that you do not do the things that you wish. But if you are led by the Spirit, you are not under the law.

Now the works of the flesh are evident, which are: adultery, fornication, uncleanness, lewdness, idolatry, sorcery, hatred, contentions, jealousies, outbursts of wrath, selfish ambitions, dissensions, heresies, envy, murders, drunkenness, revelries, and the like; of which I tell you beforehand, just as I also told *you* in time past, that those who practice such things will not inherit the kingdom of God.

But the fruit of the Spirit is love, joy, peace, longsuffering, kindness, goodness, faithfulness, gentleness, self-control. Against such there is no law. And those *who are* Christ's have crucified the flesh with its passions and desires. If we live in the Spirit, let us also walk in the Spirit. GALATIANS 5:13–25

After Paul lists all the qualities of the fruit of the Spirit, why did he then write, "Against such there is no law"?

Our capacity to love begins with receiving God's love for us. From this reservoir we pour out love toward one another. The presence of God's Spirit in us, working through us to overcome our passion for self in favor of loving others, is confirmation that we are, in fact, children of God.

Beloved, let us love one another, for love is of God; and everyone who loves is born of God and knows God. He who does not love does not know God, for God is love. In this the love of God was manifested toward us, that God has sent His only begotten Son into the world, that we might live through Him. **In this is love, not that we loved God, but that He loved us and sent His Son *to be* the propitiation for our sins. Beloved, if God so loved us, we also ought to love one another.**

No one has seen God at any time. If we love one another, God abides in us, and His love has been perfected in us. By this we know that we abide in Him, and He in us, because He has given us of His Spirit. And we have seen and testify that the Father has sent the Son *as* Savior of the world. Whoever confesses that Jesus is the Son of God, God abides in him, and he in God. And we have known and believed the love that God has for us. God is love, and he who abides in love abides in God, and God in him.

Love has been perfected among us in this: that we may have boldness in the day of judgment; because as He is, so are we in this world. There is no fear in love; but perfect love casts out fear, because fear involves torment. But he who fears has not been made perfect in love. **We love Him because He first loved us.**

If someone says, "I love God," and hates his brother, he is a liar; for he who does not love his brother whom he has seen, how can he love God whom he has not seen? And this commandment we have from Him: that he who loves God *must* love his brother also.

1 JOHN 4:7–21

With this increased capacity for God's love to flow in and through us comes increased expectation. The bar that Jesus and Paul set is higher than we can achieve on our own. But with God's love in us, it becomes quite possible.

"You have heard that it was said, *'You shall love your neighbor* and hate your enemy.' But I say to you, love your enemies, bless those who curse you, do good to those who hate you, and pray for those who spitefully use you and persecute you, that you may be sons of your Father in heaven; for He makes His sun rise on the evil and on the good, and sends rain on the just and on the unjust. For if you love those who love you, what reward have you? Do not even the tax collectors do the same? And if you greet your brethren only, what do you do more *than others?* Do not even the tax collectors do so? Therefore you shall be perfect, just as your Father in heaven is perfect."

MATTHEW 5:43–48

Owe no one anything except to love one another, for he who loves another has fulfilled the law. For the commandments, *"You shall not commit adultery," "You shall not murder," "You shall not steal," "You shall not bear false witness," "You shall not covet,"* and if *there is* any other commandment, are *all* summed up in this saying, namely, *"You shall love your neighbor as yourself."* Love does no harm to a neighbor; therefore love *is* the fulfillment of the law.

ROMANS 13:8–10

Although we may love our brother or sister, all relationships have their issues. Unfortunately, dissonance can replace the love when we leave hurts and offenses unresolved. When Peter approached Jesus with a question about forgiveness, Jesus answered the question and followed it up with a poignant parable to illustrate His point. It is forgiveness that keeps relationships connected and prevents bitterness from dividing people.

Then Peter came to Him and said, "Lord, how often shall my brother sin against me, and I forgive him? Up to seven times?"

Jesus said to him, "I do not say to you, up to seven times, but up to seventy times seven. Therefore the kingdom of heaven is like a certain king who wanted to settle accounts with his servants. And when he had begun to settle accounts, one was brought to him who owed him ten thousand talents. But as he was not able to pay, his master commanded that he be sold, with his wife and children and all that he had, and that payment be made. The servant therefore fell down before him, saying, 'Master, have patience with me, and I will pay you all.' Then the master of that servant was moved with compassion, released him, and forgave him the debt.

"But that servant went out and found one of his fellow servants who owed him a hundred denarii; and he laid hands on him and took *him* by the throat, saying, 'Pay me what you owe!' So his fellow servant fell down at his feet and begged him, saying, 'Have patience with me, and I will pay you all.' And he would not, but went and threw him into prison till he should pay the debt. So when his fellow servants saw what had been done, they were very grieved, and came and told their master all that had been done. Then his master, after he had called him, said to him, 'You wicked servant! I forgave you all that debt because you begged me. Should you not also have had compassion on your fellow servant, just as I had pity on you?' And his master was angry, and delivered him to the torturers until he should pay all that was due to him.

"So My heavenly Father also will do to you if each of you, from his heart, does not forgive his brother his trespasses."

MATTHEW 18:21–35

LOVING EXAMPLES

Now that we have a clear understanding of love as God intended it to be, it's powerful to look at how that love has been exemplified by God's people in the Bible. One of the most beautiful and inspiring stories of someone loving another as they would themselves is Jonathan and David. Jonathan, the son of King Saul, the first monarch of Israel, was next in line to reign. But when young David emerged into the limelight after killing the Philistine giant Goliath with only a slingshot, it was clear that God had other plans. Jonathan recognized God's hand on David and graciously stepped aside and even protected David. King Saul saw the same thing, but instead became driven by jealousy and insecurity.

As you read the story below from 1 Samuel 18 and 19, write down the ways that Jonathan offered David unconditional and sacrificial love.

When [David] had finished speaking to Saul, the soul of Jonathan was knit to the soul of David, and Jonathan loved him as his own soul. Saul took him that day, and would not let him go home to his father's house anymore. **Then Jonathan and David made a covenant, because he loved him as his own soul. And Jonathan took off the robe that *was* on him and gave it to David, with his armor, even to his sword and his bow and his belt.** 1 SAMUEL 18:1–4

Saul spoke to Jonathan his son and to all his servants, that they should kill David; but Jonathan, Saul's son, delighted greatly in David. So Jonathan told David, saying, "My father Saul seeks to kill you. Therefore please be on your guard until morning, and stay in a secret *place* and hide. And I will go out and stand beside my father in the field where you *are,* and I will speak with my father about you. Then what I observe, I will tell you."

Thus Jonathan spoke well of David to Saul his father, and said to him, "Let not the king sin against his servant, against David, because he has not sinned against you, and because his works *have been* very good toward you. For he took his life in his hands and killed the Philistine, and the LORD brought about a great deliverance for all Israel. You saw *it* and rejoiced. Why then will you sin against innocent blood, to kill David without a cause?"

So Saul heeded the voice of Jonathan, and Saul swore, "*As* the LORD lives, he shall not be killed." Then Jonathan called David, and Jonathan told him all these things. So Jonathan brought David to Saul, and he was in his presence as in times past. 1 SAMUEL 19:1–7

Before long, Saul jealously turned against David again and threw a spear at David with the intent of killing him. David escaped and found himself on the run. It appears the purpose of this hardship in David's life was to give him the opportunity to see God's hand in his life and to learn to trust God unreservedly. David eventually found his way safely to Jonathan. David apparently wanted to make one more attempt to come alongside Saul and serve him if Saul would accept him. David and Jonathan agreed on a plan to expose the intent of Saul's heart.

Then David fled from Naioth in Ramah, and went and said to Jonathan, "What have I done? What *is* my iniquity, and what *is* my sin before your father, that he seeks my life?"

So Jonathan said to him, "By no means! You shall not die! Indeed, my father will do nothing either great or small without first telling me. And why should my father hide this thing from me? It *is* not *so!*"

Then David took an oath again, and said, "Your father certainly knows that I have found favor in your eyes, and he has said, 'Do not let Jonathan know this, lest he be grieved.' But truly, *as* the LORD lives and *as* your soul lives, *there is* but a step between me and death."

So Jonathan said to David, "Whatever you yourself desire, I will do *it* for you."

And David said to Jonathan, "Indeed tomorrow *is* the New Moon, and I should not fail to sit with the king to eat. But let me go, that I may hide in the field until the third *day* at evening. If your father misses me at all, then say, 'David earnestly asked *permission* of me that he might run over to Bethlehem, his city, for *there is* a yearly sacrifice there for all the family.' If he says thus: '*It is* well,' your servant will be safe. But if he is very angry, be sure that evil is determined by him. Therefore you shall deal kindly with your servant, for you have brought your servant into a covenant of the LORD with you. Nevertheless, if there is iniquity in me, kill me yourself, for why should you bring me to your father?"

But Jonathan said, "Far be it from you! For if I knew certainly that evil was determined by my father to come upon you, then would I not tell you?"

Then David said to Jonathan, "Who will tell me, or what *if* your father answers you roughly?"

And Jonathan said to David, "Come, let us go out into the field." So both of them went out into the field. Then Jonathan said to David: "The LORD God of Israel *is witness!* When I have sounded out my father sometime tomorrow, *or* the third *day,* and indeed *there is* good toward David, and I do not send to you and tell you, may the LORD do so and much more to Jonathan. But if it pleases my father *to do* you evil, then I will report it to you and send you away, that you may go in safety. And the LORD be with you as He has been with my father. And you shall not only show me the kindness of the LORD while I still live, that I may not die; but you shall not cut off your kindness from my house forever, no, not when the LORD has cut off every one of the enemies of David from the face of the earth." So Jonathan made *a covenant* with the house of David, *saying,* "Let the LORD require *it* at the hand of David's enemies."

Now Jonathan again caused David to vow, because he loved him; for he loved him as he loved his own soul. Then Jonathan said to David, "Tomorrow *is* the New Moon; and you will be missed, because your seat will be empty. And *when* you have stayed three days, go down quickly and come to the place where you hid on the day of the deed; and remain by the stone Ezel. Then I will shoot three arrows to the side, as though I shot at a target; and there I will send a lad, *saying,* 'Go, find the arrows.' If I expressly say to the lad, 'Look, the arrows *are* on this side of you; get them and come'—then, as the LORD lives, *there is* safety for you and no harm. But if I say thus to the young man, 'Look, the arrows *are* beyond you'—go your way, for the LORD has sent you away. And as for the matter which you and I have spoken of, indeed the LORD *be* between you and me forever."

Then David hid in the field. And when the New Moon had come, the king sat down to eat the feast. Now the king sat on his seat, as at other times, on a seat by the wall. And Jonathan arose, and Abner sat by Saul's side, but David's place was empty. Nevertheless Saul did not say anything that day, for he thought, "Something has happened to him; he *is* unclean, surely he *is* unclean." And it happened the next day, the second *day* of the month, that David's place was empty. And Saul said to Jonathan his son, "Why has the son of Jesse not come to eat, either yesterday or today?"

So Jonathan answered Saul, "David earnestly asked *permission* of me *to go* to Bethlehem. And he said, 'Please let me go, for our family has a sacrifice in the city, and my brother has commanded me *to be there.* And now, if I have found favor in your eyes, please let me get away and see my brothers.' Therefore he has not come to the king's table."

Then Saul's anger was aroused against Jonathan, and he said to him, "You son of a perverse, rebellious *woman!* Do I not know that you have chosen the son of Jesse to your own shame and to the shame of your mother's nakedness? For as long as the son of Jesse lives on the earth, you shall not be established, nor your kingdom. Now therefore, send and bring him to me, for he shall surely die."

And Jonathan answered Saul his father, and said to him, "Why should he be killed? What has he done?" Then Saul cast a spear at him to kill him, by which Jonathan knew that it was determined by his father to kill David.

So Jonathan arose from the table in fierce anger, and ate no food the second day of the month, for he was grieved for David, because his father had treated him shamefully.

And so it was, in the morning, that Jonathan went out into the field at the time appointed with David, and a little lad *was* with him. Then he said to his lad, "Now run, find the arrows which I shoot." As the lad ran, he shot an arrow beyond him. When the lad had come to the place where the arrow was which Jonathan had shot, Jonathan cried out after the lad and said, "*Is* not the arrow beyond you?" And Jonathan cried out after the lad, "Make haste, hurry, do not delay!" So Jonathan's lad gathered up the arrows and came back to his master. But the lad did not know anything. Only Jonathan and David knew of the matter. Then Jonathan gave his weapons to his lad, and said to him, "Go, carry *them* to the city."

As soon as the lad had gone, David arose from *a place* toward the south, fell on his face to the ground, and bowed down three times. And they kissed one another; and they wept together, but David more so. Then Jonathan said to David, "Go in peace, since we have both sworn in the name of the LORD, saying, 'May the LORD be between you and me, and between your descendants and my descendants, forever.'" So he arose and departed, and Jonathan went into the city.

1 SAMUEL 20:1–42

David was a fugitive on the run from King Saul for several years. While David was hiding from Saul, the Philistines—the same enemy David defeated as a young man—attacked and defeated Israel. Jonathan was killed in battle and Saul took his own life as the enemy closed in on him. A short time later, David was inaugurated as the king of Israel. When David's kingdom was well established, he demonstrated that he hadn't forgotten his promise to show kindness to Jonathan's family by taking care of Jonathan's son Mephibosheth. In his relationship with both Jonathan and Mephibosheth and throughout his reign as king, David demonstrated his commitment to love God and others.

Of course, the ultimate model for a life of love comes from Jesus. He consistently referred to love and grace flowing first from the Father to Him and then to us. This is the secret to loving others.

"I am the good shepherd; and I know My *sheep*, and am known by My own. As the Father knows Me, even so I know the Father; and I lay down My life for the sheep. And other sheep I have which are not of this fold; them also I must bring, and they will hear My voice; and there will be one flock *and* one shepherd.

"Therefore My Father loves Me, because I lay down My life that I may take it again. No one takes it from Me, but I lay it down of Myself. I have power to lay it down, and I have power to take it again. This command I have received from My Father."

JOHN 10:14–18

WHAT WE BELIEVE

Love is the ultimate expression of becoming like Jesus. God the Father desires for us to unconditionally and sacrificially love others. Biblical love is defined in 1 Corinthians 13 and declared the Great Commandment in Mark 12. To love God and love our neighbor is the standard of God, which on our own we cannot achieve. But in Christ, a new command is issued. God pours His presence and love within us first. Then, as we receive it, we let His love pass through us to others. Jonathan provides a beautiful example of love in his relationship with David. But no one models it better than Jesus Himself. With God's love and presence in us, we can become more and more like Jesus.

BE

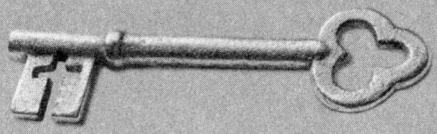

CHAPTER 22

Joy

KEY QUESTION

What gives us true happiness and contentment in life?

KEY IDEA

Despite my circumstances,
I feel inner contentment and understand
my purpose in life.

KEY VERSE

These things I have spoken to you, that My joy
may remain in you, and *that* your joy may be full.
John 15:11

OUR MAP

A person can have money, all the possessions they desire, health and even good looks, but if they don't have joy, life can be rather challenging. It is easier to find joy when things are going well. Yet some people struggle to experience this virtue even amidst life's most favorable situations. Here is some amazing news! Christ offers us joy, no matter our circumstances. True joy is rooted in the key belief that the one true God is a personal God who is involved in and cares about our daily lives. He loves us and is working out a good plan for us. When we confidently believe this in our hearts, we can rise above our circumstances and find joy in Christ alone. How can this be? We will be exploring the following Biblical concepts in this chapter:

- *Source of Joy*
- *Joyful Celebrations*
- *Joy Despite Our Circumstances*

Source of Joy

God may shower us with blessings and circumstances that bring joy to our lives, but true joy is found not in those things themselves but in their source. Joy can also be fueled and found in living out God's Word and trusting in the promises God makes to us in His Word. The psalmist declared this truth with great confidence in this song.

Preserve me, O God, for in You I put my trust.

O my soul, you have said to the Lord,
"You *are* my Lord,
My goodness is nothing apart from You."
As for the saints who *are* on the earth,
"They are the excellent ones, in whom is all my delight."

Their sorrows shall be multiplied who hasten *after*
another *god;*
Their drink offerings of blood I will not offer,
Nor take up their names on my lips.

O LORD, *You are* the portion of my inheritance and
my cup;
You maintain my lot.
The lines have fallen to me in pleasant *places;*
Yes, I have a good inheritance.

I will bless the LORD who has given me counsel;
My heart also instructs me in the night seasons.
I have set the LORD always before me;
Because *He is* at my right hand I shall not be moved.

Therefore my heart is glad, and my glory rejoices;
My flesh also will rest in hope.
For You will not leave my soul in Sheol,
Nor will You allow Your Holy One to see corruption.
You will show me the path of life;
In Your presence *is* fullness of joy;
At Your right hand *are* pleasures forevermore.

PSALM 16:1–11

God's promises find their ultimate fulfillment in His Son Jesus. Note how His arrival into our world brought joy to everyone present.

And it came to pass in those days *that* a decree went out from Caesar Augustus that all the world should be registered. This census first took place while Quirinius was governing Syria. So all went to be registered, everyone to his own city.

Joseph also went up from Galilee, out of the city of Nazareth, into Judea, to the city of David, which is called Bethlehem, because he was of the house and lineage of David, to be registered with Mary, his betrothed wife, who was with child. So it was, that while they were there, the days were completed for her to be delivered. And she brought forth her firstborn Son, and wrapped Him in swaddling cloths, and laid Him in a manger, because there was no room for them in the inn.

Now there were in the same country shepherds living out in the fields, keeping watch over their flock by night. And behold, an angel of the Lord stood before them, and the glory of the Lord shone around them, and they were greatly afraid. **Then the angel said to them, "Do not be afraid, for behold, I bring you good tidings of great joy which will be to all people. For there is born to you this day in the city of David a Savior, who is Christ the Lord.** And this *will be* the sign to you: You will find a Babe wrapped in swaddling cloths, lying in a manger."

And suddenly there was with the angel a multitude of the heavenly host praising God and saying:

> "Glory to God in the highest,
> And on earth peace, goodwill toward men!"

So it was, when the angels had gone away from them into heaven, that the shepherds said to one another, "Let us now go to Bethlehem and see this thing that has come to pass, which the Lord has made known to us." And they came with haste and found Mary and Joseph, and the Babe lying in a manger. Now when they had seen *Him,* they made widely known the saying which was told them concerning this Child. And all those who heard *it* marveled at those things which were told them by the shepherds. But Mary kept all these things and pondered *them* in her heart. Then the shepherds returned, glorifying and praising God for all the things that they had heard and seen, as it was told them. LUKE 2:1–21

Jesus taught us that spiritual growth is much like the development of fruit on a vine. He is the vine and we become the branches when we place our faith in Him. As we abide in the vine of Christ through obedience to His commands, His nutrients of joy run through our spiritual veins from the inside out and produce the ripe, juicy fruit of joy in and through our lives.

"I am the true vine, and My Father is the vinedresser. Every branch in Me that does not bear fruit He takes away; and every *branch* that bears fruit He prunes, that it may bear more fruit. You are already clean because of the word which I have spoken to you. Abide in Me, and I in you. As the branch cannot bear fruit of itself, unless it abides in the vine, neither can you, unless you abide in Me.

"I am the vine, you *are* the branches. He who abides in Me, and

I in him, bears much fruit; for without Me you can do nothing. If anyone does not abide in Me, he is cast out as a branch and is withered; and they gather them and throw *them* into the fire, and they are burned. If you abide in Me, and My words abide in you, you will ask what you desire, and it shall be done for you. By this My Father is glorified, that you bear much fruit; so you will be My disciples.

"As the Father loved Me, I also have loved you; abide in My love. If you keep My commandments, you will abide in My love, just as I have kept My Father's commandments and abide in His love.

"These things I have spoken to you, that My joy may remain in you, and *that* your joy may be full." JOHN 15:1–11

How does keeping God's commandments produce joy in our lives?

JOYFUL CELEBRATIONS

In the Old Testament, people often responded to God's blessings with joyful celebrations. Coming together intentionally to remember God stimulated joy in the hearts of the people. The annual Feast of Tabernacles especially provided an opportunity for the Israelites to celebrate God's goodness, since the focus was reminding them that God provided food and shelter during their days in the wilderness. When the people returned from captivity, it had been years since they had gathered for this joy-filled celebration. With great passion they reinstated this tradition, and the results speak for themselves.

Now on the second day the heads of the fathers' *houses* of all the people, with the priests and Levites, were gathered to Ezra the scribe, in order to understand the words of the Law. And they found written in the Law, which the LORD had commanded by Moses, that the children of Israel should dwell in booths during the feast of the seventh month, and that they should announce and proclaim in all their cities and in Jerusalem, saying, "Go out to the mountain, and bring olive branches, branches of oil trees, myrtle branches, palm branches, and branches of leafy trees, to make booths, as *it is* written."

Then the people went out and brought *them* and made themselves booths, each one on the roof of his house, or in their courtyards or the courts of the house of God, and in the open square of the Water Gate and in the open square of the Gate of Ephraim. **So the whole assembly of those who had returned from the captivity made booths and sat under the booths; for since the days of Joshua the son of Nun until that day the children of Israel had not done so. And there was very great gladness.**

NEHEMIAH 8:13–17

Another joyful celebration recorded in the Old Testament occurred when David retrieved the ark of the covenant from the Philistines. David understood the power of God's presence at the center of Israelite life and community. After he built a tent in which to store the ark, he wrote a song to celebrate God for who He is and what He had consistently done for Israel. Celebrating God's involvement in our lives evokes joy.

On that day David first delivered *this psalm* into the hand of Asaph and his brethren, to thank the LORD:

Oh, give thanks to the LORD!
Call upon His name;
Make known His deeds among the peoples!
Sing to Him, sing psalms to Him;
Talk of all His wondrous works!
Glory in His holy name;
Let the hearts of those rejoice who seek the LORD!
Seek the LORD and His strength;
Seek His face evermore!
Remember His marvelous works which He has done,
His wonders, and the judgments of His mouth,
O seed of Israel His servant,
You children of Jacob, His chosen ones!

He *is* the LORD our God;
His judgments *are* in all the earth.

Remember His covenant forever,
The word which He commanded, for a thousand
generations,
The covenant which He made with Abraham,
And His oath to Isaac,
And confirmed it to Jacob for a statute,
To Israel *for* an everlasting covenant,
Saying, "To you I will give the land of Canaan
As the allotment of your inheritance,"
When you were few in number,
Indeed very few, and strangers in it.

When they went from one nation to another,
And from *one* kingdom to another people,
He permitted no man to do them wrong;
Yes, He rebuked kings for their sakes,
Saying, "Do not touch My anointed ones,
And do My prophets no harm."

Sing to the LORD, all the earth;
Proclaim the good news of His salvation from day to day.
Declare His glory among the nations,
His wonders among all peoples.

For the LORD *is* great and greatly to be praised;
He *is* also to be feared above all gods.
For all the gods of the peoples *are* idols,
But the LORD made the heavens.
Honor and majesty *are* before Him;
Strength and gladness are in His place.

Give to the LORD, O families of the peoples,
Give to the LORD glory and strength.
Give to the LORD the glory *due* His name;
Bring an offering, and come before Him.
Oh, worship the LORD in the beauty of holiness!
Tremble before Him, all the earth.
The world also is firmly established,
It shall not be moved.

Let the heavens rejoice, and let the earth be glad;
And let them say among the nations, "The LORD reigns."
Let the sea roar, and all its fullness;
Let the field rejoice, and all that *is* in it.
Then the trees of the woods shall rejoice before the LORD,
For He is coming to judge the earth.

Oh, give thanks to the LORD, for *He is* good!
For His mercy *endures* forever.
And say, "Save us, O God of our salvation;
Gather us together, and deliver us from the Gentiles,
To give thanks to Your holy name,
To triumph in Your praise."

Blessed *be* the LORD God of Israel
From everlasting to everlasting!

And all the people said, "Amen!" and praised the LORD.

1 CHRONICLES 16:7–36

How does acknowledging God's involvement in our lives evoke joy? Israel held annual festivals and traditions to celebrate God's blessings. How do Christians accomplish this today?

JOY DESPITE OUR CIRCUMSTANCES

After the reign of David, the divided kingdom fell steadily into a dark season of disobedience. The people were led, almost without interruption, by a succession of evil kings. Habakkuk was a prophet trying desperately to get the people of Judah back on track. He asked God how long He was going to let injustice and wickedness go on before He disciplined the nation. God informed the prophet that He was going to use the Babylonians to deal with Judah's persistent disobedience. Habakkuk struggled with this idea at first but in the end found resolve. Even though God's people were going to go through a difficult season, Habakkuk knew they could retain their joy based on what God had done for them in the past and His promises for the future.

When I heard, my body trembled;
My lips quivered at *the* voice;
Rottenness entered my bones;
And I trembled in myself,
That I might rest in the day of trouble.
When he comes up to the people,
He will invade them with his troops.

Though the fig tree may not blossom,
Nor fruit be on the vines;
Though the labor of the olive may fail,
And the fields yield no food;
Though the flock may be cut off from the fold,
And there be no herd in the stalls—
Yet I will rejoice in the LORD,
I will joy in the God of my salvation.

The LORD God is my strength;
He will make my feet like deer's *feet,*
And He will make me walk on my high hills.

HABAKKUK 3:16–19

Just as God's people found joy and strength in God's promises amid dark times during Habakkuk's day, Jesus' disciples drew comfort and strength from Jesus' promises as they prepared for His death. A few hours before He was crucified, Jesus sat with them and reassured them that their grief would be short-lived—three days to be exact. After that time something was going to happen to secure their joy in any and all circumstances.

Now before the Feast of the Passover, when Jesus knew that His hour had come that He should depart from this world to the Father, having loved His own who were in the world, He loved them to the end.

JOHN 13:1

[Jesus said,] "A little while, and you will not see Me; and again a little while, and you will see Me, because I go to the Father."

Then *some* of His disciples said among themselves, "What is this that He says to us, 'A little while, and you will not see Me; and again a little while, and you will see Me'; and, 'because I go to the Father'?" They said therefore, "What is this that He says, 'A little while'? We do not know what He is saying."

Now Jesus knew that they desired to ask Him, and He said to them, "Are you inquiring among yourselves about what I said, 'A little while, and you will not see Me; and again a little while, and you will see Me'? Most assuredly, I say to you that you will weep and lament, but the world will rejoice; and you will be sorrowful, but your sorrow will be turned into joy. A woman, when she is in labor, has sorrow because her hour has come; but as soon as she has given birth to the child, she no longer remembers the anguish, for joy that a human being has been born into the world. **Therefore you now have sorrow; but I will see you again and your heart will rejoice, and your joy no one will take from you.**

"And in that day you will ask Me nothing. Most assuredly, I say to you, whatever you ask the Father in My name He will give you. Until now you have asked nothing in My name. Ask, and you will receive, that your joy may be full." JOHN 16:16–24

James introduces the book bearing his name with a thought-provoking declaration: not only can we have joy despite our difficult circumstances, but joy can grow through our difficult circumstances.

My brethren, count it all joy when you fall into various trials, knowing that the testing of your faith produces patience. But let patience have *its* perfect work, that you may be perfect and complete, lacking nothing. If any of you lacks wisdom, let him ask of God, who gives to all liberally and without reproach, and it will be given to him. But let him ask in faith, with no doubting, for he who doubts is like a wave of the sea driven and tossed by the wind. For let not that man suppose that he will receive anything from the Lord; *he is* a double-minded man, unstable in all his ways.

Let the lowly brother glory in his exaltation, but the rich in his humiliation, because as a flower of the field he will pass away. For no sooner has the sun risen with a burning heat than it withers the grass; its flower falls, and its beautiful appearance perishes. So the rich man also will fade away in his pursuits.

Blessed *is* the man who endures temptation; for when he has been approved, he will receive the crown of life which the Lord has promised to those who love Him. Let no one say when he is tempted, "I am tempted by God"; for God cannot be tempted by evil, nor does He Himself tempt anyone. But each one is tempted when he is drawn away by his own desires and enticed. Then, when desire has conceived, it gives birth to sin; and sin, when it is full-grown, brings forth death.

Do not be deceived, my beloved brethren. Every good gift and every perfect gift is from above, and comes down from the Father of lights, with whom there is no variation or shadow of turning.

JAMES 1:2–17

How can difficult circumstances actually produce joy? What role do our attitudes play in being able to experience joy?

One person whose joy seemed to grow despite his circumstances was the apostle Paul, who wrote a joyful treatise of sorts while under house arrest and chained to a Roman guard. In a passionate letter to the church at Philippi, Paul fervently expressed his joy in Christ. Half of the lessons on increasing our joy are "taught" explicitly by Paul. Half of the lessons are "caught" implicitly by observing how Paul found joy despite his circumstances. At the letter's opening, notice how he found joy in the people God had placed in his life. Then we learn that Paul even saw his imprisonment as a blessing, for it helped bring attention to the gospel message.

Paul and Timothy, bondservants of Jesus Christ,

To all the saints in Christ Jesus who are in Philippi, with the bishops and deacons:

Grace to you and peace from God our Father and the Lord Jesus Christ.

I thank my God upon every remembrance of you, always in every prayer of mine making request for you all with joy,

for your fellowship in the gospel from the first day until now, being confident of this very thing, that He who has begun a good work in you will complete *it* until the day of Jesus Christ; just as it is right for me to think this of you all, because I have you in my heart, inasmuch as both in my chains and in the defense and confirmation of the gospel, you all are partakers with me of grace. For God is my witness, how greatly I long for you all with the affection of Jesus Christ.

PHILIPPIANS 1:1–8

But I want you to know, brethren, that the things *which happened* to me have actually turned out for the furtherance of the gospel, so that it has become evident to the whole palace guard, and to all the rest, that my chains are in Christ; and most of the brethren in the Lord, having become confident by my chains, are much more bold to speak the word without fear.

Some indeed preach Christ even from envy and strife, and some also from goodwill: The former preach Christ from selfish ambition, not sincerely, supposing to add affliction to my chains; but the latter out of love, knowing that I am appointed for the defense of the gospel. **What then? Only *that* in every way, whether in pretense or in truth, Christ is preached; and in this I rejoice, yes, and will rejoice.**

For I know that this will turn out for my deliverance through your prayer and the supply of the Spirit of Jesus Christ.

PHILIPPIANS 1:12–19

Paul also instructed the Philippian believers how to rise above the fear spurred by those who opposed them. He invited them to remove grumbling and arguing from their vocabulary as a means to increase their joy. The ultimate source of joy is in knowing Christ better, so Paul encouraged his readers to put the past behind them and stay focused on the future, giving all their troubles to God and celebrating His blessings continuously.

Do all things without complaining and disputing, that you may become blameless and harmless, children of God without fault in the midst of a crooked and perverse generation, among whom you shine as lights in the world, holding fast the word of life, so that I may rejoice in the day of Christ that I have not run in vain or labored in vain.

Yes, and if I am being poured out *as a drink offering* on the sacrifice and service of your faith, I am glad and rejoice with you all. For the same reason you also be glad and rejoice with me.

PHILIPPIANS 2:14–18

Finally, my brethren, rejoice in the Lord. For me to write the same things to you *is* not tedious, but for you *it is* safe.

Beware of dogs, beware of evil workers, beware of the mutilation! For we are the circumcision, who worship God in the Spirit, rejoice in Christ Jesus, and have no confidence in the flesh, though I also might have confidence in the flesh. If anyone else thinks he may have confidence in the flesh, I more so: circumcised the eighth day, of the stock of Israel, *of* the tribe of Benjamin, a Hebrew of the Hebrews; concerning the law, a Pharisee; concerning zeal, persecuting the church; concerning the righteousness which is in the law, blameless.

But what things were gain to me, these I have counted loss for Christ. Yet indeed I also count all things loss for the excellence of the knowledge of Christ Jesus my Lord, for whom I have suffered the loss of all things, and count them as rubbish, that I may gain Christ and be found in Him, not having my own righteousness, which *is* from the law, but that which *is* through faith in Christ, the righteousness which is from God by faith; that I may know Him and the power of His resurrection, and the fellowship of His sufferings, being conformed to His death, if, by any means, I may attain to the resurrection from the dead.

Not that I have already attained, or am already perfected; but I press on, that I may lay hold of that for which Christ Jesus has also laid hold of me. Brethren, I do not count myself to have apprehended; but one thing *I do,* forgetting those things which are behind and reaching forward to those things which are ahead, I press toward the goal for the prize of the upward call of God in Christ Jesus.

Therefore let us, as many as are mature, have this mind; and if in anything you think otherwise, God will reveal even this to you.

Nevertheless, to *the degree* that we have already attained, let us walk by the same rule, let us be of the same mind.

Brethren, join in following my example, and note those who so walk, as you have us for a pattern. For many walk, of whom I have told you often, and now tell you even weeping, *that they are* the enemies of the cross of Christ: whose end *is* destruction, whose god *is their* belly, and *whose* glory *is* in their shame—who set their mind on earthly things. For our citizenship is in heaven, from which we also eagerly wait for the Savior, the Lord Jesus Christ, who will transform our lowly body that it may be conformed to His glorious body, according to the working by which He is able even to subdue all things to Himself. PHILIPPIANS 3:1–21

Therefore, my beloved and longed-for brethren, my joy and crown, so stand fast in the Lord, beloved. PHILIPPIANS 4:1

Rejoice in the Lord always. Again I will say, rejoice!

PHILIPPIANS 4:4

Paul wrapped up his thoughts by disclosing the secret to contentment despite life's varying circumstances.

But I rejoiced in the Lord greatly that now at last your care for me has flourished again; though you surely did care, but you lacked opportunity. Not that I speak in regard to need, for I have learned in whatever state I am, to be content: I know how to be abased, and I know how to abound. **Everywhere and in all things I have learned both to be full and to be hungry, both to abound and to suffer need. I can do all things through Christ who strengthens me.** PHILIPPIANS 4:10–13

Paul said he had learned how to be content even when he had plenty. Why is it sometimes difficult for people who have plenty to be content?

Like Paul, the apostle Peter also taught through his letters to the Christians scattered throughout Asia Minor that believers are in a position to experience joy in spite of, and even because of, their difficult circumstances. The same is true for followers of Jesus today.

Blessed *be* the God and Father of our Lord Jesus Christ, who according to His abundant mercy has begotten us again to a living hope through the resurrection of Jesus Christ from the dead, to an inheritance incorruptible and undefiled and that does not fade away, reserved in heaven for you, who are kept by the power of God through faith for salvation ready to be revealed in the last time.

In this you greatly rejoice, though now for a little while, if need be, you have been grieved by various trials, that the genuineness of your faith, *being* much more precious than gold that perishes, though it is tested by fire, may be found to praise, honor, and glory at the revelation of Jesus Christ, whom having not seen you love. **Though now you do not see *Him*, yet believing, you rejoice with joy inexpressible and full of glory, receiving the end of your faith—the salvation of *your* souls.** 1 PETER 1:3–9

Beloved, do not think it strange concerning the fiery trial which is to try you, as though some strange thing happened to you; but **rejoice to the extent that you partake of Christ's sufferings, that when His glory is revealed, you may also be glad with exceeding joy.** If you are reproached for the name of Christ, blessed *are you,* for the Spirit of glory and of God rests upon you. On their part He is blasphemed, but on your part He is glorified. But let none of you suffer as a murderer, a thief, an evildoer, or as a busybody in other people's matters. Yet if *anyone suffers* as a Christian, let him not be ashamed, but let him glorify God in this matter.

1 PETER 4:12–16

Therefore humble yourselves under the mighty hand of God, that He may exalt you in due time, casting all your care upon Him, for He cares for you.

Be sober, be vigilant; because your adversary the devil walks about like a roaring lion, seeking whom he may devour. Resist him, steadfast in the faith, knowing that the same sufferings are experienced by your brotherhood in the world. But may the God of all grace, who called us to His eternal glory by Christ Jesus, after you have suffered a while, perfect, establish, strengthen, and settle *you*. To Him *be* the glory and the dominion forever and ever. Amen.

1 PETER 5:6–11

How often do you joyfully acknowledge God's goodness in your life? Identify one good thing God has given to you or done for you in the past week and take a moment to celebrate that with someone else.

WHAT WE BELIEVE

If we want to experience true joy, we must anchor our lives in the source of that joy—God Himself. Saturating our minds in the key beliefs and practices of the Christian faith can help draw us closer to God. The closer we are to Him, the more confidence we will have as we face each day. Like the Israelites did, we can celebrate even God's smallest blessings in our lives. Christ offers contentment and happiness not limited by circumstances. Because of God's integrity, faithfulness and promises, we can surmount any circumstances with both smiles on our faces and true joy in our hearts. As Christians, we share the knowledge of this virtue with those God places in our lives so that they too can experience the deep and never-ending well of God's joy.

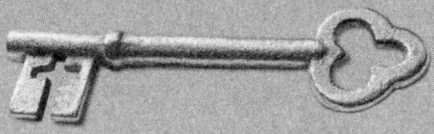

CHAPTER

23

Peace

KEY QUESTION

Where do I find strength to battle anxiety and fear?

KEY IDEA

I am free from anxiety because I have found peace with God, peace with others and peace with myself.

KEY VERSE

Be anxious for nothing, but in everything by prayer and supplication, with thanksgiving, let your requests be made known to God; and the peace of God, which surpasses all understanding, will guard your hearts and minds through Christ Jesus.
Philippians 4:6–7

OUR MAP

Most of us think of peace as a feeling. We want to trade our anxiety, depression and fear for calm and tranquility. There are many harmful and temporal ways people attempt to achieve this feeling, most notoriously by using alcohol or drugs. Biblical peace, however, starts not with the feeling of peace but with the source of peace, namely a strong and healthy relationship with God and with others. Where does one find the strength to battle anxiety and fear? In right relationships.

In this chapter we will discover how to find:

- *Peace With God*
- *Peace With Others*
- *Peace With Yourself (Inner Peace)*

Peace With God

Peace with God is made possible only through the Prince of Peace. When Christ establishes His eternal kingdom, societal peace will be the norm. Around 700 years before Jesus was born, Isaiah foretold of Jesus' arrival on earth and the far-reaching impact of His reign.

> **For unto us a Child is born,**
> **Unto us a Son is given;**
> **And the government will be upon His shoulder.**
> **And His name will be called**
> **Wonderful, Counselor, Mighty God,**
> **Everlasting Father, Prince of Peace.**
> Of the increase of *His* government and peace
> *There will be* no end,
> Upon the throne of David and over His kingdom,
> To order it and establish it with judgment and justice
> From that time forward, even forever.
> The zeal of the LORD of hosts will perform this. ISAIAH 9:6–7

Jesus Christ is the Prince of Peace, not only in the future kingdom of heaven, but also in our lives as well. The pouring out of His lifeblood produced the possibility of a life of peace between us and God today.

In the following two passages from Romans 5 and Ephesians 2, look for all the references to "peace" and similar terms such as "reconciled," "brought near" and "together." How does Jesus Christ establish peace between us and God and with each other?

Therefore, having been justified by faith, we have peace with God through our Lord Jesus Christ, through whom also we have access by faith into this grace in which we stand, and rejoice in hope of the glory of God. And not only *that,* but we also glory in tribulations, knowing that tribulation produces perseverance; and perseverance, character; and character, hope. Now hope does not disappoint, because the love of God has been poured out in our hearts by the Holy Spirit who was given to us.

For when we were still without strength, in due time Christ died for the ungodly. For scarcely for a righteous man will one die; yet perhaps for a good man someone would even dare to die. But God demonstrates His own love toward us, in that while we were still sinners, Christ died for us. Much more then, having now been justified by His blood, we shall be saved from wrath through Him. For if when we were enemies we were reconciled to God through the death of His Son, much more, having been reconciled, we shall be saved by His life. And not only *that,* but we also rejoice in God through our Lord Jesus Christ, through whom we have now received the reconciliation. ROMANS 5:1–11

In Paul's day, there were enormous barriers of cultural prejudice and religious isolation between Jews and Gentiles. The Jews arrogantly despised the pagan Gentiles and viewed them contemptuously as the "uncircumcised." Those attitudes went both ways; for instance, the Greeks divided all people into two classes—Greeks and barbarians. But these barriers came crashing down because of Christ. Through the saving work of Jesus' death and resurrection, all believers share citizenship in God's kingdom of peace.

And you *He made alive,* who were dead in trespasses and sins, in which you once walked according to the course of this world, according to the prince of the power of the air, the spirit who now works in the sons of disobedience, among whom also we all once conducted ourselves in the lusts of our flesh, fulfilling the desires of the flesh and of the mind, and were by nature children of wrath, just as the others.

But God, who is rich in mercy, because of His great love with which He loved us, even when we were dead in trespasses, made us alive together with Christ (by grace you have been saved), and raised *us* up together, and made *us* sit together in the heavenly *places* in Christ Jesus, that in the ages to come He might show the exceeding riches of His grace in *His* kindness toward us in Christ Jesus. For by grace you have been saved through faith, and that not of yourselves; *it is* the gift of God, not of works, lest anyone should boast. For we are His workmanship, created in Christ Jesus for good works, which God prepared beforehand that we should walk in them.

Therefore remember that you, once Gentiles in the flesh—who are called Uncircumcision by what is called the Circumcision made in the flesh by hands—that at that time you were without Christ, being aliens from the commonwealth of Israel and strangers from the covenants of promise, having no hope and without God in the world. But now in Christ Jesus you who once were far off have been brought near by the blood of Christ.

For He Himself is our peace, who has made both one, and has broken down the middle wall of separation, having abolished in His flesh the enmity, *that is*, the law of commandments *contained* in ordinances, so as to create in Himself one new man *from* the two, *thus* making peace, and that He might reconcile them both to God in one body through the cross, thereby putting to death the enmity. And He came and preached peace to you who were afar off and to those who were near. For through Him we both have access by one Spirit to the Father.

Now, therefore, you are no longer strangers and foreigners, but fellow citizens with the saints and members of the household of God, having been built on the foundation of the apostles and prophets, Jesus Christ Himself being the chief corner*stone,* in whom the whole building, being fitted together, grows into a holy temple in the Lord, in whom you also are being built together for a dwelling place of God in the Spirit. EPHESIANS 2:1–22

PEACE WITH OTHERS

While the Bible is brimming with examples of hostility and fighting, it also contains notable examples of people striving for peace. For instance, in the Old Testament, Abram (later named Abraham) and his wife, Sarai (later named Sarah), and nephew Lot moved to Canaan and lived as nomadic shepherds. When conflict arose between the two men regarding space and land, Abram took the initiative to end their dispute. Although Abram, as the elder, would normally have first pick of the land, he put the peace of the family above his own rights.

Then Abram went up from Egypt, he and his wife and all that he had, and Lot with him, to the South. Abram *was* very rich in livestock, in silver, and in gold. And he went on his journey from the South as far as Bethel, to the place where his tent had been at the beginning, between Bethel and Ai, to the place of the altar which he had made there at first. And there Abram called on the name of the LORD.

Lot also, who went with Abram, had flocks and herds and tents. Now the land was not able to support them, that they might dwell together, for their possessions were so great that they could not dwell together. And there was strife between the herdsmen of Abram's livestock and the herdsmen of Lot's livestock. The Canaanites and the Perizzites then dwelt in the land.

So Abram said to Lot, "Please let there be no strife between you and me, and between my herdsmen and your herdsmen; for we *are* brethren. *Is* not the whole land before you? Please separate from me. If *you take* the left, then I will go to the right; or, if *you go* to the right, then I will go to the left."

And Lot lifted his eyes and saw all the plain of Jordan, that it *was* well watered everywhere (before the LORD destroyed Sodom and Gomorrah) like the garden of the LORD, like the land of Egypt as you go toward Zoar. Then Lot chose for himself all the plain of Jordan, and Lot journeyed east. And they separated from each other. Abram dwelt in the land of Canaan, and Lot dwelt in the cities of the plain and pitched *his* tent even as far as Sodom. But the men of Sodom *were* exceedingly wicked and sinful against the LORD.

And the LORD said to Abram, after Lot had separated from him: "Lift your eyes now and look from the place where you are—northward, southward, eastward, and westward; for all the land which you see I give to you and your descendants forever. And I will make your descendants as the dust of the earth; so that if a man could number the dust of the earth, *then* your descendants also could be numbered. Arise, walk in the land through its length and its width, for I give it to you."

Then Abram moved *his* tent, and went and dwelt by the terebinth trees of Mamre, which *are* in Hebron, and built an altar there to the LORD. GENESIS 13:1–18

During the early part of his reign, King Solomon had a special encounter with God. His response to that encounter led to greater peace with God and a greater ability to discern right from wrong in his administration. Wise and just ruling resolves conflicts properly and leads to greater peace with others in the long run. The same principles apply to our lives today. (Note: Solomon's obedience to God is found in the shift in the location of his sacrifices to God from where he started on the high place of Gibeon to where he worshipped after his dream.)

Solomon loved the LORD, walking in the statutes of his father David, except that he sacrificed and burned incense at the high places.

Now the king went to Gibeon to sacrifice there, for that *was* the great high place: Solomon offered a thousand burnt offerings on that altar. At Gibeon the LORD appeared to Solomon in a dream by night; and God said, "Ask! What shall I give you?"

And Solomon said: "You have shown great mercy to Your servant David my father, because he walked before You in truth, in righteousness, and in uprightness of heart with You; You have continued this great kindness for him, and You have given him a son to sit on his throne, as *it is* this day. Now, O LORD my God, You have made Your servant king instead of my father David, but I *am* a little child; I do not know *how* to go out or come in. And Your servant *is* in the midst of Your people whom You have chosen, a great people, too numerous to be numbered or counted. Therefore give to Your servant an understanding heart to judge Your people, that I may discern between good and evil. For who is able to judge this great people of Yours?"

The speech pleased the Lord, that Solomon had asked this thing. Then God said to him: "Because you have asked this thing, and have not asked long life for yourself, nor have asked riches for yourself, nor have asked the life of your enemies, but have asked for yourself understanding to discern justice, behold, I have done according to your words; see, I have given you a wise and understanding heart, so that there has not been anyone like you before you, nor shall any like you arise after you. And I have also given you what you have not asked: both riches and honor, so that there shall not be anyone like you among the kings all your days. So if you walk in My ways, to keep My statutes and My commandments, as your father David walked, then I will lengthen your days."

Then Solomon awoke; and indeed it had been a dream. And he came to Jerusalem and stood before the ark of the covenant of the LORD, offered up burnt offerings, offered peace offerings, and made a feast for all his servants. 1 KINGS 3:3–15

The outcome of Solomon's decision is recorded below. If we want greater peace in our lives, we should first seek to live in obedience to God and then apply His wisdom to find peace in our relationships with others.

Judah and Israel *were* as numerous as the sand by the sea in multitude, eating and drinking and rejoicing. So Solomon reigned over all kingdoms from the River *to* the land of the Philistines, as far as the border of Egypt. *They* brought tribute and served Solomon all the days of his life.

Now Solomon's provision for one day was thirty kors of fine flour, sixty kors of meal, ten fatted oxen, twenty oxen from the pastures, and one hundred sheep, besides deer, gazelles, roebucks, and fatted fowl.

For he had dominion over all *the region* on this side of the River from Tiphsah even to Gaza, namely over all the kings on

this side of the River; and he had peace on every side all around him. And Judah and Israel dwelt safely, each man under his vine and his fig tree, from Dan as far as Beersheba, all the days of Solomon. 1 KINGS 4:20–25

Another example of people in the Bible striving for peace is found in the life of Jesus. In the Sermon on the Mount, Jesus encourages us to make living at peace with one another one of our top priorities, even above acts of worship. God makes it clear throughout Scripture that He values obedience over sacrifice. So if we are not at peace in our relationships, Jesus urges us not to keep performing acts of worship, but to pursue reconciliation first.

"You have heard that it was said to those of old, *'You shall not murder,* and whoever murders will be in danger of the judgment.' But I say to you that whoever is angry with his brother without a cause shall be in danger of the judgment. And whoever says to his brother, 'Raca!' shall be in danger of the council. But whoever says, 'You fool!' shall be in danger of hell fire. **Therefore if you bring your gift to the altar, and there remember that your brother has something against you, leave your gift there before the altar, and go your way. First be reconciled to your brother, and then come and offer your gift.** Agree with your adversary quickly, while you are on the way with him, lest your adversary deliver you to the judge, the judge hand you over to the officer, and you be thrown into prison. Assuredly, I say to you, you will by no means get out of there till you have paid the last penny." MATTHEW 5:21–26

Living at peace, even with fellow followers of Jesus, can be a challenge. We each think and feel differently. Naturally there are bound to be conflicts. The church in New Testament times was made up of both Jews and Gentiles. Many Jewish converts held on to the rituals of the Old Testament Law regarding diet and festivals. Some Jewish followers gladly left these rules behind in favor of their new freedom in Christ. Because the Gentiles had little regard for these traditions, it created tension in their communities. Paul instructed the church in Rome how to experience peace even amid intense disagreement.

Receive one who is weak in the faith, *but* not to disputes over doubtful things. For one believes he may eat all things, but he who is weak eats *only* vegetables. Let not him who eats despise him who does not eat, and let not him who does not eat judge him who eats; for God has received him. Who are you to judge another's servant? To his own master he stands or falls. Indeed, he will be made to stand, for God is able to make him stand.

One person esteems *one* day above another; another esteems every day *alike.* Let each be fully convinced in his own mind. He who observes the day, observes *it* to the Lord; and he who does not observe the day, to the Lord he does not observe *it.* He who eats, eats to the Lord, for he gives God thanks; and he who does not eat, to the Lord he does not eat, and gives God thanks. For none of us lives to himself, and no one dies to himself. For if we live, we live to the Lord; and if we die, we die to the Lord. Therefore, whether we live or die, we are the Lord's. For to this end Christ died and rose and lived again, that He might be Lord of both the dead and the living. But why do you judge your brother? Or why do you show contempt for your brother? For we shall all stand before the judgment seat of Christ. For it is written:

> *"As I live, says the* LORD,
> *Every knee shall bow to Me,*
> *And every tongue shall confess to God."*

So then each of us shall give account of himself to God. Therefore let us not judge one another anymore, but rather resolve this, not to put a stumbling block or a cause to fall in *our* brother's way.

I know and am convinced by the Lord Jesus that *there is* nothing unclean of itself; but to him who considers anything to be unclean, to him *it is* unclean. Yet if your brother is grieved because of *your* food, you are no longer walking in love. Do not destroy with your food the one for whom Christ died. Therefore do not let your good be spoken of as evil; for the kingdom of God is not eating and drinking, but righteousness and peace and joy in the Holy Spirit. For he who serves Christ in these things *is* acceptable to God and approved by men.

Therefore let us pursue the things *which make* for peace and the things by which one may edify another. Do not destroy the work of God for the sake of food. All things indeed *are* pure, but *it is* evil for the man who eats with offense. *It is* good neither to eat meat nor drink wine nor *do anything* by which your brother stumbles or is offended or is made weak. Do you have faith? Have *it* to yourself before God. Happy *is* he who does not condemn himself in what he approves. But he who doubts is condemned if he eats, because *he does* not *eat* from faith; for whatever *is* not from faith is sin.

We then who are strong ought to bear with the scruples of the weak, and not to please ourselves. Let each of us please *his* neighbor for *his* good, leading to edification. For even Christ did not please Himself; but as it is written, *"The reproaches of those who reproached You fell on Me."* For whatever things were written before were written for our learning, that we through the patience and comfort of the Scriptures might have hope. Now may the God of patience and comfort grant you to be like-minded toward one another, according to Christ Jesus, that you may with one mind *and* one mouth glorify the God and Father of our Lord Jesus Christ.

Therefore receive one another, just as Christ also received us, to the glory of God. Now I say that Jesus Christ has become a servant to the circumcision for the truth of God, to confirm the promises *made* to the fathers, and that the Gentiles might glorify God for *His* mercy, as it is written:

> *"For this reason I will confess to You among the Gentiles,*
> *And sing to Your name."*

And again he says:

> *"Rejoice, O Gentiles, with His people!"*

And again:

> *"Praise the* LORD*, all you Gentiles!*
> *Laud Him, all you peoples!"*

And again, Isaiah says:

> *"There shall be a root of Jesse;*
> *And He who shall rise to reign over the Gentiles,*
> *In Him the Gentiles shall hope."*

Now may the God of hope fill you with all joy and peace in believing, that you may abound in hope by the power of the Holy Spirit. ROMANS 14:1—15:13

"Doubtful things" are areas where there is more than one acceptable option or opinion, so we must each decide with conviction and yet respect others who choose differently. What are "doubtful things" for Christians today?

Many of the New Testament letters helped to resocialize the church to live in God's kingdom—a kingdom of righteousness, peace and joy. Paul offered specific instruction to believers in the various churches regarding how to achieve this divine vision through Christ. Believers were to set their sights on living at peace with everyone to the best of their ability.

If then you were raised with Christ, seek those things which are above, where Christ is, sitting at the right hand of God. Set your mind on things above, not on things on the earth. For you died, and your life is hidden with Christ in God. When Christ *who is* our life appears, then you also will appear with Him in glory.

Therefore put to death your members which are on the earth: fornication, uncleanness, passion, evil desire, and covetousness, which is idolatry. Because of these things the wrath of God is coming upon the sons of disobedience, in which you yourselves once walked when you lived in them.

But now you yourselves are to put off all these: anger, wrath, malice, blasphemy, filthy language out of your mouth. Do not lie to one another, since you have put off the old man with his deeds, and have put on the new *man* who is renewed in knowledge according to the image of Him who created him, where there is neither Greek nor Jew, circumcised nor uncircumcised, barbarian, Scythian, slave *nor* free, but Christ *is* all and in all.

Therefore, as *the* elect of God, holy and beloved, put on tender mercies, kindness, humility, meekness, longsuffering; bearing with one another, and forgiving one another, if anyone has a complaint against another; even as Christ forgave you, so you also *must do.*

But above all these things put on love, which is the bond of perfection. **And let the peace of God rule in your hearts, to which also you were called in one body;** and be thankful. Let the word of Christ dwell in you richly in all wisdom, teaching and admonishing one another in psalms and hymns and spiritual songs, singing with grace in your hearts to the Lord. And whatever you do in word or deed, *do* all in the name of the Lord Jesus, giving thanks to God the Father through Him. COLOSSIANS 3:1–17

Repay no one evil for evil. Have regard for good things in the sight of all men. If it is possible, as much as depends on you, live peaceably with all men. Beloved, do not avenge yourselves, but *rather* give place to wrath; for it is written, *"Vengeance is Mine, I will repay,"* says the Lord. Therefore

> *"If your enemy is hungry, feed him;*
> *If he is thirsty, give him a drink;*
> *For in so doing you will heap coals of fire on his head."*

Do not be overcome by evil, but overcome evil with good.

ROMANS 12:17–21

After reading Paul's counsel to the churches at Colosse and Rome below from Romans 12, how would you describe the principles that promote peace in our relationships with one another?

Paul offered a similar discourse to the church in Ephesus.

Therefore I exhort first of all that supplications, prayers, intercessions, *and* giving of thanks be made for all men, for kings and all who are in authority, that we may lead a quiet and peaceable life in all godliness and reverence. For this *is* good and acceptable in the sight of God our Savior, who desires all men to be saved and to come to the knowledge of the truth. For *there is* one God and one Mediator between God and men, *the* Man Christ Jesus, who gave Himself a ransom for all, to be testified in due time, for which I was appointed a preacher and an apostle—I am speaking the truth in Christ *and* not lying—a teacher of the Gentiles in faith and truth.

I desire therefore that the men pray everywhere, lifting up holy hands, without wrath and doubting. 1 TIMOTHY 2:1–8

How does living at peace with people outside the faith, including government leaders, promote the gospel? How do we achieve this when the government is making decisions and taking actions that conflict with our Christian faith?

Paul penned a letter to his faithful ministry partner Titus while Titus was leading the new believers on the island of Crete in the Mediterranean Sea. At this time Crete was known as an immoral, dishonest place filled with selfish people—all the ingredients for conflict and strife. Paul gave Titus tangible and practical advice to guide the believers there regarding how to live a life of peace.

Remind them to be subject to rulers and authorities, to obey, to be ready for every good work, to speak evil of no one, to be peaceable, gentle, showing all humility to all men. For we ourselves were also once foolish, disobedient, deceived, serving various lusts and pleasures, living in malice and envy, hateful and hating one another. But when the kindness and the love of God our Savior toward man appeared, not by works of righteousness which we have done, but according to His mercy He saved us, through the washing of regeneration and renewing of the Holy Spirit, whom He poured out on us abundantly through Jesus Christ our Savior, that having been justified by His grace we should become heirs according to the hope of eternal life.

This is a faithful saying, and these things I want you to affirm constantly, that those who have believed in God should be careful to maintain good works. These things are good and profitable to men.

But avoid foolish disputes, genealogies, contentions, and strivings about the law; for they are unprofitable and useless. Reject a divisive man after the first and second admonition, knowing that such a person is warped and sinning, being self-condemned.

TITUS 3:1–11

Peace With Yourself (Inner Peace)

Worry is the chief robber of peace in our lives. It prevents us from lying down and sleeping at night. It keeps us on edge during the day. Our Prince of Peace, Jesus, emphasized the immense capacity of God the Father to love and care for His people individually before they let the worries of this life overtake them.

"Therefore I say to you, do not worry about your life, what you will eat or what you will drink; nor about your body, what you will put on. Is not life more than food and the body more than clothing? Look at the birds of the air, for they neither sow nor reap nor gather into barns; yet your heavenly Father feeds them. Are you not of more value than they? Which of you by worrying can add one cubit to his stature?

"So why do you worry about clothing? Consider the lilies of the field, how they grow: they neither toil nor spin; and yet I say to you that even Solomon in all his glory was not arrayed like one of these. Now if God so clothes the grass of the field, which today is, and tomorrow is thrown into the oven, *will He* not much more *clothe* you, O you of little faith?

"Therefore do not worry, saying, 'What shall we eat?' or 'What shall we drink?' or 'What shall we wear?' For after all these things the Gentiles seek. For your heavenly Father knows that you need all these things. But seek first the kingdom of God and His righteousness, and all these things shall be added to you. Therefore do not worry about tomorrow, for tomorrow will worry about its own things. Sufficient for the day *is* its own trouble." Matthew 6:25–34

It's true that each day has enough trouble of its own. As followers of Christ, we must be prepared to deal with these troubles in the strength God provides. It might be tempting to give in to the anxiety but, as Jesus vividly illustrated to His disciples, through our faith we can find peace and remain in control.

On the same day, when evening had come, He said to them, "Let us cross over to the other side." Now when they had left the multitude, they took Him along in the boat as He was. And other little boats were also with Him. And a great windstorm arose, and the waves beat into the boat, so that it was already filling. But He was in the stern, asleep on a pillow. And they awoke Him and said to Him, "Teacher, do You not care that we are perishing?"

Then He arose and rebuked the wind, and said to the sea, "Peace, be still!" And the wind ceased and there was a great calm. But He said to them, "Why are you so fearful? How *is it* that you have no faith?" And they feared exceedingly, and said to one another, "Who can this be, that even the wind and the sea obey Him!"

MARK 4:35–41

As Paul wrapped up his personal letter to the believers at Philippi, he spoke to them directly on how to obtain a peace that "surpasses all understanding."

Rejoice in the Lord always. Again I will say, rejoice!

Let your gentleness be known to all men. The Lord *is* at hand.

Be anxious for nothing, but in everything by prayer and supplication, with thanksgiving, let your requests be made known to God; and the peace of God, which surpasses all understanding, will guard your hearts and minds through Christ Jesus.

Finally, brethren, whatever things are true, whatever things *are* noble, whatever things *are* just, whatever things *are* pure, whatever things *are* lovely, whatever things *are* of good report, if *there is* any virtue and if *there is* anything praiseworthy—meditate on these things. The things which you learned and received and heard and saw in me, these do, and the God of peace will be with you.

PHILIPPIANS 4:4–9

What is Paul's prescription
for anxiety and worry?

WHAT WE BELIEVE

The feeling of peace we long for will flow naturally when things are right in our relationships. Of greatest importance is a reconciled relationship with God, made possible through Jesus Christ. When we accept His offer of salvation, the conflict between God and us is forever eliminated. A reconciled relationship with God now becomes the source of peace in our relationships with others. The Scripture passages in this chapter lay out how we do our part to promote peace in our relationships. God's Spirit enables us to achieve this. We are also called to live at peace with ourselves by accepting God's love and forgiveness in our lives. It requires that we take the things that burden and trouble us and give them to God. When we do this we declare that God is bigger than any of our problems and that the "peace of God, which surpassess all understanding, will guard [our] hearts and [our] minds through Christ Jesus" (Philippians 4:7).

BE

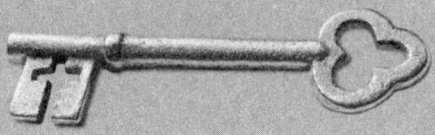

CHAPTER

24

Self-Control

KEY QUESTION

How does God free me from addictions and sinful habits?

KEY IDEA

I have the power through Christ to control myself.

KEY VERSE

For the grace of God that brings salvation has appeared
to all men, teaching us that, denying ungodliness
and worldly lusts, we should live soberly,
righteously, and godly in the present age, looking
for the blessed hope and glorious appearing
of our great God and Savior Jesus Christ.
Titus 2:11 – 13

OUR MAP

Self-control refers to the ability to control one's emotions and behavior. Everyone at some point struggles with self-control—it's the presence of the sin nature within us. So how does God help us when we've lost control and let our sinful nature take over? How does He free us from addictions and sinful habits? God's Word contains the answer.

In this chapter we will be reading about:

- *The Call and the Challenge*
- *Models of Self-Control: Bad and Good*
- *The How-Tos*

The Call and the Challenge

God desires for all of us to demonstrate self-control. However, in the face of external pressures, the battle to keep our sinful nature in check is easier said than done. The writer of Proverbs places options before us, clearly highlighting self-control.

> *He who is* slow to anger *is* better than the mighty,
> And he who rules his spirit than he who takes a city.
>
> Proverbs 16:32

> He who has knowledge spares his words,
> *And* a man of understanding is of a calm spirit. Proverbs 17:27

> **Whoever *has* no rule over his own spirit**
> ***Is like* a city broken down, without walls.** Proverbs 25:28

> A fool vents all his feelings,
> But a wise *man* holds them back. Proverbs 29:11

The benefits of having self-control are numerous. In the New Testament, Paul wrote a personal letter to his ministry partner Titus instructing him to appoint elders in the church gathered on the island of Crete. Self-control was a prominent characteristic Titus was to look for in these spiritual leaders. Paul also instructed Titus to call believers of all ages to this virtue, which obviously was much needed in Crete.

To Titus, a true son in *our* common faith:

Grace, mercy, *and* peace from God the Father and the Lord Jesus Christ our Savior.

For this reason I left you in Crete, that you should set in order the things that are lacking, and appoint elders in every city as I commanded you—if a man is blameless, the husband of one wife, having faithful children not accused of dissipation or insubordination. **For a bishop must be blameless, as a steward of God, not self-willed, not quick-tempered, not given to wine, not violent, not greedy for money, but hospitable, a lover of what is good, sober-minded, just, holy, self-controlled,** holding fast the faithful word as he has been taught, that he may be able, by sound doctrine, both to exhort and convict those who contradict.

TITUS 1:4–9

But as for you, speak the things which are proper for sound doctrine: that the older men be sober, reverent, temperate, sound in faith, in love, in patience; the older women likewise, that they be reverent in behavior, not slanderers, not given to much wine, teachers of good things—that they admonish the young women to love their husbands, to love their children, *to be* discreet, chaste, homemakers, good, obedient to their own husbands, that the word of God may not be blasphemed.

Likewise, exhort the young men to be sober-minded, in all things showing yourself *to be* a pattern of good works; in doctrine *showing* integrity, reverence, incorruptibility, sound speech that cannot be condemned, that one who is an opponent may be ashamed, having nothing evil to say of you.

Exhort bondservants to be obedient to their own masters, to be well pleasing in all *things,* not answering back, not pilfering, but showing all good fidelity, that they may adorn the doctrine of God our Savior in all things.

For the grace of God that brings salvation has appeared to all men, teaching us that, denying ungodliness and worldly lusts, we should live soberly, righteously, and godly in the present age, looking for the blessed hope and glorious appearing of our great God and Savior Jesus Christ, who gave Himself for us, that He might redeem us from every lawless deed and purify for Himself *His* own special people, zealous for good works.

Speak these things, exhort, and rebuke with all authority. Let no one despise you. TITUS 2:1–15

Paul used several different words—*temperate, discreet, sober minded* and *soberly*—to mean the same thing: self-controled. Underline these words in Titus 2:1–15, remembering that they all encourage self-control. Why do you think self-control is a key virtue required for church leaders?

MODELS OF SELF-CONTROL: BAD AND GOOD

During the days of the judges, the Philistines bullied Israel for 40 years. But time after time God raised up a special person, a judge, to deliver Israel from this oppression. God intervened in the life of a childless Israelite couple and enabled the wife to conceive and give birth to Samson, who would be used by God to set Israel free from this bondage. From conception Samson was a Nazirite—which comes from the Hebrew word meaning "separated"—and God blessed him with supernatural strength. As a spiritual and physical sign of this vow, Samson was never to cut his hair. Interestingly, this special man, one of the last judges of Israel, struggled mightily with self-control over his sexual passions; and ironically, he was particularly attracted to Philistine women. Eventually Samson let his lack of self-control get the best of him.

Now Samson went to Gaza and saw a harlot there, and went in to her. *When* the Gazites *were told,* "Samson has come here!" they surrounded *the place* and lay in wait for him all night at the gate of the city. They were quiet all night, saying, "In the morning, when it is daylight, we will kill him." And Samson lay *low* till midnight; then he arose at midnight, took hold of the doors of the gate of the city and the two gateposts, pulled them up, bar and all, put *them* on his shoulders, and carried them to the top of the hill that faces Hebron.

Afterward it happened that he loved a woman in the Valley of Sorek, whose name *was* Delilah. And the lords of the Philistines came up to her and said to her, "Entice him, and find out where his great strength *lies,* and by what *means* we may overpower him, that we may bind him to afflict him; and every one of us will give you eleven hundred *pieces* of silver."

So Delilah said to Samson, "Please tell me where your great strength *lies,* and with what you may be bound to afflict you."

And Samson said to her, "If they bind me with seven fresh bowstrings, not yet dried, then I shall become weak, and be like any *other* man."

So the lords of the Philistines brought up to her seven fresh bowstrings, not yet dried, and she bound him with them. Now *men were* lying in wait, staying with her in the room. And she said to him, "The Philistines *are* upon you, Samson!" But he broke the bowstrings as a strand of yarn breaks when it touches fire. So the secret of his strength was not known.

Then Delilah said to Samson, "Look, you have mocked me and told me lies. Now, please tell me what you may be bound with."

So he said to her, "If they bind me securely with new ropes that have never been used, then I shall become weak, and be like any *other* man."

Therefore Delilah took new ropes and bound him with them, and said to him, "The Philistines *are* upon you, Samson!" And *men were* lying in wait, staying in the room. But he broke them off his arms like a thread.

Delilah said to Samson, "Until now you have mocked me and told me lies. Tell me what you may be bound with."

And he said to her, "If you weave the seven locks of my head into the web of the loom"—

So she wove *it* tightly with the batten of the loom, and said to him, "The Philistines *are* upon you, Samson!" But he awoke from his sleep, and pulled out the batten and the web from the loom.

Then she said to him, "How can you say, 'I love you,' when your heart *is* not with me? You have mocked me these three times, and have not told me where your great strength *lies.*" And it came to pass, when she pestered him daily with her words and pressed him, *so* that his soul was vexed to death, that **he told her all his heart, and said to her, "No razor has ever come upon my head, for I *have been* a Nazirite to God from my mother's womb. If I**

am shaven, then my strength will leave me, and I shall become weak, and be like any *other* man."

When Delilah saw that he had told her all his heart, she sent and called for the lords of the Philistines, saying, "Come up once more, for he has told me all his heart." So the lords of the Philistines came up to her and brought the money in their hand. Then she lulled him to sleep on her knees, and called for a man and had him shave off the seven locks of his head. Then she began to torment him, and his strength left him. And she said, "The Philistines *are* upon you, Samson!" So he awoke from his sleep, and said, "I will go out as before, at other times, and shake myself free!" But he did not know that the LORD had departed from him.

Then the Philistines took him and put out his eyes, and brought him down to Gaza. They bound him with bronze fetters, and he became a grinder in the prison. JUDGES 16:1–21

Unlike Samson, Joseph offers one of the best examples in the Bible of a man who exercised excellent self-control. Joseph was sold into slavery at the hands of his jealous brothers. The band of traveling merchants who purchased him took him from his home in Canaan to Egypt to be resold to an important official in Pharaoh's court. Although Joseph was punished by his captors for his self-control, God rewarded his faithfulness.

Now Joseph had been taken down to Egypt. And Potiphar, an officer of Pharaoh, captain of the guard, an Egyptian, bought him from the Ishmaelites who had taken him down there. The LORD was with Joseph, and he was a successful man; and he was in the house of his master the Egyptian. And his master saw that the LORD *was* with him and that the LORD made all he did to prosper in his hand. So Joseph found favor in his sight, and served him. Then he made him overseer of his house, and all *that* he had he put under his authority. So it was, from the time *that* he had made him overseer of his house and all that he had, that the LORD blessed the Egyptian's house for Joseph's sake; and the blessing of the LORD was on all that he had in the house and in the field. Thus he left all that he had in Joseph's hand, and he did not know what he had except for the bread which he ate.

Now Joseph was handsome in form and appearance.

And it came to pass after these things that his master's wife cast longing eyes on Joseph, and she said, "Lie with me."

But he refused and said to his master's wife, "Look, my master does not know what *is* with me in the house, and he has committed all that he has to my hand. *There is* no one greater in this house than I, nor has he kept back anything from me but you, because you *are* his wife. How then can I do this great wickedness, and sin against God?"

So it was, as she spoke to Joseph day by day, that he did not heed her, to lie with her *or* to be with her.

But it happened about this time, when Joseph went into the house to do his work, and none of the men of the house *was* inside, that she caught him by his garment, saying, "Lie with me." But he left his garment in her hand, and fled and ran outside. And so it was, when she saw that he had left his garment in her hand and fled outside, that she called to the men of her house and spoke to them, saying, "See, he has brought in to us a Hebrew to mock us. He came in to me to lie with me, and I cried out with a loud voice. And it happened, when he heard that I lifted my voice and cried out, that he left his garment with me, and fled and went outside."

So she kept his garment with her until his master came home. Then she spoke to him with words like these, saying, "The Hebrew servant whom you brought to us came in to me to mock me; so it happened, as I lifted my voice and cried out, that he left his garment with me and fled outside."

So it was, when his master heard the words which his wife spoke to him, saying, "Your servant did to me after this manner," that his anger was aroused. Then Joseph's master took him and put him into the prison, a place where the king's prisoners *were* confined. And he was there in the prison. But the LORD was with Joseph and showed him mercy, and He gave him favor in the sight of the keeper of the prison. And the keeper of the prison committed to Joseph's hand all the prisoners who *were* in the prison; whatever they did there, it was his doing. The keeper of the prison did not look into anything *that was* under *Joseph's* authority, because the LORD was with him; and whatever he did, the LORD made *it* prosper.

GENESIS 39:1–23

The How-Tos

The Bible offers practical instruction on how to grow in the virtue of self-control. One of the primary applications is to "flee"—flee from the person, environment or situation that tempts us to lose control. Corinth was a place given to living without boundaries. In Paul's letter, known to us as 1 Corinthians, he instructed the believers in Corinth to keep themselves out of temptation's way lest they fall.

All things are lawful for me, but all things are not helpful. All things are lawful for me, but I will not be brought under the power of any. Foods for the stomach and the stomach for foods, but God will destroy both it and them. Now the body *is* not for sexual immorality but for the Lord, and the Lord for the body. And God both raised up the Lord and will also raise us up by His power.

Do you not know that your bodies are members of Christ? Shall I then take the members of Christ and make *them* members of a harlot? Certainly not! Or do you not know that he who is joined to a harlot is one body *with her?* For *"the two,"* He says, *"shall become one flesh."* But he who is joined to the Lord is one spirit *with Him.*

Flee sexual immorality. Every sin that a man does is outside the body, but he who commits sexual immorality sins against his own body. Or do you not know that your body is the temple of the Holy Spirit *who is* in you, whom you have from God, and you are not your own? For you were bought at a price; therefore glorify God in your body and in your spirit, which are God's.

1 Corinthians 6:12–20

Therefore, my beloved, flee from idolatry. I speak as to wise men; judge for yourselves what I say. The cup of blessing which we bless, is it not the communion of the blood of Christ? The bread which we break, is it not the communion of the body of Christ? For we, *though* many, are one bread *and* one body; for we all partake of that one bread.

Observe Israel after the flesh: Are not those who eat of the sacrifices partakers of the altar? What am I saying then? That an idol is anything, or what is offered to idols is anything? Rather, that the things which the Gentiles sacrifice they sacrifice to demons and not to God, and I do not want you to have fellowship with demons. You cannot drink the cup of the Lord and the cup of demons; you cannot partake of the Lord's table and of the table of demons. Or do we provoke the Lord to jealousy? Are we stronger than He?

1 CORINTHIANS 10:14–22

Paul reiterated the charge to flee in his letters to Timothy, which he penned to give the young leader instructions regarding how to spiritually guide the church at Ephesus. He wrote about how to avoid false teachers and resist the love of money. He also urged Timothy and the church members not to keep company with people who would draw them into ungodly behaviors.

If anyone teaches otherwise and does not consent to wholesome words, *even* the words of our Lord Jesus Christ, and to the doctrine which accords with godliness, he is proud, knowing nothing, but is obsessed with disputes and arguments over words, from which come envy, strife, reviling, evil suspicions, useless wranglings of men of corrupt minds and destitute of the truth, who suppose that godliness is a *means of* gain. From such withdraw yourself.

Now godliness with contentment is great gain. For we brought nothing into *this* world, *and it is* certain we can carry nothing out. And having food and clothing, with these we shall be content. But those who desire to be rich fall into temptation and a snare, and *into* many foolish and harmful lusts which drown men in destruction and perdition. For the love of money is a root of all *kinds of* evil, for which some have strayed from the faith in their greediness, and pierced themselves through with many sorrows.

But you, O man of God, flee these things and pursue righteousness, godliness, faith, love, patience, gentleness. Fight the good fight of faith, lay hold on eternal life, to which you were also called and have confessed the good confession in the presence of many witnesses. I urge you in the sight of God who gives life to all things, and *before* Christ Jesus who witnessed the good confession before Pontius Pilate, that you keep *this* commandment without spot, blameless until our Lord Jesus Christ's appearing, which He will manifest in His own time, *He who is* the blessed and only Potentate, the King of kings and Lord of lords, who alone has immortality, dwelling in unapproachable light, whom no man has seen or can see, to whom *be* honor and everlasting power. Amen.

1 TIMOTHY 6:3–16

Flee also youthful lusts; but pursue righteousness, faith, love, peace with those who call on the Lord out of a pure heart. But avoid foolish and ignorant disputes, knowing that they generate strife. And a servant of the Lord must not quarrel but be gentle to all, able to teach, patient, in humility correcting those who are in opposition, if God perhaps will grant them repentance, so that they may know the truth, and *that* they may come to their senses *and escape* the snare of the devil, having been taken captive by him to *do* his will.

But know this, that in the last days perilous times will come: For men will be lovers of themselves, lovers of money, boasters, proud, blasphemers, disobedient to parents, unthankful, unholy, unloving, unforgiving, slanderers, without self-control, brutal, despisers of good, traitors, headstrong, haughty, lovers of pleasure rather than lovers of God, having a form of godliness but denying its power. And from such people turn away! For of this sort are those who creep into households and make captives of gullible women loaded down with sins, led away by various lusts, always learning and never able to come to the knowledge of the truth.

2 TIMOTHY 2:22—3:7

What does the company we keep have to do with our ability to be self-controlled?

A second strategy, also defensive in nature, in the fight to preserve self-control is to resist. We can tame our tongues, reduce fights and quarrels among us, control our selfish desires and mitigate against the negative influences of the world and the devil. But ultimately, complete self-control is unattainable. Our sin nature, or flesh, eventually makes us weary and weak. The ultimate solution to gain self-control is "God-control." The believer has God's presence and power within them to guide them and give them strength. As believers, we can use this strength to preserve self-control and live godly lives.

My brethren, let not many of you become teachers, knowing that we shall receive a stricter judgment. For we all stumble in many things. If anyone does not stumble in word, he *is* a perfect man, able also to bridle the whole body. Indeed, we put bits in horses' mouths that they may obey us, and we turn their whole body. Look also at ships: although they are so large and are driven by fierce winds, they are turned by a very small rudder wherever the pilot desires. Even so the tongue is a little member and boasts great things.

See how great a forest a little fire kindles! And the tongue *is* a fire, a world of iniquity. The tongue is so set among our members that it defiles the whole body, and sets on fire the course of nature; and it is set on fire by hell. For every kind of beast and bird, of reptile and creature of the sea, is tamed and has been tamed by mankind. But no man can tame the tongue. *It is* an unruly evil, full of deadly poison. With it we bless our God and Father, and with it we curse men, who have been made in the similitude of God. Out of the same mouth proceed blessing and cursing. My brethren, these things ought not to be so. Does a spring send forth fresh *water* and bitter from the same opening? Can a fig tree, my brethren, bear olives, or a grapevine bear figs? Thus no spring yields both salt water and fresh.

Who *is* wise and understanding among you? Let him show by good conduct *that* his works *are done* in the meekness of wisdom. But if you have bitter envy and self-seeking in your hearts, do not boast and lie against the truth. This wisdom does not descend from above, but *is* earthly, sensual, demonic. For where envy and self-seeking *exist,* confusion and every evil thing *are* there. But the wisdom that is from above is first pure, then peaceable, gentle, willing to yield, full of mercy and good fruits, without partiality and without hypocrisy. Now the fruit of righteousness is sown in peace by those who make peace.

Where do wars and fights *come* from among you? Do *they* not *come* from your *desires for* pleasure that war in your members? You lust and do not have. You murder and covet and cannot obtain. You fight and war. Yet you do not have because you do not ask. You ask and do not receive, because you ask amiss, that you may spend *it* on your pleasures. Adulterers and adulteresses! Do you not know that friendship with the world is enmity with God? Whoever therefore wants to be a friend of the world makes himself an enemy of God. Or do you think that the Scripture says in vain, "The Spirit who dwells in us yearns jealously"?

But He gives more grace. Therefore He says:

> *"God resists the proud,*
> *But gives grace to the humble."*

Therefore submit to God. Resist the devil and he will flee from you. Draw near to God and He will draw near to you. Cleanse *your* hands, *you* sinners; and purify *your* hearts, *you* double-minded. Lament and mourn and weep! Let your laughter be turned to mourning and *your* joy to gloom. Humble yourselves in the sight of the Lord, and He will lift you up. JAMES 3:1—4:10

Why are our tongues so difficult to control?

Peter offered similar advice in his first letter to the Christians scattered throughout the region of Asia Minor (modern-day Turkey).

Be sober, be vigilant; because your adversary the devil walks about like a roaring lion, seeking whom he may devour. Resist him, steadfast in the faith, knowing that the same sufferings are experienced by your brotherhood in the world. But may the God of all grace, who called us to His eternal glory by Christ Jesus, after you have suffered a while, perfect, establish, strengthen, and settle *you.* To Him *be* the glory and the dominion forever and ever. Amen. 1 PETER 5:8–11

The apostle Paul presented a different strategy to practice self-control in our lives—particularly in the area of sexual passions: engage these natural desires within the boundaries of God's design.

Now concerning the things of which you wrote to me:

It is good for a man not to touch a woman. Nevertheless, because of sexual immorality, let each man have his own wife, and let each woman have her own husband. Let the husband render to his wife the affection due her, and likewise also the wife to her husband. The wife does not have authority over her own body, but the husband *does.* And likewise the husband does not have authority over his own body, but the wife *does.* Do not deprive one another except with consent for a time, that you may give yourselves to fasting and prayer; and come together again so that Satan does not tempt you because of your lack of self-control. But I say this as a concession, not as a commandment. For I wish that all men were even as I myself. But each one has his own gift from God, one in this manner and another in that.

But I say to the unmarried and to the widows: It is good for them if they remain even as I am; but if they cannot exercise self-control, let them marry. For it is better to marry than to burn *with passion.*

1 Corinthians 7:1–9

Self-control is truly impossible in our own strength. Our sin natures can wear us down and get the best of us. Thankfully, we as believers have the presence and power of God within us to live a life not undermined by our inner desires and the corruption of the world. In Peter's second letter, he challenged believers to draw on this power to live productive and effective lives.

After you read this passage from Peter (see 2 Peter 1:3–11 below) and the following passage from Paul (see Galatians 5:16–25), describe in your own words how "God-control" works to bring about "self-control" in our lives.

His divine power has given to us all things that *pertain* to life and godliness, through the knowledge of Him who called us by glory and virtue, by which have been given to us exceedingly great and precious promises, that through these you may be partakers of the divine nature, having escaped the corruption *that is* in the world through lust.

But also for this very reason, giving all diligence, add to your faith virtue, to virtue knowledge, to knowledge self-control, to self-control perseverance, to perseverance godliness, to godliness brotherly kindness, and to brotherly kindness love. For if these things are yours and abound, *you* will be neither barren nor unfruitful in the knowledge of our Lord Jesus Christ. For he who lacks these things is shortsighted, even to blindness, and has forgotten that he was cleansed from his old sins.

Therefore, brethren, be even more diligent to make your call and election sure, for if you do these things you will never stumble; for so an entrance will be supplied to you abundantly into the everlasting kingdom of our Lord and Savior Jesus Christ. 2 PETER 1:3–11

Paul also stresses the importance of relying on the power of God, walking in the Spirit, to remain in control. The ultimate solution to gain self-control is "God-control."

I say then: Walk in the Spirit, and you shall not fulfill the lust of the flesh. For the flesh lusts against the Spirit, and the Spirit against the flesh; and these are contrary to one another, so that you do not do the things that you wish. But if you are led by the Spirit, you are not under the law.

Now the works of the flesh are evident, which are: adultery, fornication, uncleanness, lewdness, idolatry, sorcery, hatred, contentions, jealousies, outbursts of wrath, selfish ambitions, dissensions, heresies, envy, murders, drunkenness, revelries, and the like; of which I tell you beforehand, just as I also told *you* in time past, that those who practice such things will not inherit the kingdom of God.

But the fruit of the Spirit is love, joy, peace, longsuffering, kindness, goodness, faithfulness, gentleness, self-control. Against such there is no law. And those *who are* Christ's have crucified the flesh with its passions and desires. If we live in the Spirit, let us also walk in the Spirit. GALATIANS 5:16–25

The bottom line is that we all struggle and fall. This failure can overwhelm us with guilt that causes us to hide from God. God knows we struggle. He wants us to "come home" to Him no matter our condition. This is demonstrated beautifully in the Parable of the Lost Son.

"A certain man had two sons. And the younger of them said to *his* father, 'Father, give me the portion of goods that falls *to me.*' So he divided to them *his* livelihood. And not many days after, the younger son gathered all together, journeyed to a far country, and there wasted his possessions with prodigal living. But when he had spent all, there arose a severe famine in that land, and he began to be in want. Then he went and joined himself to a citizen of that country, and he sent him into his fields to feed swine. And he would gladly have filled his stomach with the pods that the swine ate, and no one gave him *anything.*

"But when he came to himself, he said, 'How many of my father's hired servants have bread enough and to spare, and I perish with hunger! I will arise and go to my father, and will say to him, "Father, I have sinned against heaven and before you, and I am no longer worthy to be called your son. Make me like one of your hired servants."'

"And he arose and came to his father. But when he was still a great way off, his father saw him and had compassion, and ran and fell on his neck and kissed him. And the son said to him, 'Father, I have sinned against heaven and in your sight, and am no longer worthy to be called your son.'

"But the father said to his servants, 'Bring out the best robe and put *it* on him, and put a ring on his hand and sandals on *his* feet. And bring the fatted calf here and kill *it*, and let us eat and be merry; for this my son was dead and is alive again; he was lost and is found.' And they began to be merry." LUKE 15:11–24

In what areas of your life do you struggle with self-control? How do these readings challenge you? How does the knowledge of God's grace comfort you?

WHAT WE BELIEVE

If we truly desire to become like Jesus for the sake of others, we will receive the call and challenge to be self-controlled. As we read the stories found in the Bible, we see evidence of the wreckage caused by a lack of self-control, as in the life of Samson. We also see the amazing honor and blessing that comes with self-control, as in the life of Joseph. How do we free ourselves from addictions and sinful habits? We must learn how to flee and resist the temptation before us. But the ultimate producer of self-control is God-control. As we yield our lives to God's plan, His divine power gives us the strength to say "no" to ungodliness and "yes" to His will. We have the power, through Christ, to control ourselves. Yet, when we fall, we can remember God's grace and run back to Him. He will be waiting every time with welcoming arms.

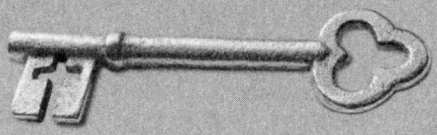

CHAPTER

25

Hope

KEY QUESTION

How do I deal with the hardships and struggles of life?

KEY IDEA

I can cope with the hardships of life
because of the hope I have in Jesus Christ.

KEY VERSE

This *hope* we have as an anchor of the soul, both sure and steadfast, and which enters the *Presence* behind the veil, where the forerunner has entered for us, *even* Jesus, having become High Priest forever according to the order of Melchizedek.
Hebrews 6:19–20

OUR MAP

We simply cannot live without hope. As our key verse above states, Christian hope is an anchor for our souls. It stabilizes us during difficult seasons because we know this is not how our story ends. It is rooted in our belief and trust in a personal God, His salvation and eternity. If we believe these truths in our hearts, then it will produce a hope that doesn't disappoint.

This chapter addresses:

- *The Need for Hope*
- *Sources of False Hope*
- *The Source of True Hope*
- *The Effect of Hope*

and how...

- *Hope Activates Faith, Faith Deepens Hope*

The Need for Hope

It is impossible to cope without hope. Job had lost everything and was running out of strength. He wanted to die. His "friends" came to comfort him. His response to his unhelpful friends is the expression of a man without hope.

Then Job answered and said:

"Oh, that my grief were fully weighed,
And my calamity laid with it on the scales!
For then it would be heavier than the sand of the sea—
Therefore my words have been rash.
For the arrows of the Almighty *are* within me;
My spirit drinks in their poison;
The terrors of God are arrayed against me.
Does the wild donkey bray when it has grass,
Or does the ox low over its fodder?
Can flavorless food be eaten without salt?
Or is there *any* taste in the white of an egg?
My soul refuses to touch them;
They *are* as loathsome food to me.

"Oh, that I might have my request,
That God would grant *me* the thing that I long for!
That it would please God to crush me,
That He would loose His hand and cut me off!
Then I would still have comfort;
Though in anguish I would exult,
He will not spare;
For I have not concealed the words of the Holy One.

"What strength do I have, that I should hope?
And what *is* my end, that I should prolong my life?
Is my strength the strength of stones?
Or is my flesh bronze?
Is my help not within me?
And is success driven from me?" JOB 6:1–13

"*Is there* not a time of hard service for man on earth?
Are not his days also like the days of a hired man?
Like a servant who earnestly desires the shade,
And like a hired man who eagerly looks for his wages,
So I have been allotted months of futility,
And wearisome nights have been appointed to me.
When I lie down, I say, 'When shall I arise,
And the night be ended?'
For I have had my fill of tossing till dawn.
My flesh is caked with worms and dust,
My skin is cracked and breaks out afresh.

**"My days are swifter than a weaver's shuttle,
And are spent without hope."** JOB 7:1–6

Have you ever felt despair like Job's?
What questions did you ask of God?

SOURCES OF FALSE HOPE

Our deep need for hope sometimes leads us to falsely put our hope in unhealthy things. False hope causes people to plan, build and risk for something that is not likely to happen. The

Bible identifies several things humans unfortunately place their hope in, only to be disappointed in the end.

As you read about the four sources of false hope,
think about which one you are most susceptible to.
What made you pick the one you did?

False hope . . . in riches.

Because of his fearless confidence in God, David was able to hurl condemnation at his enemy who trusted in wealth.

Why do you boast in evil, O mighty man?
The goodness of God *endures* continually.
Your tongue devises destruction,
Like a sharp razor, working deceitfully.
You love evil more than good,
Lying rather than speaking righteousness.
You love all devouring words,
You deceitful tongue.

God shall likewise destroy you forever;
He shall take you away, and pluck you out of *your* dwelling place,
And uproot you from the land of the living.
The righteous also shall see and fear,
And shall laugh at him, *saying,*
"Here is the man *who* did not make God his strength,
But trusted in the abundance of his riches,
***And* strengthened himself in his wickedness."**

But I *am* like a green olive tree in the house of God;
I trust in the mercy of God forever and ever.
I will praise You forever,
Because You have done *it;*
And in the presence of Your saints
I will wait on Your name, for *it is* good. PSALM 52:1–9

Paul tells Timothy to instruct the believers in Ephesus about the false hope of trusting in riches.

Command those who are rich in this present age not to be haughty, nor to trust in uncertain riches but in the living God, who gives us richly all things to enjoy. 1 TIMOTHY 6:17

False hope . . . in people.

The psalmists tell us that we will be disappointed if we place our hope in people rather than God.

***It is* better to trust in the LORD**
Than to put confidence in man.
It is better to trust in the LORD
Than to put confidence in princes. PSALM 118:8–9

Do not put your trust in princes,
***Nor* in a son of man, in whom *there is* no help.**
His spirit departs, he returns to his earth;
In that very day his plans perish. PSALM 146:3–4

The prophet Jeremiah declares the same sentiment.

Thus says the LORD:

"Cursed *is* the man who trusts in man
And makes flesh his strength,
Whose heart departs from the LORD.
For he shall be like a shrub in the desert,
And shall not see when good comes,
But shall inhabit the parched places in the wilderness,
In a salt land *which is* not inhabited." JEREMIAH 17:5–6

False hope . . . in idols.

An idol is any object we place above God. The prophet Habakkuk declares how foolish it is to place our hope in such man-made inventions.

"What profit is the image, that its maker should carve it,
The molded image, a teacher of lies,
That the maker of its mold should trust in it,
To make mute idols?

Woe to him who says to wood, 'Awake!'
To silent stone, 'Arise! It shall teach!'
Behold, it is overlaid with gold and silver,
Yet in it there is no breath at all." HABAKKUK 2:18–19

False hope . . . in human government.

It is easy and often more tangible for people to place their trust and hope in nations. Isaiah warns the people of Judah to avoid such a mistake, even with the mighty nation of Egypt.

Woe to those who go down to Egypt for help,
And rely on horses,
Who trust in chariots because *they are* many,
And in horsemen because they are very strong,
But who do not look to the Holy One of Israel,
Nor seek the LORD! ISAIAH 31:1

Now the Egyptians *are* men, and not God;
And their horses are flesh, and not spirit.
When the LORD stretches out His hand,
Both he who helps will fall,
And he who is helped will fall down;
They all will perish together. ISAIAH 31:3

THE SOURCE OF TRUE HOPE

True hope is found only in God.

Hope is only as good as the power and character of the one who guarantees it. The psalmist expresses with deep passion his trust in God as his source of hope when present times were difficult.

As the deer pants for the water brooks,
So pants my soul for You, O God.
My soul thirsts for God, for the living God.
When shall I come and appear before God?
My tears have been my food day and night,
While they continually say to me,
"Where *is* your God?"

When I remember these *things*,
I pour out my soul within me.
For I used to go with the multitude;
I went with them to the house of God,
With the voice of joy and praise,
With a multitude that kept a pilgrim feast.

Why are you cast down, O my soul?
And *why* are you disquieted within me?
Hope in God, for I shall yet praise Him
***For* the help of His countenance.**

O my God, my soul is cast down within me;
Therefore I will remember You from the land of the
Jordan,
And from the heights of Hermon,
From the Hill Mizar.
Deep calls unto deep at the noise of Your waterfalls;
All Your waves and billows have gone over me.
The LORD will command His lovingkindness in the
daytime,
And in the night His song *shall be* with me—
A prayer to the God of my life.

I will say to God my Rock,
"Why have You forgotten me?
Why do I go mourning because of the oppression of the
enemy?"
As with a breaking of my bones,
My enemies reproach me,
While they say to me all day long,
"Where *is* your God?"

Why are you cast down, O my soul?
And why are you disquieted within me?
Hope in God;
For I shall yet praise Him,
The help of my countenance and my God. PSALM 42:1–11

True hope is found in God's promises.

All the authors of the New Testament wrote on the topic of hope. It is clearly one of the unique and powerful benefits of following God. The writer of Hebrews drew on the character of God to confirm God's promises.

What promises of God can you find in the following passages from Hebrews 6; Colossians 1; 1 Peter 1; 1 Thessalonians 4 and 1 John 3?

For when God made a promise to Abraham, because He could swear by no one greater, He swore by Himself, saying, *"Surely blessing I will bless you, and multiplying I will multiply you."* And so, after he had patiently endured, he obtained the promise. For men indeed swear by the greater, and an oath for confirmation *is* for them an end of all dispute. Thus God, determining to show more abundantly to the heirs of promise the immutability of His counsel, confirmed *it* by an oath, that by two immutable things, in which it *is* impossible for God to lie, we might have strong consolation, who have fled for refuge to lay hold of the hope set before *us.*

This *hope* we have as an anchor of the soul, both sure and steadfast, and which enters the *Presence* behind the veil, where the forerunner has entered for us, *even* Jesus, having become High Priest forever according to the order of Melchizedek.

HEBREWS 6:13–20

Since God's character is rock solid, trustworthy and true, we anchor our hope in His promises to us. Paul wrote a letter to the church at Colosse while he was under house arrest in Rome. God had been unfolding His grand promise of redemption since the fall of Adam and Eve. The true and full content of this promise was a mystery to the people of the Old Testament. Now, God has fulfilled His promise and revealed it to us—the source of our hope has come.

I now rejoice in my sufferings for you, and fill up in my flesh what is lacking in the afflictions of Christ, for the sake of His body, which is the church, of which I became a minister according to the stewardship from God which was given to me for you, to fulfill the word of God, the mystery which has been hidden from ages and from generations, but now has been revealed to His saints. **To them God willed to make known what are the riches of the glory of this mystery among the Gentiles: which is Christ in you, the hope of glory.** Him we preach, warning every man and teaching every man in all wisdom, that we may present every man perfect in Christ Jesus. To this *end* I also labor, striving according to His working which works in me mightily. COLOSSIANS 1:24–29

What God has promised to all believers in Jesus enables us to endure life's hardships. Peter opened his first letter proclaiming this truth. The ultimate promise of God is our future resurrection. The hope of this promise trumps all momentary trials.

Peter, an apostle of Jesus Christ,

To the pilgrims of the Dispersion in Pontus, Galatia, Cappadocia, Asia, and Bithynia, elect according to the foreknowledge of God the Father, in sanctification of the Spirit, for obedience and sprinkling of the blood of Jesus Christ:

Grace to you and peace be multiplied.

Blessed *be* the God and Father of our Lord Jesus Christ, who according to His abundant mercy has begotten us again to a living hope through the resurrection of Jesus Christ from the dead, to an inheritance incorruptible and undefiled and that does not fade away, reserved in heaven for you, who are kept by the power of God through faith for salvation ready to be revealed in the last time.

In this you greatly rejoice, though now for a little while, if need be, you have been grieved by various trials, that the genuineness of your faith, *being* much more precious than gold that perishes, though it is tested by fire, may be found to praise, honor, and glory at the revelation of Jesus Christ, whom having not seen you love. Though now you do not see *Him,* yet believing, you rejoice with joy inexpressible and full of glory, receiving the end of your faith—the salvation of *your* souls.

Of this salvation the prophets have inquired and searched carefully, who prophesied of the grace *that would come* to you, searching what, or what manner of time, the Spirit of Christ who was in them was indicating when He testified beforehand the sufferings of Christ and the glories that would follow. To them it was revealed that, not to themselves, but to us they were ministering the things which now have been reported to you through those who have preached the gospel to you by the Holy Spirit sent from heaven—things which angels desire to look into.

Therefore gird up the loins of your mind, be sober, and rest *your* hope fully upon the grace that is to be brought to you at the revelation of Jesus Christ; as obedient children, not conforming yourselves to the former lusts, *as* in your ignorance; but as He who called you *is* holy, you also be holy in all *your* conduct, because it is written, *"Be holy, for I am holy."*

And if you call on the Father, who without partiality judges according to each one's work, conduct yourselves throughout the time of your stay *here* in fear; knowing that you were not redeemed with corruptible things, *like* silver or gold, from your aimless conduct *received* by tradition from your fathers, but with the precious blood of Christ, as of a lamb without blemish and without spot. He indeed was foreordained before the foundation of the world, but was manifest in these last times for you who through Him believe in God, who raised Him from the dead and gave Him glory, so that your faith and hope are in God.

Since you have purified your souls in obeying the truth through the Spirit in sincere love of the brethren, love one another fervently with a pure heart, having been born again, not of corruptible seed but incorruptible, through the word of God which lives and abides forever, because

> *"All flesh is as grass,*
> *And all the glory of man as the flower of the grass.*
> *The grass withers,*
> *And its flower falls away,*
> *But the word of the* LORD *endures forever."*

Now this is the word which by the gospel was preached to you.

1 PETER 1:1–25

The Christians in Thessalonica had misunderstood Paul and thought that all believers would live until Christ returns. That caused them distress when some in the church died. Paul wrote his first letter to them to clear up this matter. The promise to all believers, past and present, of being with the Lord forever is the foundation of our hope.

But I do not want you to be ignorant, brethren, concerning those who have fallen asleep, lest you sorrow as others who have no hope. For if we believe that Jesus died and rose again, even so God will bring with Him those who sleep in Jesus.

For this we say to you by the word of the Lord, that we who are alive *and* remain until the coming of the Lord will by no means precede those who are asleep. For the Lord Himself will descend from heaven with a shout, with the voice of an archangel, and with the trumpet of God. And the dead in Christ will rise first. Then we who are alive *and* remain shall be caught up together with them in the clouds to meet the Lord in the air. And thus we shall always be with the Lord. Therefore comfort one another with these words.

1 Thessalonians 4:13–18

John echoed the writings of Paul and Peter regarding the hope we have through the promised resurrection. He challenged his readers to live pure lives in anticipation of this guaranteed event.

Behold what manner of love the Father has bestowed on us, that we should be called children of God! Therefore the world does not know us, because it did not know Him. Beloved, now we are children of God; and it has not yet been revealed what we shall be, but **we know that when He is revealed, we shall be like Him, for we shall see Him as He is. And everyone who has this hope in Him purifies himself, just as He is pure.** 1 John 3:1–3

The Effect of Hope

When we hope in God's promises, the effect on our lives is profound. Even if we are going through difficulties, hope gives us the strength to continue. Isaiah prophesied that the people of Judah were about to go through 70 years of difficulty as captives of the Babylonians. Despite such suffering, Isaiah was able to confidently give the people hope because God had promised to bring them home. The exiles could live full, happy lives in a painful situation because they knew God would keep His promise.

"To whom then will you liken Me,
Or *to whom* shall I be equal?" says the Holy One.
Lift up your eyes on high,
And see who has created these *things,*
Who brings out their host by number;
He calls them all by name,
By the greatness of His might
And the strength of *His* power;
Not one is missing.

Why do you say, O Jacob,
And speak, O Israel:
"My way is hidden from the LORD,
And my just claim is passed over by my God"?
Have you not known?
Have you not heard?
The everlasting God, the LORD,
The Creator of the ends of the earth,
Neither faints nor is weary.
His understanding is unsearchable.
He gives power to the weak,
And to *those who have* no might He increases strength.
Even the youths shall faint and be weary,
And the young men shall utterly fall,
But those who wait on the LORD
Shall renew *their* strength;
They shall mount up with wings like eagles,
They shall run and not be weary,
They shall walk and not faint. ISAIAH 40:25–31

The positive effect of hope is more powerful than we realize. Simeon waited many long years without seeing the fulfillment of his hope, but he carried on, letting hope give him strength for each new day. God and His promises are the reason for our hope. When we embrace this hope, it has a dramatic effect on our daily lives. Simeon's story can give us pause to think about the impact our hope in Christ has on our ability to persevere.

And behold, there was a man in Jerusalem whose name *was* Simeon, and this man *was* just and devout, waiting for the Consolation of Israel, and the Holy Spirit was upon him. And it had been revealed to him by the Holy Spirit that he would not see death before he had seen the Lord's Christ. So he came by the Spirit into the temple. And when the parents brought in the Child Jesus, to do for Him according to the custom of the law, he took Him up in his arms and blessed God and said:

> "Lord, now You are letting Your servant depart in peace,
> According to Your word;
> For my eyes have seen Your salvation
> Which You have prepared before the face of all peoples,
> A light to *bring* revelation to the Gentiles,
> And the glory of Your people Israel."

And Joseph and His mother marveled at those things which were spoken of Him. Then Simeon blessed them, and said to Mary His mother, "Behold, this *Child* is destined for the fall and rising of many in Israel, and for a sign which will be spoken against (yes, a sword will pierce through your own soul also), that the thoughts of many hearts may be revealed." LUKE 2:25–35

What effect did God's promise to Simeon, that he would see the first arrival of Christ, have on his life? What effect should God's promise to us, that we will see the second arrival of Christ, have on our lives?

HOPE ACTIVATES FAITH, FAITH DEEPENS HOPE

Hope is available to all followers of God, but not everyone takes hold of it. It can be hard for us to trust in a God we cannot see and hold fast to fantastic promises yet to come. To activate the power of hope in our lives, we need to have faith in God and His promises. The writer of Hebrews preached this message to his readers. He then listed people from the past who placed their faith in God and experienced amazing results in their lives. God offers this same opportunity to us today. In fact, God has "something better" planned for those who know Jesus.

Now faith is the substance of things hoped for, the evidence of things not seen. For by it the elders obtained a *good* testimony.

By faith we understand that the worlds were framed by the word of God, so that the things which are seen were not made of things which are visible.

By faith Abel offered to God a more excellent sacrifice than Cain, through which he obtained witness that he was righteous, God testifying of his gifts; and through it he being dead still speaks.

By faith Enoch was taken away so that he did not see death, *"and was not found, because God had taken him"*; for before he was taken he had this testimony, that he pleased God. But without faith *it is* impossible to please *Him,* for he who comes to God must believe that He is, and *that* He is a rewarder of those who diligently seek Him.

By faith Noah, being divinely warned of things not yet seen, moved with godly fear, prepared an ark for the saving of his household, by which he condemned the world and became heir of the righteousness which is according to faith.

By faith Abraham obeyed when he was called to go out to the place which he would receive as an inheritance. And he went out, not knowing where he was going. By faith he dwelt in the land of promise as *in* a foreign country, dwelling in tents with Isaac and Jacob, the heirs with him of the same promise; for he waited for the city which has foundations, whose builder and maker *is* God.

By faith Sarah herself also received strength to conceive seed, and she bore a child when she was past the age, because she judged Him faithful who had promised. Therefore from one man, and him as good as dead, were born *as many* as the stars of the sky in multitude—innumerable as the sand which is by the seashore.

These all died in faith, not having received the promises, but having seen them afar off were assured of them, embraced *them* and confessed that they were strangers and pilgrims on the earth.

For those who say such things declare plainly that they seek a homeland. And truly if they had called to mind that *country* from which they had come out, they would have had opportunity to return. But now they desire a better, that is, a heavenly *country.* Therefore God is not ashamed to be called their God, for He has prepared a city for them.

By faith Abraham, when he was tested, offered up Isaac, and he who had received the promises offered up his only begotten *son,* of whom it was said, *"In Isaac your seed shall be called,"* concluding that God *was* able to raise *him* up, even from the dead, from which he also received him in a figurative sense.

By faith Isaac blessed Jacob and Esau concerning things to come.

By faith Jacob, when he was dying, blessed each of the sons of Joseph, and worshiped, *leaning* on the top of his staff.

By faith Joseph, when he was dying, made mention of the departure of the children of Israel, and gave instructions concerning his bones.

By faith Moses, when he was born, was hidden three months by his parents, because they saw *he was* a beautiful child; and they were not afraid of the king's command.

By faith Moses, when he became of age, refused to be called the son of Pharaoh's daughter, choosing rather to suffer affliction with the people of God than to enjoy the passing pleasures of sin, esteeming the reproach of Christ greater riches than the treasures in Egypt; for he looked to the reward.

By faith he forsook Egypt, not fearing the wrath of the king; for he endured as seeing Him who is invisible. By faith he kept the Passover and the sprinkling of blood, lest he who destroyed the firstborn should touch them.

By faith they passed through the Red Sea as by dry *land, whereas* the Egyptians, attempting to do so, were drowned.

By faith the walls of Jericho fell down after they were encircled for seven days. By faith the harlot Rahab did not perish with those who did not believe, when she had received the spies with peace.

And what more shall I say? For the time would fail me to tell of Gideon and Barak and Samson and Jephthah, also *of* David and Samuel and the prophets: who through faith subdued kingdoms, worked righteousness, obtained promises, stopped the mouths of lions, quenched the violence of fire, escaped the edge of the sword, out of weakness were made strong, became valiant in battle, turned to flight the armies of the aliens. Women received their dead raised to life again.

Others were tortured, not accepting deliverance, that they might obtain a better resurrection. Still others had trial of mockings and scourgings, yes, and of chains and imprisonment. They were stoned, they were sawn in two, were tempted, were slain with the sword. They wandered about in sheepskins and goatskins, being destitute, afflicted, tormented—of whom the world was not worthy. They wandered in deserts and mountains, *in* dens and caves of the earth.

And all these, having obtained a good testimony through faith, did not receive the promise, God having provided something better for us, that they should not be made perfect apart from us.

Therefore we also, since we are surrounded by so great a cloud of witnesses, let us lay aside every weight, and the sin which so easily ensnares *us,* and **let us run with endurance the race that is set before us, looking unto Jesus, the author and finisher of *our* faith,** who for the joy that was set before Him endured the cross, despising the shame, and has sat down at the right hand of the throne of God.

For consider Him who endured such hostility from sinners against Himself, lest you become weary and discouraged in your souls. HEBREWS 11:1—12:3

According to the writer of Hebrews, what did the Biblical heroes endure because they had hope in God? What is the "race that is set before us"? How is hope dependent on faith?

WHAT WE BELIEVE

Unfortunately, too often humans put their hope in things that overpromise and underdeliver—riches, people, idols, government. The only true source of hope is found in Jesus Christ. Christ and His promises become an anchor for our souls and the reason we can persevere. Of all the promises Jesus has made to us, the promise of eternal life with God is the most significant. No matter what we may be going through today, we know what happens in this life is not how our story ends. Our story ends, or really only begins, in the presence of God in His eternal kingdom.

BE

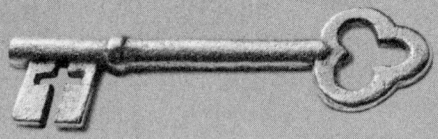

CHAPTER

26

Patience

KEY QUESTION

How does God provide the help
I need to deal with stress?

KEY IDEA

I am slow to anger and endure patiently
under the unavoidable pressures of life.

KEY VERSE

He who is slow to wrath has great understanding,
But *he who is* impulsive exalts folly.
Proverbs 14:29

OUR MAP

As with the beliefs and practices, the first half of the key virtues are more vertical or inward in nature—God plants within us His heart of love, joy, peace, self-control and hope. Now, we turn more outward and consider virtues that are felt by others when we are exhibiting them.

One virtue that is most evident when it is missing is patience. We all have stress triggers—the proverbial buttons that when pushed cause us to lose our patience. Some of these triggers are other people. The way they act, move, talk or even look can set us off. Then there are those triggers of circumstances. We are too busy; we have a wayward family member who is making destructive choices; we suffer from a physical condition or a lingering illness. But if we long to be like Jesus, becoming a more patient person is non-negotiable. So how does God provide the help we need to deal with stress? That is the focus of the Scripture in this chapter.

In our reading we will learn:

- *God Is Patient With Us*
- *Being Slow to Become Angry*
- *Persevering Under Pressure*

God Is Patient With Us

As you might suspect, God models what He desires to see in us.

> **But You, O Lord, *are* a God full of compassion, and gracious,**
> **Longsuffering and abundant in mercy and truth.**
>
> Psalm 86:15

God loved the Israelites and had a wonderful plan for them. They, however, struggled to trust God even after He proved Himself to them repeatedly in mighty ways.

The Israelites had spent 400 long years in Egypt, but now the land God had promised to Abraham for his descendants was ready. But the people had to step forward in faith. God would accomplish the rest. In the book of Exodus, we read how God, through Moses, led the people out of Egypt, and how God even parted the Red Sea.

In the book of Numbers, the people were poised to enter the promised land. They sent 12 spies into the land to scope out the situation. Upon their return, the spies reported that the size and strength of the enemy was too great. Except for Joshua and Caleb, all the spies gave in to their fear and said, "We are not able to go up against the people, for they are stronger than we." After the report was given to the people, they decided they would rather go back to Egypt and subject themselves to slavery than trust God to lay hold of a life of freedom.

As you read the passage below from Numbers 14, highlight some examples of God's patience.

So all the congregation lifted up their voices and cried, and the people wept that night. And all the children of Israel complained against Moses and Aaron, and the whole congregation said to them, "If only we had died in the land of Egypt! Or if only we had died in this wilderness! Why has the LORD brought us to this land to fall by the sword, that our wives and children should become victims? Would it not be better for us to return to Egypt?" So they said to one another, "Let us select a leader and return to Egypt."

Then Moses and Aaron fell on their faces before all the assembly of the congregation of the children of Israel.

But Joshua the son of Nun and Caleb the son of Jephunneh, *who were* among those who had spied out the land, tore their clothes; and they spoke to all the congregation of the children of Israel, saying: "The land we passed through to spy out *is* an exceedingly good land. If the LORD delights in us, then He will bring us into this land and give it to us, 'a land which flows with milk and honey.' Only do not rebel against the LORD, nor fear the people of the land, for they *are* our bread; their protection has departed from them, and the LORD *is* with us. Do not fear them."

And all the congregation said to stone them with stones. Now the glory of the LORD appeared in the tabernacle of meeting before all the children of Israel.

Then the LORD said to Moses: "How long will these people reject Me? And how long will they not believe Me, with all the signs which I have performed among them? I will strike them with the pestilence and disinherit them, and I will make of you a nation greater and mightier than they."

And Moses said to the LORD: "Then the Egyptians will hear *it,* for by Your might You brought these people up from among them, and they will tell *it* to the inhabitants of this land. They have heard that You, LORD, *are* among these people; that You, LORD, are seen face to face and Your cloud stands above them, and You go before them in a pillar of cloud by day and in a pillar of fire by night. Now *if* You kill these people as one man, then the nations which have heard of Your fame will speak, saying, 'Because the LORD was not able to bring this people to the land which He swore to give them, therefore He killed them in the wilderness.' **And now, I pray, let the power of my Lord be great, just as You have spoken, saying, 'The LORD is longsuffering and abundant in mercy, forgiving iniquity and transgression; but He by no means clears *the guilty,* visiting the iniquity of the fathers on the children to the third and fourth *generation.*' Pardon the iniquity of this people, I pray, according to the greatness of Your mercy, just as You have forgiven this people, from Egypt even until now."**

Then the LORD said: "I have pardoned, according to your word; but truly, as I live, all the earth shall be filled with the glory of the LORD—because all these men who have seen My glory and the signs which I did in Egypt and in the wilderness, and have put Me to the test now these ten times, and have not heeded My voice, they certainly shall not see the land of which I swore to their fathers, nor shall any of those who rejected Me see it." NUMBERS 14:1–23

"Except for Caleb the son of Jephunneh and Joshua the son of Nun, you shall by no means enter the land which I swore I would make you dwell in. But your little ones, whom you said would be victims, I will bring in, and they shall know the land which you have despised. But *as for* you, your carcasses shall fall in this wilderness. And your sons shall be shepherds in the wilderness forty years, and bear the brunt of your infidelity, until your carcasses are consumed in the wilderness." NUMBERS 14:30–33

Although God didn't wipe out the rebellious Israelites as they deserved, He made them wander in the wilderness for 40 years—one year for each of the 40 days the spies explored the land. Nevertheless, God patiently demonstrated His commitment to His covenant with Israel and established the next generation in the promised land.

God's patience extends beyond the Israelites to all people. God is just. In Peter's second letter he tells his readers about "the day of the Lord" when Christ will return and bring to consummation all things. This will be the day of judgment for unbelievers, but the day of redemption for believers. God demonstrates His patience toward all humanity by delaying this ultimate and final judgment in order to give more people an opportunity to reach out and take hold of His forgiveness.

Beloved, I now write to you this second epistle (in *both of* which I stir up your pure minds by way of reminder), that you may be mindful of the words which were spoken before by the holy prophets, and of the commandment of us, the apostles of the Lord and Savior, knowing this first: that scoffers will come in the last days, walking according to their own lusts, and saying, "Where is the promise of His coming? For since the fathers fell asleep, all things continue as *they were* from the beginning of creation." For this they willfully forget: that by the word of God the heavens were of old, and the earth standing out of water and in the water, by which the world *that* then existed perished, being flooded with water. But the heavens and the earth *which* are now preserved by the same word, are reserved for fire until the day of judgment and perdition of ungodly men.

But, beloved, do not forget this one thing, that with the Lord one day *is* as a thousand years, and a thousand years as one day. **The Lord is not slack concerning *His* promise, as some count slackness, but is longsuffering toward us, not willing that any should perish but that all should come to repentance.**

But the day of the Lord will come as a thief in the night, in which the heavens will pass away with a great noise, and the elements will melt with fervent heat; both the earth and the works that are in it will be burned up. Therefore, since all these things will be dissolved, what manner *of persons* ought you to be in holy conduct and godliness, looking for and hastening the coming of the day of God, because of which the heavens will be dissolved, being on fire, and the elements will melt with fervent heat? Nevertheless we, according to His promise, look for new heavens and a new earth in which righteousness dwells.

Therefore, beloved, looking forward to these things, be diligent to be found by Him in peace, without spot and blameless; and consider *that* the longsuffering of our Lord *is* salvation—as also our beloved brother Paul, according to the wisdom given to him, has written to you, as also in all his epistles, speaking in them of these things, in which are some things hard to understand, which untaught and unstable *people* twist to their own destruction, as *they do* also the rest of the Scriptures.

You therefore, beloved, since you know *this* beforehand, beware lest you also fall from your own steadfastness, being led away with the error of the wicked; but grow in the grace and knowledge of our Lord and Savior Jesus Christ.

To Him *be* the glory both now and forever. Amen. 2 Peter 3:1–18

Being Slow to Become Angry

One of the primary ideas behind the virtue of patience is taking a long time to become angry—to overheat. The Greek word carries the idea of a thermometer. If a spiritual thermometer were placed in our mouths as we faced a difficult situation, how long would it take for our temperatures to rise? As we mature, we learn to control our anger and practice patience in all circumstances.

Young David was a threat to King Saul. While popularity was not David's goal, he was beloved by the people of Israel. King Saul burned with anger and jealousy toward David. For the next several years, he pursued David, hoping to capture and kill him. David, forced to become a fugitive, proved he was a "man after God's own heart" when he waited on God's timing instead of taking matters into his own hands.

As you read 1 Samuel 24, look for examples of how David waited on God's timing. Why is this so difficult for many people to do?

Now it happened, when Saul had returned from following the Philistines, that it was told him, saying, "Take note! David *is* in the Wilderness of En Gedi." Then Saul took three thousand chosen men from all Israel, and went to seek David and his men on the Rocks of the Wild Goats. So he came to the sheepfolds by the road, where there *was* a cave; and Saul went in to attend to his needs. (David and his men were staying in the recesses of the cave.) Then the men of David said to him, "This is the day of which the LORD said to you, 'Behold, I will deliver your enemy into your hand, that you may do to him as it seems good to you.'" And David arose and secretly cut off a corner of Saul's robe. Now it happened afterward that David's heart troubled him because he had cut Saul's robe. And he said to his men, "The LORD forbid that I should do this thing to my master, the LORD's anointed, to stretch out my hand against him, seeing he *is* the anointed of the LORD." So David restrained his servants with *these* words, and did not allow them to rise against Saul. And Saul got up from the cave and went on *his* way.

David also arose afterward, went out of the cave, and called out to Saul, saying, "My lord the king!" And when Saul looked behind him, David stooped with his face to the earth, and bowed down. And David said to Saul: "Why do you listen to the words of men who say, 'Indeed David seeks your harm'? Look, this day your eyes have seen that the LORD delivered you today into my hand in the cave, and *someone* urged *me* to kill you. But *my eye* spared you, and I said, 'I will not stretch out my hand against my lord, for he *is* the LORD's anointed.' Moreover, my father, see! Yes, see the corner of your robe in my hand! For in that I cut off the corner of your robe, and did not kill you, know and see that *there is* neither evil nor rebellion in my hand, and I have not sinned against you. Yet you hunt my life to take it. Let the LORD judge between you and me, and let the LORD avenge me on you. But my hand shall not be against you. As the proverb of the ancients says, 'Wickedness proceeds from the wicked.' But my hand shall not be against you. After whom has the king of Israel come out? Whom do you pursue? A dead dog? A flea? Therefore let the LORD be judge, and judge between you and me, and see and plead my case, and deliver me out of your hand."

So it was, when David had finished speaking these words to

Saul, that Saul said, "*Is* this your voice, my son David?" And Saul lifted up his voice and wept. Then he said to David: "You *are* more righteous than I; for you have rewarded me with good, whereas I have rewarded you with evil. And you have shown this day how you have dealt well with me; for when the LORD delivered me into your hand, you did not kill me. For if a man finds his enemy, will he let him get away safely? Therefore may the LORD reward you with good for what you have done to me this day. And now I know indeed that you shall surely be king, and that the kingdom of Israel shall be established in your hand. Therefore swear now to me by the LORD that you will not cut off my descendants after me, and that you will not destroy my name from my father's house."

So David swore to Saul. And Saul went home, but David and his men went up to the stronghold. 1 SAMUEL 24:1–22

Saul returned home, but his jealousy remained. As the days passed, Saul allowed his anger against David to fester and grow. Once again Saul led three thousand troops on a mission to capture and kill David.

Now the Ziphites came to Saul at Gibeah, saying, "Is David not hiding in the hill of Hachilah, opposite Jeshimon?" Then Saul arose and went down to the Wilderness of Ziph, having three thousand chosen men of Israel with him, to seek David in the Wilderness of Ziph. And Saul encamped in the hill of Hachilah, which *is* opposite Jeshimon, by the road. But David stayed in the wilderness, and he saw that Saul came after him into the wilderness. David therefore sent out spies, and understood that Saul had indeed come.

So David arose and came to the place where Saul had encamped. And David saw the place where Saul lay, and Abner the son of Ner, the commander of his army. Now Saul lay within the camp, with the people encamped all around him. Then David answered, and said to Ahimelech the Hittite and to Abishai the son of Zeruiah, brother of Joab, saying, "Who will go down with me to Saul in the camp?"

And Abishai said, "I will go down with you."

So David and Abishai came to the people by night; and there Saul lay sleeping within the camp, with his spear stuck in the ground by his head. And Abner and the people lay all around him. Then Abishai said to David, "God has delivered your enemy into your hand this day. Now therefore, please, let me strike him at once with the spear, right to the earth; and I will not *have to strike* him a second time!"

But David said to Abishai, "Do not destroy him; for who can stretch out his hand against the LORD's anointed, and be guiltless?" David said furthermore, "*As* the LORD lives, the LORD shall strike him, or his day shall come to die, or he shall go out to battle and perish. The LORD forbid that I should stretch out my hand against the LORD's anointed. But please, take now the spear and the jug of water that *are* by his head, and let us go." So David took the spear and the jug of water *by* Saul's head, and they got away; and no man saw or knew *it* or awoke. For they *were* all asleep, because a deep sleep from the LORD had fallen on them.

Now David went over to the other side, and stood on the top of a hill afar off, a great distance *being* between them. And David called out to the people and to Abner the son of Ner, saying, "Do you not answer, Abner?"

Then Abner answered and said, "Who *are* you, calling out to the king?"

So David said to Abner, "*Are* you not a man? And who *is* like you in Israel? Why then have you not guarded your lord the king? For one of the people came in to destroy your lord the king. This thing that you have done *is* not good. *As* the LORD lives, you deserve to die, because you have not guarded your master, the LORD's anointed. And now see where the king's spear *is,* and the jug of water that *was* by his head."

Then Saul knew David's voice, and said, "*Is* that your voice, my son David?"

David said, "*It is* my voice, my lord, O king." And he said, "Why does my lord thus pursue his servant? For what have I done, or what evil *is* in my hand? Now therefore, please, let my lord the king hear the words of his servant: If the LORD has stirred you up against me, let Him accept an offering. But if *it is* the children of men, *may* they *be* cursed before the LORD, for they have driven me out this day from sharing in the inheritance of the LORD, saying, 'Go, serve other gods.' So now, do not let my blood fall to the earth before the face of the LORD. For the king of Israel has come out to seek a flea, as when one hunts a partridge in the mountains."

Then Saul said, "I have sinned. Return, my son David. For I will harm you no more, because my life was precious in your eyes this day. Indeed I have played the fool and erred exceedingly."

And David answered and said, "Here is the king's spear. Let one of the young men come over and get it. May the LORD repay every man *for* his righteousness and his faithfulness; for the LORD delivered you into *my* hand today, but I would not stretch out my hand against the LORD's anointed. **And indeed, as your life was valued much this day in my eyes, so let my life be valued much in the eyes of the LORD, and let Him deliver me out of all tribulation."**

Then Saul said to David, "*May* you *be* blessed, my son David! You shall both do great things and also still prevail."

So David went on his way, and Saul returned to his place.

1 SAMUEL 26:1–25

Saul was critically wounded in a battle against the Philistines and eventually died after falling on his own sword. When David got word of the death of Saul and his son Jonathan, he refused to celebrate victory for himself and instead grieved the loss of Israel's king. In the course of time, David became king of his own tribe, Judah, and seven years later he was crowned king of all Israel. During those long years, from when he was chosen to be king at age 15 to the day of his coronation 15 years later, David waited for God to work out His plan.

David's son Solomon took the throne of Israel after David's death. In Proverbs, Solomon shares from his amazing reservoir of God-instilled wisdom. Listen to and learn from what he wrote about patience.

As you read Proverbs 14:29; 15:18; 16:32; 19:11 and 25:15 below, ponder these two questions: How does patience defuse a conflict? How do impatience and rashness escalate it?

He who is slow to wrath has great understanding,
But *he who is* impulsive exalts folly.

PROVERBS 14:29

A wrathful man stirs up strife,
But *he who is* slow to anger allays contention.

PROVERBS 15:18

He who is slow to anger *is* better than the mighty,
And he who rules his spirit than he who takes a city.

PROVERBS 16:32

The discretion of a man makes him slow to anger,
And his glory *is* to overlook a transgression. PROVERBS 19:11

By long forbearance a ruler is persuaded,
And a gentle tongue breaks a bone. PROVERBS 25:15

In the New Testament, James offers this advice to use in our relationships with others—particularly those who "push our buttons."

So then, my beloved brethren, let every man be swift to hear, slow to speak, slow to wrath; for the wrath of man does not produce the righteousness of God. JAMES 1:19–20

PERSEVERING UNDER PRESSURE

Another aspect of patience is holding up under the pressures of life, waiting on the Lord for resolution. The apostle John wrote of an elderly man stricken with paralysis who discovered this reality when he met Jesus.

After this there was a feast of the Jews, and Jesus went up to Jerusalem. Now there is in Jerusalem by the Sheep *Gate* a pool, which is called in Hebrew, Bethesda, having five porches. In these lay a great multitude of sick people, blind, lame, paralyzed, waiting for the moving of the water. For an angel went down at a certain time into the pool and stirred up the water; then whoever stepped in first, after the stirring of the water, was made well of whatever disease he had. Now a certain man was there who had an infirmity thirty-eight years. When Jesus saw him lying there, and knew that he already had been *in that condition* a long time, He said to him, "Do you want to be made well?"

The sick man answered Him, "Sir, I have no man to put me into the pool when the water is stirred up; but while I am coming, another steps down before me."

Jesus said to him, "Rise, take up your bed and walk." And immediately the man was made well, took up his bed, and walked.

And that day was the Sabbath. The Jews therefore said to him who was cured, "It is the Sabbath; it is not lawful for you to carry your bed."

He answered them, "He who made me well said to me, 'Take up your bed and walk.'"

Then they asked him, "Who is the Man who said to you, 'Take up your bed and walk'?" But the one who was healed did not know who it was, for Jesus had withdrawn, a multitude being in *that* place. Afterward Jesus found him in the temple, and said to him, "See, you have been made well. Sin no more, lest a worse thing come upon you."

The man departed and told the Jews that it was Jesus who had made him well. JOHN 5:1–15

Sometimes the Lord's resolution is physical healing, sometimes it is not. The apostle Paul discovered a different plan from God and came to terms with its good purpose in his life. (Note: Paul did not disclose the specifics of his chronic problem. Some believe it was some sort of eye disease.)

And lest I should be exalted above measure by the abundance of the revelations, a thorn in the flesh was given to me, a messenger of Satan to buffet me, lest I be exalted above measure. Concerning this thing I pleaded with the Lord three times that it might depart from me. And He said to me, "My grace is sufficient for you, for My strength is made perfect in weakness." Therefore most gladly I will rather boast in my infirmities, that the power of Christ may rest upon me. Therefore I take pleasure in infirmities, in reproaches, in needs, in persecutions, in distresses, for Christ's sake. For when I am weak, then I am strong. 2 CORINTHIANS 12:7–10

Can you discern why God healed the lame man and not Paul? How does trusting in God's goodness give us the strength to live patiently with our suffering?

In the book of Job we read of a most unusual conversation taking place in heaven between God and Satan. The outcome of this conversation would gravely affect the life of a righteous man named Job. What unfolds is the ultimate test of patience. Will Job curse God or will he offer up his praise to God?

There was a man in the land of Uz, whose name *was* Job; and that man was blameless and upright, and one who feared God and shunned evil. And seven sons and three daughters were born to him. Also, his possessions were seven thousand sheep, three thousand camels, five hundred yoke of oxen, five hundred female donkeys, and a very large household, so that this man was the greatest of all the people of the East.

And his sons would go and feast *in their* houses, each on his *appointed* day, and would send and invite their three sisters to eat and drink with them. So it was, when the days of feasting had run their course, that Job would send and sanctify them, and he would rise early in the morning and offer burnt offerings *according to* the number of them all. For Job said, "It may be that my sons have sinned and cursed God in their hearts." Thus Job did regularly.

Now there was a day when the sons of God came to present themselves before the LORD, and Satan also came among them. And the LORD said to Satan, "From where do you come?"

So Satan answered the LORD and said, "From going to and fro on the earth, and from walking back and forth on it."

Then the LORD said to Satan, "Have you considered My servant Job, that *there is* none like him on the earth, a blameless and upright man, one who fears God and shuns evil?"

So Satan answered the LORD and said, "Does Job fear God for nothing? Have You not made a hedge around him, around his household, and around all that he has on every side? You have blessed the work of his hands, and his possessions have increased in the land. But now, stretch out Your hand and touch all that he has, and he will surely curse You to Your face!"

And the LORD said to Satan, "Behold, all that he has *is* in your power; only do not lay a hand on his *person*."

So Satan went out from the presence of the LORD.

Now there was a day when his sons and daughters *were* eating and drinking wine in their oldest brother's house; and a messenger came to Job and said, "The oxen were plowing and the donkeys feeding beside them, when the Sabeans raided *them* and took them away—indeed they have killed the servants with the edge of the sword; and I alone have escaped to tell you!"

While he *was* still speaking, another also came and said, "The fire of God fell from heaven and burned up the sheep and the servants, and consumed them; and I alone have escaped to tell you!"

While he *was* still speaking, another also came and said, "The Chaldeans formed three bands, raided the camels and took them away, yes, and killed the servants with the edge of the sword; and I alone have escaped to tell you!"

While he *was* still speaking, another also came and said, "Your sons and daughters *were* eating and drinking wine in their oldest brother's house, and suddenly a great wind came from across the wilderness and struck the four corners of the house, and it fell on the young people, and they are dead; and I alone have escaped to tell you!"

Then Job arose, tore his robe, and shaved his head; and he fell to the ground and worshiped. And he said:

> "Naked I came from my mother's womb,
> And naked shall I return there.
> The LORD gave, and the LORD has taken away;
> Blessed be the name of the LORD."

In all this Job did not sin nor charge God with wrong.

Again there was a day when the sons of God came to present themselves before the LORD, and Satan came also among them to present himself before the LORD. And the LORD said to Satan, "From where do you come?"

Satan answered the LORD and said, "From going to and fro on the earth, and from walking back and forth on it."

Then the LORD said to Satan, "Have you considered My servant Job, that *there is* none like him on the earth, a blameless and upright man, one who fears God and shuns evil? And still he holds fast to his integrity, although you incited Me against him, to destroy him without cause."

So Satan answered the LORD and said, "Skin for skin! Yes, all that a man has he will give for his life. But stretch out Your hand now, and touch his bone and his flesh, and he will surely curse You to Your face!"

And the LORD said to Satan, "Behold, he *is* in your hand, but spare his life."

So Satan went out from the presence of the LORD, and struck Job with painful boils from the sole of his foot to the crown of his head. And he took for himself a potsherd with which to scrape himself while he sat in the midst of the ashes.

Then his wife said to him, "Do you still hold fast to your integrity? Curse God and die!"

But he said to her, "You speak as one of the foolish women speaks. Shall we indeed accept good from God, and shall we not accept adversity?" In all this Job did not sin with his lips.

Now when Job's three friends heard of all this adversity that had come upon him, each one came from his own place—Eliphaz the Temanite, Bildad the Shuhite, and Zophar the Naamathite. For they had made an appointment together to come and mourn with him, and to comfort him. And when they raised their eyes from afar, and did not recognize him, they lifted their voices and wept; and each one tore his robe and sprinkled dust on his head toward heaven. So they sat down with him on the ground seven days and seven nights, and no one spoke a word to him, for they saw that *his* grief was very great. JOB 1:1—2:13

Job's three friends did their best work when they merely sat silently with Job in the ashes. But they didn't stay silent. They felt an obligation to open their mouths and interpret the tragedy that befell Job. They suggested it could only be Job's sin that would cause such a catastrophe. Of course, this wasn't true. Understandably, Job contemplated giving up; he also had straightforward questions for God and defended himself. But Job never cursed

God as Satan claimed he would. Job's patience in the face of trials is a model for us. In the end, God restored Job.

And so it was, after the LORD had spoken these words to Job, that the LORD said to Eliphaz the Temanite, "My wrath is aroused against you and your two friends, for you have not spoken of Me *what is* right, as My servant Job *has.* Now therefore, take for yourselves seven bulls and seven rams, go to My servant Job, and offer up for yourselves a burnt offering; and My servant Job shall pray for you. For I will accept him, lest I deal with you *according to your* folly; because you have not spoken of Me *what is* right, as My servant Job *has.*"

So Eliphaz the Temanite and Bildad the Shuhite *and* Zophar the Naamathite went and did as the LORD commanded them; for the LORD had accepted Job. And the LORD restored Job's losses when he prayed for his friends. Indeed the LORD gave Job twice as much as he had before. Then all his brothers, all his sisters, and all those who had been his acquaintances before, came to him and ate food with him in his house; and they consoled him and comforted him for all the adversity that the LORD had brought upon him. Each one gave him a piece of silver and each a ring of gold.

Now the LORD blessed the latter *days* of Job more than his beginning; for he had fourteen thousand sheep, six thousand camels, one thousand yoke of oxen, and one thousand female donkeys. He also had seven sons and three daughters. And he called the name of the first Jemimah, the name of the second Keziah, and the name of the third Keren-Happuch. In all the land were found no women *so* beautiful as the daughters of Job; and their father gave them an inheritance among their brothers.

After this Job lived one hundred and forty years, and saw his children and grandchildren *for* four generations. So Job died, old and full of days.

JOB 42:7–17

Do you struggle more with being patient with other people or dealing with unavoidable pressures in your life? What is one thing you learned from this chapter that might help you?

WHAT WE BELIEVE

Not all our stories are the same, yet we are all called to respond with patience. Patience is a key virtue that we must work to develop. Our cultivation of it pleases God, who is patient with us. Showing patience positively affects our relationships and brings great joy to our lives and community. If we trust God and have a passion to treat others the way He treats us, we will learn more each day how to be slow to anger and tolerate the unavoidable pressures of life.

BE

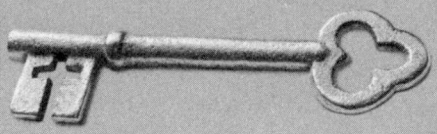

CHAPTER

27

Kindness/Goodness

KEY QUESTION

What does it mean to do the right thing?
How do I know?

KEY IDEA

I choose to be kind and good
in my relationships with others.

KEY VERSE

See that no one renders evil for evil
to anyone, but always pursue what is good
both for yourselves and for all.
1 Thessalonians 5:15

OUR MAP

The virtues of kindness and goodness found in the list of the fruit of the Spirit in Galatians 5:22 are almost always spoken of together and rightfully so. While the meaning behind these two words in the original Greek is similar, they are less like twins and more like cousins. Both indicate how to respond to others from a deep, moral inner conviction of what is the right thing to do for the sake of the other person. The content for our conviction flows from the ten key beliefs embraced and owned in our hearts. Kindness involves doing something deemed positive by the recipient. Goodness, however, sometimes entails tough love for the benefit of another because it will genuinely help them. This could involve speaking the truth in love or even withholding something that could harm them. But at the end of the day both virtues involve seeking the best for others. How do we know the right thing to do? This chapter will help greatly as we read about:

- *Our Kind and Good God*
- *Stories of Kindness: Rahab*
- *Stories of Kindness: David*
- *Stories of Kindness: The Dinner Guest*
- *Stories of Kindness: Paul, Onesimus and Philemon*
- *Stories of Kindness: Onesiphorus*
- *Teachings on Goodness*

Our Kind and Good God

As with all the virtues, our God is the perfect example. This psalm was likely written after the Israelites returned from captivity in Babylon and was recited each year at one of the annual religious festivals. Throughout their history the Israelites cried out to God for mercy and help. Each time God responded from a tender and kind heart. As we look back on our own life we will see the same pattern of response from God.

Oh, give thanks to the Lord, for *He is* good!
For His mercy *endures* forever.
Let the redeemed of the Lord say *so*,

Whom He has redeemed from the hand of the enemy,
And gathered out of the lands,
From the east and from the west,
From the north and from the south.

They wandered in the wilderness in a desolate way;
They found no city to dwell in.
Hungry and thirsty,
Their soul fainted in them.
Then they cried out to the LORD in their trouble,
And He delivered them out of their distresses.
And He led them forth by the right way,
That they might go to a city for a dwelling place.
Oh, that *men* would give thanks to the LORD *for* His goodness,
And *for* His wonderful works to the children of men!
For He satisfies the longing soul,
And fills the hungry soul with goodness.

Those who sat in darkness and in the shadow of death,
Bound in affliction and irons—
Because they rebelled against the words of God,
And despised the counsel of the Most High,
Therefore He brought down their heart with labor;
They fell down, and *there was* none to help.
Then they cried out to the LORD in their trouble,
And He saved them out of their distresses.
He brought them out of darkness and the shadow of death,
And broke their chains in pieces.
Oh, that *men* would give thanks to the LORD *for* His goodness,
And *for* His wonderful works to the children of men!
For He has broken the gates of bronze,
And cut the bars of iron in two.

Fools, because of their transgression,
And because of their iniquities, were afflicted.
Their soul abhorred all manner of food,
And they drew near to the gates of death.

Then they cried out to the LORD in their trouble,
And He saved them out of their distresses.
He sent His word and healed them,
And delivered *them* from their destructions.
Oh, that *men* would give thanks to the LORD *for* His goodness,
And *for* His wonderful works to the children of men!
Let them sacrifice the sacrifices of thanksgiving,
And declare His works with rejoicing.

Those who go down to the sea in ships,
Who do business on great waters,
They see the works of the LORD,
And His wonders in the deep.
For He commands and raises the stormy wind,
Which lifts up the waves of the sea.
They mount up to the heavens,
They go down again to the depths;
Their soul melts because of trouble.
They reel to and fro, and stagger like a drunken man,
And are at their wits' end.
Then they cry out to the LORD in their trouble,
And He brings them out of their distresses.
He calms the storm,
So that its waves are still.
Then they are glad because they are quiet;
So He guides them to their desired haven.
Oh, that *men* would give thanks to the LORD *for* His goodness,
And *for* His wonderful works to the children of men!
Let them exalt Him also in the assembly of the people,
And praise Him in the company of the elders.

He turns rivers into a wilderness,
And the watersprings into dry ground;
A fruitful land into barrenness,
For the wickedness of those who dwell in it.
He turns a wilderness into pools of water,
And dry land into watersprings.

There He makes the hungry dwell,
That they may establish a city for a dwelling place,
And sow fields and plant vineyards,
That they may yield a fruitful harvest.
He also blesses them, and they multiply greatly;
And He does not let their cattle decrease.

When they are diminished and brought low
Through oppression, affliction, and sorrow,
He pours contempt on princes,
And causes them to wander in the wilderness *where there is* no way;
Yet He sets the poor on high, far from affliction,
And makes *their* families like a flock.
The righteous see *it* and rejoice,
And all iniquity stops its mouth.

Whoever *is* wise will observe these *things,*
And they will understand the lovingkindness of the LORD.

PSALM 107:1–43

Write your own psalm. Start with the same opening words of Psalm 107: "Oh, give thanks to the LORD, for *He is* good! For His mercy *endures* forever. Let the redeemed of the LORD say *so*." Then record an act of kindness and goodness that God has shown toward you.

STORIES OF KINDNESS: RAHAB

The Bible contains many stories of kindness throughout its pages. In the Old Testament, Joshua, Israel's great and courageous leader, sent two spies to scope out the land of Canaan in preparation for the conquest. While they were deep in enemy territory, God used a most unusual character to show them kindness.

Joshua the son of Nun sent out two men from Acacia Grove to spy secretly, saying, "Go, view the land, especially Jericho."

So they went, and came to the house of a harlot named Rahab, and lodged there. And it was told the king of Jericho, saying,

"Behold, men have come here tonight from the children of Israel to search out the country."

So the king of Jericho sent to Rahab, saying, "Bring out the men who have come to you, who have entered your house, for they have come to search out all the country."

Then the woman took the two men and hid them. So she said, "Yes, the men came to me, but I did not know where they *were* from. And it happened as the gate was being shut, when it was dark, that the men went out. Where the men went I do not know; pursue them quickly, for you may overtake them." (But she had brought them up to the roof and hidden them with the stalks of flax, which she had laid in order on the roof.) Then the men pursued them by the road to the Jordan, to the fords. And as soon as those who pursued them had gone out, they shut the gate.

Now before they lay down, she came up to them on the roof, and said to the men: "I know that the LORD has given you the land, that the terror of you has fallen on us, and that all the inhabitants of the land are fainthearted because of you. For we have heard how the LORD dried up the water of the Red Sea for you when you came out of Egypt, and what you did to the two kings of the Amorites who *were* on the other side of the Jordan, Sihon and Og, whom you utterly destroyed. And as soon as we heard *these things,* our hearts melted; neither did there remain any more courage in anyone because of you, for the LORD your God, He *is* God in heaven above and on earth beneath. Now therefore, I beg you, swear to me by the LORD, since I have shown you kindness, that you also will show kindness to my father's house, and give me a true token, and spare my father, my mother, my brothers, my sisters, and all that they have, and deliver our lives from death."

So the men answered her, "Our lives for yours, if none of you tell this business of ours. And it shall be, when the LORD has given us the land, that we will deal kindly and truly with you."

Then she let them down by a rope through the window, for her house *was* on the city wall; she dwelt on the wall. And she said to them, "Get to the mountain, lest the pursuers meet you. Hide there three days, until the pursuers have returned. Afterward you may go your way."

So the men said to her: "We *will be* blameless of this oath of yours which you have made us swear, unless, *when* we come into the land, you bind this line of scarlet cord in the window through which you let us down, and unless you bring your father, your mother, your brothers, and all your father's household to your own home. So it shall be *that* whoever goes outside the doors of your house into the street, his blood *shall be* on his own head, and we *will be* guiltless. And whoever is with you in the house, his blood *shall be* on our head if a hand is laid on him. And if you tell this business of ours, then we will be free from your oath which you made us swear."

Then she said, "According to your words, so *be* it." And she sent them away, and they departed. And she bound the scarlet cord in the window.

They departed and went to the mountain, and stayed there three days until the pursuers returned. The pursuers sought *them* all along the way, but did not find *them.* So the two men returned, descended from the mountain, and crossed over; and they came to Joshua the son of Nun, and told him all that had befallen them. And they said to Joshua, "Truly the LORD has delivered all the land into our hands, for indeed all the inhabitants of the country are fainthearted because of us."

JOSHUA 2:1–24

With the hand of God obviously on their side, the Israelites conquered the city of Jericho, and Rahab was rewarded for her act of kindness.

Joshua rose early in the morning, and the priests took up the ark of the LORD. Then seven priests bearing seven trumpets of rams' horns before the ark of the LORD went on continually and blew with the trumpets. And the armed men went before them. But the rear guard came after the ark of the LORD, while *the priests* continued blowing the trumpets. And the second day they marched around the city once and returned to the camp. So they did six days.

But it came to pass on the seventh day that they rose early, about the dawning of the day, and marched around the city seven times in the same manner. On that day only they marched around the city seven times. And the seventh time it happened, when the priests blew the trumpets, that Joshua said to the people: "Shout, for the LORD has given you the city! Now the city shall be doomed by the LORD to destruction, it and all who *are* in it. Only Rahab the harlot shall live, she and all who *are* with her in the house, because she hid the messengers that we sent. And you, by all means abstain from the accursed things, lest you become accursed when you take of the accursed things, and make the camp of Israel a curse, and trouble it. But all the silver and gold, and vessels of bronze and iron, *are* consecrated to the LORD; they shall come into the treasury of the LORD."

So the people shouted when *the priests* blew the trumpets. And it happened when the people heard the sound of the trumpet, and the people shouted with a great shout, that the wall fell down flat. Then the people went up into the city, every man straight before him, and they took the city. And they utterly destroyed all that *was* in the city, both man and woman, young and old, ox and sheep and donkey, with the edge of the sword.

But Joshua had said to the two men who had spied out the country, "Go into the harlot's house, and from there bring out the woman and all that she has, as you swore to her." And the young men who had been spies went in and brought out Rahab, her father, her mother, her brothers, and all that she had. So they brought out all her relatives and left them outside the camp of Israel. But they burned the city and all that *was* in it with fire. Only the silver and gold, and the vessels of bronze and iron, they put into the treasury of the house of the LORD. **And Joshua spared Rahab the harlot, her father's household, and all that she had. So she dwells in Israel to this day, because she hid the messengers whom Joshua sent to spy out Jericho.** JOSHUA 6:12–25

How do you reconcile Rahab's decision to lie about the spies' whereabouts with her act of kindness?

STORIES OF KINDNESS: DAVID

The prophet Samuel anointed David, when he was just a teenager, to be Israel's next king. His coronation, however, was a number of years away. Over the next several years God would use the rebellious heart of King Saul to grow David's trust in God. Before David took off running from King Saul, Jonathan, Saul's son and successor to the throne, had a sobering conversation with David. Jonathan acknowledged and accepted God's plan for David, not himself, to be the next king. However, he made one request of the future king of Israel.

[Jonathan said,] "If it pleases my father *to do* you evil, then I will report it to you and send you away, that you may go in safety. And the LORD be with you as He has been with my father. **And you shall not only show me the kindness of the LORD while I still live, that I may not die; but you shall not cut off your kindness from my house forever, no, not when the LORD has cut off every one of the enemies of David from the face of the earth."** So Jonathan made *a covenant* with the house of David, *saying,* "Let the LORD require *it* at the hand of David's enemies." 1 SAMUEL 20:13–16

Fast-forward many years. Saul and Jonathan were both dead, and David was king. All potential threats from the old royal house of Saul had been neutralized, and David remembered his promise to Jonathan.

David said, "Is there still anyone who is left of the house of Saul, that I may show him kindness for Jonathan's sake?"

And *there was* a servant of the house of Saul whose name *was* Ziba. So when they had called him to David, the king said to him, "*Are* you Ziba?"

He said, "At your service!"

Then the king said, "*Is* there not still someone of the house of Saul, to whom I may show the kindness of God?"

And Ziba said to the king, "There is still a son of Jonathan *who is* lame in *his* feet."

So the king said to him, "Where *is* he?"

And Ziba said to the king, "Indeed he *is* in the house of Machir the son of Ammiel, in Lo Debar."

Then King David sent and brought him out of the house of Machir the son of Ammiel, from Lo Debar.

Now when Mephibosheth the son of Jonathan, the son of Saul,

had come to David, he fell on his face and prostrated himself. Then David said, "Mephibosheth?"

And he answered, "Here is your servant!"

So David said to him, "Do not fear, for I will surely show you kindness for Jonathan your father's sake, and will restore to you all the land of Saul your grandfather; and you shall eat bread at my table continually."

Then he bowed himself, and said, "What *is* your servant, that you should look upon such a dead dog as I?"

And the king called to Ziba, Saul's servant, and said to him, "I have given to your master's son all that belonged to Saul and to all his house. You therefore, and your sons and your servants, shall work the land for him, and you shall bring in *the harvest,* that your master's son may have food to eat. But Mephibosheth your master's son shall eat bread at my table always." Now Ziba had fifteen sons and twenty servants.

Then Ziba said to the king, "According to all that my lord the king has commanded his servant, so will your servant do."

"As for Mephibosheth," *said the king,* "he shall eat at my table like one of the king's sons." Mephibosheth had a young son whose name *was* Micha. And all who dwelt in the house of Ziba *were* servants of Mephibosheth. So Mephibosheth dwelt in Jerusalem, for he ate continually at the king's table. And he was lame in both his feet.

2 Samuel 9:1–13

Stories of Kindness: The Dinner Guest

The Jewish religious leaders in Jesus' day held exclusive dinner parties. Only invited guests of significant public standing were allowed to attend. Upon arrival, the host would seat guests in order of importance. On one occasion when Jesus was invited to eat at the table of a well-known Pharisee, He took advantage of the opportunity to teach a lesson, first about humility and then about the kind of people who should be on the guest list of such occasions.

Now it happened, as [Jesus] went into the house of one of the rulers of the Pharisees to eat bread on the Sabbath, that they watched Him closely.

Luke 14:1

So [Jesus] told a parable to those who were invited, when He noted how they chose the best places, saying to them: "When you are invited by anyone to a wedding feast, do not sit down in the best place, lest one more honorable than you be invited by him; and he who invited you and him come and say to you, 'Give place to this man,' and then you begin with shame to take the lowest place. But when you are invited, go and sit down in the lowest place, so that when he who invited you comes he may say to you, 'Friend, go up higher.' Then you will have glory in the presence of those who sit at the table with you. For whoever exalts himself will be humbled, and he who humbles himself will be exalted."

Then He also said to him who invited Him, "When you give a dinner or a supper, do not ask your friends, your brothers, your relatives, nor rich neighbors, lest they also invite you back, and you be repaid. **But when you give a feast, invite *the* poor, *the* maimed, *the* lame, *the* blind. And you will be blessed, because they cannot repay you; for you shall be repaid at the resurrection of the just."**

LUKE 14:7–14

Jesus was teaching us to do exactly what David did for Mephibosheth. Why does it matter that we invite people into our lives who cannot reciprocate? Can you think of a way to include someone in your activities who is usually left out?

STORIES OF KINDNESS: PAUL, ONESIMUS AND PHILEMON

While Paul was in prison, likely in Rome, he met a slave named Onesimus, who may have stolen from his master before running away. Through Paul's ministry, Onesimus became a Christian and eventually returned to his master. As it turned out, the master, a man name Philemon, was a Christian and Paul's close friend. Paul sent Onesimus home with a personal letter he had written to give to Philemon. The letter encouraged Philemon to exercise kindness toward his slave and accept Onesimus, not as a slave but as a Christian brother.

As you read Philemon 1–25 below, note how Paul models kindness in his appeal to Philemon. Would you have honored Paul's request? Why or why not?

Paul, a prisoner of Christ Jesus, and Timothy *our* brother,

To Philemon our beloved *friend* and fellow laborer, to the beloved Apphia, Archippus our fellow soldier, and to the church in your house:

Grace to you and peace from God our Father and the Lord Jesus Christ.

I thank my God, making mention of you always in my prayers, hearing of your love and faith which you have toward the Lord Jesus and toward all the saints, that the sharing of your faith may become effective by the acknowledgment of every good thing which is in you in Christ Jesus. For we have great joy and consolation in your love, because the hearts of the saints have been refreshed by you, brother.

Therefore, though I might be very bold in Christ to command you what is fitting, *yet* for love's sake I rather appeal *to you*—being such a one as Paul, the aged, and now also a prisoner of Jesus Christ—I appeal to you for my son Onesimus, whom I have begotten *while* in my chains, who once was unprofitable to you, but now is profitable to you and to me.

I am sending him back. You therefore receive him, that is, my own heart, whom I wished to keep with me, that on your behalf he might minister to me in my chains for the gospel. But without your consent I wanted to do nothing, that your good deed might not be by compulsion, as it were, but voluntary.

For perhaps he departed for a while for this *purpose,* that you might receive him forever, no longer as a slave but more than a slave—a beloved brother, especially to me but how much more to you, both in the flesh and in the Lord.

If then you count me as a partner, receive him as *you would* me. But if he has wronged you or owes anything, put that on my account. I, Paul, am writing with my own hand. I will repay—not to mention to you that you owe me even your own self besides. Yes, brother, let me have joy from you in the Lord; refresh my heart in the Lord.

Having confidence in your obedience, I write to you, knowing that you will do even more than I say. But, meanwhile, also prepare a guest room for me, for I trust that through your prayers I shall be granted to you.

Epaphras, my fellow prisoner in Christ Jesus, greets you, *as do* Mark, Aristarchus, Demas, Luke, my fellow laborers.

The grace of our Lord Jesus Christ *be* with your spirit. Amen.

PHILEMON 1–25

STORIES OF KINDNESS: ONESIPHORUS

While Paul spent his years in ministry encouraging others to show kindness, from time to time he found himself on the receiving end and was grateful. At the end of his ministry and life, from a cold dungeon Paul penned his last letter to his prodigy Timothy, who was pastoring the church at Ephesus. Life in this season had been extremely hard for Paul. In the letter, he shared with Timothy his gratitude for one particular believer.

This you know, that all those in Asia have turned away from me, among whom are Phygellus and Hermogenes. **The Lord grant mercy to the household of Onesiphorus, for he often refreshed me, and was not ashamed of my chain; but when he arrived in Rome, he sought me out very zealously and found *me*.** The Lord grant to him that he may find mercy from the Lord in that Day—and you know very well how many ways he ministered *to me* at Ephesus.

2 TIMOTHY 1:15–18

TEACHINGS ON GOODNESS

Jesus left us instructions for being good to others that are both practical and radical. Remember that kindness is doing something that the recipient feels positively about, but goodness means doing the right thing for a person, even when it may not make them feel good. Goodness is sometimes called "tough love," because it involves speaking the truth or withholding something harmful for the ultimate benefit of the recipient.

Write down a list of every principle you discover from the teachings of Jesus, Peter and Paul on how to not only do the kind thing but also the right thing in our relationships. Which principle speaks to you the most? Why?

"But I say to you who hear: Love your enemies, do good to those who hate you, bless those who curse you, and pray for those who spitefully use you. To him who strikes you on the *one* cheek, offer the other also. And from him who takes away your cloak, do not withhold *your* tunic either. Give to everyone who asks of you. And from him who takes away your goods do not ask *them* back. **And just as you want men to do to you, you also do to them likewise.**

"But if you love those who love you, what credit is that to you? For even sinners love those who love them. And if you do good to those who do good to you, what credit is that to you? For even sinners do the same. And if you lend *to those* from whom you hope to receive back, what credit is that to you? For even sinners lend to sinners to receive as much back. But love your enemies, do good, and lend, hoping for nothing in return; and your reward will be great, and you will be sons of the Most High. For He is kind to the unthankful and evil. Therefore be merciful, just as your Father also is merciful.

"Judge not, and you shall not be judged. Condemn not, and you shall not be condemned. Forgive, and you will be forgiven. Give, and it will be given to you: good measure, pressed down, shaken together, and running over will be put into your bosom. For with the same measure that you use, it will be measured back to you."

And He spoke a parable to them: "Can the blind lead the blind? Will they not both fall into the ditch? A disciple is not above his teacher, but everyone who is perfectly trained will be like his teacher. And why do you look at the speck in your brother's eye, but do not perceive the plank in your own eye? Or how can you say to your brother, 'Brother, let me remove the speck that *is* in your eye,' when you yourself do not see the plank that *is* in your own eye? Hypocrite! First remove the plank from your own eye, and then you will see clearly to remove the speck that is in your brother's eye.

"For a good tree does not bear bad fruit, nor does a bad tree bear good fruit. For every tree is known by its own fruit. For *men* do not gather figs from thorns, nor do they gather grapes from a bramble bush. **A good man out of the good treasure of his heart brings forth good; and an evil man out of the evil treasure of his heart brings forth evil. For out of the abundance of the heart his mouth speaks."** LUKE 6:27–45

Two good men who were followers of Jesus—the apostles Peter and Paul—offered instruction to the early believers on living a life of kindness and goodness. The Scripture passages below remind us how the goodness we show to others can enlighten the world about our good God. In other words, the way we treat people is a reflection of our relationship with God.

Finally, all *of you be* of one mind, having compassion for one another; love as brothers, *be* tenderhearted, *be* courteous; not returning evil for evil or reviling for reviling, but on the contrary blessing, knowing that you were called to this, that you may inherit a blessing. For

"He who would love life
And see good days,
Let him refrain his tongue from evil,
And his lips from speaking deceit.
Let him turn away from evil and do good;
Let him seek peace and pursue it.
For the eyes of the LORD *are* on the righteous,
And His ears are open to their prayers;
But the face of the LORD *is* against those who do evil."

And who *is* he who will harm you if you become followers of what is good? But even if you should suffer for righteousness' sake, *you are* blessed. *"And do not be afraid of their threats, nor be troubled."* But sanctify the Lord God in your hearts, and always *be* ready to *give* a defense to everyone who asks you a reason for the hope that is in you, with meekness and fear; having a good conscience, that when they defame you as evildoers, those who revile your good conduct in Christ may be ashamed. For *it is* better, if it is the will of God, to suffer for doing good than for doing evil.

1 Peter 3:8–17

We then who are strong ought to bear with the scruples of the weak, and not to please ourselves. Let each of us please *his* neighbor for *his* good, leading to edification. Romans 15:1–2

All things are lawful for me, but not all things are helpful; all things are lawful for me, but not all things edify. **Let no one seek his own, but each one the other's *well-being.*** 1 Corinthians 10:23–24

And let us not grow weary while doing good, for in due season we shall reap if we do not lose heart. Therefore, as we have opportunity, let us do good to all, especially to those who are of the household of faith. Galatians 6:9–10

Let all bitterness, wrath, anger, clamor, and evil speaking be put away from you, with all malice. **And be kind to one another, tenderhearted, forgiving one another, even as God in Christ forgave you.**

Therefore be imitators of God as dear children. And walk in love, as Christ also has loved us and given Himself for us, an offering and a sacrifice to God for a sweet-smelling aroma.

Ephesians 4:31—5:2

See that no one renders evil for evil to anyone, but always pursue what is good both for yourselves and for all.

1 Thessalonians 5:15

In all things [show] yourself *to be* a pattern of good works; in doctrine *[show]* integrity, reverence, incorruptibility. Titus 2:7

Remind them to be subject to rulers and authorities, to obey, to be ready for every good work, to speak evil of no one, to be peaceable, gentle, showing all humility to all men. For we ourselves were also once foolish, disobedient, deceived, serving various lusts and pleasures, living in malice and envy, hateful and hating one another. **But when the kindness and the love of God our Savior toward man appeared, not by works of righteousness which we have done, but according to His mercy He saved us,** through the washing of regeneration and renewing of the Holy Spirit, whom He poured out on us abundantly through Jesus Christ our Savior, that having been justified by His grace we should become heirs according to the hope of eternal life.

This is a faithful saying, and these things I want you to affirm constantly, that those who have believed in God should be careful to maintain good works. These things are good and profitable to men. TITUS 3:1–8

And let our *people* also learn to maintain good works, to *meet* urgent needs, that they may not be unfruitful. TITUS 3:14

WHAT WE BELIEVE

Throughout history God has consistently showed His kindness and goodness to all people. If God's love is in us, we will seek to show that love to the people in our lives. Most often we will engage in positive acts of kindness toward others. However, occasionally we can help someone by issuing some tough love—a confrontation, a rebuke, a refusal. We have many great examples in the Bible to look to, including Rahab, David, Jesus, Paul and Onesiphorus. We have also been given many practical principles to guide our demonstration of both random and intentional acts of goodness and kindness. Pick one principle and one person in your life with the most need and give it a try!

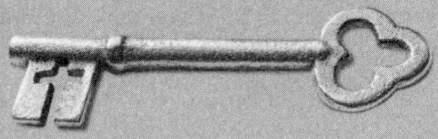

CHAPTER

28

Faithfulness

KEY QUESTION

Why is it important to be loyal
and committed to God and others?

KEY IDEA

I have established a good name with God
and others based on my loyalty to those relationships.

KEY VERSE

Let not mercy and truth forsake you; bind them around
your neck, write them on the tablet of your heart, *and*
so find favor and high esteem in the sight of God and man.
Proverbs 3:3–4

OUR MAP

As with all the other key virtues, faithfulness benefits the people in our lives. When we are faithful to them, they are blessed. And over time, as our key verse expresses, our faithfulness to others also has a reciprocal benefit. First, we win favor. As needs emerge in our lives, people will be inclined to help us. Second, we establish a good name. When our name is mentioned, even when we are not present, it is spoken with high regard. A good name established through a life of faithfulness is a boundless gift to pass on to our children. Most of all, faithfulness pleases God, who is always loyal and committed to us. Our loyalty and commitment to others reflects the love God has shown us. Yet because of our sinful nature, we struggle to be faithful. That is where God and His presence in our lives come into play.

In this chapter we will read Scripture passages that address the following subjects to instruct and inspire us:

- *God's Faithfulness*
- *Called to Faithfulness*
- *Stories of Faithfulness: Joseph*
- *Stories of Faithfulness: Ruth*
- *Stories of Faithfulness: Mary*

God's Faithfulness

Many of the authors of the Bible recorded their reflections about God's faithfulness. In the Song of Moses, recorded in Deuteronomy 32, Moses exalts the faithfulness of the covenant-keeping God.

As you read the passages below from Deuteronomy 32; Psalm 36 and Lamentations 3, highlight the phrases that best express God's faithfulness to you.

"Give ear, O heavens, and I will speak;
And hear, O earth, the words of my mouth.
Let my teaching drop as the rain,

My speech distill as the dew,
As raindrops on the tender herb,
And as showers on the grass.
For I proclaim the name of the LORD:
Ascribe greatness to our God.
He is the Rock, His work *is* perfect;
For all His ways *are* justice,
A God of truth and without injustice;
Righteous and upright *is* He." DEUTERONOMY 32:1–4

Likewise, while living in a world with so much uncertainty, the author of Psalm 36 took great comfort in the extent of God's devotion.

Your mercy, O LORD, *is* in the heavens;
Your faithfulness *reaches* to the clouds.
Your righteousness *is* like the great mountains;
Your judgments *are* a great deep;
O LORD, You preserve man and beast.

How precious *is* Your lovingkindness, O God!
Therefore the children of men put their trust under the shadow of Your wings.
They are abundantly satisfied with the fullness of Your house,
And You give them drink from the river of Your pleasures.
For with You *is* the fountain of life;
In Your light we see light. PSALM 36:5–9

While God always remained faithful, the Israelites did not, and He disciplined them for it. God called the prophet Jeremiah to warn the southern kingdom of Judah of God's just punishment. In 586 BC Jerusalem and the temple were destroyed and the people were exiled to Babylon. The author (ancient tradition credits Jeremiah with writing Lamentations) of this series of alphabetic acrostic poems lamented about what he saw and felt but also reminded the people of God's consistent faithfulness.

Remember my affliction and roaming,
The wormwood and the gall.
My soul still remembers
And sinks within me.
This I recall to my mind,
Therefore I have hope.

***Through* the Lord's mercies we are not consumed,**
Because His compassions fail not.
***They are* new every morning;**
Great *is* Your faithfulness.
"The LORD *is* my portion," says my soul,
"Therefore I hope in Him!" LAMENTATIONS 3:19–24

CALLED TO FAITHFULNESS

The writers of the wisdom books call the reader to a life of faithfulness and also highlight its rich rewards in their lives.

My son, do not forget my law,
But let your heart keep my commands;
For length of days and long life
And peace they will add to you.

Let not mercy and truth forsake you;
Bind them around your neck,
Write them on the tablet of your heart,
***And* so find favor and high esteem**
In the sight of God and man.

Trust in the LORD with all your heart,
And lean not on your own understanding;
In all your ways acknowledge Him,
And He shall direct your paths. PROVERBS 3:1–6

Most men will proclaim each his own goodness,
But who can find a faithful man? PROVERBS 20:6

A faithful man will abound with blessings,
But he who hastens to be rich will not go unpunished.
PROVERBS 28:20

Why will a faithful person be richly blessed,
and one eager to get rich be punished?

The calling Paul shared with the Corinthians concerning his own life applies to all followers of Christ.

Let a man so consider us, as servants of Christ and stewards of the mysteries of God. Moreover it is required in stewards that one be found faithful. 1 CORINTHIANS 4:1–2

STORIES OF FAITHFULNESS: JOSEPH

God built Israel from scratch, starting with Abraham, to reveal His plan to provide a way for people to come back into a relationship with Him. Israel's faithfulness to God over the next 2,000 years was sketchy at best. However, a few Israelites, such as Joseph, did display a tenacious faithfulness both to God and to others.

At the age of seventeen, Joseph, one of the twelve sons of Jacob, had two consecutive dreams in which his brothers bowed down to him. The brothers were furious with their younger brother, whom their dad already favored. So they plotted together one day and sold Joseph to a caravan of Ishmaelites who ultimately sold him into slavery in Egypt. The brothers returned home and lied to their father, telling him that Joseph had been mauled to death by a ferocious animal. Jacob was crushed. Joseph, however, was prospering despite his brothers' jealous attempts to destroy him.

As you read Joseph's story, look back at our key verse from Proverbs 3:3–4. How did Joseph live out the truth of this verse?

Now Joseph had been taken down to Egypt. And Potiphar, an officer of Pharaoh, captain of the guard, an Egyptian, bought him from the Ishmaelites who had taken him down there. The LORD was with Joseph, and he was a successful man; and he was in the house of his master the Egyptian. And his master saw that the LORD *was* with him and that the LORD made all he did to prosper in his hand. So Joseph found favor in his sight, and served him. Then he made him overseer of his house, and all *that* he had he put under his authority. So it was, from the time *that* he had made him overseer of his house and all that he had, that the LORD blessed the Egyptian's house for Joseph's sake; and the blessing of the LORD was on all that he had in the house and in the field. Thus he left all that he had in Joseph's hand, and he did not know what he had except for the bread which he ate. GENESIS 39:1–6

As part of God's master plan, Joseph rose again only to be cast into another "pit." Potiphar's wife tried to seduce Joseph, but Joseph maintained his integrity and faithfulness to both Potiphar and God by resisting the temptation. Because he rejected her, Potiphar's wife made false accusations against Joseph, and he was thrown into prison. But God was with him there too and lifted him up yet again.

It came to pass after these things *that* the butler and the baker of the king of Egypt offended their lord, the king of Egypt. And Pharaoh was angry with his two officers, the chief butler and the chief baker. So he put them in custody in the house of the captain of the guard, in the prison, the place where Joseph *was* confined. And the captain of the guard charged Joseph with them, and he served them; so they were in custody for a while.

Then the butler and the baker of the king of Egypt, who *were* confined in the prison, had a dream, both of them, each man's dream in one night *and* each man's dream with its *own* interpretation. And Joseph came in to them in the morning and looked at them, and saw that they *were* sad. So he asked Pharaoh's officers who *were* with him in the custody of his lord's house, saying, "Why do you look *so* sad today?"

And they said to him, "We each have had a dream, and *there is* no interpreter of it."

So Joseph said to them, "Do not interpretations belong to God? Tell *them* to me, please."

Then the chief butler told his dream to Joseph, and said to him, "Behold, in my dream a vine *was* before me, and in the vine *were* three branches; it *was* as though it budded, its blossoms shot forth, and its clusters brought forth ripe grapes. Then Pharaoh's cup *was* in my hand; and I took the grapes and pressed them into Pharaoh's cup, and placed the cup in Pharaoh's hand."

And Joseph said to him, "This *is* the interpretation of it: The three branches *are* three days. Now within three days Pharaoh will lift up your head and restore you to your place, and you will put Pharaoh's cup in his hand according to the former manner, when you were his butler. But remember me when it is well with you, and please show kindness to me; make mention of me to Pharaoh, and get me out of this house. For indeed I was stolen away from the land of the Hebrews; and also I have done nothing here that they should put me into the dungeon."

When the chief baker saw that the interpretation was good, he said to Joseph, "I also *was* in my dream, and there *were* three white baskets on my head. In the uppermost basket *were* all kinds of baked goods for Pharaoh, and the birds ate them out of the basket on my head."

So Joseph answered and said, "This *is* the interpretation of it: The three baskets *are* three days. Within three days Pharaoh will lift off your head from you and hang you on a tree; and the birds will eat your flesh from you."

Now it came to pass on the third day, *which was* Pharaoh's birthday, that he made a feast for all his servants; and he lifted up the head of the chief butler and of the chief baker among his servants. Then he restored the chief butler to his butlership again, and he placed the cup in Pharaoh's hand. But he hanged the chief baker, as Joseph had interpreted to them. Yet the chief butler did not remember Joseph, but forgot him. GENESIS 40:1–23

Joseph sat in prison two more years. It wasn't until Pharaoh had a dream that none of his magicians or wise men could interpret that the restored cupbearer finally remembered Joseph, and Joseph was brought from the dungeon to explain the dream's meaning. As he stood before the king, Joseph maintained his faithfulness to God.

Then Pharaoh sent and called Joseph, and they brought him quickly out of the dungeon; and he shaved, changed his clothing, and came to Pharaoh. And Pharaoh said to Joseph, "I have had a dream, and *there is* no one who can interpret it. But I have heard it said of you *that* you can understand a dream, to interpret it."

So Joseph answered Pharaoh, saying, "*It is* not in me; God will give Pharaoh an answer of peace."

Then Pharaoh said to Joseph: "Behold, in my dream I stood on the bank of the river. Suddenly seven cows came up out of the river, fine looking and fat; and they fed in the meadow. Then behold, seven other cows came up after them, poor and very ugly and gaunt, such ugliness as I have never seen in all the land of Egypt. And the gaunt and ugly cows ate up the first seven, the fat cows. When they had eaten them up, no one would have known that they had eaten them, for they *were* just as ugly as at the beginning. So I awoke. Also I saw in my dream, and suddenly seven heads came up on one stalk, full and good. Then behold, seven heads, withered, thin, *and* blighted by the east wind, sprang up after them. And the thin heads devoured the seven good heads. So I told *this* to the magicians, but *there was* no one who could explain *it* to me."

Then Joseph said to Pharaoh, "The dreams of Pharaoh *are* one; God has shown Pharaoh what He *is* about to do: The seven good cows *are* seven years, and the seven good heads *are* seven years; the dreams *are* one. And the seven thin and ugly cows which came up after them *are* seven years, and the seven empty heads blighted by the east wind are seven years of famine. This *is* the thing which I have spoken to Pharaoh. God has shown Pharaoh what He *is* about to do. Indeed seven years of great plenty will come throughout all the land of Egypt; but after them seven years of famine will arise, and all the plenty will be forgotten in the land of Egypt; and the famine will deplete the land. So the plenty will not be known in the land because of the famine following, for it *will be* very severe. And the dream was repeated to Pharaoh twice because the thing *is* established by God, and God will shortly bring it to pass.

"Now therefore, let Pharaoh select a discerning and wise man, and set him over the land of Egypt. Let Pharaoh do *this,* and let him appoint officers over the land, to collect one-fifth *of the produce* of the land of Egypt in the seven plentiful years. And let them gather all the food of those good years that are coming, and store up grain under the authority of Pharaoh, and let them keep food in the cities. Then that food shall be as a reserve for the land for the seven years of famine which shall be in the land of Egypt, that the land may not perish during the famine."

So the advice was good in the eyes of Pharaoh and in the eyes of all his servants. And Pharaoh said to his servants, "Can we find *such a one* as this, a man in whom *is* the Spirit of God?"

Then Pharaoh said to Joseph, "Inasmuch as God has shown you all this, *there is* no one as discerning and wise as you. You shall be over my house, and all my people shall be ruled according to your word; only in regard to the throne will I be greater than you." And Pharaoh said to Joseph, "See, I have set you over all the land of Egypt."

Then Pharaoh took his signet ring off his hand and put it on Joseph's hand; and he clothed him in garments of fine linen and put a gold chain around his neck. And he had him ride in the second chariot which he had; and they cried out before him, "Bow the knee!" So he set him over all the land of Egypt. Pharaoh also said to Joseph, "I *am* Pharaoh, and without your consent no man may lift his hand or foot in all the land of Egypt." And Pharaoh called Joseph's name Zaphnath-Paaneah. And he gave him as a wife Asenath, the daughter of Poti-Pherah priest of On. So Joseph went out over *all* the land of Egypt.

Joseph was thirty years old when he stood before Pharaoh king of Egypt. And Joseph went out from the presence of Pharaoh, and went throughout all the land of Egypt. GENESIS 41:14–46

Just as Joseph had predicted, seven years of bumper crops were followed by seven years of famine throughout the land. Joseph made sure Egypt saved up enough food during the good years to survive the hard years. Although he was now a rich and influential man, Joseph stayed faithful to his promise to help Egypt survive the famine. Meanwhile, back in Joseph's homeland, his father and brothers began to talk about where they might be able to find more food for their families. Joseph's long-ago dream was about to come true.

When Jacob saw that there was grain in Egypt, Jacob said to his sons, "Why do you look at one another?" And he said, "Indeed

I have heard that there is grain in Egypt; go down to that place and buy for us there, that we may live and not die."

So Joseph's ten brothers went down to buy grain in Egypt. But Jacob did not send Joseph's brother Benjamin with his brothers, for he said, "Lest some calamity befall him." And the sons of Israel went to buy *grain* among those who journeyed, for the famine was in the land of Canaan.

Now Joseph *was* governor over the land; and it was he who sold to all the people of the land. And Joseph's brothers came and bowed down before him with *their* faces to the earth.

GENESIS 42:1–6

From pit to pinnacle. It took 21 years for Joseph's dreams to come to pass, but through it all God was faithful. Joseph also stayed faithful to God, whether his circumstances were terribly unjust or tremendously prosperous. Through the faithfulness of God and Joseph, the emerging nation of Israel survived the famine. As a result, Joseph was reunited with his father and enjoyed a position of prosperity and blessing for more than 70 years until his death.

Throughout the Bible, God never calls us to be successful. He calls us to be faithful. As we saw in Joseph's life, sometimes success follows faithfulness, sometimes it doesn't. What do you think about this? How are you doing at being faithful?

STORIES OF FAITHFULNESS: RUTH

Fast-forward to the period in Israel's history when the Israelites occupied the land of Canaan. One of the most heart warming stories of faithfulness and loyalty does not involve an Israelite but a young Moabite woman.

Now it came to pass, in the days when the judges ruled, that there was a famine in the land. And a certain man of Bethlehem, Judah, went to dwell in the country of Moab, he and his wife and his two sons. The name of the man *was* Elimelech, the name of his wife *was* Naomi, and the names of his two sons *were* Mahlon and Chilion—Ephrathites of Bethlehem, Judah. And they went to the country of Moab and remained there. Then Elimelech, Naomi's husband, died; and she was left, and her two sons. Now they took wives of the women of Moab: the name of the one *was* Orpah, and the name of the other Ruth. And they dwelt there about ten years. Then both Mahlon and Chilion also died; so the woman survived her two sons and her husband.

Then she arose with her daughters-in-law that she might return from the country of Moab, for she had heard in the country of Moab that the LORD had visited His people by giving them bread. Therefore she went out from the place where she was, and her two daughters-in-law with her; and they went on the way to return to the land of Judah. And Naomi said to her two daughters-in-law, "Go, return each to her mother's house. The LORD deal kindly with you, as you have dealt with the dead and with me. The LORD grant that you may find rest, each in the house of her husband."

So she kissed them, and they lifted up their voices and wept. And they said to her, "Surely we will return with you to your people."

But Naomi said, "Turn back, my daughters; why will you go with me? *Are* there still sons in my womb, that they may be your husbands? Turn back, my daughters, go—for I am too old to have a husband. If I should say I have hope, *if* I should have a husband tonight and should also bear sons, would you wait for them till they were grown? Would you restrain yourselves from having husbands? No, my daughters; for it grieves me very much for your sakes that the hand of the LORD has gone out against me!"

Then they lifted up their voices and wept again; and Orpah kissed her mother-in-law, but Ruth clung to her.

And she said, "Look, your sister-in-law has gone back to her people and to her gods; return after your sister-in-law."

But Ruth said:

> **"Entreat me not to leave you,**
> ***Or to* turn back from following after you;**
> **For wherever you go, I will go;**
> **And wherever you lodge, I will lodge;**
> **Your people *shall be* my people,**
> **And your God, my God.**

Where you die, I will die,
And there will I be buried.
The LORD do so to me, and more also,
If *anything but* death parts you and me."

When she saw that she was determined to go with her, she stopped speaking to her.

Now the two of them went until they came to Bethlehem. And it happened, when they had come to Bethlehem, that all the city was excited because of them; and the women said, "*Is* this Naomi?"

But she said to them, "Do not call me Naomi; call me Mara, for the Almighty has dealt very bitterly with me. I went out full, and the LORD has brought me home again empty. Why do you call me Naomi, since the LORD has testified against me, and the Almighty has afflicted me?"

So Naomi returned, and Ruth the Moabitess her daughter-in-law with her, who returned from the country of Moab. Now they came to Bethlehem at the beginning of barley harvest. RUTH 1:1–22

God demonstrated His faithfulness to Naomi and Ruth through Boaz, their close relative, who provided for their needs and married Ruth. Boaz and Ruth had a son named Obed, who had a son named Jesse, who had a son named David—who became the greatest king of Israel.

STORIES OF FAITHFULNESS: MARY

The prophet Micah prophesied that the Messiah would come from David's town of Bethlehem. A thousand years after David lived, the time had come for the Messiah to be born from the tribe of Judah, the family of David, in the city of Bethlehem. God would pull this off through Ruth's very young descendant Mary. Her response to a shocking announcement shows us her heart of faithfulness.

Now in the sixth month the angel Gabriel was sent by God to a city of Galilee named Nazareth, to a virgin betrothed to a man whose name was Joseph, of the house of David. The virgin's name *was* Mary. And having come in, the angel said to her, "Rejoice, highly favored *one,* the Lord *is* with you; blessed *are* you among women!"

But when she saw *him,* she was troubled at his saying, and considered what manner of greeting this was. **Then the angel said to her, "Do not be afraid, Mary, for you have found favor with God. And behold, you will conceive in your womb and bring forth a Son, and shall call His name JESUS. He will be great, and will be called the Son of the Highest; and the Lord God will give Him the throne of His father David. And He will reign over the house of Jacob forever, and of His kingdom there will be no end."**

Then Mary said to the angel, "How can this be, since I do not know a man?"

And the angel answered and said to her, "*The* Holy Spirit will come upon you, and the power of the Highest will overshadow you; therefore, also, that Holy One who is to be born will be called the Son of God. Now indeed, Elizabeth your relative has also conceived a son in her old age; and this is now the sixth month for her who was called barren. For with God nothing will be impossible."

Then Mary said, "Behold the maidservant of the Lord! Let it be to me according to your word." And the angel departed from her.

Now Mary arose in those days and went into the hill country with haste, to a city of Judah, and entered the house of Zacharias and greeted Elizabeth. And it happened, when Elizabeth heard the greeting of Mary, that the babe leaped in her womb; and Elizabeth was filled with the Holy Spirit. Then she spoke out with a loud voice and said, "Blessed *are* you among women, and blessed *is* the fruit of your womb! But why *is* this *granted* to me, that the mother of my Lord should come to me? For indeed, as soon as the voice of your greeting sounded in my ears, the babe leaped in my womb for joy. Blessed *is* she who believed, for there will be a fulfillment of those things which were told her from the Lord."

And Mary said:

"My soul magnifies the Lord,
And my spirit has rejoiced in God my Savior.
For He has regarded the lowly state of His maidservant;

For behold, henceforth all generations will call me blessed.
For He who is mighty has done great things for me,
And holy *is* His name.
And His mercy *is* on those who fear Him
From generation to generation.
He has shown strength with His arm;
He has scattered *the* proud in the imagination of their hearts.
He has put down the mighty from *their* thrones,
And exalted *the* lowly.
He has filled *the* hungry with good things,
And *the* rich He has sent away empty.
He has helped His servant Israel,
In remembrance of *His* mercy,
As He spoke to our fathers,
To Abraham and to his seed forever."

And Mary remained with her about three months, and returned to her house.

LUKE 1:26–56

Mary committed herself, as "the maidservant of the Lord," to be faithful to God's plan, and she extolled God's faithfulness. After visiting her relative Elizabeth, Mary—now about three months pregnant—returned to her home in Nazareth. But Nazareth was at least a three-day trip from Bethlehem. How then was the prophecy, that the Messiah would come from the town of Bethlehem, going to be fulfilled?

And it came to pass in those days *that* a decree went out from Caesar Augustus that all the world should be registered. This census first took place while Quirinius was governing Syria. So all went to be registered, everyone to his own city.

Joseph also went up from Galilee, out of the city of Nazareth, into Judea, to the city of David, which is called Bethlehem, because he was of the house and lineage of David, to be registered with Mary, his betrothed wife, who was with child. So it was, that while they were there, the days were completed for her to be delivered. And she brought forth her firstborn Son, and wrapped Him in swaddling cloths, and laid Him in a manger, because there was no room for them in the inn.

Now there were in the same country shepherds living out in the fields, keeping watch over their flock by night. And behold, an angel of the Lord stood before them, and the glory of the Lord shone around them, and they were greatly afraid. Then the angel said to them, "Do not be afraid, for behold, I bring you good tidings of great joy which will be to all people. For there is born to you this day in the city of David a Savior, who is Christ the Lord. And this *will be* the sign to you: You will find a Babe wrapped in swaddling cloths, lying in a manger."

And suddenly there was with the angel a multitude of the heavenly host praising God and saying:

> "Glory to God in the highest,
> And on earth peace, goodwill toward men!"

So it was, when the angels had gone away from them into heaven, that the shepherds said to one another, "Let us now go to Bethlehem and see this thing that has come to pass, which the Lord has made known to us." And they came with haste and found Mary and Joseph, and the Babe lying in a manger. Now when they had seen *Him,* they made widely known the saying which was told them concerning this Child. And all those who heard *it* marveled at those things which were told them by the shepherds. But Mary kept all these things and pondered *them* in her heart. Then the shepherds returned, glorifying and praising God for all the things that they had heard and seen, as it was told them.

And when eight days were completed for the circumcision of the Child, His name was called JESUS, the name given by the angel before He was conceived in the womb. LUKE 2:1–21

Based on what you have learned about faithfulness, who are some of the most faithful people you know? How have they found honor and a good name in your sight? In the sight of others? If it is possible, let them know.

WHAT WE BELIEVE

Throughout the Bible, God called believers to be faithful to His assignments for them, no matter how difficult. In fact, it was often amid the difficult seasons that they discovered the trustworthiness of God the most. When they aligned their lives to God's story, He was with them and accomplished great things through them. All believers have the opportunity to open their lives to God's will and demonstrate their faithfulness. The results of such faithfulness can be both great and beautiful as God works through those who believe.

BE

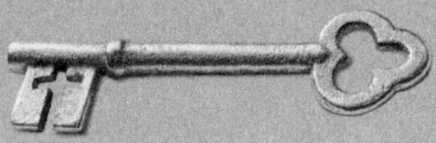

CHAPTER

29

Gentleness

KEY QUESTION

How do I demonstrate thoughtfulness and consideration?

KEY IDEA

I am thoughtful, considerate and calm
in my dealings with others.

KEY VERSE

Let your gentleness be known to all men.
The Lord *is* at hand.
Philippians 4:5

OUR MAP

Nothing kills a family, a friendship, a neighborhood or even a church like pride, arrogance, anger, closed ears and raised voices. Since God is all about community, He calls His followers to be gentle. The New Testament word for "gentleness" comes from a medical word and is associated with a mild medication. Essentially, we might say a gentle person is someone who is easy on our stomachs. The person who lacks gentleness causes our stomach to double up in knots. God wants us to be healing agents in the lives of those around us. So how do we learn how to demonstrate thoughtfulness and consideration to others? That is the focus of this chapter, with Scripture concentrated on:

- *Gentle Jesus*
- *Nuggets on Gentleness*
- *Stories of Gentleness: Abigail*
- *Stories of Gentleness: David*
- *Stories of Gentleness: Paul*

Look at the key verse again. Why do you think Paul put these two sentences together?

Gentle Jesus

Throughout the Bible we find stories and people who reinforce the fact that gentleness is a character trait that God has intended for us. Jesus, of course, is our greatest example of someone who displayed gentleness in His dealings with others. This is particularly true in His relationship with Peter. At the Last Supper on the night before Jesus was crucified, Peter told Jesus he would die for Him. Jesus, predicting Peter's future betrayal, corrected him. Jesus had already predicted the betrayal of Judas, who had just stepped out of the room.

So, when [Judas] had gone out, Jesus said, "Now the Son of Man is glorified, and God is glorified in Him. If God is glorified in Him, God will also glorify Him in Himself, and glorify Him immediately. Little children, I shall be with you a little while longer. You will seek Me; and as I said to the Jews, 'Where I am going, you cannot come,' so now I say to you. A new commandment I give to you, that you love one another; as I have loved you, that you also love one another. By this all will know that you are My disciples, if you have love for one another."

Simon Peter said to Him, "Lord, where are You going?"

Jesus answered him, "Where I am going you cannot follow Me now, but you shall follow Me afterward."

Peter said to Him, "Lord, why can I not follow You now? I will lay down my life for Your sake."

Jesus answered him, "Will you lay down your life for My sake? Most assuredly, I say to you, the rooster shall not crow till you have denied Me three times." JOHN 13:31–38

Peter could not imagine betraying his master. He had left everything to follow Jesus. However, when Jesus was arrested later that evening Peter's fear overcame his faith.

Then the detachment *of troops* and the captain and the officers of the Jews arrested Jesus and bound Him. And they led Him away to Annas first, for he was the father-in-law of Caiaphas who was high priest that year. Now it was Caiaphas who advised the Jews that it was expedient that one man should die for the people.

And Simon Peter followed Jesus, and so *did* another disciple. Now that disciple was known to the high priest, and went with Jesus into the courtyard of the high priest. But Peter stood at the door outside. Then the other disciple, who was known to the high priest, went out and spoke to her who kept the door, and brought Peter in. **Then the servant girl who kept the door said to Peter, "You are not also *one* of this Man's disciples, are you?"**

He said, "I am not."

Now the servants and officers who had made a fire of coals stood there, for it was cold, and they warmed themselves. And Peter stood with them and warmed himself.

The high priest then asked Jesus about His disciples and His doctrine.

Jesus answered him, "I spoke openly to the world. I always taught in synagogues and in the temple, where the Jews always meet, and in secret I have said nothing. Why do you ask Me? Ask those who have heard Me what I said to them. Indeed they know what I said."

And when He had said these things, one of the officers who stood by struck Jesus with the palm of his hand, saying, "Do You answer the high priest like that?"

Jesus answered him, "If I have spoken evil, bear witness of the evil; but if well, why do you strike Me?"

Then Annas sent Him bound to Caiaphas the high priest.

Now Simon Peter stood and warmed himself. Therefore they said to him, "You are not also *one* of His disciples, are you?"

He denied *it* and said, "I am not!"

One of the servants of the high priest, a relative *of him* whose ear Peter cut off, said, "Did I not see you in the garden with Him?" Peter then denied again; and immediately a rooster crowed.

JOHN 18:12–27

Sometime between Jesus' resurrection and ascension to heaven, He appeared to seven of His disciples who had gone fishing. With a heart of gentleness, Jesus restored Peter's relationship with Him and reinstated Peter to a position of special responsibility in the church.

After these things Jesus showed Himself again to the disciples at the Sea of Tiberias, and in this way He showed *Himself:* Simon Peter, Thomas called the Twin, Nathanael of Cana in Galilee, the *sons* of Zebedee, and two others of His disciples were together. Simon Peter said to them, "I am going fishing."

They said to him, "We are going with you also." They went out and immediately got into the boat, and that night they caught nothing. But when the morning had now come, Jesus stood on the shore; yet the disciples did not know that it was Jesus. Then Jesus said to them, "Children, have you any food?"

They answered Him, "No."

And He said to them, "Cast the net on the right side of the boat, and you will find *some.*" So they cast, and now they were not able to draw it in because of the multitude of fish.

Therefore that disciple whom Jesus loved said to Peter, "It is the Lord!" Now when Simon Peter heard that it was the Lord, he put on *his* outer garment (for he had removed it), and plunged into the sea. But the other disciples came in the little boat (for they were not far from land, but about two hundred cubits), dragging the net with fish. Then, as soon as they had come to land, they saw a fire of coals there, and fish laid on it, and bread. Jesus said to them, "Bring some of the fish which you have just caught."

Simon Peter went up and dragged the net to land, full of large fish, one hundred and fifty-three; and although there were so many, the net was not broken. Jesus said to them, "Come *and* eat breakfast." Yet none of the disciples dared ask Him, "Who are You?"—knowing that it was the Lord. Jesus then came and took the bread and gave it to them, and likewise the fish.

This *is* now the third time Jesus showed Himself to His disciples after He was raised from the dead.

So when they had eaten breakfast, Jesus said to Simon Peter, "Simon, *son* of Jonah, do you love Me more than these?"

He said to Him, "Yes, Lord; You know that I love You."

He said to him, "Feed My lambs."

He said to him again a second time, **"Simon, *son* of Jonah, do you love Me?"**

He said to Him, "Yes, Lord; You know that I love You."

He said to him, "Tend My sheep."

He said to him the third time, **"Simon, *son* of Jonah, do you love Me?"** Peter was grieved because He said to him the third time, "Do you love Me?"

And he said to Him, "Lord, You know all things; You know that I love You."

Jesus said to him, "Feed My sheep. Most assuredly, I say to you, when you were younger, you girded yourself and walked where you wished; but when you are old, you will stretch out your hands, and another will gird you and carry *you* where you do not wish." This He spoke, signifying by what death he would glorify God. And when He had spoken this, He said to him, "Follow Me."

JOHN 21:1–19

Some have suggested that Jesus asked Simon Peter if he loved Him three times to help restore Peter from the three times he had denied Jesus. Do you think this was Jesus' intent? Do you think this would have helped you if you were in Peter's sandals?

Peter's relationship was fully restored by Jesus' gentle invitation. The rest of the New Testament tells us how Peter fulfilled this mission given to him by Jesus. He spoke the Word of God boldly and provided leadership to God's people. Peter isn't the only one Jesus spoke to with gentleness. Jesus invites all people to receive His gift of peace and rest.

"Come to Me, all *you* who labor and are heavy laden, and I will give you rest. Take My yoke upon you and learn from Me, for I am gentle and lowly in heart, and you will find rest for your souls. For My yoke *is* easy and My burden is light."

MATTHEW 11:28–30

NUGGETS ON GENTLENESS

The New Testament offers us wonderful nuggets on being thoughtful, considerate and calm. Jesus offered up powerful insights and encouragement in the Sermon on the Mount.

As you read Jesus' nuggets of wisdom on gentleness, identify the one that most speaks to you. Why did you choose this one?

"Blessed *are* the meek,
For they shall inherit the earth." MATTHEW 5:5

"You have heard that it was said, *'An eye for an eye and a tooth for a tooth.'* But I tell you not to resist an evil person. **But whoever slaps you on your right cheek, turn the other to him also.** If anyone wants to sue you and take away your tunic, let him have *your* cloak also. And whoever compels you to go one mile, go with him two. Give to him who asks you, and from him who wants to borrow from you do not turn away." MATTHEW 5:38–42

"Judge not, that you be not judged. For with what judgment you judge, you will be judged; and with the measure you use, it will be measured back to you. And why do you look at the speck in your brother's eye, but do not consider the plank in your own eye? Or how can you say to your brother, 'Let me remove the speck from your eye'; and look, a plank *is* in your own eye? Hypocrite! First remove the plank from your own eye, and then you will see clearly to remove the speck from your brother's eye."

MATTHEW 7:1–5

Inspired by the life and teaching of Jesus and led by the Spirit, the apostles offered further understanding of and encouragement about gentleness.

But the fruit of the Spirit is love, joy, peace, longsuffering, kindness, goodness, faithfulness, gentleness, self-control. Against such there is no law. GALATIANS 5:22–23

Walk worthy of the calling with which you were called, with all lowliness and gentleness, with longsuffering, bearing with one another in love. EPHESIANS 4:1–2

***"Be angry, and do not sin"*: do not let the sun go down on your wrath, nor give place to the devil.** Let him who stole steal no longer, but rather let him labor, working with *his* hands what is good, that he may have something to give him who has need. **Let no corrupt word proceed out of your mouth, but what is good for necessary edification, that it may impart grace to the hearers.** And do not grieve the Holy Spirit of God, by whom you were sealed for the day of redemption. Let all bitterness, wrath, anger, clamor, and evil speaking be put away from you, with all malice. And be kind to one another, tenderhearted, forgiving one another, even as God in Christ forgave you. EPHESIANS 4:26–32

And you, fathers, do not provoke your children to wrath, but bring them up in the training and admonition of the Lord.

EPHESIANS 6:4

Therefore, as *the* elect of God, holy and beloved, put on tender mercies, kindness, humility, meekness, longsuffering.

COLOSSIANS 3:12

This *is* a faithful saying: If a man desires the position of a bishop, he desires a good work. A bishop then must be blameless, the husband of one wife, temperate, sober-minded, of good behavior, hospitable, able to teach; not given to wine, not violent, not greedy for money, but gentle, not quarrelsome, not covetous; one who rules his own house well, having *his* children in submission with all reverence. 1 TIMOTHY 3:1–4

Do not rebuke an older man, but exhort *him* as a father, younger men as brothers, older women as mothers, younger women as sisters, with all purity. 1 TIMOTHY 5:1–2

For the love of money is a root of all *kinds of* evil, for which some have strayed from the faith in their greediness, and pierced themselves through with many sorrows.

But you, O man of God, flee these things and pursue righteousness, godliness, faith, love, patience, gentleness. 1 TIMOTHY 6:10–11

And a servant of the Lord must not quarrel but be gentle to all, able to teach, patient, in humility correcting those who are in opposition, if God perhaps will grant them repentance, so that they may know the truth, and *that* they may come to their senses *and escape* the snare of the devil, having been taken captive by him to *do* his will. 2 TIMOTHY 2:24–26

Remind them to be subject to rulers and authorities, to obey, to be ready for every good work, to speak evil of no one, to be peaceable, gentle, showing all humility to all men. TITUS 3:1–2

The wisdom that is from above is first pure, then peaceable, gentle, willing to yield, full of mercy and good fruits, without partiality and without hypocrisy. Now the fruit of righteousness is sown in peace by those who make peace. JAMES 3:17–18

Look at Ephesians 4:26–32 again. How do we "give place to the devil" in our lives when we let the sun go down while we are still angry?

Paul encouraged two Christian women in the church at Philippi to reconcile their differences and then urged the entire congregation to put their gentleness on public display in light of the Lord's arrival.

I implore Euodia and I implore Syntyche to be of the same mind in the Lord. And I urge you also, true companion, help these women who labored with me in the gospel, with Clement also, and the rest of my fellow workers, whose names *are* in the Book of Life.

Rejoice in the Lord always. Again I will say, rejoice!

Let your gentleness be known to all men. The Lord *is* at hand. PHILIPPIANS 4:2–5

Likewise, Peter told his readers that a thoughtful, considerate and calm gentleness is key in a marriage relationship.

Wives, likewise, *be* submissive to your own husbands, that even if some do not obey the word, they, without a word, may be won by the conduct of their wives, when they observe your chaste conduct *accompanied* by fear. **Do not let your adornment be *merely* outward—arranging the hair, wearing gold, or putting on *fine* apparel—rather *let it be* the hidden person of the heart, with the incorruptible *beauty* of a gentle and quiet spirit, which is very precious in the sight of God.** 1 PETER 3:1–4

Husbands, likewise, dwell with *them* with understanding, giving honor to the wife, as to the weaker vessel, and as *being* heirs together of the grace of life, that your prayers may not be hindered.

1 PETER 3:7

Stories of Gentleness: Abigail

As you read the next three stories from 1 Samuel 25;
2 Samuel 16 and 1 Thessalonians 2,
find the ways anger is stirred up and look
for how gentleness affects tense situations.

Samuel anointed young David to be the next king of Israel, but the reigning King Saul hated David, causing David to flee as a fugitive. David was on the run from Saul when he encountered a couple who displayed opposite qualities—Abigail was wise and gentle, while Nabal was foolish and cruel. When David asked Nabal for reasonable payment for the protection that he and his men had voluntarily rendered for Nabal's benefit, Nabal's response was harsh and rude. Abigail repaired the situation with gentleness and diplomacy.

Then Samuel died; and the Israelites gathered together and lamented for him, and buried him at his home in Ramah. And David arose and went down to the Wilderness of Paran.

Now *there was* a man in Maon whose business *was* in Carmel, and the man *was* very rich. He had three thousand sheep and a thousand goats. And he was shearing his sheep in Carmel. The name of the man *was* Nabal, and the name of his wife Abigail. And *she was* a woman of good understanding and beautiful appearance; but the man *was* harsh and evil in *his* doings. He *was of the house of* Caleb.

When David heard in the wilderness that Nabal was shearing his sheep, David sent ten young men; and David said to the young men, "Go up to Carmel, go to Nabal, and greet him in my name. And thus you shall say to him who lives *in prosperity:* 'Peace *be* to you, peace to your house, and peace to all that you have! Now I have heard that you have shearers. Your shepherds were with us, and we did not hurt them, nor was there anything missing from them all the while they were in Carmel. Ask your young men, and they will tell you. Therefore let *my* young men find favor in your eyes, for we come on a feast day. Please give whatever comes to your hand to your servants and to your son David.'"

So when David's young men came, they spoke to Nabal according to all these words in the name of David, and waited.

Then Nabal answered David's servants, and said, "Who *is* David, and who *is* the son of Jesse? There are many servants nowadays who break away each one from his master. Shall I then take my bread and my water and my meat that I have killed for my shearers, and give *it* to men when I do not know where they *are* from?"

So David's young men turned on their heels and went back; and they came and told him all these words. Then David said to his men, "Every man gird on his sword." So every man girded on his sword, and David also girded on his sword. And about four hundred men went with David, and two hundred stayed with the supplies.

Now one of the young men told Abigail, Nabal's wife, saying, "Look, David sent messengers from the wilderness to greet our master; and he reviled them. But the men *were* very good to us, and we were not hurt, nor did we miss anything as long as we accompanied them, when we were in the fields. They were a wall to us both by night and day, all the time we were with them keeping the sheep. Now therefore, know and consider what you will do, for harm is determined against our master and against all his household. For he *is such* a scoundrel that *one* cannot speak to him."

Then Abigail made haste and took two hundred *loaves* of bread, two skins of wine, five sheep already dressed, five seahs of roasted *grain,* one hundred clusters of raisins, and two hundred cakes of figs, and loaded *them* on donkeys. And she said to her servants, "Go on before me; see, I am coming after you." But she did not tell her husband Nabal.

So it was, *as* she rode on the donkey, that she went down under cover of the hill; and there were David and his men, coming down toward her, and she met them. Now David had said, "Surely in vain I have protected all that this *fellow* has in the wilderness, so that nothing was missed of all that *belongs* to him. And he has repaid me evil for good. May God do so, and more also, to the enemies of David, if I leave one male of all who *belong* to him by morning light."

Now when Abigail saw David, she dismounted quickly from the donkey, fell on her face before David, and bowed down to the ground. So she fell at his feet and said: "On me, my lord, *on* me *let* this iniquity *be!* And please let your maidservant speak in your ears, and hear the words of your maidservant. Please, let not my lord regard this scoundrel Nabal. For as his name *is,* so *is* he: Nabal *is* his name, and folly *is* with him! But I, your maidservant, did not see the young men of my lord whom you sent. Now therefore, my lord, *as* the LORD lives and *as* your soul lives, since the LORD has held you back from coming to bloodshed and from avenging yourself with your own hand, now then, let your enemies and those who seek harm for my lord be as Nabal. And now this present which your maidservant has brought to my lord, let it be given to the young men who follow my lord. Please forgive the trespass of your maidservant. For the LORD will certainly make for my lord an enduring house, because my lord fights the battles of the LORD, and evil is not found in you throughout your days. Yet a man has risen to pursue you and seek your life, but the life of my lord shall be bound in the bundle of the living with the LORD your God; and the lives of your enemies He shall sling out, *as from* the pocket of a sling. And it shall come to pass, when the LORD has done for my lord according to all the good that He has spoken concerning you, and has appointed you ruler over Israel, that this will be no grief to you, nor offense of heart to my lord, either that you have shed blood without cause, or that my lord has avenged himself. But when the LORD has dealt well with my lord, then remember your maidservant."

Then David said to Abigail: "Blessed *is* the LORD God of Israel, who sent you this day to meet me! And blessed *is* your advice and blessed *are* you, because you have kept me this day from coming to bloodshed and from avenging myself with my own hand. For indeed, *as* the LORD God of Israel lives, who has kept me back from hurting you, unless you had hurried and come to meet me, surely by morning light no males would have been left to Nabal!" So David received from her hand what she had brought him, and said to her, "Go up in peace to your house. See, I have heeded your voice and respected your person."

Now Abigail went to Nabal, and there he was, holding a feast in his house, like the feast of a king. And Nabal's heart *was* merry within him, for he *was* very drunk; therefore she told him nothing, little or much, until morning light. So it was, in the morning, when the wine had gone from Nabal, and his wife had told him these things, that his heart died within him, and he became *like* a stone. Then it happened, *after* about ten days, that the LORD struck Nabal, and he died.

So when David heard that Nabal was dead, he said, "Blessed *be* the LORD, who has pleaded the cause of my reproach from the hand of Nabal, and has kept His servant from evil! For the LORD has returned the wickedness of Nabal on his own head."

And David sent and proposed to Abigail, to take her as his wife. When the servants of David had come to Abigail at Carmel, they spoke to her saying, "David sent us to you, to ask you to become his wife."

Then she arose, bowed her face to the earth, and said, "Here is your maidservant, a servant to wash the feet of the servants of my lord." So Abigail rose in haste and rode on a donkey, attended by five of her maidens; and she followed the messengers of David, and became his wife. 1 SAMUEL 25:1–42

STORIES OF GENTLENESS: DAVID

Our gentleness toward others is tested most when things are not going well for us—when we are frustrated, tired or discouraged. David was now king of Israel, but his son Absalom had conspired against him to take the throne. Uncertain of the extent of Absalom's support, David feared being trapped in Jerusalem and wanted to spare the city a bloodbath. So he fled as a fugitive once again. On his way out of Jerusalem, David experienced a situation that was nearly unbearable. How would he respond?

Now when King David came to Bahurim, there was a man from the family of the house of Saul, whose name *was* Shimei the son of Gera, coming from there. He came out, cursing continuously as he came. And he threw stones at David and at all the servants of King David. And all the people and all the mighty men *were* on his right hand and on his left. Also Shimei said thus when he cursed: "Come out! Come out! You bloodthirsty man, you rogue! The LORD has brought upon you all the blood of the house of Saul, in whose place you have reigned; and the LORD has delivered the kingdom into the hand of Absalom your son. So now you *are caught* in your own evil, because you are a bloodthirsty man!"

Then Abishai the son of Zeruiah said to the king, "Why should this dead dog curse my lord the king? Please, let me go over and take off his head!"

But the king said, "What have I to do with you, you sons of Zeruiah? So let him curse, because the LORD has said to him, 'Curse David.' Who then shall say, 'Why have you done so?'"

And David said to Abishai and all his servants, "See how my son who came from my own body seeks my life. How much more now *may this* Benjamite? Let him alone, and let him curse; for so the LORD has ordered him. It may be that the LORD will look on my affliction, and that the LORD will repay me with good for his cursing this day." And as David and his men went along the road, Shimei went along the hillside opposite him and cursed as he went, threw stones at him and kicked up dust. Now the king and all the people who *were* with him became weary; so they refreshed themselves there. 2 SAMUEL 16:5–14

STORIES OF GENTLENESS: PAUL

Like David, Paul carried great responsibility on his shoulders and was often challenged by others and undermined in his work. It would have been easy for Paul to lose his temper with the new believers he sought to encourage in Christ. But he didn't. In his first letter to the church of Thessalonica, Paul laid out his effective approach of gentleness in ministering to them. It's an approach we would be wise to emulate with the people God has placed in our lives.

For you yourselves know, brethren, that our coming to you was not in vain. But even after we had suffered before and were spitefully treated at Philippi, as you know, we were bold in our God to speak to you the gospel of God in much conflict. For our exhortation *did* not *come* from error or uncleanness, nor *was it* in deceit.

But as we have been approved by God to be entrusted with the gospel, even so we speak, not as pleasing men, but God who tests our hearts. For neither at any time did we use flattering words, as you know, nor a cloak for covetousness—God *is* witness. Nor did we seek glory from men, either from you or from others, when we might have made demands as apostles of Christ. But we were gentle among you, just as a nursing *mother* cherishes her own children. So, affectionately longing for you, we were well pleased to impart to you not only the gospel of God, but also our own lives, because you had become dear to us. For you remember, brethren, our labor and toil; for laboring night and day, that we might not be a burden to any of you, we preached to you the gospel of God.

You *are* witnesses, and God *also,* how devoutly and justly and blamelessly we behaved ourselves among you who believe; as you know how we exhorted, and comforted, and charged every one of you, as a father *does* his own children, that you would walk worthy of God who calls you into His own kingdom and glory.

For this reason we also thank God without ceasing, because when you received the word of God which you heard from us, you welcomed *it* not *as* the word of men, but as it is in truth, the word of God, which also effectively works in you who believe.

1 THESSALONIANS 2:1–13

WHAT WE BELIEVE

Gentleness is rooted in our belief in humanity. When we see people the way God sees them, we are compelled to treat them well. A gentle person, according to God's vision, is thoughtful. They think before they talk or act. A gentle person is considerate. They consistently put themselves in other people's shoes and act accordingly. A gentle person is calm. They are known for their even temper and positive energy. Jesus modeled this for us in so many of His relationships. We can also find positive examples of gentleness in the stories of Abigail, David and Paul. Also pay attention to the lives of men like Nabal. Sometimes looking at a negative example can be eye-opening. Go back to the nuggets on gentleness you read earlier in the chapter. Pick just one suggestion and try it for seven days and see if it doesn't make a difference in your life and the lives of those God has purposefully placed around you.

BE

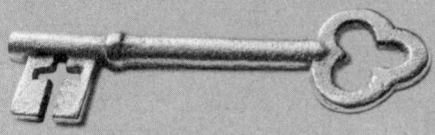

CHAPTER

30

Humility

KEY QUESTION

What does it mean to value others before myself?

KEY IDEA

I choose to esteem others above myself.

KEY VERSE

Let nothing *be done* through selfish ambition or conceit, but in lowliness of mind let each esteem others better than himself. Let each of you look out not only for his own interests, but also for the interests of others.
Philippians 2:3–4

OUR MAP

Humility is a driving virtue in the Christian life and community. Choosing to esteem others above oneself encourages harmony and love. The opposite of humility is pride. Prideful people typically believe they are better than others. They strive to get their way at the expense of others or boast as a way of boosting low self-esteem. When a person possesses Biblical humility, they draw from internal "God-esteem." They have received God's unconditional love and embraced their inherent worth as God's child—their identity in Christ. From this belief they are capable of lifting others up. This chapter will provide us with God's Word on the matter:

- *Christ As Our Example*
- *God Resists the Proud, Gives Grace to the Humble*
- *The Paradox of Humility*
- *God's Requirement*

Christ As Our Example

Jesus is our supreme example of humility. The God of the universe could have ridden into our world on a white horse with a serious entourage and fanfare. Instead He came to us as a baby born in a stable to poor parents.

And it came to pass in those days *that* a decree went out from Caesar Augustus that all the world should be registered. This census first took place while Quirinius was governing Syria. So all went to be registered, everyone to his own city.

Joseph also went up from Galilee, out of the city of Nazareth, into Judea, to the city of David, which is called Bethlehem, because he was of the house and lineage of David, to be registered with Mary, his betrothed wife, who was with child. So it was, that while they were there, the days were completed for her to be delivered. **And she brought forth her firstborn Son, and wrapped Him in swaddling cloths, and laid Him in a manger, because there was no room for them in the inn.**

Now there were in the same country shepherds living out in the fields, keeping watch over their flock by night. And behold, an angel of the Lord stood before them, and the glory of the Lord shone around them, and they were greatly afraid. Then the angel said to them, "Do not be afraid, for behold, I bring you good tidings of great joy which will be to all people. For there is born to you this day in the city of David a Savior, who is Christ the Lord. And this *will be* the sign to you: You will find a Babe wrapped in swaddling cloths, lying in a manger."

And suddenly there was with the angel a multitude of the heavenly host praising God and saying:

> "Glory to God in the highest,
> And on earth peace, goodwill toward men!"

So it was, when the angels had gone away from them into heaven, that the shepherds said to one another, "Let us now go to Bethlehem and see this thing that has come to pass, which the Lord has made known to us." And they came with haste and found Mary and Joseph, and the Babe lying in a manger. Now when they had seen *Him,* they made widely known the saying which was told them concerning this Child. And all those who heard *it* marveled at those things which were told them by the shepherds. But Mary kept all these things and pondered *them* in her heart. Then the shepherds returned, glorifying and praising God for all the things that they had heard and seen, as it was told them. LUKE 2:1–20

As Jesus was coming to the end of His time on earth, He wanted to impress upon His disciples the importance of humility. He does so in an unforgettable way.

Now before the Feast of the Passover, when Jesus knew that His hour had come that He should depart from this world to the Father, having loved His own who were in the world, He loved them to the end.

And supper being ended, the devil having already put it into the heart of Judas Iscariot, Simon's *son,* to betray Him, **Jesus, knowing that the Father had given all things into His hands, and that He had come from God and was going to God, rose from supper and laid aside His garments, took a towel and girded Himself. After that, He poured water into a basin and began to wash the disciples' feet, and to wipe *them* with the towel with which He**

was girded. Then He came to Simon Peter. And *Peter* said to Him, "Lord, are You washing my feet?"

Jesus answered and said to him, "What I am doing you do not understand now, but you will know after this."

Peter said to Him, "You shall never wash my feet!"

Jesus answered him, "If I do not wash you, you have no part with Me."

Simon Peter said to Him, "Lord, not my feet only, but also *my* hands and *my* head!"

Jesus said to him, "He who is bathed needs only to wash *his* feet, but is completely clean; and you are clean, but not all of you." For He knew who would betray Him; therefore He said, "You are not all clean."

So when He had washed their feet, taken His garments, and sat down again, He said to them, "Do you know what I have done to you? You call Me Teacher and Lord, and you say well, for *so* I am. If I then, *your* Lord and Teacher, have washed your feet, you also ought to wash one another's feet. For I have given you an example, that you should do as I have done to you. Most assuredly, I say to you, a servant is not greater than his master; nor is he who is sent greater than he who sent him. If you know these things, blessed are you if you do them."

JOHN 13:1–17

Servant leadership is what Jesus modeled while on earth. What other ways can we demonstrate this principle besides washing someone's feet?

Following in the steps of his Savior, the apostle Paul wrote a tender letter to the church at Philippi instructing them to practice humility. He cited Jesus as their model.

Therefore if *there is* any consolation in Christ, if any comfort of love, if any fellowship of the Spirit, if any affection and mercy, fulfill my joy by being like-minded, having the same love, *being* of one accord, of one mind. *Let* nothing *be done* through selfish ambition or conceit, but in lowliness of mind let each esteem others better than himself. Let each of you look out not only for his own interests, but also for the interests of others.

Let this mind be in you which was also in Christ Jesus, who, being in the form of God, did not consider it robbery to be equal with God, but made Himself of no reputation, taking the form of a bondservant, *and* coming in the likeness of men. And being found in appearance as a man, He humbled Himself and became obedient to *the point of* death, even the death of the cross. Therefore God also has highly exalted Him and given Him the name which is above every name, that at the name of Jesus every knee should bow, of those in heaven, and of those on earth, and of those under the earth, and *that* every tongue should confess that Jesus Christ *is* Lord, to the glory of God the Father.

Therefore, my beloved, as you have always obeyed, not as in my presence only, but now much more in my absence, work out your own salvation with fear and trembling; for it is God who works in you both to will and to do for *His* good pleasure. PHILIPPIANS 2:1–13

What do you think was involved when Jesus "made Himself of no reputation?" What was He before? Why did He do this?

GOD RESISTS THE PROUD, GIVES GRACE TO THE HUMBLE

Throughout the Bible we find a pattern—God opposes the proud but grants favor to the humble. The following passages from Psalms and Proverbs are brief, but their messages are powerful.

As you read the Scripture passages below from Psalms and Proverbs, write down all the ways God resists the proud and gives grace to the humble.

The wicked in *his* pride persecutes the poor;
Let them be caught in the plots which they have devised.

For the wicked boasts of his heart's desire;
He blesses the greedy *and* renounces the LORD.

The wicked in his proud countenance does not seek *God;*
God *is* in none of his thoughts. PSALM 10:2–4

For You will save the humble people,
But will bring down haughty looks. PSALM 18:27

Good and upright *is* the LORD;
Therefore He teaches sinners in the way.
The humble He guides in justice,
And the humble He teaches His way. PSALM 25:8–9

The LORD lifts up the humble;
He casts the wicked down to the ground. PSALM 147:6

The curse of the LORD *is* on the house of the wicked,
But He blesses the home of the just.
Surely He scorns the scornful,
But gives grace to the humble. PROVERBS 3:33–34

When pride comes, then comes shame;
But with the humble *is* wisdom. PROVERBS 11:2

Pride *goes* before destruction,
And a haughty spirit before a fall.
Better *to be* of a humble spirit with the lowly,
Than to divide the spoil with the proud. PROVERBS 16:18–19

Before destruction the heart of a man is haughty,
And before honor *is* humility. PROVERBS 18:12

A haughty look, a proud heart,
And the plowing of the wicked *are* sin. PROVERBS 21:4

A proud *and* haughty *man*—"Scoffer" *is* his name;
He acts with arrogant pride. PROVERBS 21:24

By humility *and* the fear of the LORD
***Are* riches and honor and life.** PROVERBS 22:4

Do not exalt yourself in the presence of the king,
And do not stand in the place of the great;
For *it is* better that he say to you,
"Come up here,"
Than that you should be put lower in the presence
of the prince,
Whom your eyes have seen. PROVERBS 25:6–7

A man's pride will bring him low,
But the humble in spirit will retain honor. PROVERBS 29:23

An example of God opposing the proud and granting favor to the humble can be found in the story of a young Hebrew man named Daniel, who was taken captive from Jerusalem to Babylon in 605 BC. There, after three years of training, Daniel was given a responsible post in King Nebuchadnezzar's service. Through divine wisdom, Daniel was able to interpret dreams, and he soon became one of the most prominent figures in the royal court. God used Daniel to teach Nebuchadnezzar a memorable lesson in humility. The book of Daniel includes the following letter that the king wrote to his subjects regarding his experience.

Nebuchadnezzar the king,

To all peoples, nations, and languages that dwell in all the earth:

Peace be multiplied to you.

I thought it good to declare the signs and wonders that the Most High God has worked for me.

How great *are* His signs,
And how mighty His wonders!
His kingdom *is* an everlasting kingdom,
And His dominion *is* from generation to generation.

I, Nebuchadnezzar, was at rest in my house, and flourishing in my palace. I saw a dream which made me afraid, and the thoughts on my bed and the visions of my head troubled me. Therefore I issued a decree to bring in all the wise *men* of Babylon before me, that they might make known to me the interpretation of the dream.

Then the magicians, the astrologers, the Chaldeans, and the soothsayers came in, and I told them the dream; but they did not make known to me its interpretation. But at last Daniel came before me (his name *is* Belteshazzar, according to the name of my god; in him *is* the Spirit of the Holy God), and I told the dream before him, *saying:* "Belteshazzar, chief of the magicians, because I know that the Spirit of the Holy God *is* in you, and no secret troubles you, explain to me the visions of my dream that I have seen, and its interpretation.

"These *were* the visions of my head *while* on my bed:

I was looking, and behold,
A tree in the midst of the earth,
And its height was great.
The tree grew and became strong;
Its height reached to the heavens,
And it could be seen to the ends of all the earth.
Its leaves *were* lovely,
Its fruit abundant,
And in it *was* food for all.
The beasts of the field found shade under it,
The birds of the heavens dwelt in its branches,
And all flesh was fed from it.

"I saw in the visions of my head *while* on my bed, and there was a watcher, a holy one, coming down from heaven. He cried aloud and said thus:

'Chop down the tree and cut off its branches,
Strip off its leaves and scatter its fruit.
Let the beasts get out from under it,
And the birds from its branches.
Nevertheless leave the stump and roots in the earth,
Bound with a band of iron and bronze,
In the tender grass of the field.
Let it be wet with the dew of heaven,
And *let* him graze with the beasts
On the grass of the earth.
Let his heart be changed from *that of* a man,

Let him be given the heart of a beast,
And let seven times pass over him.

'This decision *is* by the decree of the watchers,
And the sentence by the word of the holy ones,
In order that the living may know
That the Most High rules in the kingdom of men,
Gives it to whomever He will,
And sets over it the lowest of men.'

"This dream I, King Nebuchadnezzar, have seen. Now you, Belteshazzar, declare its interpretation, since all the wise *men* of my kingdom are not able to make known to me the interpretation; but you *are* able, for the Spirit of the Holy God *is* in you."

Then Daniel, whose name *was* Belteshazzar, was astonished for a time, and his thoughts troubled him. *So* the king spoke, and said, "Belteshazzar, do not let the dream or its interpretation trouble you."

Belteshazzar answered and said, "My lord, *may* the dream concern those who hate you, and its interpretation concern your enemies!

"The tree that you saw, which grew and became strong, whose height reached to the heavens and which *could be* seen by all the earth, whose leaves *were* lovely and its fruit abundant, in which *was* food for all, under which the beasts of the field dwelt, and in whose branches the birds of the heaven had their home—it *is* you, O king, who have grown and become strong; for your greatness has grown and reaches to the heavens, and your dominion to the end of the earth.

"And inasmuch as the king saw a watcher, a holy one, coming down from heaven and saying, 'Chop down the tree and destroy it, but leave its stump and roots in the earth, *bound* with a band of iron and bronze in the tender grass of the field; let it be wet with the dew of heaven, and let him graze with the beasts of the field, till seven times pass over him'; **this is the interpretation, O king, and this is the decree of the Most High, which has come upon my lord the king: They shall drive you from men, your dwelling shall be with the beasts of the field, and they shall make you eat grass like oxen. They shall wet you with the dew of heaven, and**

seven times shall pass over you, till you know that the Most High rules in the kingdom of men, and gives it to whomever He chooses.

"And inasmuch as they gave the command to leave the stump *and* roots of the tree, your kingdom shall be assured to you, after you come to know that Heaven rules. **Therefore, O king, let my advice be acceptable to you; break off your sins by *being* righteous, and your iniquities by showing mercy to *the* poor. Perhaps there may be a lengthening of your prosperity."**

All *this* came upon King Nebuchadnezzar. At the end of the twelve months he was walking about the royal palace of Babylon. The king spoke, saying, "Is not this great Babylon, that I have built for a royal dwelling by my mighty power and for the honor of my majesty?"

While the word *was still* in the king's mouth, a voice fell from heaven: "King Nebuchadnezzar, to you it is spoken: the kingdom has departed from you! And they shall drive you from men, and your dwelling *shall be* with the beasts of the field. They shall make you eat grass like oxen; and seven times shall pass over you, until you know that the Most High rules in the kingdom of men, and gives it to whomever He chooses."

That very hour the word was fulfilled concerning Nebuchadnezzar; he was driven from men and ate grass like oxen; his body was wet with the dew of heaven till his hair had grown like eagles' *feathers* and his nails like birds' *claws*.

And at the end of the time I, Nebuchadnezzar, lifted my eyes to heaven, and my understanding returned to me; and I blessed the Most High and praised and honored Him who lives forever:

> For His dominion *is* an everlasting dominion,
> And His kingdom *is* from generation to generation.
> All the inhabitants of the earth *are* reputed as nothing;
> He does according to His will in the army of heaven
> And *among* the inhabitants of the earth.
> No one can restrain His hand
> Or say to Him, "What have You done?"

At the same time my reason returned to me, and for the glory of my kingdom, my honor and splendor returned to me. My counselors and nobles resorted to me, I was restored to my kingdom, and excellent majesty was added to me. Now I, Nebuchadnezzar, praise and extol and honor the King of heaven, all of whose works *are* truth, and His ways justice. **And those who walk in pride He is able to put down.**

DANIEL 4:1–37

James, the brother of Jesus, wrote a practical book of application for the first followers of Jesus. Contained in the letter is a "cost-benefit" analysis between pride and humility from which all of us can learn.

Where do wars and fights *come* from among you? Do *they* not *come* from your *desires for* pleasure that war in your members? You lust and do not have. You murder and covet and cannot obtain. You fight and war. Yet you do not have because you do not ask. You ask and do not receive, because you ask amiss, that you may spend *it* on your pleasures. Adulterers and adulteresses! Do you not know that friendship with the world is enmity with God? Whoever therefore wants to be a friend of the world makes himself an enemy of God. Or do you think that the Scripture says in vain, "The Spirit who dwells in us yearns jealously"?

But He gives more grace. Therefore He says:

> ***"God resists the proud,***
> ***But gives grace to the humble."***

Therefore submit to God. Resist the devil and he will flee from you. Draw near to God and He will draw near to you. Cleanse *your* hands, *you* sinners; and purify *your* hearts, *you* double-minded. Lament and mourn and weep! Let your laughter be turned to mourning and *your* joy to gloom. Humble yourselves in the sight of the Lord, and He will lift you up.

Do not speak evil of one another, brethren. He who speaks evil of a brother and judges his brother, speaks evil of the law and judges the law. But if you judge the law, you are not a doer of the law but a judge. There is one Lawgiver, who is able to save and to destroy. Who are you to judge another?

Come now, you who say, "Today or tomorrow we will go to such and such a city, spend a year there, buy and sell, and make a profit"; whereas you do not know what *will happen* tomorrow. For what *is* your life? It is even a vapor that appears for a little time and then vanishes away. Instead you *ought* to say, "If the Lord wills, we shall live and do this or that." But now you boast in your arrogance. All such boasting is evil.

Therefore, to him who knows to do good and does not do *it*, to him it is sin. JAMES 4:1–17

In Peter's first letter to the growing group of Christians in Asia Minor, he instructed believers of all ages to practice the virtue of humility.

The elders who are among you I exhort, I who am a fellow elder and a witness of the sufferings of Christ, and also a partaker of the glory that will be revealed: Shepherd the flock of God which is among you, serving as overseers, not by compulsion but willingly, not for dishonest gain but eagerly; nor as being lords over those entrusted to you, but being examples to the flock; and when the Chief Shepherd appears, you will receive the crown of glory that does not fade away.

Likewise you younger people, submit yourselves to *your* elders. Yes, all of *you* be submissive to one another, and be clothed with humility, for

"God resists the proud,
But gives grace to the humble."

Therefore humble yourselves under the mighty hand of God, that He may exalt you in due time. 1 PETER 5:1–6

THE PARADOX OF HUMILITY

A paradox is a statement that seems contrary to common sense and yet is true. Some might believe that a humble person always loses out, gets overlooked and comes in dead last, while someone with less humility always wins, gets noticed and comes in first. But the Bible teaches the opposite. There are great blessings in store for people who demonstrate humility. It doesn't mean humble people will always "win" or "come in first" in a worldly sense, but it does mean that they will experience true contentment and joy.

As you read the Scripture passage from Matthew 5 below, identify all of God's paradoxes (such as, rejoice when people persecute you). Have you seen the truth in any of these paradoxes in your own experience?

And seeing the multitudes, He went up on a mountain, and when He was seated His disciples came to Him. Then He opened His mouth and taught them, saying:

"Blessed *are* the poor in spirit,
For theirs is the kingdom of heaven.
Blessed *are* those who mourn,
For they shall be comforted.
Blessed *are* the meek,
For they shall inherit the earth.
Blessed *are* those who hunger and thirst for righteousness,
For they shall be filled.
Blessed *are* the merciful,
For they shall obtain mercy.
Blessed *are* the pure in heart,
For they shall see God.
Blessed *are* the peacemakers,
For they shall be called sons of God.
Blessed *are* those who are persecuted for righteousness' sake,
For theirs is the kingdom of heaven.

"Blessed are you when they revile and persecute you, and say all kinds of evil against you falsely for My sake. Rejoice and be exceedingly glad, for great *is* your reward in heaven, for so they persecuted the prophets who were before you." MATTHEW 5:1–12

It was not uncommon for large crowds of people to follow and gather around Jesus to hear Him teach and watch Him perform all kinds of miracles. On one such occasion, after Jesus healed a demon-possessed boy, a disagreement broke out among the disciples. Before pride got the best of them, Jesus reiterated the role of humility in a believer's life.

Now it happened on the next day, when they had come down from the mountain, that a great multitude met Him. Suddenly a man from the multitude cried out, saying, "Teacher, I implore You, look on my son, for he is my only child. And behold, a spirit seizes him, and he suddenly cries out; it convulses him so that he foams *at the mouth;* and it departs from him with great difficulty, bruising him. So I implored Your disciples to cast it out, but they could not."

Then Jesus answered and said, "O faithless and perverse generation, how long shall I be with you and bear with you? Bring your son here." And as he was still coming, the demon threw him down and convulsed *him.* Then Jesus rebuked the unclean spirit, healed the child, and gave him back to his father.

And they were all amazed at the majesty of God.

But while everyone marveled at all the things which Jesus did, He said to His disciples, "Let these words sink down into your ears, for the Son of Man is about to be betrayed into the hands of men." But they did not understand this saying, and it was hidden from them so that they did not perceive it; and they were afraid to ask Him about this saying.

Then a dispute arose among them as to which of them would be greatest. And Jesus, perceiving the thought of their heart, took a little child and set him by Him, and said to them, **"Whoever receives this little child in My name receives Me; and whoever receives Me receives Him who sent Me. For he who is least among you all will be great."** LUKE 9:37–48

This question of which of Jesus' disciples would be the greatest arose on a number of occasions. You would think the message would have eventually sunk in, but it hadn't. As Jesus was on His way to Jerusalem for the last time, the brothers James and John—two disciples from Jesus' inner circle—approached Him with a request.

James and John, the sons of Zebedee, came to Him, saying, "Teacher, we want You to do for us whatever we ask."

And He said to them, "What do you want Me to do for you?"

They said to Him, "Grant us that we may sit, one on Your right hand and the other on Your left, in Your glory."

But Jesus said to them, "You do not know what you ask. Are you able to drink the cup that I drink, and be baptized with the baptism that I am baptized with?"

They said to Him, "We are able."

So Jesus said to them, "You will indeed drink the cup that I drink, and with the baptism I am baptized with you will be baptized; but to sit on My right hand and on My left is not Mine to give, but *it is for those* for whom it is prepared."

And when the ten heard *it,* they began to be greatly displeased with James and John. But Jesus called them to *Himself* and said to them, "You know that those who are considered rulers over the Gentiles lord it over them, and their great ones exercise authority over them. Yet it shall not be so among you; **but whoever desires to become great among you shall be your servant. And whoever of you desires to be first shall be slave of all. For even the Son of Man did not come to be served, but to serve, and to give His life a ransom for many."** MARK 10:35–45

Jesus did acknowledge one individual who got it right. What He said next was in keeping with the paradox of humility.

"Assuredly, I say to you, among those born of women there has not risen one greater than John the Baptist; but he who is least in the kingdom of heaven is greater than he." MATTHEW 11:11

What was John's secret to success? John gave perhaps the most succinct description of how to become humble in a powerful conversation with his disciples.

After these things Jesus and His disciples came into the land of Judea, and there He remained with them and baptized. Now John also was baptizing in Aenon near Salim, because there was much water there. And they came and were baptized. For John had not yet been thrown into prison.

Then there arose a dispute between *some* of John's disciples and the Jews about purification. And they came to John and said to him, "Rabbi, He who was with you beyond the Jordan, to whom you have testified—behold, He is baptizing, and all are coming to Him!"

John answered and said, "A man can receive nothing unless it has been given to him from heaven. You yourselves bear me witness, that I said, 'I am not the Christ,' but, 'I have been sent before Him.' He who has the bride is the bridegroom; but the friend of the bridegroom, who stands and hears him, rejoices greatly because of the bridegroom's voice. Therefore this joy of mine is fulfilled. **He must increase, but I *must* decrease.** He who comes from above is above all; he who is of the earth is earthly and speaks of the earth. He who comes from heaven is above all. JOHN 3:22–31

People who struggle with humility are often caught boasting or bragging about themselves. In 2 Corinthians, Paul responded to criticism he received about his ministry. Using a unique style of writing, almost tongue-in-cheek, Paul introduced his readers to a proper form of boasting.

Whatever anyone is bold—I speak foolishly—I am bold also.

Are they Hebrews? So *am* I. Are they Israelites? So *am* I. Are they the seed of Abraham? So *am* I. Are they ministers of Christ?—I speak as a fool—I *am* more: in labors more abundant, in stripes above measure, in prisons more frequently, in deaths often. From the Jews five times I received forty *stripes* minus one. Three times I was beaten with rods; once I was stoned; three times I was shipwrecked; a night and a day I have been in the deep; *in* journeys often, *in* perils of waters, *in* perils of robbers, *in* perils of *my own* countrymen, *in* perils of the Gentiles, *in* perils in the city, *in* perils in the wilderness, *in* perils in the sea, *in* perils among false brethren; in weariness and toil, in sleeplessness often, in hunger and thirst, in fastings often, in cold and nakedness—besides the other things, what comes upon me daily: my deep concern for all the churches. Who is weak, and I am not weak? Who is made to stumble, and I do not burn *with indignation?*

If I must boast, I will boast in the things which concern my infirmity. 2 CORINTHIANS 11:21–30

And lest I should be exalted above measure by the abundance of the revelations, a thorn in the flesh was given to me, a messenger of Satan to buffet me, lest I be exalted above measure. Concerning this thing I pleaded with the Lord three times that it might depart from me. And He said to me, "My grace is sufficient for you, for My strength is made perfect in weakness." Therefore most gladly I will rather boast in my infirmities, that the power of Christ may rest upon me. Therefore I take pleasure in infirmities, in reproaches, in needs, in persecutions, in distresses, for Christ's sake. **For when I am weak, then I am strong.** 2 Corinthians 12:7–10

Although he eventually became one of Christ's most trusted followers, Paul had not always been a humble servant of Jesus. He once had been arrogant and violent, a vehement persecutor of Christians. In his first letter to Timothy, the apostle wrote honestly and openly about this amazing shift in his life.

And I thank Christ Jesus our Lord who has enabled me, because He counted me faithful, putting *me* into the ministry, although I was formerly a blasphemer, a persecutor, and an insolent man; but I obtained mercy because I did *it* ignorantly in unbelief. And the grace of our Lord was exceedingly abundant, with faith and love which are in Christ Jesus. This *is* a faithful saying and worthy of all acceptance, that Christ Jesus came into the world to save sinners, of whom I am chief. **However, for this reason I obtained mercy, that in me first Jesus Christ might show all longsuffering, as a pattern to those who are going to believe on Him for everlasting life.** Now to the King eternal, immortal, invisible, to God who alone is wise, *be* honor and glory forever and ever. Amen.

1 Timothy 1:12–17

God's Requirement

What does God require from us? Micah, a prophet to Israel and Judah in the eighth century BC, answered this question with convicting succinctness. What God required then, He still requires of us today.

With what shall I come before the Lord,
And bow myself before the High God?

Shall I come before Him with burnt offerings,
With calves a year old?
Will the LORD be pleased with thousands of rams,
Ten thousand rivers of oil?
Shall I give my firstborn *for* my transgression,
The fruit of my body *for* the sin of my soul?

He has shown you, O man, what *is* good;
And what does the LORD require of you
But to do justly,
To love mercy,
And to walk humbly with your God? MICAH 6:6–8

Micah tells us that God requires us to act justly, love mercy and walk humbly with Him. How are these actions related?

WHAT WE BELIEVE

One of the most amazing pieces of evidence that we are becoming more and more like Jesus is the virtue of humility. Believers do not lift others up because they think lowly of themselves. No, they are able to esteem others above themselves because they have accepted the high esteem they have found through faith in Christ. Because we are freed from the struggle to prove we are somebody special, we can humble ourselves and look instead to build up others. When we do, it signals God's presence within us. Look to the supreme example of Jesus. Remember, God opposes the proud but grants favor to the humble. Don't let the world fool you; a humble person wins out at the end of the day and at the end of eternity. God requires His followers to act justly, love mercy and walk humbly before Him. It's a requirement that leads to great blessing. Remember, "I can do all things through Christ who strengthens me" (Philippians 4:13).

Epilogue

You have just finished reading stories of real people who lived in ancient times and encountered the one true God. They were invited to take part in the unfolding of God's Grand Love Story.

Many believed; many did not. But for all it was a journey. We see this in one particular story from the Bible. A man brought his boy to Jesus to deliver him from demon possession. Jesus asked the father how long his son had been like this. The father replied that he had been afflicted since childhood. "And often he has thrown him both into the fire and into the water to destroy him. But if You can do anything, have compassion on us and help us."

"Jesus said to him, 'If you can believe, all things *are* possible to him who believes.'

"Immediately the father of the child cried out and said with tears, 'Lord, I believe; help my unbelief!'" (Mark 9:22–24).

Right now, Jesus invites you to believe—to believe in Him and to believe the truths taught in the pages of Scripture that guide our lives daily and into eternity. Be honest, like the man who spoke with Jesus. Tell Jesus about your doubts and invite Him to help you with your unbelief. He will. He doesn't want you to merely believe these truths are the right answer. He wants you to take them in your heart where they will affect how you will live.

Here is the promise: what you once thought was impossible will now be possible. The more you believe, the more you see and discover the power of God. The more you believe, the more He changes you from the inside out to become the kind of person you have only dreamed about—filled with love, joy, peace, forbearance, kindness, goodness, faithfulness, gentleness and self-control. These virtues are displayed in your life like fruit on a tree for others to taste and enjoy.

When we *think* and *act* like Jesus, empowered by His presence within us, little by little we *become* like Jesus. This is not only the most truthful and abundant way to live, but it is truly the best gift we can give to our family and others whom God sovereignly places into our lives.

So, spiritual pilgrim, BELIEVE.

"Oh, taste and see that the LORD *is good" (Psalm 34:8).*

Chart of References

Chapter 1: God

Genesis 1:1
Psalm 19:1–4
Romans 1:20
Deuteronomy 6:1–9
Joshua 24:1–31
1 Kings 18:16–40
Genesis 2:4–9
Genesis 2:15–24
John 1:1–5
Luke 3:1–6
Luke 3:15–18
Luke 3:21–23
Acts 17:16–34
2 Corinthians 13:14

Chapter 2: Personal God

Genesis 16:1–16
Genesis 21:1–21
Psalm 8:1–9
Psalm 23:1–6
Psalm 139:1–18
Psalm 145:1–21
2 Kings 20:1–7
Jeremiah 1:1–19
Jeremiah 29:1–14
Matthew 6:25–34
Romans 8:12–13
Romans 8:26–39
James 1:1–18

Chapter 3: Salvation

Genesis 2:8–9
Genesis 2:15–17
Genesis 3:1–24
Exodus 11:1—12:13
Exodus 12:21–31
Isaiah 52:13—53:12
Matthew 26:1–4
Matthew 27:27—28:10
John 3:1–21
Acts 2:36–41
Romans 5:12–21
Romans 10:1–13
Ephesians 1:3–14

Chapter 4: The Bible

Exodus 3:1—4:17
Luke 24:27–49
2 Peter 1:1–21
Exodus 19:1–9
Exodus 19:16–19
Exodus 20:1–21
Matthew 4:1–11
2 Timothy 3:10–17
Isaiah 40:6–8
Isaiah 55:6–13
Hebrews 4:12–13
Deuteronomy 4:1–2
Proverbs 30:5–6
Revelation 22:18–19

Chapter 5: Identity in Christ

Genesis 17:1–7
Genesis 17:17
Genesis 17:19
Genesis 21:1–7
Jeremiah 31:31–34
John 1:9–13
Hebrews 10:1–18
Luke 19:1–9
Romans 3:10–26
Romans 5:1–2
Romans 5:6–11
Romans 6:1–7
Romans 8:1–25
Ephesians 2:1—3:21
1 Corinthians 3:16–17
1 Corinthians 6:19
1 Corinthians 12:12–14
1 Peter 1:1–5
1 Peter 1:22–23
1 Peter 2:4–10

Chapter 6: Church

Genesis 12:1–9
Genesis 15:1–6
Genesis 15:7–21
Matthew 16:13–19
Acts 1:1–11
Acts 2:1–41
Acts 8:1–8
Acts 8:14–17
Acts 8:25
Acts 9:31
Acts 11:1–18
Acts 11:19–26
Acts 13:1–3
Acts 13:38–52
Acts 20:17—21:1
Ephesians 4:1–16
Revelation 2:1–7

Chapter 7: Humanity

Genesis 1:1–31
Genesis 4:1–5
Genesis 4:6–16
Jude 1–16
Romans 1:18–32
Romans 2:17–24
Romans 3:9–20
Hosea 1:1–3
Hosea 3:1–3
Hosea 11:1–11
John 1:4
John 1:7
John 1:11–12
John 3:16
John 3:36
John 4:14
John 5:24
John 6:35
John 6:37
John 6:51
John 6:54
John 7:38
John 8:12
John 8:51
John 10:9
John 11:26
John 12:31–32
Matthew 18:1–14
Luke 6:27–36
Philemon 1–25

Chapter 8: Compassion

Nehemiah 9:1–38
Romans 3:21–26
1 John 4:7–10
Deuteronomy 24:10–15
Deuteronomy 24:17–22
Deuteronomy 25:5–10
Ruth 2:1–23
Ruth 4:13–17
Luke 10:25–37
Matthew 25:31–46
James 1:19—2:13

Chapter 9: Stewardship

Psalm 24:1–10
Psalm 50:1–23
Matthew 25:14–30
Genesis 1:26–30
1 Samuel 1:1–28
1 Samuel 2:18–21
Deuteronomy 12:5–7
Malachi 3:6–12
Luke 16:1–15
Mark 12:41–44
1 Kings 17:1–24
Romans 12:10–13
Hebrews 13:2
1 Peter 4:9
3 John 2–8
1 Corinthians 6:12–20
1 Corinthians 10:23—11:1

Chapter 10: Eternity

2 Kings 2:1–18
Luke 16:19–31
1 Corinthians 15:1–28
1 Corinthians 15:35–58
1 Thessalonians 4:13—5:11
2 Peter 3:1–18
Revelation 20:11—22:21
John 14:1–7

Chapter 11: Worship

Psalm 95:1–7
Isaiah 1:11–20
Matthew 23:1–28
Exodus 15:1–21
Daniel 6:1–27
Acts 16:16–35
Hebrews 10:1–25
Luke 22:7–30
Colossians 3:1–17

Chapter 12: Prayer

Psalm 66:16–20
Mark 1:32–35
Luke 6:12–16
Mark 6:39–46
Matthew 26:36–46
Psalm 77:1–20
Ecclesiastes 5:1–3
Judges 6:1—7:22
Psalm 25:1–15
Genesis 18:20–33
2 Kings 20:1–11
Luke 11:1–13
Philippians 4:6–9

Chapter 13: Bible Study

Deuteronomy 6:13–25
Deuteronomy 31:9–13
Joshua 1:1–9
Nehemiah 7:73—9:3
Psalm 19:7–14
Psalm 119:9–24
Psalm 119:33–40
Psalm 119:97–112
Matthew 13:1–23
John 14:15–27
1 Corinthians 2:1–16
1 Timothy 4:1–16
2 Timothy 2:14–16
Hebrews 5:9—6:3

Chapter 14: Single-Mindedness

Exodus 20:2–3
Deuteronomy 6:1–9
Matthew 6:19–24
Philippians 3:1–14
2 Chronicles 20:1–30
John 8:12–30
Matthew 14:22–33
Acts 5:12–42
Deuteronomy 29:16—30:20
Romans 12:1–2
Colossians 3:1–4
Colossians 3:15–17

Chapter 15: Total Surrender

Exodus 20:1–7
Daniel 3:1–28
Esther 3:1—4:16
Luke 9:23–26
Luke 22:24–62
Acts 6:8—7:60
Acts 21:4–14
Philippians 1:12–21

Chapter 16: Biblical Community

Genesis 2:4–25
Ecclesiastes 4:8–12
Exodus 25:1–9
Exodus 40:1–17
Exodus 40:34–35
2 Chronicles 7:1–3
Ephesians 2:11–22
Acts 2:1–4
Acts 2:42–47
Acts 4:32–37
Hebrews 10:19–25
Matthew 18:20
Nehemiah 2:11—3:32
Nehemiah 6:15
Romans 12:4–5
Romans 12:10
Romans 13:8
Romans 15:5–7
Romans 15:14
Galatians 5:13
Galatians 6:2
Ephesians 4:1–2
Ephesians 5:21
1 Thessalonians 5:9–11
Hebrews 13:1–3
Hebrews 13:15–16
Acts 18:1–3
Acts 18:18–19
Acts 18:24–26
1 Corinthians 16:19
Romans 16:3–4
1 John 1:1–7
1 John 2:7–11
1 John 3:16–18

Chapter 17: Spiritual Gifts

Exodus 35:30—36:1
Daniel 2:1–47
John 14:15–31
Acts 2:1–21
Romans 12:4–8
1 Corinthians 12:4–31
Matthew 25:14–30
1 Peter 4:7–11
Ephesians 4:1–16

Chapter 18: Offering My Time

Jonah 1:1—2:10
Haggai 1:1–15
Luke 2:41–52
Exodus 16:1–30
Exodus 18:5–27
Proverbs 31:10–31
John 7:1–16
Matthew 25:31–46
Ephesians 5:15–17
Galatians 6:7–10

Chapter 19: Giving My Resources

Genesis 28:10–22
Exodus 35:4–29
Exodus 36:3–7
1 Chronicles 29:1–18
Proverbs 3:9–10
Proverbs 11:24–25
Proverbs 11:28
Ecclesiastes 5:10–20
Matthew 2:1–12
Matthew 6:1–4
Matthew 6:19–24
Luke 12:13–21
Mark 12:41–44
Luke 6:32–36
Acts 4:32–37
2 Corinthians 8:1—9:15

Chapter 20: Sharing My Faith

Genesis 12:1–4
2 Corinthians 5:14–21
2 Kings 5:1–15
Matthew 5:13–16
Acts 2:42–47
1 Corinthians 9:19–23
Psalm 40:1–10
Acts 1:1–8
Acts 8:1–8
Acts 8:26–40
Acts 20:17–24
Ephesians 6:19–20
Colossians 4:2–6
Jonah 3:1—4:11
John 4:3–42
Romans 10:1–15

Chapter 21: Love

1 Corinthians 13:1–13
Deuteronomy 6:4–9
Leviticus 19:17–18
Mark 12:28–34
John 13:31–35
Galatians 5:13–25
1 John 4:7–21
Matthew 5:43–48
Romans 13:8–10
Matthew 18:21–35
1 Samuel 18:1–4
1 Samuel 19:1–7
1 Samuel 20:1–42
John 10:14–18

Chapter 22: Joy

Psalm 16:1–11
Luke 2:1–21
John 15:1–11
Nehemiah 8:13–17
1 Chronicles 16:7–36
Habakkuk 3:16–19
John 13:1
John 16:16–24
James 1:2–17
Philippians 1:1–8
Philippians 1:12–19
Philippians 2:14–18
Philippians 3:1–21
Philippians 4:1
Philippians 4:4
Philippians 4:10–13
1 Peter 1:3–9
1 Peter 4:12–16
1 Peter 5:6–11

Chapter 23: Peace

Isaiah 9:6–7
Romans 5:1–11
Ephesians 2:1–22
Genesis 13:1–18
1 Kings 3:3–15
1 Kings 4:20–25
Matthew 5:21–26
Romans 14:1—15:13
Colossians 3:1–17
Romans 12:17–21
1 Timothy 2:1–8
Titus 3:1–11
Matthew 6:25–34
Mark 4:35–41
Philippians 4:4–9

Chapter 24: Self-Control

Proverbs 16:32
Proverbs 17:27
Proverbs 25:28
Proverbs 29:11
Titus 1:4–9
Titus 2:1–15
Judges 16:1–21
Genesis 39:1–23
1 Corinthians 6:12–20
1 Corinthians 10:14–22
1 Timothy 6:3–16
2 Timothy 2:22—3:7
James 3:1—4:10
1 Peter 5:8–11
1 Corinthians 7:1–9
2 Peter 1:3–11
Galatians 5:16–25
Luke 15:11–24

Chapter 25: Hope

Job 6:1–13
Job 7:1–6
Psalm 52:1–9
1 Timothy 6:17
Psalm 118:8–9
Psalm 146:3–4
Jeremiah 17:5–6
Habakkuk 2:18–19
Isaiah 31:1
Isaiah 31:3
Psalm 42:1–11
Hebrews 6:13–20
Colossians 1:24–29
1 Peter 1:1–25
1 Thessalonians 4:13–18
1 John 3:1–3
Isaiah 40:25–31
Luke 2:25–35
Hebrews 11:1—12:3

Chapter 26: Patience

Psalm 86:15
Numbers 14:1–23
Numbers 14:30–33
2 Peter 3:1–18
1 Samuel 24:1–22
1 Samuel 26:1–25
Proverbs 14:29
Proverbs 15:18
Proverbs 16:32
Proverbs 19:11
Proverbs 25:15
James 1:19–20
John 5:1–15
2 Corinthians 12:7–10
Job 1:1—2:13
Job 42:7–17

Chapter 27: Kindness/Goodness

Psalm 107:1–43
Joshua 2:1–24
Joshua 6:12–25
1 Samuel 20:13–16
2 Samuel 9:1–13
Luke 14:1
Luke 14:7–14
Philemon 1–25
2 Timothy 1:15–18
Luke 6:27–45
1 Peter 3:8–17
Romans 15:1–2
1 Corinthians 10:23–24
Galatians 6:9–10
Ephesians 4:31—5:2
1 Thessalonians 5:15
Titus 2:7
Titus 3:1–8
Titus 3:14

Chapter 28: Faithfulness

Deuteronomy 32:1–4
Psalm 36:5–9
Lamentations 3:19–24
Proverbs 3:1–6
Proverbs 20:6
Proverbs 28:20
1 Corinthians 4:1–2
Genesis 39:1–6
Genesis 40:1–23
Genesis 41:14–46
Genesis 42:1–6
Ruth 1:1–22
Luke 1:26–56
Luke 2:1–21

Chapter 29: Gentleness

John 13:31–38
John 18:12–27
John 21:1–19
Matthew 11:28–30
Matthew 5:5
Matthew 5:38–42
Matthew 7:1–5
Galatians 5:22–23
Ephesians 4:1–2
Ephesians 4:26–32
Ephesians 6:4
Colossians 3:12
1 Timothy 3:1–4
1 Timothy 5:1–2
1 Timothy 6:10–11
2 Timothy 2:24–26
Titus 3:1–2
James 3:17–18
Philippians 4:2–5
1 Peter 3:1–4
1 Peter 3:7
1 Samuel 25:1–42
2 Samuel 16:5–14
1 Thessalonians 2:1–13

Chapter 30: Humility

Luke 2:1–20
John 13:1–17
Philippians 2:1–13
Psalm 10:2–4
Psalm 18:27
Psalm 25:8–9
Psalm 147:6
Proverbs 3:33–34
Proverbs 11:2
Proverbs 16:18–19
Proverbs 18:12
Proverbs 21:4
Proverbs 21:24
Proverbs 22:4
Proverbs 25:6–7
Proverbs 29:23
Daniel 4:1–37
James 4:1–17
1 Peter 5:1–6
Matthew 5:1–12
Luke 9:37–48
Mark 10:35–45
Matthew 11:11
John 3:22–31
2 Corinthians 11:21–30
2 Corinthians 12:7–10
1 Timothy 1:12–17
Micah 6:6–8

BELIEVE

POWERED BY ZONDERVAN

Dear Reader,

Notable researcher George Gallup Jr. summarized his findings on the state of American Christianity with this startling revelation: "Churches face no greater challenge…than overcoming biblical illiteracy, and the prospects for doing so are formidable because **the stark fact is, many Christians don't know what they believe or why.**"

The problem is not that people lack a hunger for God's Word. Research tells us that the number one thing people want from their church is for it to help them understand the Bible, and that Bible engagement is the number one catalyst for spiritual growth. Nothing else comes close.

This is why I am passionate about the book you're holding in your hands: *Believe*—a Bible engagement experience to anchor every member of your family in the key teachings of Scripture.

The *Believe* experience helps you answer three significant questions: Can you clearly articulate the essentials of the faith? Would your neighbors or coworkers identify you as a Christian based on their interactions with you and your family? Is the kingdom of God expanding in your corner of the world?

Grounded in Scripture, *Believe* is a spiritual growth experience for all ages, taking each person on a journey toward becoming more like Jesus in their beliefs, actions, and character. There is one edition for adults, one for students, and two versions for children. All four age-appropriate editions of *Believe* unpack the 10 key beliefs, 10 key practices, and 10 key virtues of a Christian, so that everyone in your family and your church can learn together to be more like Jesus.

When these timeless truths are understood, believed in the heart, and applied to our daily living, they will transform a life, a family, a church, a city, a nation, and even our world.

Imagine thousands of churches and hundreds of thousands of individuals all over the world who will finally be able to declare—**"I know what I believe and why, and in God's strength I will seek to live it out all the days of my life."** It could change the world. It has in the past; it could happen again.

In Him,

Randy Frazee
General Editor, *Believe*

LIVING THE STORY OF THE BIBLE TO BECOME LIKE JESUS

Teach your whole family how to live the story of the Bible!

- **Adults** – Unlocks the 10 key beliefs, 10 key practices, and 10 key virtues that help people live the story of the Bible. Bible Study DVD and Study Guide also available.
- ***Think, Act, Be Like Jesus*** – A companion to *Believe*, this fresh resource by pastor Randy Frazee will help readers develop a personal vision for spiritual growth and a simple plan for getting started on the *Believe* journey.
- **Students** – This edition contains fewer Scriptures than the adult edition, but with transitions and fun features to engage teens and students. Bible Study DVD also available.
- **Children** – With a Kids' Edition for ages 8-12, a Storybook for ages 4-8, a coloring book for toddlers, and four levels of curriculum for toddlers, preschool, early elementary, and later elementary, children of all ages will learn how to think, act, and be like Jesus.
- **Churches** – *Believe* is flexible, affordable, and easy to use with your whole church.
- **Spanish** – All *Believe* resources are also available in Spanish.

FOR ADULTS

9780310443834

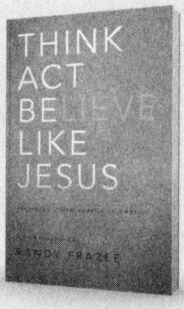

9780310250173

FOR STUDENTS

9780310745617

FOR CHILDREN

Ages 8–12
9780310746010

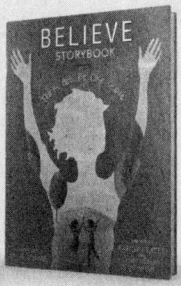

Ages 4–8
9780310745907

Ages 2–5
9780310752226

FOR CHURCHES

Campaign Kit 9780310681717

BelieveTheStory.com

BELIEVE

POWERED BY ZONDERVAN

THE STORY

POWERED BY ZONDERVAN

READ THE STORY. EXPERIENCE THE BIBLE.

Here I am, 50 years old. I have been to college, seminary, engaged in ministry my whole life, my dad is in ministry, my grandfather was in ministry, and ***The Story* has been one of the most unique experiences of my life**. The Bible has been made fresh for me. It has made God's redemptive plan come alive for me once again.
—Seth Buckley, Youth Pastor,
Spartanburg Baptist Church, Spartanburg, SC

As my family and I went through *The Story* together, the more I began to believe and the more real [the Bible] became to me, and **it rubbed off on my children and helped them with their walk with the Lord**. *The Story* inspired conversations we might not normally have had.
—Kelly Leonard, Parent, Shepherd of the Hills Christian Church, Porter Ranch, CA

We have people reading *The Story*—some devour it and can't wait for the next week. Some have never really read the Bible much, so it's exciting to see a lot of adults reading the Word of God for the first time. I've heard wonderful things from people who are long-time readers of Scripture. They're excited about how it's all being tied together for them. It just seems to make more sense.
—Lynnette Schulz,
Director of Worship
Peace Lutheran Church,
Eau Claire, WI

FOR ADULTS

9780310950974

FOR TEENS

Ages 13+
9780310722809

FOR KIDS

Ages 8–12
9780310719250

TheStory.com

Dive into the Bible in a whole new way!

The Story is changing lives, making it easy for any person, regardless of age or biblical literacy level, to understand the Bible.

The Story comes in five editions, one for each age group from toddlers to adults. All five editions are organized chronologically into 31 chapters with selected Scripture from Genesis to Revelation. The additional resources create an engaging group Bible-reading experience, whether you read *The Story* with your whole church, in small groups, or with your family.

- **Adults** – Read the Bible as one compelling story, from Genesis to Revelation. Available in NIV, KJV, NKJV, large print, imitation leather, and audio editions. Curriculum DVD and Participant's Guide also available.
- **Teens** – Teen edition of *The Story*, with special study helps and features designed with teens in mind. Curriculum DVD also available.
- **Children** – With a Kids' Edition for ages 8-12, a Storybook Bible for ages 4-8, a Storybook Bible for toddlers, fun trading cards, and three levels of curriculum for preschool, early elementary, and later elementary, children of all ages will learn how their story fits into God's story.
- **Churches** – *The Story* is flexible, affordable, and easy to use with your church, in any ministry, from nursery to adult Sunday school, small groups to youth group…and even the whole church.
- **Spanish** – *The Story* resources are also available in Spanish.

FOR CHILDREN

Ages 4–8
9780310719755

Ages 2–5
9780310719274

FOR CHURCHES

Campaign Kit 9780310941538

THE STORY

POWERED BY ZONDERVAN